D0379060

Southern California
for Kids

Southern California for Kids

45 One-Day Itineraries from Los Angeles to San Diego

By Kay And Tom Sanger

CLARKSON N. POTTER, INC./PUBLISHERS
NEW YORK

Copyright © 1990 by Kay Sanger and Tom Sanger

All rights reserved. No part of this book may be reproduced or transmitted
in any form or by any means, electronic or mechanical, including photo-
copying, recording, or by any information storage and retrieval system,
without permission in writing from the publisher.

Published by Clarkson N. Potter, Inc., distributed by Crown Publishers,
Inc., 201 East 50th Street, New York, New York 10022

CLARKSON N. POTTER, POTTER and colophon are trademarks of
Clarkson N. Potter, Inc.

Manufactured in the United States of America

Design by Jan Melchior
Maps by David Lindroth

Library of Congress Cataloging-in-Publication Data

Sanger, Kay.
    Southern California for kids: 45 one-day itineraries from Los
Angeles to San Diego/by Kay and Tom Sanger. — 1st ed.
      p.   cm.
      1. California, Southern—Description and travel—Guide-books.
    2. Family recreation—California, Southern—Guide-books.
    3. Children—Travel—California, Southern—Guide-books.   I. Sanger,
Tom.   II. Title.
    F867.S22   1990
    917.9404'53—dc20   90-7031
                                                                          CIP

ISBN 0-517-57347-4

10 9 8 7 6 5 4 3 2 1

First Edition

To Kristin and Ted, our travel advisers

Contents

Introduction

"What are we going to do today?"

If you've ever been at a loss for an answer when the kids come up with this question, then this book is for you.

Southern California is filled with exciting experiences for children; the trick is knowing where to find them. How about a train museum where you can actually ride the rails? A park where you can walk the dusty streets of an old western-movie set? A place where you can dig for giant ground sloth bones?

It's hard enough for visitors, but even long-time residents don't always know where to find some of the best attractions for children. We recognize the feeling. For most of two decades, we have been going places in Southern California with children, not only as parents on family outings but also in our roles as teachers and leaders of various parent-child programs.

Based on information accumulated during those years, this book presents more than five hundred attractions, parks, and restaurants, covering Southern California from San Diego to Santa Barbara and from the eastern deserts to the Channel Islands in the Pacific Ocean.

Lots of kids gave candid appraisals of the places highlighted in this book, telling us which ones they found the most fun or the least interesting. Not only have we included the places the kids liked best, but, keeping in mind that adults usually drive kids to these destinations and pay for them, we've provided information to help the grown-ups decide whether they, too, would like to visit a particular place.

While the book is aimed at fun places for children, we recognize that the term covers a broad range of ages—from infants to teenagers—and interests. In view of this, we've included everything from parks with toddler play equipment to haunts teens would prefer. Where appropriate, our descriptions suggest what age group would be most interested in which activities. But our book isn't simply a list of places with descriptions. We tell you where attractions are in relation to one another. We let you know if a museum is across the street from a park where you can picnic and the kids can play, or down the street from a particularly good child-oriented restaurant. If there are places to rent bikes, boats, or roller skates nearby, we tell you how to find them.

How to Use This Book

Southern California for Kids is divided into 11 chapters that correspond to geographic areas. The chapters are divided into sections according to the proximity of various travel destinations in a given area. Each chapter includes from three to six sections describing local attractions. At the end of each section, a directory of the attractions provides addresses, phone numbers, hours of operation, costs of admission, and directions from the nearest freeway. All destinations are within a 2½-hour drive or less from the center of Los Angeles.

Most of the sections can be used as itineraries for a day's visit to the area. You may not want or be able to see everything suggested in one day, but you'll be able to choose from a number of activities to make up a satisfying itinerary on your own. The description of each attraction should let you know whether it will be of interest to your children and just how long it might keep them entertained.

In choosing the places to feature, we give particular emphasis to free and inexpensive attractions. We recommend parks where you can picnic and restaurants that are not in the expensive bracket. For the most part, we have left out fast-food chain restaurants. You will be able to find those on your own; they are plentiful enough in Southern California to be located near most of the attractions we suggest. The same is true of small chain amusement parks. Whether they offer miniature golf, small racing cars, or video arcades, you should be able to find them listed in the local phone book, and one is pretty much like another.

At the end of the book you'll find a chapter listing annual events in Southern California, grouped by month, that are of particular interest to kids. We've included a brief description of each event to help you decide which ones will be most appropriate for your children. You will need to call to find out the exact dates and locations of the events.

We have designed this book with families in mind, but youth-group leaders and teachers will also find it useful. Most places listed are open to the public on a drop-in basis, but if you have more than ten children in a group, it's best to call ahead to make a reservation. Many attractions offer lower rates for groups.

In fact, it's best to call ahead no matter what the size of your group. The hours of operation and prices of admission given were in effect at the time this book went to press, but these can change as quickly as a child's interests. What was a pumpkin patch with pony rides last year may be this year's used-car lot.

A word about transportation. It is possible to get around in Southern California without a car, but at some sacrifice to convenience. Public transport can be excellent within given areas. Orange County Rapid Transit District and Southern California Rapid Transit District (which covers Los Angeles County and some parts of Orange County) have information packages and programs geared to children and family vacationers. The cities of Long Beach, San Diego, Santa Barbara, and Santa Monica offer excellent local transit services. If you do not have transit passes or coupons, you'll need exact change for the bus, and transfers between transit jurisdictions can be time-consuming unless your destination is a major attraction or lies on a well-traveled route.

Other transportation alternatives include tour buses, taxis (rarely sighted anywhere besides airports, hotels, and major business centers), and the train. Amtrak operates daily scheduled passenger service and some tour packages between Los Angeles, San Diego, and Santa Barbara. You'll find the details in the appropriate sections.

If you forsake public transit for the family auto or a rental car, you will gain considerable flexibility. Be sure to allow extra time to negotiate our increasingly busy freeways. You'll find area maps and directions to each destination in this book, but it's always a good idea to carry a more detailed local map if you have questions about where you are going. Maps are available from the chambers of commerce or visitors' bureaus in most areas or at gas stations and book stores.

One final piece of advice concerns Southern California weather. Visitors expect each day to be sunny and perfect for sight-seeing. While this is nearly always the case *somewhere* in Southern California, the area has many microclimates. It can be uncomfortably hot in the valleys and deserts between May and October, so don't plan your midday hikes then. In winter, these same areas can be quite cool, especially in the early morning hours. Weather at the beaches can be cloudy and cool all morning in spring and early summer. Because of California's low humidity, temperatures often vary by about 20 degrees between midday and evening. For greatest comfort and fewer complaints, dress the kids in layers that can be removed or put on during different times of the day.

With a full tank of gas, a trusty map, and a copy of *Southern California for Kids*, you have everything you need to answer the children the next time they ask, "What are we going to do today?"

Southern California
for Kids

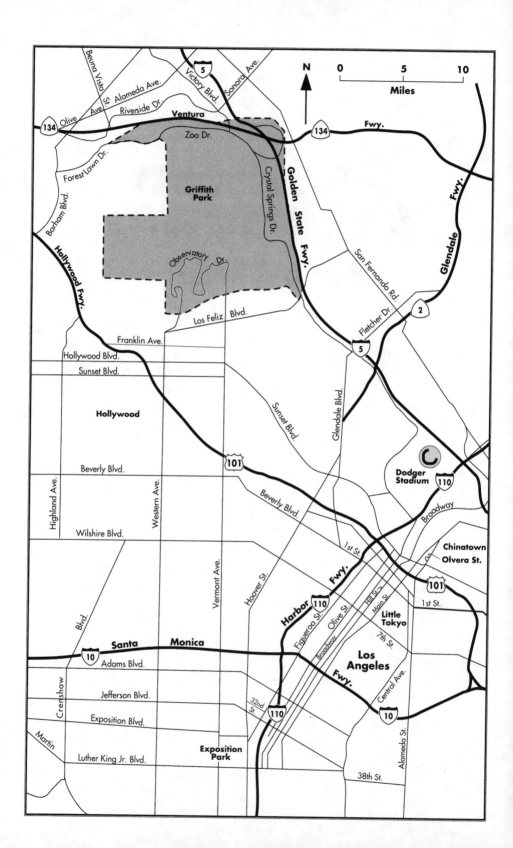

1

Los Angeles

With more than 3 million residents in its 465 square miles, Los Angeles is a vast landscape that often confounds those who go in search of its center. There are, in fact, many "centers" in the nation's second largest city. In this section, we focus on downtown and its surrounding communities and attractions; L.A.'s beaches, valleys, mountains, and harbor areas are examined elsewhere in this book.

Most families considering a day's outing often bypass this downtown region, preferring to visit better-known children's attractions and theme parks in nearby areas or even in the next county. As a result, they miss some of Southern California's richest treats for kids: The heart of Los Angeles boasts the largest municipal park in the nation, one of the finest collections of science and natural history museums in any American city, and the lure of the movie industry.

The problem, especially for out-of-town tourists, is transportation. Although downtown's Union Station is a handy jumping-off place for catching trains to the north coast or south to San Diego, mass rapid transit within the city is its Achilles' heel. Los Angeles is hard at work fixing the situation. Its downtown streets reflect the construction chaos that is a consequence of building a combination subway and light-rail system in a mature city. In Civic Center you will find a convenient shuttle-bus system, but elsewhere you are likely to rely on the family car or a rental car (if you're from out of town) to get around. In the city, parking can range from $5 to $20 a day depending on the facility and its location. But the effort and the cost are small prices to pay for the rewarding experiences waiting for kids in the heart of Los Angeles.

DOWNTOWN LOS ANGELES
Fun among the Skyscrapers

Downtown Los Angeles is growing up—the city's dynamic skyline is evidence of its rise as a commercial center of the Pacific Rim—but it isn't all business. Tucked away amid the shiny new skyscrapers are several attractions for families.

If the youngsters are up to walking a few miles, one of the best ways to appreciate the city is on foot. Or if walking is impractical, take the DASH, a shuttle-bus system that covers downtown's highlights (every day except Sunday) for only 25 cents a ride. The gray DASH bus-stop signs have maps showing the route, or you can pick up a route map on the bus.

For most local residents, downtown refers to the area roughly bounded by the Hollywood Freeway to the north, the Santa Monica Freeway to the south, the Harbor Freeway to the west, and Golden State Freeway to the east. During weekdays, the city is alive with office workers and most restaurants and attractions are open. On weekends, some of the attractions and restaurants close, but the crowds are much smaller and traffic is more manageable. As with most big cities today, whenever you go you are likely to see homeless people in downtown L.A., a fact you may want to discuss with younger children in advance.

If you want a map for your downtown stroll, stop in at the Los Angeles Visitor Information Center in the Hilton Hotel at 7th and Figueroa streets. The best place to start your walking tour is a few blocks away at 4th and Hope streets. If you're driving, park in the multi-story Arco Plaza Garage on Flower Street across from the futuristic Bonaventure Hotel. (Be sure you don't park beneath the Arco Plaza itself; the walk is much longer.) Take the elevators to the very top of the garage, then walk around to the right, past the YMCA Building to the 4th and Hope street intersection.

Cross the intersection and head north to the Wells Fargo Center. Between the Center's two tall, trapezoidal office towers you will find the two-story Wells Fargo Court building. Inside is a fountain courtyard with a variety of snack stands and shops on the ground floor, and a large cafeteria and oriental restaurant upstairs.

Go around the fountain court and step outside to the **Wells Fargo History Museum,** a must for any youngster learning about the days of the Pony Express and California gold rush. Sponsored by Wells Fargo Bank, the free museum includes exhibits and displays that vividly portray frontier life. An authentic stagecoach sits near the entrance. Six-guns, strongboxes, miner's tools, real gold nuggets, and a replica of an early Wells Fargo office help make the history come alive. In the back of the museum, be sure to see a stagecoach mock-up that shows how the Concord coaches were built. Climb aboard the mock-up and get a feeling for the cramped quarters and rocking ride that nineteenth-century travelers had to endure on the long journey west. A small auditorium plays a video of the company's history and periodically shows the 1939 westerns "Wells Fargo" and John Ford's classic "Stagecoach." At the museum's General Store you can buy books and memorabilia. The hottest-selling item for kids is a hunk of iron pyrites ("fool's gold") for 75 cents.

From the museum, walk through the Wells Fargo Center to Grand Avenue. Across the street and up to the left is the **Museum of Contemporary Art (MOCA),** with its distinctive red sandstone walls and pyramid-shaped skylights. MOCA concentrates on art from 1940 to the present, and the unconventional nature of the paintings, sculptures, photographs, and experimental pieces will fascinate most youngsters.

To resume your tour, continue north on Grand Avenue to 1st Street. Across the street to the left is the **Los Angeles Music Center** and its three theaters: the Ahmanson Theater, Dorothy Chandler Pavilion, and Mark Taper Forum. At the pavilion, the Los Angeles Philharmonic offers six "Symphonies for Youth" that introduce music to elementary-school children in special hour-long concerts during the school year.

If you're not going to a performance, turn right and head down 1st Street four blocks to the **Los Angeles Times** at 1st and Broadway. One of the largest and most successful newspapers in America, the *Los Angeles Times* has been published since 1882. The newspaper offers free one-hour guided tours weekdays at 11:15 A.M. and 3 P.M. Youngsters age ten and older see the process of making a daily newspaper, from the reporters in the newsroom to the bundled copies of the paper heading out the door to newsstands.

Two blocks past the Times Building on 1st Street, a fast food stand sells a specialty you are likely to find only in Los Angeles—the kosher burrito. Made with pastrami instead of traditional shredded beef, this burrito is a pleasing combination of Jewish and Mexican cuisines. The stand provides only a few places to sit, but you can take your snack across the street for an impromptu picnic on the grounds of City Hall.

From the corner of 1st and Main streets, walk north on Main past City Hall and its distinctive stair-step pyramid tower. After crossing Temple Street on Main, you will see the Los Angeles Mall on your right. At the north end of the mall is the **Los Angeles Children's Museum.** The museum is at street level, while most of the mall, with its shops and fast food restaurants, is one level below on an open courtyard. Plans for the museum involve taking over the entire mall to create the Los Angeles Children's Plaza, with expanded exhibits, a theater, and an outdoor playground.

Today's 15,000-square-foot museum is tailored for kids from 2 to 12, but youngsters of almost any age will find something to intrigue them in the semichaotic whirl of exhibits. Budding reporters give news broadcasts from a TV studio complete with cameras, microphones, and a weather map. Young performers make their own music or drama in a recording studio, or become part of the show with actors and mimes at the museum's Performance Center. Other exhibit areas highlight health, art, and music. There's a bus for kids to play on, blocks for them to build with, and an animation center, designed by Walt Disney Co., where their drawings come to life. At "Sticky City" kids create sculptures from Velcro-covered shapes of foam rubber. For children under three, "Soft Space" offers a gentle environment away from the bigger children. In the summer, the museum conducts its Inside L.A. tours, taking children to behind-the-scenes places like a dugout at Dodger Stadium or a space simulation lab. A gift shop sells educational toys and children's books. Kids can hold birthday parties at the museum.

To resume your walking tour, continue north on Main Street and cross over the Hollywood Freeway. Be sure to look down at the walls on both sides of the freeway to see a few of the many murals that were painted in Los Angeles before the city hosted the 1984 Olympics.

On the other side of the freeway, you enter **El Pueblo de Los Angeles State Historic Park,** a 44-acre preserve of historic buildings and a commercial marketplace that commemorate the founding of Los Angeles in 1781. The historic park includes 27 buildings built between 1818 and 1926; a few have been restored as museums and three are of interest to kids. The 1884 Sepulveda House on Olvera Street doubles as a museum of early Los Angeles and the park's visitors center, where you can buy books on the city's history and other items. You also can pick up a self-guided walking tour of the park's historic sites. In the park's Plaza, the Old Plaza Firehouse, built in 1884, is now a firefighting museum. Across the Plaza, the 1818 Avila Adobe has been restored as a museum depicting the days of Spanish California.

The entire area is loosely referred to as **Olvera Street,** site of an open-air Mexican market where merchants sell a variety of Mexican goods and handicrafts—a souvenir-hunter's dream. In addition to the market and Sepulveda House, there are four restaurants on Olvera Street. At the least expensive one, La Luz del Dia, kids enjoy watching tortillas being made by hand while you order your food at a counter. Seating is at long tables, family style. After eating, stop at one of the street's bakeries and sample a churro, a long donut stick rolled in powdered sugar and cinnamon.

To complete your tour, walk over to Los Angeles Street on the east side of the plaza where it joins Alameda Street. Go across Alameda to **Union Station,** the large white building reminiscent of California's mission architecture. Youngsters will be impressed by the three-story-high open beam ceiling in the station's waiting room. The terminal is where you come to catch Amtrak trains to San Diego, Santa Barbara, and points in between. Out front you also can catch the DASH to take you back to your starting place. *Please note:* DASH stops running at 6 P.M. weekdays and 5 P.M. Saturday.

Los Angeles holds other attractions for kids, but they are mostly beyond walking distance from downtown. Ten blocks west of downtown on 1st Street the **Bob Baker Marionette Theater** keeps alive both the art of puppetry and children's imaginations. When not on tour in the United States or Canada, the Baker troupe entertains younger children with fast-paced musical shows featuring some very ingenious marionettes. After the show, children go backstage to see how marionettes are made. The $7 ticket price includes the workshop tour and refreshments. Although it is located near a freeway underpass, where chain-link fences and padlocks are needed to ensure security, the theater has been going strong for 27 years and shows no signs of flagging popularity.

North of Civic Center, just off Pasadena Freeway (State Highway 110), you can immerse the youngsters in the sights, sounds, smells, and tastes of Southern California's Hispanic heritage at **Lawry's California Center.** Built by the spice company as a showplace for its products, the center is an open-air restaurant that features Mexican cuisine. The ambience is embellished with whitewashed Spanish architecture, colorful gardens of exotic flowers and cascading fountains, and the occasional band of strolling musicians (*mariachis*). On weekdays, take a free guided tour of the spicemaker's plant at the center to see test kitchens and production facilities. Children must be at least fourth-graders to take the tour.

Other attractions, though not specifically geared to children, hold great promise for family outings. Two of the city's largest ethnic groups, the Japanese and the Chinese, live in distinct communities on the edges of Civic Center. **Little Tokyo** is just east of City Hall off 1st Street, while **Chinatown** lies north across the Hollywood Freeway beyond Olvera Street. Chinatown's primary tourist area lies along North Broadway. Dragons abound as architectural and design motifs, small shops offer ethnic wares and inexpensive toys, and restaurants range from Chinese to Italian to Continental. Meanwhile, in Little Tokyo, the toy stores in the shopping malls off 1st Street feature the latest battery-powered items, and small, specialty Japanese and Korean restaurants. At the northeast edge of Little Tokyo, **The Temporary Contemporary** displays modern works of art that often fascinate youngsters. This huge warehouselike facility was the temporary home of MOCA while the Bunker Hill museum was being built, hence its name.

East of Little Tokyo, in an area of old warehouses fast becoming a fashionable neighborhood for artists, is one of the city's more unusual art museums. The **Museum of Neon Art (MONA)** preserves the artistry of those who work with gas and glass tubing through a series of changing exhibitions. Not all works on display are neon. For some "kinetic" pieces, you can push a button or pull a lever to make them work. Kids enjoy the museum's bright lights and action. You may want to visit MONA's small gift shop to see the books and novelties on sale.

Attractions

BOB BAKER MARIONETTE THEATER, 1345 West 1st Street, Los Angeles. (Exit Harbor Freeway [110] south at 2nd Street; right on Beaudry Avenue; left on 2nd Street; theater is near intersection of 2nd and 1st streets.) (213) 250-9995. Reservations required. Shows Tuesday–Friday, 10:30 A.M.; Saturday and Sunday, 2:30 P.M. Admission: $7 per person (includes tour and refreshments).

CHINATOWN, centered along North Broadway from 700 block to 1000 block. (Exit Pasadena Freeway [110] southbound at Hill Street; left on Vignes; left on Broadway to Chinatown. Exit Hollywood Freeway [101] eastbound at Broadway; north to Chinatown.)

EL PUEBLO DE LOS ANGELES STATE HISTORIC PARK, 845 North Alameda Street, Los Angeles. (Exit Hollywood Freeway [101] southbound at Broadway; straight on Aliso Street across Broadway to Main Street; left to park. Exit Hollywood Freeway [101] westbound at Aliso Street;

straight onto Arcadia Street and continue to Main Street; right to park.) (213) 628-0605. Visitors center open Monday–Friday, 10 A.M.–3 P.M.; Saturday, 10 A.M.–4:30 P.M. Free.

- *Avila Adobe.* Open Tuesday–Friday, 10 A.M.–3 P.M.; Saturday and Sunday, 10 A.M.–4:30 P.M. Free.
- *Old Plaza Firehouse.* Open Tuesday–Friday, 10 A.M.–3 P.M; Saturday and Sunday, 10 A.M.–4:30 P.M. Free.
- *Olvera Street.* Open daily, 10 A.M.–8 P.M.

HOLOGRAPHIC VISIONS, 300 South Grand Avenue, Los Angeles. (Exit Hollywood Freeway [101] southbound at Temple Street; straight across Temple on Hope Street to 1st Street; left to Grand Avenue and gallery. Exit Hollywood Freeway [101] northbound at Grand Avenue; south to gallery.) (213) 687-7171. Open Thursday and Friday, 11 A.M.–8 P.M.; Tuesday–Sunday, 11 A.M.–6 P.M. Free.

LAWRY'S CALIFORNIA CENTER, 570 West Avenue 26, Los Angeles. (Exit Pasadena Freeway [110] northbound at Figueroa Street; right to Avenue 26; left to Lawry's Center.) (213) 225-2491. Open daily, 10:30 A.M.–10 P.M. Free.

LITTLE TOKYO, centered along 1st Street between Main and Alameda streets. (Exit Hollywood Freeway [101] at Alameda Street; south to 1st Street; right to Little Tokyo.)

LOS ANGELES CHILDREN'S MUSEUM, 310 North Main Street, Los Angeles. (Exit Hollywood Freeway [101] southbound at Broadway; continue straight across Broadway on Aliso Street to Los Angeles Street; right to museum. Exit Hollywood Freeway [101] northbound at Alameda Street; left to Aliso Street; right to Los Angeles Street; left to museum.) (213) 687-8800. Open, summer vacation: Monday–Friday, 11:30 A.M.–5 P.M.; Saturday and Sunday, 10 A.M.–5 P.M. School year: Wednesday and Thursday, 2 P.M.–4 P.M.; Saturday and Sunday, 10 A.M.–5 P.M. Adults, children, $4; under 2, free (all children must be accompanied by an adult).

LOS ANGELES MUSIC CENTER, 135 North Grand Avenue, Los Angeles. (Exit Hollywood Freeway [101] southbound at Temple Street; east to Grand Avenue; right to center. Exit Hollywood Freeway [101] northbound at Grand Avenue; south to center.) (213) 972-7475. Los Angeles Philharmonic

Symphonies for Youth, (213) 972-0703. Call theaters for performances, times, and ticket prices: Ahmanson Theater, (213) 972-7403; Dorothy Chandler Pavilion, (213) 972-7200; Mark Taper Forum, (213) 972-7353.

LOS ANGELES TIMES, 202 West 1st Street, Los Angeles. (Exit Hollywood Freeway [101] southbound at Broadway; south to 1st Street and Times Building. Exit Hollywood Freeway [101] northbound at Spring Street; south at 1st Street and Times Building.) (213) 237-5757. Tours, Monday–Friday, 11:15 A.M. and 3 P.M. Free (children must be ten years old to participate).

MUSEUM OF CONTEMPORARY ART, 250 South Grand Avenue, Los Angeles. (Exit Hollywood Freeway [101] southbound at Temple Street; continue across Temple on Hope Street to 1st Street; left to Grand Avenue; right to museum. Exit Hollywood Freeway [101] northbound at Grand Avenue; south to museum.) (213) 626-6222. Open Tuesday–Sunday, 11 A.M.–6 P.M.; Thursday until 8 P.M. Adults, $4; seniors and students, $2; under 12, free. (Admission free 5–8 P.M. Thursday.) Tickets also good for same-day admission to the Temporary Contemporary.

MUSEUM OF NEON ART, 704 Tracton Avenue, Los Angeles. (Exit Hollywood Freeway [101] at Alameda Street; south to Tracton Avenue; left to museum.) (213) 617-1580. Open Tuesday–Saturday, 11 A.M.–5 P.M. Adults, $2.50; students, $1; under 16, free.

OLVERA STREET (see listing for El Pueblo de Los Angeles State Historic Park).

THE TEMPORARY CONTEMPORARY, 152 North Central Avenue, Los Angeles. (Exit Harbor Freeway [110] at Alameda Street; south to 1st Street; right to Central Avenue; right to museum.) (213) 262-6222. Open Tuesday–Sunday, 11 A.M.–6 P.M.; Thursday until 8 P.M. Adults, $4; seniors and students, $2; under 12, free. (Admission free 5–8 P.M. Thursday.) Tickets also good for same-day admission to Museum of Contemporary Art.

UNION STATION, 800 North Alameda Street, Los Angeles. (Exit Hollywood Freeway [101] at Alameda Street; north to station.) (213) 683-6873.

WELLS FARGO HISTORY MUSEUM, 333 South Grand Avenue, Los Angeles. (Exit Hollywood Freeway [101] southbound at Temple Street; straight across Temple on Hope Street to 1st Street; left to Grand Avenue;

right to museum. Exit Hollywood Freeway [101] northbound at Grand Avenue; south to museum.) (213) 253-7166. Open Monday–Friday (except bank holidays), 9 A.M.–5 P.M. Free.

For More Information

Chinese Chamber of Commerce, 978 Broadway, Room 206, Los Angeles, CA 90012; (213) 617-0396.

Los Angeles Visitors Information Center, 695 South Figueroa Street (in the Los Angeles Hilton Hotel). (213) 689-8822. Open, Monday–Saturday, 8 A.M.–5 P.M.

Japanese Chamber of Commerce of Southern California, 244 South San Pedro Street, Los Angeles, CA 90012; (213) 626-3067.

EXPOSITION PARK
Acres of Roses and Museums

Minutes south of downtown Los Angeles, just west of the Harbor Freeway (I-110) at Exposition Boulevard, is one of the finest collections of museums in the nation. The museums of Natural History and Science and Industry sit in the welcoming grassy expanse of Exposition Park. A little more than a century ago the park was an agricultural marketplace; today it is the site of the city's historic Coliseum and home of the 1932 and 1984 Olympic Games.

Though not as well known as the famous sports edifice, the museums and their energetic curatorial staffs always seem to be on the move, constantly refurbishing and expanding their exhibits. Children with inquiring minds, active imaginations, and a penchant for pushing buttons likely will run out of energy before they run out of museum exhibits to explore.

At the **Natural History Museum of Los Angeles County,** you will find one of the most comprehensive natural-history collections in the world. Permanent exhibits examine the worlds of mammals, birds, fish, gems, fossils, insects, and plants. But for every youngster, a "must" attraction is the museum's Discovery Center, located off the Rotunda at the east end of the building's ground floor. The center closes at 3 P.M., two hours before the rest of the museum, so you'll need to plan accordingly.

The center's appeal is that it gives kids a chance to touch, stroke, manipulate, and even wear the kinds of objects they can only look at behind glass in the rest of the museum. Youngsters grind corn with Indian stone tools, watch the squiggly patterns sounds make on an oscilloscope, stroke the fur of an Alaskan brown bear, make crayon rubbings of fossils, dress up in historic costumes, and do much more. At The Box Office in the middle of the center, you'll check out a discovery box with your child. These large wooden boxes, with such colorful titles as "The Eyes Have It" and "The Write Stuff," contain games that teach simple lessons in the earth and life sciences. Another favorite with kids is an interactive video with several different two-minute programs on dinosaurs. On Sunday, after the center closes at 3 P.M., youngsters attend bimonthly Whale's Tales programs. Kids might see a dinosaur puppet show, learn about bears, or delve into any other natural-science topic during these special sessions. The center posts topics for future programs, but be sure to sign up early. Youngsters also can join the museum's Discovery Club ($10/year) to attend special children's openings of exhibits, sign up in advance for the museum's children's programs, and receive a club newsletter.

Children will find plenty to interest them in the rest of the museum, too. Near the central foyer on the ground floor, three exhibits never fail to fascinate most youngsters. The Egyptian mummy Pu, wrapped in ancient cloth bindings, lies in a glass case. Look closely and you'll see his teeth and his toes. East of the foyer, Megamouth, a huge member of the shark family, lies in a long case with his mouth agape. West of the foyer, in a similar case, a giant specimen of the rare oarfish lies in state. These creatures are among the strangest any child is ever likely to see. In the center of the foyer two dinosaur skeletons are locked in combat as they might have been in life many millions of years ago.

Elsewhere in the museum kids especially like to explore huge mammal halls that have detailed dioramas depicting the mounted animals in their natural habitats. Another favorite is the Hall of Gems, a darkened room lit dramatically to emphasize the natural beauty of crystalline rock formations and cut gemstones. In front of the fossil exhibit, the giant skull of a tyrannosaurus dwarfs most children. By the way, most of the museum's fine fossil collection will not be on permanent display until a new exhibit hall is built in a few years. You can see a separate and extensive collection of Ice Age fossils at the George C. Page Museum at the La Brea Tar Pits (see Beverly Hills and the Mid-Wilshire District in chapter 2).

The museum offers workshops and classes for youngsters throughout the year, in conjunction with its exhibits. Most classes are two hours long. Prices vary, and you will need to preregister for the popular sessions. During the summer, the museum sponsors week-long classes for kids from kindergarten through sixth grade.

Before you leave, visit the Dinosaur Shop near the south entrance. Aimed at kids, the shop sells dinosaur souvenirs, juvenile books, models, and educational toys and games on a wide range of topics. Across the foyer near the north entrance, the museum stocks a large bookstore which also has a children's section. If you get hungry, there's a cafeteria in the museum basement.

An easy stroll east of the Natural History Museum brings you to the **California Museum of Science and Industry,** second in size only to the Smithsonian Institution among the nation's science museums. Its many displays and interactive exhibits invite kids to learn about earthquakes, mathematics, aeronautics, energy, even economics, and have fun doing it. The huge facility is actually several museums in one: Aerospace Hall, Kinsey Hall of Health, Mark Taper Hall of Economics and Finance, and Technology Hall.

At the entrance to the museum's main structure (Ahmanson Building), kids are immediately captivated by an odd contraption of metal tubing and red balls that demonstrates the principle of kinetic energy. In Technology Hall to your left in this main building, youngsters assemble a bicycle by computer and then operate a factory to manufacture their product. The award-winning Mathematica exhibit graphically displays such principles as probability, multiplication, geometry, and orbital mechanics. The Energy Experience teaches youngsters the nature of energy and how to conserve it through the use of interactive touch TV screens.

Downstairs youngsters feel the shaking, rumbling terror of an earthquake in an exhibit on quakes. Very young children should probably pass up this frightening experience and head around the corner to see chicks hatching in the museum's incubator.

Back on the main floor near the entrance, the transportation exhibit holds a special fascination for many youngsters. On the second level of this exhibit two electric trains endlessly circle the entire room, traveling through tiny cities, past harbors, across deserts, and through miniature mountains in an elaborate diorama. A few steps from the trains is one of the museum's most popular stops—a McDonald's restaurant with all the fast food trimmings. Munch your burgers in an adjacent seating area or take them across the street to the fragrant seven-acre Rose Garden.

Just south of the Ahmanson Building, exhibits in the Mark Taper Hall of Economics and Finance manage to make this "dismal science" entertaining through the use of computers, push buttons, video displays, and imagination. When you enter the exhibit area you receive a "credit card" that helps personalize many of the learning experiences. At the Bongo Bead Exchange youngsters learn about supply and demand through computer bidding with other kids. Computers also help teach vivid lessons about savings, interest rates, and balancing a budget. Obviously, in this bright, open, inviting hall, all the learning isn't limited to the kids.

East of the Ahmanson Building, the Kinsey Hall of Health also dispenses "credit cards" to visitors. Using the cards, kids conduct a self-checkup of their pulse, breathing, weight, height, and reaction to stress. In the Food-works exhibit, a video waitress encourages youngsters to improve their eating habits. Other displays explain how the body works, birth and reproduction, and the perils of substance abuse.

One of the most popular stops for kids is Aerospace Hall, across the street to the north of Kinsey Hall. The building is easy to spot because it has a Lockheed F-104 Starfighter mounted dramatically on its facade. On the ground floor, where an Air Force T-38 jet trainer and a P-51 World War II fighter are suspended overhead, youngsters soak up exhibits on flight and the history of aviation. Kids take the controls to "fly" a model F-16 jet fighter through roll-and-pitch maneuvers. Using a propeller engine, jet engine, or rocket engine, youngsters learn about the principles of lift and propulsion.

In the hall's upstairs gallery, kids come face to face with several space-craft, including Mercury and Gemini capsules and a communications satellite. They'll learn about weather with an interactive computer exhibit that includes actual satellite photos. Be sure to see the 13-minute multi-screen slide show "Windows on the Universe," which tells the story of space exploration. The show's loud rumbling soundtrack may be a bit too intense for very little ones. The show runs every half hour between 10 A.M. and 4 P.M.

Immediately east of Aerospace Hall, movies on the huge five-story screen of the **Mitsubishi IMAX Theater** will take you and the kids as close as you are likely to come to space travel and a variety of other adventures.

Before leaving the Museum of Science and Industry, the kids probably will want to visit the gift center in Aerospace Hall or the Ahmanson Building. The aerospace center concentrates on a space and aviation theme, with models of airplanes and spacecraft, books, buttons, posters, and space ice cream. At the larger center in the main building, the selection is broader.

Another museum hallmark is the excellent array of classes and **children's workshops** it offers. Sessions are held in summer and on weekends during the school year. With other students in their grade level, kids learn about such subjects as the planets, insects, and electricity. There are also classes for parents and children to take together.

The **California Afro-American Museum** occupies a striking building just east of Kinsey Hall. Children will like the openness of the museum's 13,000-square-foot sculpture court at the entrance, enclosed beneath bronze-tinted glass. In the galleries just off the court, displays document the Afro-American experience in the United States through art, science, religion, sports, and politics. Though none of the permanent exhibits are designed just for kids, the museum's gift shop carries black children's books and dolls. The museum also sponsors summer art workshops for children as well as adults.

One more museum in the area is not located in Exposition Park but is well worth visiting. The **Skirball Museum** on the campus of Hebrew Union College is the largest museum of Judaica in the West. The museum is north of Exposition Park at 32nd and Hoover streets (on the other side of the University of Southern California campus from the park). The Skirball concentrates on Jewish fine art and religious objects, but kids will be most interested in its archaeology exhibit. In a cross-section view of a mound (called a *tell*), youngsters see how artifacts are deposited in layers with the oldest ones, from the fourth millennium B.C., at the bottom. Museum docents use a model of a Bronze Age granary to explain how archaeologists uncover ancient secrets. Other displays trace the development of language and explain pottery making. Call the museum to arrange a docent tour during the week, or take the regularly scheduled tour at 1 P.M. on Sunday.

Just south of the Skirball Museum, on the University of Southern California campus, the **Children's Film and Television Center of America** monthly screens short films for kids. The films are from independent filmmakers, studios, and TV stations. The 15-year-old, nonprofit center was established to promote quality films for children, and each year it sponsors a week-long International Film Festival.

Attractions

CALIFORNIA AFRO-AMERICAN MUSEUM, 600 State Drive, Los Angeles. (Exit Harbor Freeway [110] at Exposition Boulevard; west to Flower Street; left to Figueroa Street; left to Museum Drive; right to museum.) (213) 744-7432. Open daily, 10 A.M.–5 P.M. Free. Parking $1.

CALIFORNIA MUSEUM OF SCIENCE AND INDUSTRY, 700 State Drive, Los Angeles. (See directions to California Afro-American Museum.) (213) 744-7400. Open daily, 10 A.M.–5 P.M. Free. Parking $1.

- *Mitsubishi IMAX Theater:* (213) 744-2015. Adults, $5 (one show), $7.50 (two shows), $9 (three shows); ages 3–17 and students with valid I.D., $3.50; seniors, $3.50.
- *Children's Science Workshops:* (213) 744-7440.

CHILDREN'S FILM AND TELEVISION CENTER OF AMERICA, 850 West 34th Street, Los Angeles. (Films shown on USC campus. Exit Harbor Freeway [110] at Exposition Boulevard; west to campus at Figueroa Street.) (213) 740-3339 (call for time and exact locations of theaters). Adults, $3; ages 3–16, $2; under 3 and members, free.

NATURAL HISTORY MUSEUM OF LOS ANGELES COUNTY, 900 Exposition Boulevard, Los Angeles. (Exit Harbor Freeway [110] at Exposition Boulevard; west to Menlo Avenue; left to parking.) (213) 744-3466. Open Tuesday–Sunday, 10 A.M.–5 P.M. Adults, $3; ages 13–17 and seniors, $1.50; ages 5–12, 75 cents. Free to all first Tuesday of each month.

- *Discovery Center:* (213) 744-3335. Open Tuesday–Sunday, 11 A.M.–3 P.M. Free with museum admission.
- *Children's classes information,* (213) 744-3333.

SKIRBALL MUSEUM, 32nd Street at Hoover Street, Los Angeles. (Exit Harbor Freeway [110] at Figueroa Street; south to Jefferson Boulevard; right to Hoover Street; right to 32nd Street and museum. (213) 749-3424. Open Tuesday–Friday, 11 A.M.–4 P.M.; Sunday, 10 A.M.–5 P.M. Free.

For More Information

Greater Los Angeles Visitors and Convention Bureau, 515 South Figueroa Street, 11th Floor, Los Angeles, CA 90071; (213) 689-8822.

H O L L Y W O O D
Stargazing Past and Present

Hollywood has been associated with the glamour of movie stars and film-making since the 1920s. Despite its fascinating image, the movie capital in recent years has disappointed visitors with its tawdriness. On a walking tour of Hollywood Boulevard, you'll glimpse the former glamour in only a handful of museums and attractions, tucked in among T-shirt shops and souvenir stands. All this may change in a few years when the city fathers complete an ambitious redevelopment plan. Still, the area is full of history and quite safe during the day, and for children with an interest in movies, Hollywood is a must-see attraction. But the city has more to offer than movie lore, including a summer series of children's concerts given daily and an art center with free weekly art workshops for families.

Start your tour at the De Mille barn, where in 1913 Hollywood's full-length feature filmmaking first began with Cecil B. De Mille's production of *The Squaw Man*. The barn is now the home of the **Hollywood Studio Museum** on Highland Avenue.

Kids who have never heard of De Mille or the early screen stars will watch the museum's snappy two-minute video and come away with an appreciation for the simple stories and free-wheeling methods used by the early filmmakers. The museum displays cameras and equipment used by the fledgling industry, and costumes and props from famous films. In De Mille's re-created office you'll see his ancient typewriter and the large wooden wastebasket he put his feet on to keep them dry when water ran through his office after the barn's stalls were cleaned.

During the summer, a shuttle bus runs between the museum and the famous landmark across the street, the **Hollywood Bowl.** The 17,000-seat outdoor amphitheater is the setting for evening concerts presented by the Los Angeles Philharmonic during summer months. Children's favorites are the bowl's pop concerts with fireworks finales, given several times during the season.

On weekday mornings at 9:30 and 10:30 during July and August, take the kids to **Open House at Hollywood Bowl.** These one-hour concerts, which change each week for a six-week session, are designed for children from ages 3 to early teens. Each show presents international entertainers, such as dancers, musicians, puppeteers, and mimes. The programs are held at an outdoor theater in the box-office plaza adjacent to the bowl. Dress for hot weather at the bowl on summer days. Wear sunscreen or a hat and also bring along two spoons for each child so the kids can enjoy the Open House tradition of making music with spoons.

After each performance at 10:30 and 11:30 A.M., educators hold workshops—organized by age group—in activities related to the show, such as puppet making and folk dancing. You'll need to sign up for these popular workshops in advance. Afterward you can go up the outdoor escalator to see the bowl and perhaps hear an orchestra rehearsing for an evening performance. There are shaded picnic tables and snack bars in the park near the theater. The adjacent **Hollywood Bowl Museum** highlights the history of the bowl with displays of musical instruments and photos of famous performers and conductors.

To continue your tour of old Hollywood, drive a few blocks south on Highland Avenue to Hollywood Boulevard, for a two-block walking tour of its famous sites. Turn right (west) on Hollywood Boulevard and right again on Orchid to park in one of the large lots.

Start your walking tour just around the corner at Hollywood's most famous landmark, **Mann's Chinese Theatre,** the lavish pagoda-style movie theater, known for most of its life as Grauman's Chinese, built by Sid Grauman in 1927. It is best known for the movie-star handprints and footprints embedded in the cement forecourt. Many of the "signatures" will be familiar to the younger set—Donald Duck's footprints and *Star Wars'* robots' body prints. Kids can wander around and match their hands and feet to the prints of their favorite stars. Children have fun discovering other famous features also traced in the cement—George Burns's cigar, Harpo Marx's harp, and the hoofprints of Roy Rogers's horse Trigger. Child-star Shirley Temple's footprints are of particular interest to younger children. You may want to interrupt your tour here to take in a movie at the theater. The exotic interior, built during an era when movie houses were palaces, is worth a look.

Continue your tour walking east on Hollywood Boulevard along the Walk of Fame. Black-and-gold metal stars bearing the names of Hollywood entertainers dot the sidewalks on both sides of the street. Children will recognize many of the names, starting with Mickey Mouse in front of Mann's Chinese Theatre. Walk east across Highland Boulevard to the **Hollywood Wax Museum** to see what those stars looked like. The museum displays nearly two hundred life-size figures of famous entertainers. Kids may recognize many, such as Superman and Mr. T. There's also a chamber of horrors more appropriate for older kids, full of such characters as Count Dracula and the Wolfman.

Cross Hollywood Boulevard at Highland Avenue and walk a half block south on Highland to the **Max Factor Beauty Museum.** Housed in the makeup salon built by Max Factor in 1935, the free museum contains celebrity makeup rooms and antique cosmetic devices. Exhibits explain how Factor created the first makeup for movies. You'll see hairpieces used by stars, early Max Factor products such as nose putty, and the Scroll of Fame, one of the largest collections of famous film-star autographs.

If the kids are hungry at this point, you will find several fast food restaurants in the area. One block west of Highland Avenue on Hollywood Boulevard, **Hollywood on Location** evokes Hollywood's heyday with its 1950s soda fountain. Children enjoy sitting on the round silver stools at the counter where they can eat hot dogs and sandwiches and play their favorite rock and roll songs at counter juke box selectors.

Adjacent to the small restaurant is a souvenir shop and an exhibit of intricate models, **Hollywood in Miniature.** Set in a darkened exhibit area, the models recreate places important to the movie industry in the 1930s. Kids like watching the lights come up on each of the scenes, which include the Malibu beach colony (complete with rolling surf), Paramount Studios, and Grauman's Chinese Theatre.

Walk west on Hollywood Boulevard for one more block to get a better look at the ornate architecture of the real Chinese Theatre across the street. On the next corner is the **Hollywood Roosevelt Hotel,** which has been restored to its original (1927) glory. The hotel has been home to many famous stars and was the site of the first Academy Awards presentations. The lobby is worth a walk-through to see the hand-painted ceilings and historical displays of Hollywood and the movie industry on the mezzanine.

Finish your tour of Hollywood by stepping across the street to **C. C. Brown's,** an old-fashioned ice-cream parlor, for a hot-fudge sundae. A Hollywood tradition since 1929, C. C. Brown's retains its original high-backed, chocolate-colored mahogany booths. The menu includes nearly two dozen mouth-watering sundaes, as well as sandwiches and soups, sure to please weary stargazers.

When you've had your fill of film history, drive two miles east on Hollywood Boulevard to see, and perhaps create, more contemporary art. **Barnsdall Art Park** overlooks the northeast corner of Hollywood from a small hill. Once an estate owned by oil heiress Aline Barnsdall, the park is now the site of an art center that offers classes for kids, an art gallery, and a home designed by Frank Lloyd Wright that you can tour. Elsewhere in the 13-acre park, you will find children's play areas and picnic tables.

Most interesting for children is the **Junior Arts Center,** a facility operated by the City of Los Angeles Cultural Affairs Department, which offers studio art workshops for kids ages 3 to 18. Classes cover such subjects as painting, clay sculpture, illustration, and theater arts, and cost about $20 for the eight-week sessions. Many of the workshops for 3- to 6-year-olds are designed for parents and children together.

Every Sunday from 2 to 4 P.M. the center sponsors free art workshops for the whole family called Sunday Open Sunday. You don't need to register for these drop-in classes and all materials are provided. Workshops in the past have offered classes in clay mask making, cloth printing, and mural painting. A gallery at the center features changing exhibits by adults and children.

Plan to visit the adjacent **Municipal Art Gallery** when you come to the park for a workshop. The gallery has changing exhibits by contemporary artists, mostly from Southern California. Many exhibits contain works that invite interaction, and docents with the museum's education department will point out those works of greatest interest to kids.

The most striking building on the hill is **Hollyhock House,** the home Frank Lloyd Wright designed for Aline Barnsdall in 1920. You can take a guided tour of the sprawling concrete and stucco home. Indoors and out you'll see the geometric hollyhock motif that gives the house its name. Older children interested in design will find the tour most interesting. The hilly park surrounding the buildings has fine views of Hollywood, with picnic tables and a children's play area.

Attractions

BARNSDALL ART PARK, 4800 Hollywood Boulevard, Hollywood. (Exit Hollywood Freeway [101] at Hollywood Boulevard; east to park.)

• *Hollyhock House:* (213) 662-7272. Guided tours, Tuesday–Thursday, 10 and 11 A.M. and 12 and 1 P.M.; Saturday and the first 3 Sundays of the month, 12, 1, 2, and 3 P.M. Adults, $1.50; seniors, $1; ages 12 and under, free. Buy tickets at the adjacent Municipal Art Gallery.
• *Junior Arts Center:* (213) 485-4474. Sunday Open Sunday, every Sunday, 2–4 P.M. Free. Eight-week Studio Art Workshops for children ages 3–18 held year round. Call for schedule. Prices vary, but most are about $20.
• *Municipal Art Gallery:* (213) 485-4581. Open Tuesday–Sunday, 12:30–5 P.M. Adults, $1; ages 12 and under, free.

HOLLYWOOD BOWL, 2301 North Highland Avenue, Hollywood. (Exit Hollywood Freeway [101] at Highland Avenue; south to bowl.) (213) 850-2000. Evening concerts. Tuesday–Saturday, 8:30 P.M. (July–September), some Sundays. Open house at Hollywood Bowl children's concerts: (213) 850-2077. Monday–Friday, 9:30 A.M. and 10:30 A.M. (July–August). Concert tickets for ages 3 and up, $2.50. Workshops, $1.

HOLLYWOOD BOWL MUSEUM, 2301 North Highland Avenue, Hollywood. (See directions to Hollywood Bowl above.) (213) 850-2058. Open June 30–September 15, Monday–Sunday, 9:30 A.M.–8:30 P.M. (concert days); 9:30 A.M.–4:30 P.M. (other days); September–June, 9:30 A.M.–4:30 P.M. Free.

HOLLYWOOD STUDIO MUSEUM, 2100 North Highland Avenue, Hollywood. (Exit Hollywood Freeway [101] at Highland Avenue; south to museum.) (213) 874-2276. Call museum for hours. Adults, $3.50; seniors and students, $2.50; under 12, $1.50.

(**Note:** All directions to the following attractions are given from the intersection of Highland Avenue and Hollywood Boulevard. To reach this intersection, exit Hollywood Freeway [101] northbound at Hollywood Boulevard; west to intersection. Exit [101] southbound at Highland Avenue; south to intersection.)

C. C. BROWN'S, 7007 Hollywood Boulevard, Hollywood. (West of Highland Avenue.) (213) 462-9262. Open Monday–Thursday, 1–11 P.M.; Friday and Saturday, 1 P.M.–midnight.

HOLLYWOOD IN MINIATURE, 6834 Hollywood Boulevard, Hollywood. (West of Highland Avenue.) (213) 466-7758. Open daily, 7 A.M.–2 A.M. Free.

HOLLYWOOD ON LOCATION, 6824 Hollywood Boulevard, Hollywood. (West of Highland Avenue.) (213) 466-7758. Open daily, 7 A.M.– 2 A.M.

HOLLYWOOD ROOSEVELT HOTEL, 7000 Hollywood Boulevard, Hollywood. (West of Highland Avenue.) (213) 466-7000.

HOLLYWOOD WAX MUSEUM, 6767 Hollywood Boulevard, Hollywood. (East of Highland Avenue.) (213) 462-8860. Open Sunday–Thursday, 10 A.M.–midnight; Friday and Saturday, 10 A.M.–2 A.M. Adults, $7; senior citizens and ages 13–17, $6; ages 6–12, $5; under 6, free.

MANN'S CHINESE THEATRE, 6925 Hollywood Boulevard, Hollywood. (West of Highland Avenue.) (213) 464-8111. Forecourt open 24 hours. Free. Theater open daily, noon–midnight. Call for film schedule.

MAX FACTOR BEAUTY MUSEUM AND RETAIL STORE, 1666 North Highland Avenue, Hollywood. (South of Hollywood Boulevard.) (213) 463-6668. Open Monday–Saturday, 10 A.M.–4 P.M. Museum is free.

For More Information

Hollywood Chamber of Commerce, 6255 Sunset Boulevard, #911, Hollywood, CA 90028; (213) 469-8311.

GRIFFITH PARK
Big Park for a Big City

Many Angelenos don't realize that one of the world's largest municipal parks lies within their city's borders. **Griffith Park**'s 4,107 acres hold a wide variety of attractions to delight children. You'll find 53 miles of mountainous hiking and bridle trails to explore, museums, a theater, a zoo, a planetarium, sports facilities, and pony and train rides. You could spend several full days exploring this park with kids.

Plan to spend most of a day when you visit the **Los Angeles Zoo,** located at the north end of the park. The hilly 110-acre zoo displays more than two thousand animals, many in environments that simulate their natural habitats.

Start your tour with kids at Adventure Island, the recently renovated children's zoo located near the main entrance. In place of the former barnyard petting zoo, Adventure Island now provides an environment where kids learn about animals with the use of computers and interactive exhibits. In a cave behind a waterfall, children discover a dark glass wall where they touch hidden sensors that illuminate pictures of animals. At the Southwestern Desert area, kids play a computer game to learn about the live reptiles in the exhibit. Elsewhere they poke their heads up into Plexiglas domes to imitate prairie dogs and see them up close in their dens. In sculptured masks of a bee, mountain lion, and rabbit, youngsters look through special optical lenses to learn about each animal's vision. Large, low windows in the animal care nursery allow kids to see baby animals unable to stay with their natural mothers. The new Spanish-hacienda–style petting zoo allows kids to pet the animals—at the animals' discretion—through a split-rail fence.

The rest of the zoo is divided into five geographical areas with animals indigenous to a particular continent exhibited together. The apes, monkeys, and elephants in the African section always attract attention. You can ride an elephant nearby, too. In the Eurasia area you'll see Siberian tigers and black leopards, while South American favorites include jaguars and giant Galapagos turtles. In the North American section, there are animals seldom seen on the continent today, such as bison and mountain lions. The Australian section has kangaroos, wallabies, and, of course, koala bears. The nearby Ahmanson Koala House showcases these lovable nocturnal animals in a nighttime environment. An aquatic section features otters and seals, and at the reptile house you'll view poisonous snakes from behind the safety of a glass window.

Don't try to see the entire zoo on foot with young children. It's spread out over hilly terrain and involves a lot of walking, so you may want to pick just a few areas to visit. When it's time to eat, the zoo has two shady picnic areas and fast food concessions nearby. Southern California's mild winter months are an ideal time to visit the zoo because summer temperatures often hover around 90 degrees. If you do go in summer, start your visit early in the day, and plan frequent rest stops to see the daily animal shows. Two of the shows are designed especially for children: "Animals and You" presents animals close-up in a small theater and "The Zoopeteers" perform an animal puppet show.

Near the zoo at the north end of the park is **Travel Town Museum,** another favorite attraction for kids. This transportation museum showcases locomotives, airplanes, fire engines, streetcars, and automobiles in displays that children can touch. When you enter the museum you'll cross the tracks of the only working railroad in the collection, a small-scale steam-engine train that chugs around Travel Town every 15 minutes. Buy tickets at the station if you want to take the seven-minute ride. Then enter the large museum building on the left to see a collection of firefighting equipment used in Los Angeles from 1869 to 1940. Look for the brightly painted circus wagon and some antique cars, too. Through large windows at the back of the museum you'll often see members of the East Valley Lines N Scale Model Railroad Club running model trains through elaborate miniature town and country settings.

Outside you'll find more than forty steam locomotives and other railroad cars displayed on tracks. Climb up stairs into the locomotive cabs to imagine what it was like to drive the huge iron horses, but be sure not to let the kids climb on top or under the equipment. At the back of the park, youngsters can ride an earlier form of travel—ponies or pony-powered small stage-coaches. Bring a picnic to enjoy at one of the tables set up in a shady area near the entrance. There's also an adjacent snack bar. This area is often used for birthday parties. For a more private celebration, depending on the weather, you can rent an air-conditioned or a heated train car.

If you're in Griffith Park on a Sunday with kids who like trains, plan to visit the **Los Angeles Live Steamers,** who run a scale-model steam train on a track east of Travel Town. Members of the group operate the miniature railroad each Sunday between 11 A.M. and 5 P.M. Visitors are welcome to climb aboard for a free ride.

Across the Ventura Freeway (101) from Travel Town you can go for a ride of a different sort. The Griffith Park Livery Stable at the **Los Angeles Equestrian Center** rents horses for trail rides in the park. Children need to be at least 12 to ride alone. The Equestrian Center's huge arena is the site of regularly scheduled horse shows and polo matches that children might enjoy, and an Irish Fair in June with medieval games and market.

Near the zoo is the park's newest attraction, the **Gene Autry Western Heritage Museum.** The trilevel California-mission–style building houses exhibits that chronicle the development of the American West from the time of the Spanish Conquistadores in the sixteenth century to the cattle ranchers of today. Walt Disney Imagineering designed the permanent exhibit spaces in the museum's six themed galleries. Indians, explorers, pioneers, and cowboys come alive in dramatically lit displays that are accompanied by music and sound effects. There's also a section devoted to Hollywood's portrayal of the West. In one exhibit kids can sit on a saddle and see themselves star in a western movie on a screen, thanks to moviemaking techniques that combine two images. You're welcome to bring along a video camera to record the event, if you wish. The museum sponsors western history classes for children during the summer.

Near the museum there's another place for children to ride in a saddle—at Griffith Park's popular **Merry-Go-Round.** Built in 1926, the well-preserved carousel's brightly painted horses gallop four abreast. You can ride the carousel daily in summer and on weekends in winter. Festive strains of organ music drift from the carousel to the children's playground and picnic areas nearby. In this area there are tennis courts, where you can play for free, and two of the park's four public golf courses.

Drive south on Griffith Park Drive to visit more attractions for kids. In the southeast corner of the park, the **Griffith Park & Southern Railroad** offers children another chance to ride on a miniature train. Adjacent to the train is a different kind of ride, the **SR2 Ride Simulator.** The 12-seat, space-age–looking vehicle gives you the sensation of high-speed travel while you stay firmly planted on the ground. Hydraulic motion and sound effects are synchronized with a film to make you feel as if you are moving. Strap yourself in and you'll soon be speeding along on a bobsled, roller coaster, or a low-flying airplane. The three-minute ride would probably frighten young children, but older ones will love it. Next door, there are **Pony and Stagecoach Rides.** The ponies walk or trot in two separate lanes around a safe oval track. You can walk around the rail with the ponies if youngsters are frightened. For those who don't want to climb into a saddle, there are more sedate wagon and stagecoach rides.

There's more to delight kids on the west side of the park. Perched on a hill above the city, **Griffith Park Observatory** houses an astronomical museum, a planetarium, and a large telescope for public viewing. From parking lots on either side of the observatory grounds, you'll have a spectacular view of the Los Angeles basin.

As you enter the observatory, stop to watch the 240-pound brass Foucault pendulum that swings while the earth's rotation causes it to knock over pegs on the floor. The Hall of Science has galleries on both sides of the pendulum with interactive educational exhibits. Push buttons beneath a model of the observatory to open doors to the telescope and rotate the dome. Nearby, look through a periscope to see the terrain outside. In the gallery at the other end of the hall, take the push-button astronomy and constellation quizzes. Make your own earthquake by jumping in front of a seismograph that records your movements with red ink on a turning drum. Compare that with the seismograph recordings of recent Southern California earthquakes. Near the planetarium entrance, weigh yourself on a scale that shows you how heavy you would be on the Moon, on Mars, or on Jupiter.

Regularly scheduled shows in the planetarium cover dramatic and educational astronomic events, such as comets and eclipses, and present theories on the death of the dinosaurs. Purchase tickets at the box office near the pendulum. On the ceiling of the 75-foot planetarium dome, a projector that looks like a giant ant reproduces the night sky at any time of the year. Rest your head on the back of your chair to enjoy the one-hour narrated productions. Children under 5 are not allowed at these shows, but may attend a show specially designed for preschoolers, presented at 1:30 P.M. on weekends in winter and daily in summer.

Teenagers and older children enjoy the Laserium shows presented at the planetarium in the evenings. The intense colors of laser images combine with rock, jazz, or classical music to create an entertaining experience.

On a clear night, plan a visit to the observatory between seven and ten o'clock so the kids can look at the heavens through the Zeiss telescope. There's no charge to look through the largest public telescope in California, which is often trained on one of the nearer planets or comets.

Attractions

GENE AUTRY WESTERN HERITAGE MUSEUM, 4700 Zoo Drive, Los Angeles. (Exit Golden State Freeway [5] at Zoo Drive; follow signs to the museum.) (213) 667-2000. Open Tuesday–Sunday, 10 A.M.–5 P.M. Adults, $4.75; seniors, $3.50; ages 2–12, $2.

GRIFFITH PARK & SOUTHERN RAILROAD AND SR2 RIDE SIM-ULATOR. On the east side of Crystal Springs Drive near Los Feliz Boulevard, Griffith Park. (Exit Golden State Freeway [5] at Los Feliz Boulevard;

west to Crystal Springs Drive; right to attractions.) (213) 664-6788. Open in summer: 10 A.M.–5 P.M. weekdays; 10 A.M.–6 P.M. weekends. Open in winter: 10 A.M.–4:30 P.M. weekdays; 10 A.M.–5 P.M. weekends. Railroad admission: adults, $1.50; children, $1.25. SR2 admission: $1.25 per person.

GRIFFITH PARK OBSERVATORY AND PLANETARIUM, 2800 East Observatory Road, Los Angeles. (Exit Hollywood Freeway [101] at Vermont Avenue; north to East Observatory Road; left to observatory. Exit Golden State Freeway [5] at Los Feliz Boulevard; west to Vermont Avenue; right to East Observatory Road; left to observatory.) (213) 664-1191. Hall of Science open in summer: Sunday–Friday, 12:30 P.M.–10 P.M.; Saturday, 11:30 A.M.–10 P.M.; open in winter: Tuesday–Friday, 2 P.M.–10 P.M.; Saturday, 11:30 A.M.–10 P.M.; Sunday, 12:30–10 P.M. Free. Planetarium shows in summer: Monday–Friday, 1:30, 3, and 8 P.M.; Saturday and Sunday, 1:30, 3, 4:30, and 8 P.M.; in winter: Tuesday–Friday, 3 and 8 P.M.; Saturday and Sunday, 1:30, 3, 4:30, and 8 P.M. Ages 16 and over, $2.75; ages 5–15 and seniors, $1.50.

LOS ANGELES EQUESTRIAN CENTER, 480 Riverside Drive (at corner of Riverside Drive and Main Street), Burbank. (Exit Ventura Freeway [134] at Buena Vista Street; east on Riverside Drive to Main Street. Exit Golden State Freeway [5] at Western Avenue; south to Riverside Drive; right to Main Street.) Equestrian shows, (818) 840-9066. Griffith Park Livery Stable horse rentals, (818) 840-8401. Daily, 8 A.M.–4 P.M.; ages 13 and up, $13 per hour, 1 or 2 hour rides. No reservations.

LOS ANGELES LIVE STEAMERS, on Zoo Drive, west of Victory Drive. (Exit Ventura Freeway [134] at Forest Lawn Drive; follow signs to attraction.) Rides every Sunday, 11 A.M.–5 P.M. Free.

LOS ANGELES ZOO, 5333 Zoo Drive, Los Angeles. (Exit Ventura Freeway [134] eastbound at Victory Boulevard; right and follow signs to zoo. Exit Golden State Freeway [5] at Zoo Drive and follow signs to zoo. (818) 666-4090. Open daily, 10 A.M.–5 P.M. Ages 13 and up, $5.50; ages 2–12, $2.25; seniors, $4.50; under 2, free. Guided tours, third grade and up, (213) 666-5133.

PONY AND STAGECOACH RIDES, on Crystal Springs Drive near Los Feliz Boulevard. (Exit Golden State Freeway [5] at Los Feliz Boulevard; west to Crystal Springs Drive; north to rides.) (213) 664-3266. Open in summer:

10 A.M.–5 P.M. weekdays; 10 A.M.–5:30 P.M. weekends; open in winter: Tuesday–Friday, 10 A.M.–4:30 P.M.; 10 A.M.–5 P.M. weekends. Twice around pony track, $1; wagon rides, $1.

TRAVEL TOWN MUSEUM, on Zoo Drive near Griffith Park Drive. (Exit Ventura Freeway [134] at Forest Lawn Drive; continue an eighth of a mile to entrance.) (213) 662-5874. Open Monday–Friday, 10 A.M.–5 P.M.; Saturday, Sunday, and holidays, 10 A.M.–6 P.M. Free. School tours Tuesday, Thursday, and Friday, 10–11 A.M.; reservations required.

For More Information

Greater Los Angeles Convention and Visitors Bureau, 515 South Figueroa Street, 11th Floor, Los Angeles, CA 90071; (213) 689-8822.

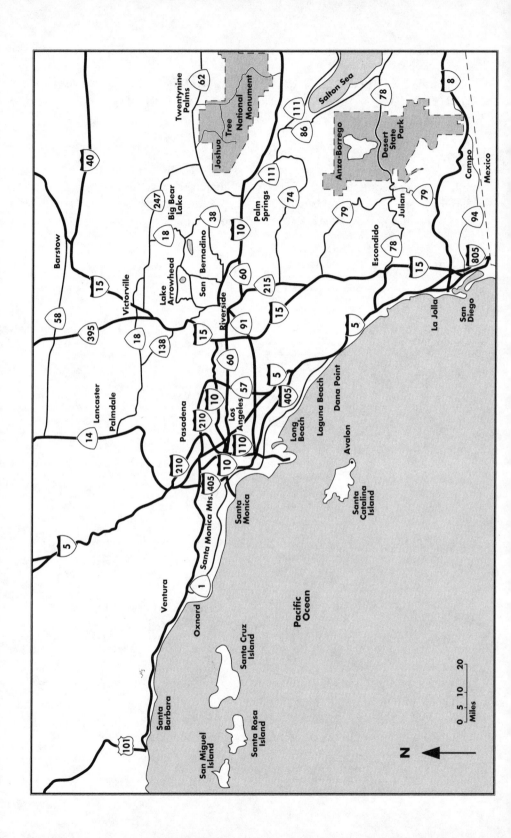

2

Los Angeles: Westside

In Los Angeles, the Westside is as much a state of being as it is a place. The geographic area stretches roughly from Beverly Hills west to the beach communities. The social landscape tends to be affluent, tolerant, and appreciative of the arts.

As a result, many family attractions on the Westside are related to the arts. In its museums, children see classical treasures from ancient Greece and feudal Japan. At its festivals and workshops, kids inspired by folk art from many lands create their own artworks. But not all Westside attractions are cultural. You also will find a historic merry-go-round, movie stars, and a fascinating collection of Ice Age fossils.

A major influence on Westside lifestyles and attractions is its beaches. From Leo Carrillo Beach near the western end of Los Angeles County to Marina del Rey on Santa Monica Bay, the beaches form a collective recreational resource of subtle variations. Tide pooling, surfing, kite flying, sailing, and sunbathing are among the most popular pursuits.

Sections in this chapter focus on three main areas: Beverly Hills and the Mid-Wilshire District, Santa Monica and Malibu, and the beaches. In planning a day's itinerary from any of these sections, you'll need to keep a few things in mind. While attractions are no more expensive on the Westside than in other parts of the city, other amenities, such as parking and restaurants, can cost more. The attractions in these sections are close to one another, but are probably too numerous to be covered in a single day or weekend. They will be much more enjoyable if taken in small doses.

BEVERLY HILLS AND THE MID-WILSHIRE DISTRICT

Tar Pits and Star Maps

Beverly Hills. The name conjures up images of wealth: chic clothing stores, exclusive art galleries, and Rolls-Royces. Hardly the place you would expect to find diversions for kids. The truth is, Beverly Hills and the nearby Mid-Wilshire District of Los Angeles offer a variety of big attractions and small pleasures, enough to satisfy the whole family.

A good place to start your day is at the museums in Hancock Park in the Mid-Wilshire District. The park, on Wilshire Boulevard just east of Fairfax Avenue, is the site of both the George C. Page Museum and the Los Angeles County Museum of Art. But it's the park's most unusual attraction, the Rancho La Brea Tar Pits, that likely will hold a special fascination for most youngsters.

The tar pits, sticky black asphalt beds, have trapped animal life for thousands of years and today are yielding one of the world's richest collections of Ice Age fossils. Behind the art museum, a small round building encloses an observation pit showing exactly how the fossils appear as they are uncovered in the tar. In front of the Page Museum, one of the largest asphalt "pools" is fenced off, but a two-story viewing station gives youngsters a good look at the goo. Life-size statues depicting a family of mammoths show how the animals might have been trapped there more than ten thousand years ago. By the way, Hancock Park has large stretches of open lawn, shade trees, and tables, everything you might need for a picnic before or after visiting the museums.

The **George C. Page Museum** houses a fine collection of fossils taken from the tar pits, plus displays and dioramas that document life in the Pleistocene epoch. Many youngsters equate the word *fossil* with dinosaur, and they often are initially disappointed to find the museum has no dinosaur skeletons (see Exposition Park section). But one look at the skeletons of the huge imperial mammoth or the formidable saber-toothed cat, and most kids forget their disappointment.

The museum's exhibits are laid out in an uncrowded gallery that surrounds a tranquil interior garden. Special lighting techniques let you see skeletons of a saber-toothed cat and an Ice Age woman "come alive." Kids enjoy one interactive exhibit that encourages them to pull rods similar in size to animals' legs out of tar. You can watch workers in the museum's paleontology lab clean and categorize fossils. Slide and video presentations tell of the area's history and explain how plants and animals became trapped in the tar. The museum also has a small but well-stocked gift and book store.

Immediately west of the Page Museum, the **Los Angeles County Museum of Art** has one of the broadest public collections of art on the West Coast. The museum's collection is too comprehensive for youngsters to cover in one visit, so you should plan to see only a few of the highlights most interesting to them. If the kids get hungry, the museum has a cafeteria adjacent to the Leo S. Bing Theater.

The museum's Ahmanson Building contains art from around the world, ranging from prehistory to the modern era. American and European classical paintings share the stage with a comprehensive collection of Pre-Columbian art, and there are exhibits of glass, costumes, and textiles. The new Robert O. Anderson Gallery is devoted entirely to twentieth-century painting and sculpture. The museum's most recent addition is the Pavilion for Japanese Art. Be sure the kids see the fine collection of netsuke, fanciful tiny carvings that depict animals, Japanese mythic deities, and comic human figures.

In addition to school tours and art classes given year-round, the art museum offers special programs for kids. During the summer months Sundays in the Museum is aimed at families and includes art workshops, storytellers, poetry readings, dance performances, or other artistic expressions that often relate to a special exhibit at the museum. Call for program information and be sure to arrive early. Admission to the programs is on a first come, first served basis.

Almost directly across Wilshire Boulevard from the Page Museum is an art museum that began as a restaurant. The **Craft and Folk Art Museum** displays changing exhibits that feature folk art from around the world. The colorful displays are often quite appealing to youngsters and the museum welcomes them with an active educational program. Sunday Family Night is a once-a-month drop-in program that features music or storytelling and an art workshop related to a holiday or museum exhibit. While new quarters are being built, the museum occupies temporary space in the May Co. department store at the corner of Wilshire Boulevard and Fairfax Avenue. The museum's most popular event by far, however, is the biennial Festival of the Masks, which draws a hundred thousand people to Hancock Park on the last weekend of October (held only in even numbered years). The festival includes mask-making demonstrations and workshops, ethnic food, and entertainment. Kids can join in the highlight of the festival, the Parade of Masks down Wilshire Boulevard on Sunday morning.

Just north of Hancock Park, on Fairfax Avenue at 3rd Street, is **Farmer's Market,** a tourist destination since the 1930s, when Southern California produce was the envy of the nation. Numbered among its 160 businesses today are art galleries, clothing stores, gift shops, jewelry stores, bakeries, and restaurants. If it all seems a bit too tourist oriented, you get the picture. Yet the crowds, the merchandise, and particularly the food make the market a fun stop, even for kids. Be sure not to miss the marvelous machine that turns peanuts into peanut butter "right before your eyes." You can buy a picnic lunch at the market to enjoy in Hancock Park.

Just north of Farmer's Market you'll see **CBS Television City.** This massive network broadcast and production facility doesn't offer tours, but you can get free tickets to live tapings at the box office every day from 9 A.M. to 5 P.M. Youngsters must be at least 14 years old to attend most shows, although some will admit children as young as 8 years old.

Two of L.A.'s most enjoyable restaurants for kids are nearby. **Ed Debevic's** is a 1950s-style diner that is sure to entertain any youngster. The food is better than average, reasonably priced, and served in a fun-filled atmosphere by waiters and waitresses who actually have to audition for their jobs. Signs everywhere in the restaurant implore you to try Ed's meat loaf. Another proclaims, "If you're a good customer, you'll order more." The menu, which comes in a plastic folder, offers standard diner fare, including burgers, spaghetti, and something called wets, french fries with gravy.

For a different but no less frantic atmosphere, try the **Hard Rock Café.** Rock 'n' roll is the theme of this restaurant chain and the café is filled with R&R memorabilia: guitars, posters, photos, and concert ads. Like Ed Debevic's, the Hard Rock offers a standard, though expanded, café menu, with prices slightly higher than Ed's. Both restaurants sell T-shirts and souvenir merchandise.

The Hard Rock is actually part of Beverly Center, a multistory shopping mall with upscale clothing stores, bookstores, a huge toy shop, and a top floor full of more places to eat, as well as multiple movie theaters.

You are more likely to spot a celebrity in nearby Beverly Hills than anywhere else in Los Angeles. Indeed, celebrities, or at least their homes, are a local industry. Several tour companies in Beverly Hills and Los Angeles offer guided excursions to movie-stars' homes. If the kids are eager for this kind of stargazing, the tours are probably your best choice, since the guides know the routes, the homes, and the history.

The alternative is to buy one of the maps to stars' homes sold at local gift shops and newsstands and on several street corners along Sunset Boulevard. Driving unfamiliar streets and trying to figure out if the hedge in front of you belongs to a celebrity or the neighbor next door can be frustrating for you and disappointing for the kids. The maps, however, do make memorable souvenirs.

To see movie stars in action, try **Hollywood on Location.** Since 1982, this Beverly Hills–based company has been directing people to Los Angeles locations on a daily basis to watch movies, TV series, and music videos being filmed. The service includes a listing of who and what are being filmed, the schedule, and a map directing you to the site. The listing includes about 35 locations, almost all within ten miles of the company's headquarters. You need to make a reservation for the day you want to go. A less expensive alternative is to contact the **Motion Picture Coordination Office** in Hollywood, which can provide limited information on filming around town.

Visitors to Beverly Hills often are surprised that the city offers a number of programs for children through the **Beverly Hills Recreation and Parks Department.** These programs are aimed at all ages, from preschoolers to teenagers, and even include family field trips and day care. There is a charge for these programs. The **Beverly Hills Library** offers Saturday story hours at 10:30 A.M. for children ages 3 to 5, and at 4 P.M. for youngsters 6 to 10 years old. In each case the children are treated to a half hour of stories, singing or games, and a movie. The well-equipped children's library has recently moved to a spacious new facility with computers for kids' use, an extensive video library, and more than 35,000 children's book titles. The parks department and library programs are free, but children must be registered in advance. You need not be a Beverly Hills resident to take part.

For exercise, try two of the area's great recreational parks. **Roxbury Park,** at the corner of Roxbury Drive and Olympic Boulevard, is the site of many Recreation and Parks Department activities for children. Less than a mile southwest is **Rancho Park,** the largest public park in the area. With a golf course, tennis courts, playing fields, play equipment, picnic tables, and acres of green grass, Rancho Park has something for every child.

Across Pico Boulevard and just west of the park, the Century City Playhouse hosts the **Burbage Theater Ensemble,** which presents plays for children most Saturdays and occasional Sunday afternoons. The presentations are geared to children and structured to allow them to participate in the action. Birthday parties are welcome and the theater has facilities to accommodate them. Be sure to call the theater in advance to determine if a play is scheduled for the weekend you plan to come.

With **Junior Programs of California** the bill of fare is more varied. Presentations might involve magicians, puppeteers, ballet dancers, and actors in hour-long programs aimed at elementary school children. The productions are given on weekends from October through April at various locations around Los Angeles County. To find out where the productions will be given, call the group's offices in West Los Angeles.

Attractions

(**Note:** Directions to all attractions are given from a starting point at Wilshire Boulevard and Fairfax Avenue. To get to this point, exit Santa Monica Freeway [10] at Fairfax Avenue; north to Wilshire Boulevard.)

BEVERLY HILLS PUBLIC LIBRARY, 444 North Rexford Drive, Beverly Hills. (West on Wilshire Boulevard; right on Rexford Drive to library.) (213) 285-1101. Story Hour, Saturday, 10:30 A.M. and 4 P.M. Free.

BEVERLY HILLS RECREATION AND PARKS DEPARTMENT, 330 North Foothill Road, Beverly Hills. (West on Wilshire Boulevard; right on Rexford Drive; right on Foothill Road to parks building.) (213) 285-2537. Call for listing of children's programs. Free.

BURBAGE THEATER ENSEMBLE, Century City Playhouse, 10508 West Pico Boulevard, Los Angeles. (West on Wilshire Boulevard; left at Beverly Drive; right on Pico Boulevard to theater.) (213) 839-3322. Open most Saturdays, 1 P.M. Call theater for program dates and prices.

CBS TELEVISION CITY, 7800 Beverly Boulevard, Los Angeles. (North on Fairfax Avenue to Beverly Boulevard.) (213) 852-4002. Ticket office open Monday–Sunday, 9 A.M.–5 P.M. Tapings are free, most for ages 14 and older.

CRAFT AND FOLK ART MUSEUM, May Co., Wilshire Boulevard at Fairfax Avenue, Los Angeles. Temporary exhibition space on 4th floor. (213) 937-5544. Open Tuesday–Sunday, 11:30 A.M.–5 P.M. Adults, $1.50; seniors and students, $1; children, 75 cents.

ED DEBEVIC'S, 134 North La Cienega Boulevard, Beverly Hills. (West on Wilshire Boulevard; right on La Cienega to diner.) (213) 659-1952. Open Monday–Thursday, 11:30 A.M.–midnight; Friday–Saturday, 11:30 A.M.–1 A.M.; Sunday, 11:30 A.M.–11 P.M.

FARMER'S MARKET, 6333 West 3rd Street, Los Angeles. (North on Fairfax Avenue to 3rd Street.) (213) 933-9211. Summer hours: Monday–Saturday, 9 A.M.–7 P.M.; Sunday, 10 A.M.–6 P.M. Winter hours: Monday–Saturday, 9 A.M.–6:30 P.M.; Sunday, 10 A.M.–5 P.M.

GEORGE C. PAGE MUSEUM, 5801 Wilshire Boulevard, Los Angeles. (East on Wilshire Boulevard to museum.) (213) 936-2230. Open Tuesday–Sunday, 10 A.M.–5 P.M. Adults, $3; seniors and students, $1.50; ages 6–12, 75 cents. (Free the second Tuesday of each month.)

HARD ROCK CAFÉ, 8600 Beverly Boulevard, Los Angeles. (North on Fairfax Avenue; left on Beverly Boulevard to café.) (213) 276-7605. Open Monday–Friday, 11 A.M.–11 P.M.; Saturday and Sunday, 11:30 A.M.–11:30 P.M.

HOLLYWOOD ON LOCATION, 8644 Wilshire Boulevard, Beverly Hills. (West on Wilshire Boulevard to office.) (213) 659-9165. Must call for reservations. Open Monday–Friday, 9:30 A.M.–4:30 P.M. Fee: $29 per car.

JUNIOR PROGRAMS OF CALIFORNIA, 2030 Comstock Avenue, Los Angeles. (213) 271-6402. Call for productions, locations, and dates.

LOS ANGELES COUNTY MUSEUM OF ART, 5905 Wilshire Boulevard, Los Angeles. (East on Wilshire Boulevard to museum.) (213) 857-6111. Open Tuesday–Friday, 10 A.M.–5 P.M.; Saturday and Sunday, 10 A.M.–6 P.M. Adults, $3; students, seniors, $1.50; ages 6–12, 75 cents.

MOTION PICTURE COORDINATION OFFICE, 6922 Hollywood Boulevard, Hollywood. (North on Fairfax Avenue to Hollywood Boulevard; right to office.) (213) 485-5324. Call for information and shooting schedules.

RANCHO PARK, 2459 Motor Avenue, Los Angeles. (West on Wilshire Boulevard to Beverly Drive; left to Pico Boulevard; right to Motor Avenue and park.) Open daily.

ROXBURY PARK, 471 South Roxbury Drive, Beverly Hills. (West on Wilshire Boulevard to Roxbury Drive; left to park.) (213) 550-4761. Open daily.

For More Information

Beverly Hills Visitors Bureau, 239 South Beverly Drive, Beverly Hills, CA 90212; (213) 271-8174 or (800) 334-2210.

Los Angeles Visitors and Convention Bureau, 515 South Figueroa Street, 11th Floor, Los Angeles, CA 90071; (213) 689-8822.

SANTA MONICA AND MALIBU
Culture by the Bay

Most families visit Santa Monica and Malibu for the beaches and seaside recreation. Yet these two communities have many other attractions that children enjoy. Thanks to active citizens in both affluent cities, you'll find art and drama programs for children, plus seven museums, including a new children's museum, with exhibits to interest kids. This happy marriage of beaches and culture can help you design a number of successful visits to the area.

A good place to start a day's adventure in Santa Monica is at **Angels Attic,** a museum that features antique dollhouses, dolls, and toys. The museum is housed in a renovated 1895 Queen Anne Victorian home painted light blue with white gingerbread trim and it looks like a dollhouse itself. On the ground floor, you'll walk through rooms filled with 60 doll houses, many with the original period furniture and some with tiny electric lights and antique dolls. You'll see a replica of Anne Hathaway's cottage, an 1800s upper-class Mexican home, and even a furnished Cheyenne Indian tepee dating from 1864. Each dwelling reflects the architecture and furnishings of the time in which it was built, providing kids with an easy-to-learn social history lesson. While children can't touch the exhibits, they can see the houses easily because most are placed at their eye level.

Kids who have little interest in dolls may be fascinated by the museum's collection of antique toys. A miniature train chugs around a room that also displays a working model of a carousel with tiny painted horses. Look for a miniature Noah's ark with 150 pairs of carved wooden animals. Go upstairs to see a fine doll collection and a small book and toy store that sells some inexpensive miniatures to help kids furnish their own dollhouses. If you have time, plan to enjoy afternoon tea on the porch or in the backyard garden.

A few blocks north on 11th Street, the **Westside Children's Museum** resides in temporary quarters in a former school. This little museum has ambitious plans to teach children about Santa Monica's past, present, and future. When completed, the museum's centerpiece will be a recreated Southern California Indian village with interactive exhibits. Until it finds a permanent home, the children's museum is open on some weekends only, for workshops and performances designed for kids and their families. Past programs have included a computer workshop, a teddy bear clinic, and Indian dance performances.

South of the museum on 4th Street, the **Santa Monica Playhouse** features live theater for the family every Saturday and Sunday afternoon, at one and three o'clock. Adults and teens make up the casts of these plays. During summer, kids ages 4 to 15 can enroll in a four-week workshop to learn about acting and theater production.

If the kids are more interested in creating visual arts, try the **Westside Arts Center.** This nonprofit center provides creative arts experiences for both children and adults. On weekends, the center often has low-cost, drop-in festival art workshops. At mini workshops for 5- to 12-year-olds and their families, participants visit nearby mountains or beaches to create art projects that focus on the environment. The center teaches art studio classes to kids on a weekly basis, too, but you'll need to call for a schedule of these changing programs.

Two blocks north of the center is the **Children's Book and Music Center.** This store has an excellent selection of books, records, videotapes, and musical instruments for children. Youngsters can listen to records or tapes and preview videos of children's movie classics before you buy. The store has a large selection of musical instruments that children also can try out before buying. Bring your preschool children, ages 2 to 6, to a free storytime at the store, held the first and third Saturdays of the month at 10 A.M.

Let the kids stretch their legs nearby at **Palisades Park.** The narrow palm-lined park stretches for a mile between Colorado Avenue and San Vicente Boulevard on the palisades above Santa Monica Beach. On weekends it's a popular spot for people-watchers and sunset picnics. Pick up maps and information on the area at the **Visitor Information Center** in the south end of the park at the foot of Santa Monica Boulevard. The kiosk is open daily between 10 A.M. and 4 P.M. Then walk south about half a block to see the **Camera Obscura.** The camera's mirror reflects images from outside the building onto a table inside, which lets kids "spy" on people in the park. You can look through the camera on weekdays from 9 A.M. to 4 P.M. and on weekends from 11 A.M. to 4 P.M. There's no fee, but you'll need to obtain a key from the Senior Recreation Center next door. If you want to picnic in the park, head for the north end, where it's less crowded.

On the south side of Santa Monica Freeway (10), you'll find three museums (two are quite new) and a planetarium that will interest children.

The **Museum of Flying** at Santa Monica Municipal Airport displays aircraft from all over the world, including planes from the airport's former Donald Douglas Museum and Library. The museum showcases the history of aviation in Santa Monica where aerospace pioneer Donald Douglas, Sr., started Douglas Aircraft. In the bright, three-story hangarlike building, you'll see nearly twenty vintage airplanes hanging from the ceiling or parked on the ground, including a P-51 Mustang and a 1930s Spitfire. Be sure to see the Douglas World Cruiser *New Orleans,* one of four open-cockpit biplanes that left from Santa Monica Airport (then Clover Field) in 1924 on the first around-the-world flight. Kiosks near the aircraft present audiovisual information about each plane. Rotating exhibits explore future technologies and individual achievements in aviation.

After you've seen the museum, walk next door to Clover Park, where you can watch contemporary aircraft taking off. Or for a bird's-eye view, head for the sod-roofed observation area on top of the airport's Clover Field Terminal and Administration Building on the south side of the airport. Bring a picnic and spread a blanket out on the lawn of this park in the sky. A railing surrounds the grass, but you'll still have a magnificent view of the mountains and the city as well as the runway. For an even higher view, climb up to the observation deck and sit on bleachers to watch planes touch down below.

If you didn't bring a picnic and the kids are hungry, stop at the **Kitty Hawk** nearby on the airport grounds. This moderately priced restaurant serves breakfast and lunch only, with such kid favorites as hamburgers, pancakes, and spaghetti.

At **Santa Monica College Planetarium,** a few blocks west of the airport, you'll scan the skies for more distant objects. Housed on the second floor of the Technology Building at the college, the planetarium offers weekly shows on Friday nights at 7 and 8 P.M. Lean back in your chair in the circular theater to see the night sky reproduced on the dome ceiling. There is no minimum age limit at these shows, so children can learn about the heavens at an early age. On clear nights after the shows, take the kids up to the telescope to view the sky.

To reach the next two museums, drive south on Ocean Park Boulevard so you can see the murals painted on the walls of the boulevard's 4th Street underpass. On one side of the 600-foot-long underpass, you'll see the *Whale Mural,* which features Southern California marine life. On the other side is

Unbridled, depicting a herd of colorful horses fleeing the carousel at the Santa Monica Pier.

Continue south on Ocean Park to Main Street to see another of Santa Monica's famous murals, *Early Ocean Park.* Painted on a building at the southeast corner of this intersection, the vivid mural recreates scenes from Ocean Park's past.

Across the street is the **Santa Monica Heritage Museum,** housed in an 1891 building that was the former home of Roy Jones, son of the founder of Santa Monica. The museum showcases the area's history. Docents who take visitors on tours of the house point out items of specific interest to children. The dark green dining room exhibits furnishings from the Victorian era, while the lighter living room reflects design elements popular in 1915. Changing exhibits in the upstairs galleries feature contemporary art, historical displays, and photography. The museum holds art workshops and toy shows for children to correspond with changing exhibits.

A block north on Main Street, the **Santa Monica Museum of Art** houses contemporary art in the 8,300-square-foot Edgemar Center, a former egg warehouse. The 1908 structure is big enough to hold very large artworks. There are no programs just for kids, but the unusual exhibitions, including video art, performance art, and sound and light sculptures, often appeal to children. Adjacent to the museum are restaurants and an ice-cream shop.

North of Santa Monica in Malibu, kids have a chance to see ancient art at the **J. Paul Getty Museum.** Located on a bluff overlooking the ocean, the building is a recreation of a first-century Roman house that stood near the city of Herculaneum, overlooking the Bay of Naples. The museum is a cultural treasure that will mean most to kids old enough to understand how long ago two thousand years is. The lovely garden in front of the colonnaded building has plants and wall paintings that approximate those that might have decorated the original villa.

Indoors, kids will be interested in an exhibit that explains the devastation of the villa in the volcanic eruption of Vesuvius. They also will relate to the lifelike ancient sculptures of animals and people displayed on the ground floor. On the upper level, look for European paintings and drawings on subjects that might be of interest to your children. Have them look for the painting on the ceiling that depicts people gazing down on them. Try to go on a docent-led tour; docents at this museum are very good at making the ancient world come alive for kids. Before visiting the museum, you'll need to call for parking reservations, as there is limited space in the lots.

To go from ancient Rome to not-so-ancient California, drive north on Pacific Coast Highway to the historic **Adamson House and Malibu Lagoon**

Museum. Located between Malibu Lagoon State Beach and the Malibu Pier, the 1929 Spanish Colonial Revival house was the home of the last family to own all of the land that is now Malibu. You'll tour the home with a docent to see bathrooms and floors laid with colorful tiles made in Malibu between 1926 and 1932. The floor in one hallway is decorated with a tile-made design of a Persian rug, complete with fringe. Kids will spot old kitchen appliances, a huge wooden radio in the living room, and the black telephone that was part of an intercom system.

A museum in the former garage displays artifacts from the Chumash Indians who once lived on the site and explains the unusual history of Malibu. Outside, look at some of the home's beautiful tilework. Have the kids find the one upside-down tile in the peacock fountain on the back patio, and the wrought-iron spider in a gate nearby. There is more to see in this area, at the Malibu Lagoon next door and at adjacent Surfrider Beach. See the following section on Westside Beaches for information.

Attractions

ADAMSON HOUSE AND MALIBU LAGOON MUSEUM, 23200 Pacific Coast Highway, Malibu. (Exit Santa Monica Freeway [10] at its western end and continue north on Pacific Coast Highway [1] about five miles to the entrance, which is well signed; left into museum drive or adjacent parking lot.) (213) 456-8432. Docent-led tours: Wednesday–Sunday, 10 A.M.–2 P.M. Free.

ANGELS ATTIC, 516 Colorado Avenue, Santa Monica. (Exit Santa Monica Freeway [10] at 5th Street; north to Colorado; right to street parking.) (213) 394-8331. Open Thursday–Sunday, 12:30–4:30 P.M. Adults, $4; seniors and students, $3; under 12, $2.

CHILDREN'S BOOK AND MUSIC CENTER, 2500 Santa Monica Boulevard, Santa Monica. (Exit Santa Monica Freeway [10] westbound at 26th Street/Cloverfield Boulevard; north to Santa Monica Boulevard; right to store.) (213) 829-0215. Open Monday–Saturday, 9 A.M.–5 P.M.; Wednesday until 7 P.M.; closed Sunday except during December when it's open 10 A.M.–5 P.M. Preschool storytime, first and third Saturday, 10 A.M. Free.

J. PAUL GETTY MUSEUM, 17985 Pacific Coast Highway, Malibu. (Exit Santa Monica Freeway [10] at its western end and continue north on Pacific Coast Highway [1] to driveway just south of Coastline Drive; right into parking lot.) Parking reservations are required; (213) 458-2003. Open Tuesday–Sunday, 10 A.M.–5 P.M. Closed Monday and holidays. Free.

KITTY HAWK, 3300 Airport Avenue, Santa Monica. (Exit Santa Monica Freeway [10] at Bundy Drive South; south to Airport Avenue; right to restaurant.) (213) 398-0540. Open daily, 7 A.M.–4 P.M., for breakfast and lunch.

MUSEUM OF FLYING, 2772 Donald Douglas Loop North, Santa Monica. (Exit Santa Monica Freeway [10] at Bundy Drive South; south to Ocean Park Boulevard; right to 31st Street; left to end of street and follow sign to right and museum.) (213) 392-8822. Open September–May: Thursday–Sunday, 10 A.M.–6 P.M.; June–August: Tuesday–Sunday, 10 A.M.–6 P.M. Adults, $4; seniors, $3; ages 13–17, $2; ages 3–12, $1; under 3, free.

PALISADES PARK, along Ocean Avenue between Colorado Avenue and San Vicente Boulevard. (Exit Santa Monica Freeway [10] westbound at 4th Street; north to Broadway; left to park.)

• Visitor Information Center, 1430 Ocean Avenue, Santa Monica. (In park, between Santa Monica Boulevard and Broadway.) (213) 393-7593. Open daily, 10 A.M.–4 P.M.
• Camera Obscura, 1450 Ocean Avenue, Santa Monica. (In park, at the end of Broadway, in the south end of Senior Recreation Center.) (213) 394-1227. Open weekdays, 9 A.M.–4 P.M.; weekends, 11 A.M.–4 P.M. Get key at Senior Recreation Center. Free.

SANTA MONICA COLLEGE PLANETARIUM, 1900 Pico Boulevard, Santa Monica. (Exit Santa Monica Freeway [10] westbound at 26th Street/Cloverfield Boulevard; south on Cloverfield; right on Pico Boulevard to college.) Free parking in lot off Pico Boulevard. Planetarium shows every Friday night during school year, 7 and 8 P.M. Seats for each show: $2.

SANTA MONICA HERITAGE MUSEUM, 2612 Main Street, Santa Monica. (Exit Santa Monica Freeway [10] at 4th Street; south to Ocean Park Boulevard; right to Main Street; left to museum.) (213) 392-8537. Open Thursday–Saturday, 11 A.M.–4 P.M.; Sunday, 12–4 P.M. Free.

SANTA MONICA PLAYHOUSE, 1211 4th Street, Santa Monica. (Exit Santa Monica Freeway [10] at 4th Street; north to Playhouse.) (213) 394-9779. Shows on Saturday and Sunday, 1 and 3 P.M. All seats: $5.

SANTA MONICA MUSEUM OF ART, 2437 Main Street, Santa Monica. (Exit Santa Monica Freeway [10] at 4th Street; south to Ocean Park

Boulevard; right to Main Street; right to museum.) (213) 399-0433. Open, Wednesday–Thursday, 11 A.M.–8 P.M.; Friday–Saturday, 4 P.M.–6 P.M. Suggested donation: $3; seniors, artists, students, $1; under 12, 50 cents.

WESTSIDE ARTS CENTER, 2320 Arizona Avenue, Santa Monica. (Exit Santa Monica Freeway [10] westbound at 26th Street/Cloverfield Boulevard; north on Cloverfield; left on Santa Monica Boulevard; right on 23rd Street; right on Arizona.) (213) 453-3966. Drop-in program hours vary; call for schedule. Approximate cost of programs: $4–$5 per person.

WESTSIDE CHILDREN'S MUSEUM, 1302 11th Street, Santa Monica. (Exit Santa Monica Freeway [10] at Lincoln Boulevard; north to Arizona Avenue; right to museum.) (213) 451-5524. Workshop and performance admission: adults, $5; children, $2. Call for schedule.

For More Information:

Santa Monica Convention and Visitors Bureau, Box 5278C, Santa Monica, CA 90405; (213) 393-7593.

WESTSIDE BEACHES
Bathing, Biking, and Boating

There's a giant sandbox that stretches along L.A.'s coast. From Malibu in the west to Palos Verdes in the south, dozens of public beaches wait for kids to come and play. Each offers a slightly different kind of experience. Some have tide pools, while others boast good surfing waves, fishing piers, or children's play equipment.

This section lists beaches from northwest to southeast that have special attractions for children. Each provides lifeguards and restrooms, and some have food concessions. You can choose the beaches that best suit the interests and ages of your children. Be forewarned, though, that these beaches are tremendously popular on summer weekends. If you plan to go on a weekend, you'll need to arrive before 10 A.M. to find a place to park and a choice patch of sand. Another good time to arrive with young children is after 3 P.M., when the crowds are leaving. You'll avoid the most dangerous hours of sun, and you might even want to bring along a dinner picnic to enjoy while watching the sunset. Summer weekdays or winter weekends are delightful and quieter times to spend a day at the beach with kids.

Point Mugu State Park has four miles of beach that lie along a rugged, undeveloped stretch of land between Malibu and Oxnard just northwest of the Los Angeles County line. The most exciting feature of this beach area for kids is the huge sand dune that rises above Pacific Coast Highway on the inland side. Kids love sliding, rolling, and running pell-mell to the bottom of the dune. The beaches—Sycamore Cove, La Jolla Beach, and Point Mugu Beach—are wide sandy swatches with some rock outcrops and tide pools and they are not as crowded as beaches closer to the city in the south. Surf can be rough here as it splashes on rocks near the shore. You can camp and picnic under shady sycamores near the beach or in Sycamore Canyon. There are tables and grills at both sites.

To the southeast is Malibu, perhaps L.A.'s most famous shore. There are nearly a dozen public beaches in Malibu, but the following have the most to offer children: **Leo Carrillo State Beach** near the Los Angeles County line has two miles of shore with two beach areas separated by a rocky bluff. Wave and wind conditions make this a good body-surfing and wind-surfing spot. Youngsters will feel like real adventurers climbing on the rocks or exploring the tunnels and caves carved into the rocks by the sea. It's fun to find a protected little spot for a picnic on this beach, or you can eat at tables on the top of the bluff that rises behind the beach. You can camp at this beach, but there is no market or snack shop. Inland from the beach, older kids may want to explore some of the 11 miles of hiking trails that wind through chaparral-covered hills.

Drive southeast on Pacific Coast Highway (PCH) a little farther and you'll come to **Zuma Beach County Park.** This wide stretch of sand runs almost five miles and is popular with families and surfers. You'll find a picnic area and food concessions near the parking lot, plus volleyball courts and children's play equipment on the sand. Body surfing is popular at Zuma, but the seas can produce dangerous rip tides. It's a good idea to check with the lifeguards for information on surf conditions.

Westward Beach at **Point Dume State Reserve** is really a southern extension of Zuma Beach. Located at the base of a sandstone cliff topped with houses and condominiums, this wide beach is seldom crowded because there isn't much parking space nearby. This is a good beach to visit in the winter for sand play and picnicking. A quarter-mile trail south of the houses leads to the top of the bluff. Walk up the trail for a terrific view of the ocean and Point Dume. To avoid the steepest climb to the top, stay to the left when the trail branches. On weekends during the winter whale-watch season, you'll find a park ranger stationed at the top who will help you spot migrating whales through binoculars. The ranger also will have whalebone and baleen for kids to examine.

Malibu Lagoon State Beach offers variety for kids of different ages. The lagoon is a rich tidal estuary, full of marine life and birds that stop off during their migrations between Alaska and South America. Walk along the board-walk to observe the salt marsh up close or take one of the weekend hikes guided by park rangers. Signs along the trail help you identify the birds so you'll know whether you are watching a blue heron, egret, or one of the other species that frequent the area. Docents from the William O. Douglas Outdoor Classroom lead Babes at the Beach hikes through the wetland for children ages 3 months to 3 years accompanied by adults. Reservations are required for these hikes. There are picnic tables near the parking lot, and if you need extra food, you'll find a market across the street.

West of the lagoon, the park's white sandy beach is nice for strolling. It is bordered by Malibu Colony Drive, along which are lavish beach homes owned by the rich and famous. Adjacent to the lagoon on the east side is the gracious Adamson House, which you can tour Wednesday through Sunday (see preceding section on Santa Monica/Malibu).

Kids who like to surf will want to spend their time in the water at **Surfrider Beach,** east of Adamson House. This is Malibu's most famous surfing beach. This is where surfing got its start in California, and where Annette met Frankie in those 1960 surfing movie classics. Long, gently rolling waves at this beach give surfers a lasting ride, making it a good place for youngsters to learn. Competition is keen, though, and many surfing contests are held here during the year. Swimming is restricted in some areas because of the surfing activity. If the kids want to try surfing, rent a board at **Zuma Jay's,** a Malibu institution located just south of the beach at the end of Malibu Pier. Surfboards rent for $15 a day and boogie boards for $5. For a good look at the coast, walk out on **Malibu Pier.** This is also a good place from which to fish, and remember, you don't need a license to fish from any of the piers along the ocean. When the children are hungry, stop for lunch at the **Malibu Inn** across Pacific Coast Highway from the pier. The decor is eye-popping for kids, with a huge stuffed bear, and old surfboards and movie props hanging from the ceilings and walls. It's a comfortable place where you can wear your beach clothes indoors or outside on the patio. The menu includes sandwiches, hamburgers, and salads.

Will Rogers State Beach extends for two miles along PCH below the cliffs of Pacific Palisades. It's a good swimming beach with volleyball courts and children's play equipment on the sand. You'll have to arrive early because the narrow parking lot that parallels the beach fills up quickly with families on summer weekends.

Santa Monica State Beach, L.A.'s most convenient and popular beach, lies at the western end of Santa Monica Freeway (10). On hot summer weekends, thousands of people come here to cool off. The beach is very wide and the long walk to the shoreline can seem especially so if you're carrying a lot of paraphernalia for young children. Near the parking lot you'll find snack bars, play equipment, and volleyball courts.

Santa Monica Pier juts out from the beach at the foot of Colorado Boulevard. The pier's main feature is a carousel, built in 1922. Kids of all ages love to take a whirl on one of the 46 hand-carved and colorfully painted horses while the old Wurlitzer organ belts out carnival tunes. The carefully renovated pavilion that houses the carousel has been used in many films, including the Newman/Redford movie *The Sting*. During the summer months, visit a small children's amusement park that is set up next to the pavilion and features kiddie rides and a ferris wheel. Walk farther out on the pier to find other amusements, including bumper cars, arcade games, and novelty shops. You can fish from the pier, too. Snack bars offer an array of choices from hot dogs to seafood.

On the last Sunday of January, March, June, and October, the pier holds a kite festival open to all kite enthusiasts. Kids and adults alike fly all kinds of colorful kites in what becomes a party atmosphere. Every Thursday evening at 7:30 P.M. during July and August the pier features its Twilight Dance Series. Bring the kids to this free concert at the west end of the pier to hear a variety of musical styles, including jazz, reggae, and country. When the beat is strong, the audience gets up to dance. It's very informal, so the children can join in on the fun.

A bike path that starts less than a mile north of the pier runs along the beach for 19 miles, from Santa Monica south to Torrance Beach. The cement path is an ideal place to ride bikes with children because there is no auto traffic except for a short stretch around Marina del Rey. Rent bikes or roller skates at **Sea Mist Rentals** at the foot of the Santa Monica Pier. This is a great activity for the winter, when there are fewer people at the beach.

On bikes or skates, head south from the pier toward Venice. You'll pass a pair of large beach chairs sitting on the beach. No ordinary chairs, these have long pipes extending from their backs that vibrate in the wind and produce musical sounds.

If the kids have the stamina, ride down to **Venice City Beach,** unsurpassed in Los Angeles for people-watching. On Sunday, the two-mile boardwalk north of Washington Street takes on a carnival atmosphere. The bike path merges with the boardwalk for a few blocks. Vendors set up makeshift shops along the boardwalk selling T-shirts, jewelry, and other items. Serious roller skaters, break dancers, and musicians entertain along the street. At

Muscle Beach near 18th Avenue, young weightlifters demonstrate their strength and ripple their biceps for an appreciative audience. You may have to walk your bikes for a block or two through this section.

When the bike path heads down the hill and back toward the shore, you'll have a quieter stretch to ride along again. You may want to stop at one of the areas with play equipment and picnic tables on the sand near the bike path. You can buy sandwiches, ice cream, and cold drinks at snack shops and markets along this strip. If you didn't rent bikes or skates in Santa Monica, you can get them at **Spokes 'n Stuff,** which operates three rental kiosks in Venice along the bike path, at Rose Avenue, Venice Boulevard, and Washington Street. The 1,100-foot **Venice Pier** at the end of Washington Street is another good place for fishing.

The bike path heads east along Washington Street for less than a mile and then turns right at the duck pond near Mildred Avenue into **Marina del Rey,** home to six thousand boats and numerous upscale condominiums and restaurants. Two areas in the marina are of special interest to children.

Marina del Rey Public Beach, along Admiralty Way at the west end of Basin D between Palawan Way and Panay Way, is probably L.A.'s safest beach for children. The protected marina beach has no ocean waves and the shallow, roped-off swimming area is carefully watched by lifeguards. You could spend a whole day at this beach with children because everything you need is close to hand. A short way from the water's edge there's a children's playground, showers, a snack bar, and covered picnic tables.

At the other end of the marina on Fiji Way, **Fisherman's Village** offers other kinds of recreation for kids. This Cape Cod–style group of shops and restaurants has a number of fast food kiosks centered around a courtyard with picnic tables. You can choose between hamburgers, pizza, and Mexican food for a casual outdoor meal with kids. Of course, if you want to spend more money for a meal, the Village has several fine restaurants.

From a dock nearby, **Hornblower Dining Yachts** offers narrated cruises of the harbor aboard riverboat-styled craft that depart every hour. On the cruise you'll see the thousands of private boats moored in the harbor, including some that belong to Hollywood stars and other celebrities.

If you would rather skipper your own boat, head over to Mindanao Way to **Rent-a-Sail,** where you can rent boats from 14 to 25 feet long. For an active outing, you can ride bikes to the dock from Venice, go sailing for an hour or two, and then ride back to the bike-rental kiosk or your car.

At the end of Mindanao Way you'll find **Burton Chace Park,** a wide strip of green grass at the end of a jetty, surrounded by water on three sides. There's a fence around the park so kids can't fall into the water. It's a good place to watch some of the yachts that use the marina. This park gets very crowded on Sunday, and the free concerts that take place here on summer Sundays bring in more people. On Saturday and during the week, when it's less busy, the park is a good place to fly a kite.

Attractions

LEO CARRILLO STATE BEACH, 36000 block of Pacific Coast Highway at Mulholland Highway, south of the Ventura County line in Malibu. (Follow Santa Monica Freeway [10] to its western end; continue north and west on PCH [1] to beach.) (805) 499-2112 or (818) 706-1310. Day-use parking: $4.

MALIBU INN, 22969 Pacific Coast Highway, Malibu (across from the Malibu Pier). (Follow Santa Monica Freeway [10] to its western end; continue north and west on PCH to restaurant.) (213) 456-6060. Restaurant open daily, 11:30–8:30.

MALIBU LAGOON STATE BEACH, 23200 Pacific Coast Highway, Malibu. (Follow Santa Monica Freeway [10] to its western end; continue north and west on PCH a quarter of a mile past Malibu Pier and 1½ miles east of Malibu Canyon Road.) (213) 456-9497 or (818) 706-1310. Parking: $4. For Babes at the Beach call: (818) 706-1310.

MALIBU PIER, 23000 block of Pacific Coast Highway, Malibu. (Follow Santa Monica Freeway [10] to its western end; continue north and west on PCH west to pier.) Open daily.

MARINA DEL REY, at the west end of the Marina Expressway (90).

• *Burton Chace Park,* 13650 Mindanao Way, Marina del Rey. (Follow Marina Freeway [90] to the end; continue on Marina Expressway to Mindanao Way; left to end of street.) (213) 870-6782. Open daily.
• *Fisherman's Village,* 13763 Fiji Way. (Follow Marina Freeway [90] to the end; continue on Marina Expressway to Mindanao Way; left to Admiralty Way; left to Fiji Way; right to village.) (213) 823-5411. Open daily. Summer hours: 10 A.M.–10 P.M. Winter hours: 10 A.M.–9 P.M.
• *Hornblower Dining Yachts,* 13755 Fiji Way, at Fisherman's Village, Marina del Rey. (See directions above.) (213) 301-9900. Harbor Cruise summer hours: daily every hour from 11 A.M.–4 P.M. Winter hours: Wednesday–Sunday, every hour from 11 A.M.–4 P.M. 45-minute narrated tour: adults, $5; ages 2–12, $4; seniors, $3.50; under 2, free.

• *Marina del Rey Public Beach*, off Admiralty Way between Palawan Way and Panay Way. (Follow Marina Freeway [90] to the end; continue on Marina Expressway to Mindanao Way; left to Admiralty Way; right to beach.)
• *Rent-a-Sail*, 13560 Mindanao Way, Marina del Rey. (Follow Marina Freeway [90] to the end; continue on Marina Expressway to Mindanao Way; left to parking lot.) (213) 822-1868. Open daily, 11 A.M.–5 P.M. Boat rentals: $15–$35 per hour.

POINT MUGU STATE PARK, on Pacific Coast Highway, four miles west of the Los Angeles/Ventura County line. (Follow Santa Monica Freeway [10] to its western end; continue north and west on PCH to park.) (805) 987-3303. Enter park at Sycamore Canyon Campground. Parking: $4.

SANTA MONICA PIER, at west end of Colorado Avenue, Santa Monica. (Exit Santa Monica Freeway [10] at 4th Street; north to Colorado Avenue; west to pier.) (213) 458-8900. Open daily.

• *Sea Mist Rentals*, 1619 Ocean Front Walk, Santa Monica, at the foot of the Santa Monica Pier. (See directions to pier above.) (213) 395-7076. Open daily. Summer hours: Monday–Friday, 10 A.M.–6 P.M.; Saturday and Sunday, 9 A.M.–7 P.M. Winter hours: Monday–Friday, 11 A.M.–4:30 P.M.; Saturday and Sunday, 10 A.M.–5 P.M. Rent bikes, roller skates, and boogie boards: $4 an hour.

SANTA MONICA STATE BEACH, west of Pacific Coast Highway, Santa Monica. (Follow Santa Monica Freeway [10] to its western end; continue north on PCH; beach parking lots are on left side of the street.) (213) 394-3266. Parking: $4.

SPOKES 'N STUFF, at three kiosks along Ocean Front Walk in Venice: Rose Avenue, Venice Boulevard, and Washington Street. (Exit San Diego Freeway [405] at Washington Boulevard; west and continue straight on Washington Street to Ocean Front Walk.) (213) 306-3332. Open daily. Summer hours: daily 10 A.M.–6 P.M. Winter hours: Monday–Friday, 11 A.M.–5 P.M.; Saturday and Sunday, 10 A.M.–6 P.M. Bike rentals: $3–$5 per hour.

SURFRIDER BEACH, 23200 block of Pacific Coast Highway, east of Malibu Canyon Road, Malibu. (Follow Santa Monica Freeway [10] to its western end; continue north and west on PCH to beach.) (818) 706-1310. Parking: $4.

VENICE CITY BEACH, along Ocean Front Walk, Venice. (Exit San

Diego Freeway [405] at Washington Boulevard; west and continue straight on Washington Street to beach.) (213) 394-3266. Open daily. Parking: $4.

VENICE PIER, at foot of Washington Street, Venice Beach. (See directions above.) Open daily.

WESTWARD BEACH AT POINT DUME STATE RESERVE, at southern end of Zuma Beach. (See directions to Zuma Beach County Park.)

WILL ROGERS STATE BEACH, 16000 block of Pacific Coast Highway, Pacific Palisades, northwest of Chautauqua Boulevard. (Follow Santa Monica Freeway [10] to its western end; continue north on PCH to beach.) (213) 394-3266. Open daily. Parking: $4.

ZUMA BEACH COUNTY PARK, 30000 block of Pacific Coast Highway, north of Kanan/Dume Road, Malibu. (Follow Santa Monica Freeway [10] to its western end; continue north and west on PCH to beach.) (213) 457-9891. Open daily. Parking: $4.

ZUMA JAY'S, 22775 Pacific Coast Highway (500 yards south of the Malibu Pier), Malibu. (See directions to pier above.) (213) 456-8044. Open daily, 10 A.M.–5 P.M. Surfboard rentals: $15 a day; boogie-board rentals: $5 a day.

For More Information

Santa Monica Convention and Visitors Bureau, Box 5278C, Santa Monica, CA 90405; (213) 393-7593.

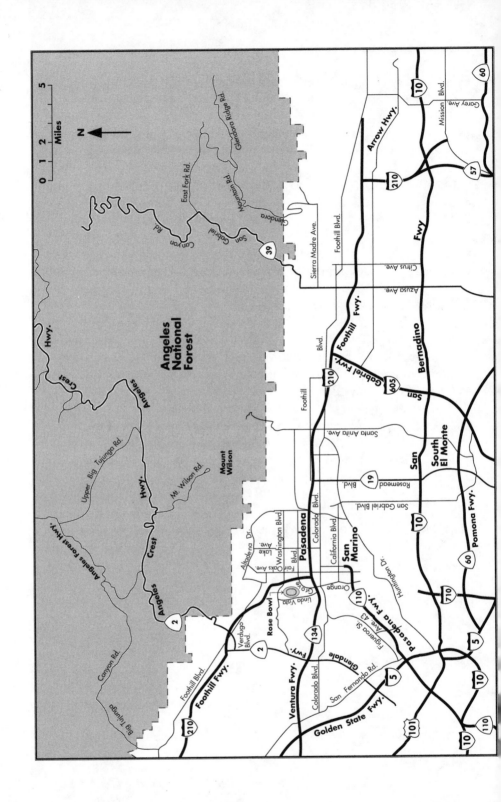

3

San Gabriel Valley and Mountains

San Gabriel Valley lies east of downtown Los Angeles and south of the San Gabriel Mountains. Once a ranching and citrus-growing region, the valley now is packed with more than thirty suburbs. The most famous of these is Pasadena, known for its dazzling New Year's Day parade. But Pasadena is much more than a parade, and the valley is much more than Pasadena.

If attractions in San Gabriel Valley have a dominant theme, it is history. Many of the area's museums are located in historic homes. Some of its biggest attractions were created before the turn of the century. Yet all this history doesn't mean the kids must endure long stretches of boredom on family outings to the area. In the hands of a skilled docent, the halls and rooms of historic houses come alive with the lifestyle and gadgetry of nineteenth-century America.

You'll find more active pursuits in the valley's many parks and in a children's museum that draws youngsters into a variety of activities. Most active of all are the numerous year-round recreational opportunities in the San Gabriel Mountains. In summer, there's hiking, fishing, and camping. In winter, it's skiing and snow play, and all within an hour's drive of downtown Los Angeles.

PASADENA
Kids Love a Parade

Each New Year's Day, the nation's attention focuses on Pasadena, one of Southern California's most venerable communities. The weather is usually mild and the sky a clear blue as flower-covered floats glide down Orange Grove Boulevard for the annual **Tournament of Roses Parade.** Locals jest that the parade and the collegiate football game that follows in the Rose Bowl have done more to encourage snowbound easterners to move to California than any other event.

Kids love a parade, and they especially like the idea of seeing Pasadena's televised Rose Parade live. If you decide to attend the parade, there are several ways you can be sure your children will have a good view. The simplest is also the most expensive: buy tickets and sit in assigned grandstand seats. You'll need to make reservations with the grandstand operator, **Sharp Seating Company,** at least two months in advance.

If you want to sit or stand on the curb for free, you'll have to be clever to find a spot that is not already crowded. To do this, you have two choices: arrive early and stand at the beginning of the parade route, or arrive after the parade starts and stand near the end. These two areas are usually less crowded than the middle sections, most of which are staked out the night before by young people who use the streets for a giant slumber party. If you choose the former, arrive at least one hour before the parade starts (8:20 A.M.) and park near the formation area, which includes streets around Orange Grove Boulevard south of Del Mar Boulevard. The parade officially starts at Orange Grove and Del Mar, proceeding north on Orange Grove to Colorado Boulevard where it turns east to Sierra Madre Boulevard. This is where you should plan to be by at least 9:30 A.M. to see the parade at its conclusion. Try to park on the north side of Foothill Freeway (210) to see the parade after it passes under the freeway on Sierra Madre Boulevard.

However you choose to see the parade, there are several things to keep in mind. Dress warmly in layered clothing because it is very cold in Pasadena on winter mornings, even though it may warm up later in the day. When choosing a place to stand along the parade route, make sure you are on the right side of the parade (from the marchers' point of view) because all the TV cameras are positioned on that side and the floats are designed with this in mind. Make sure you aren't standing where telephone wires stretch across the street. Floats with moving parts that elevate will not be able to raise them near you. You can bring folding chairs to sit on while you wait for the parade to start, but you'll find that most spectators stand up when the parade comes by. You may want to bring a stepladder to make sure the kids can see over the standing crowds, even if you end up near the back of the spectator strip.

If you decide not to attend the parade, there are other ways you can see the floats in person. During the week before the parade you can watch crews decorating floats at the **Rosemont Pavilion** and at the **Rose Palace,** both in Pasadena. Teenagers might even be able to help, as some floats recruit volunteers at the last minute. After the parade, catch the floats on display for several days along Sierra Madre Boulevard between Paloma Street and Sierra Madre Villa Avenue. It's a good chance to see close up the intricate use of flowers and plants on the floats.

During the rest of the year, Pasadena settles back into its comfortable role as a pleasant residential community. Yet this suburb has a different feeling from many communities in Southern California because of its rich heritage and traditions. The city boasts many tree-lined streets with stately homes built in the early 1900s. Today, a number of these fine mansions and gardens are open to the public, along with a handful of museums. If this sounds like a place for "The Little Old Lady from Pasadena" of rock and roll fame, with nothing to interest kids, think again.

Pasadena has a children's museum, lovely parks to play in, and outstanding art and cultural museums with special programs just for kids. To plan a successful day in the Pasadena area, choose one museum to visit for an hour or two, basing your choice on the ages and interests of the children. Then plan a picnic and some recreation at a park or in the natural wilderness of the San Gabriel Mountains, a short drive from the city limits.

Take your preschool and elementary-school children to **Kidspace Museum** near the center of Pasadena. Housed in a former junior high school auditorium, the museum encourages youngsters to touch and manipulate its interactive exhibits. Herman the Robot greets visitors at the door. Once inside, children are free to explore on their own. Some like to be stars at the KKID TV studio, while budding DJs practice at the KFUN radio station. Nearby, other kids climb aboard a fire engine or into a Malibu Grand Prix car, and still others live out their fantasies by dressing up as football players or firefighters. In the museum's most popular exhibit, kids crawl through a carpeted human habitrail called the Ant Wall. Next to it, they can observe a live colony of California harvester ants crawling through their tunnels. Elsewhere, children learn about human anatomy with manipulative skeletons and fabric puzzles of body parts. During daily workshops, offered free with museum admission, museum staff and volunteers involve children in such activities as face painting, Polaroid photography, or storytelling. Outside, there are picnic tables and a sandy play area. You can rent the museum for birthday parties during either public or private hours.

The **Pacific Asia Museum** a few blocks away appeals more to older children. This is the only institution in Southern California that specializes in the art and culture of Asia and the Pacific Basin. Changing exhibits often include costumes, toys, and masks that appeal to children. The museum's Chinese-palace–style architecture is as much a fascination for children as its exhibits. The building's green tile roof and marble carvings are visible from the street. In the central Chinese courtyard, stone lions guard a pool filled with bright koi fish. Visit the Student's Gallery through one of the graceful archways near the entrance. The gallery displays folk art and household objects that complement the changing exhibits in the main gallery. On the third Saturday of every month, the museum holds Free-Day–Fun-Day, with varying programs for the entire family, such as dance performances and Asian art workshops.

Nearby on Colorado Boulevard is **Vromans Book Store,** a Pasadena institution with two floors of books for sale. Most of the second floor is devoted to children's books, with more than five thousand titles, including picture books, young-adult fiction, and activity books. Tables and chairs in one section allow kids to peruse their selections before buying.

Across the street is another Pasadena institution, **Stottlemyer's Theatrical Delicatessen.** The deli has more than a hundred sandwiches to choose from, most named after famous people. Kids' favorites include the Snoopy Sandwich with peanut butter and jelly, and the Miss Piggy, with ham and cheese in a croissant. You can sit at tables along the sidewalk outside or at red leather booths in the restaurant.

A few blocks west on Colorado, at the **Norton Simon Museum,** you'll have one of the best opportunities in Southern California to introduce the kids to famous artists and artworks. The museum's exhibits span 2,500 years, many of the pieces on loan from Simon's personal collections. Without having to walk too far, you can show children the works of old masters, such as Rembrandt and Reubens, or of impressionists, such as Cézanne and Degas. Kids may relate especially well to some of the large contemporary pieces and the Asian and Indian sculpture found elsewhere in the museum. The outdoor sculpture garden features works by Rodin and Moore as well as a fountain that never fails to attract children. The museum offers docent-led tours for school groups.

Across the street and down two blocks, there's a special toy and book store for kids, **A Child's Fancy.** The place is crammed with children's books, educational toys, and dolls. Books include classics, high-quality picture books, and illustrated fiction. There are several former librarians on staff to help you make selections. Kids are drawn to the large choice of dolls displayed in and around a three-story dollhouse. Elsewhere in the same shopping complex, you can buy baked goods and sandwiches.

For a more complete meal, head for the **Rose City Diner** a few blocks west. This fifties-style restaurant serves home-cooked food at reasonable prices. There's pot roast, spaghetti, cinnamon rolls, and, of course, hamburgers. At the soda fountain, kids can order banana splits and root-beer floats. The diner's color scheme is rose, in keeping with Pasadena's theme, and walls are lined with photographs of the city in the 1950s, including past Rose Parade queens. It's a tradition to help decorate the place by blowing toothpicks through straws up to the ceiling, where they stick in the acoustical tiles.

Not far away is the **Ambassador Auditorium,** a lavish hall that hosts world-renowned performers, many of whom will interest kids. Recent programs included Chinese acrobats, circus acts, and mimes. During the school year, the auditorium presents a Family Pops Series that features musical favorites for all ages.

One of Pasadena's most intriguing mansions is nearby and open for tours. **Gamble House,** built in 1908 by Pasadena architects Greene and Greene, is a masterpiece example of the California Craftsman-style bungalow. The wood-shingle home still holds most of the furniture that was designed and built by the Greene brothers for the Cincinnati-based Gamble family (of Procter and Gamble.) Docents lead small groups on informative tours through the house. Although older children would probably find the home most interesting, younger kids can be well entertained by a lively docent. Elementary-school children visit the house regularly on tours led by trained seventh-grade student docents. Kids are quick to notice design elements that are repeated on Tiffany windows, carved wood moldings, and furniture, so the tour becomes a game of finding these motifs.

Nearby is **Brookside Park,** an oak- and eucalyptus-studded grassy strip that meanders along the arroyo north toward the Rose Bowl. Kids like to explore the woodsy areas. Other attractions here include a playground, picnic tables, and tennis courts. The area of the park near the Rose Bowl is flat and open, and a good place to fly a kite.

The **Rose Bowl** itself is an impressive place to visit. Built in 1902, the stadium is home to the UCLA football team and the famous New Year's Day football game between the Big Ten Conference and the Pacific Athletic Conference college teams. You can tour the Rose Bowl on weekdays between 9 A.M. and 4 P.M. Enter through Gate B and walk through Tunnel 28 to view the 104,000-seat stadium. Kids often enjoy shopping for bargains at the Rose Bowl Flea Market held at the bowl on the second Sunday of each month.

Another fascinating mansion is the headquarters for the **Huntington Library, Art Collections, and Botanical Gardens,** located south of Pasadena in San Marino. This complex is one of Southern California's most famous cultural attractions. Built by railroad tycoon Henry E. Huntington, the mansion now houses the Huntington Art Gallery, a collection that features eighteenth-century English and French art. Famous works include Gainsborough's *Blue Boy* and Laurence's *Pinkie.*

Manuscripts in the Huntington Library next door represent nine centuries of literature. You'll see hand-painted manuscripts, first printings of Shakespeare's plays, and a Gutenberg Bible. Most of these works are behind glass, but you're welcome to touch the vellum (parchment) pages of a fifteenth-century choirbook. Kids who have studied American history may be interested to see original letters handwritten by George Washington, Thomas Jefferson, and Abraham Lincoln.

If you have small children, you'll want to spend most of your time outside in the 140-acre Botanical Gardens, where there are 12 different environments to explore. Kids will probably enjoy most the Japanese garden, where there's a huge temple bell, a red arched bridge over a koi pond, and a furnished sixteenth-century teahouse. You can make a game of discovering cacti of unusual shapes in the desert garden and smelling the blossoms in the fragrant rose garden. You can't picnic on the grounds, but you can buy snacks and light lunches at the Patio Restaurant or enjoy English tea at the Earth Garden Restaurant on weekend afternoons.

While you're in San Marino, stop in at El Molino Viejo (The Old Mill). Built in 1816 by Indians from the San Gabriel Mission, it was the first water-powered gristmill in Southern California. Although only the millstones remain from the original structure, the adobe building that stands nearby, with its red-tile roof and gardenlike grounds, is a gracious reminder of California's early Spanish days. Down in the basement, kids will be intrigued by a scale model of the mill that has moving parts and small Indian dolls using the machinery.

A ten-minute drive away, in Highland Park, the **Southwest Museum** fascinates children of all ages. It sits atop a hill like a Spanish fortress and contains one of the most extensive collections of Native American art and artifacts in the United States. You can enter the museum from the parking-lot level on the hill, but the most exciting entrance is down below on Museum Drive where there is street parking. This entrance resembles a Mayan temple and leads to a dark tunnel lined with dioramas of Southwest Indian life. Very young children might find the entrance a little frightening. At the end of the tunnel, an elevator takes you up several floors to the galleries.

Well-designed exhibits, many at kids' eye level, showcase the diversity of American Indian life. Kids will notice tribal differences in costumes, weapons, and art. They'll see huge totem poles carved by Northwest Coast Indians and a full-size teepee made by a Plains Indian tribe. In the California Hall, kids can crawl into a replica of a cave painted with Chumash Indian rock art designs. Children also like to enter a model of a Northern California plank house by crawling through a low doorway, while adults usually prefer to walk through a larger opening nearby. A fine collection of Hopi Kachina dolls interests young people too. Before you leave, visit the museum shop, which carries a fine selection of Indian-made art objects and books.

To see how European settlers lived in the nineteenth century, visit the museum's satellite facility, **Casa de Adobe.** Located down the hill from the museum, the adobe is filled with nineteenth-century furnishings to re-create that period of California history. Through doorways you'll peek around thick adobe walls to view the kitchen with its wood-burning stove, the bedrooms with tiny beds, and the simple family chapel. While young children may not be very interested in the contents of the rooms, they will enjoy the patio fountain that splashes into a pool filled with fish and water lilies.

Sycamore Grove Park across the street from the museum is a good place for the kids to run off some steam. The park has picnic tables and a playground with climbing equipment under tall sycamore trees.

Near the museum on Avenue 43, the **Lummis House,** or **El Alisal,** is an unusual house that's worth a visit. Charles Fletcher Lummis, the writer and archaeologist who founded the Southwest Museum, built this house by himself, using arroyo rocks and old telegraph poles. Now the site of the Historical Society of California, the charming house contains memorabilia and photos taken by Lummis of Indian ceremonies and pueblos. Look for the windowpanes Lummis made from positive photographic glass plates of these scenes. Docent-led tours for schoolchildren emphasize the garden Lummis planted that contains drought-resistant plants.

Across the freeway off Avenue 43 is an outdoor architectural museum of sorts, **Heritage Square.** Eight buildings built from 1865 to 1914 sit in a villagelike setting around the ten-acre square. All have been relocated from other sites in Southern California. The eclectic group includes Victorian houses, a Methodist church, and the Palms Railroad Depot. You can tour three of the buildings and see the restoration process taking place at the others when the square is open on weekends. The tour is most appropriate for older children, but even a short visit to walk around the square gives kids a feeling for small-town California at the turn of the last century.

Attractions

A CHILD'S FANCY, 140 West Colorado Boulevard, Pasadena. (Exit Ventura Freeway [134] at San Rafael Avenue/Linda Vista Avenue; south to Colorado Boulevard; east to store.) (818) 793-4085. Open Monday–Saturday 10 A.M.–6 P.M. (Friday to 9 P.M.); Sunday, 12–5 P.M.

AMBASSADOR AUDITORIUM, 300 West Green Street, Pasadena. (Exit Ventura Freeway [134] eastbound at Colorado Boulevard; east to Orange Grove Boulevard; right to Green Street; left to auditorium entrance. Exit Ventura Freeway [134] westbound at San Rafael Avenue; south to Colorado Boulevard; left to Orange Grove Boulevard; right to Green Street; left to auditorium entrance.) (818) 304-6166. Family Pop Series between September and June. Call for series schedule.

BROOKSIDE PARK, along Arroyo Boulevard, Pasadena. (Exit Ventura Freeway [134] at San Rafael Avenue/Linda Vista Avenue; north on Linda Vista Avenue to Seco Street; right to Arroyo Boulevard; left or right to park.) (818) 793-7193. Open daily.

EL MOLINO VIEJO, 1120 Old Mill Road, San Marino. (Follow Pasadena Freeway [State 110] north to the end; continue north on Arroyo Parkway to California Boulevard; right to Oak Knoll Avenue; right to Old Mill Road; left to entrance.) (818) 449-5450. Open Tuesday–Sunday, 1–4 P.M. Free.

GAMBLE HOUSE, 4 Westmoreland Place, Pasadena. (Exit Ventura Freeway [134] at San Rafael Avenue/Linda Vista Avenue; south to Colorado Boulevard; left to Orange Grove Boulevard; left to Arroyo Terrace; left to Westmoreland Place; right to house.) (818) 793-3334. Open Thursday–Sunday, noon–3 P.M. Adults, $4; seniors, $3; full-time students, $2; under 18, free.

HERITAGE SQUARE, 3800 Homer Street, Los Angeles. (Exit Pasadena Freeway [State 110] at Avenue 43; east to Homer Street; right to end of street.) (818) 796-2898. Open Saturday and Sunday, 12–4 P.M. Self-guided tours on Saturday, guided tours on Sunday. Adults, $4.50; seniors and ages 13–17, $3; 12 and under, free.

HUNTINGTON LIBRARY, ART COLLECTIONS, AND BOTANICAL GARDENS, 1151 Oxford Road, San Marino. (Follow Pasadena Freeway [State 110] north to end; continue north on Arroyo Parkway to California Boulevard; right to Allen Avenue; right to entrance. Exit Foothill Freeway [210] at Hill Avenue; south to California Boulevard; left to Allen Avenue; right to entrance.) (818) 405-2275. Open Tuesday–Sunday, 1–4:30 P.M. Advance reservations required on Sunday, (818) 405-2141. Free, but $2 donation per adult is suggested.

KIDSPACE MUSEUM, 390 South El Molino Avenue, Pasadena. (Follow Pasadena Freeway [State 110] north to the end; continue north on Arroyo Parkway to California Boulevard; right to El Molino Avenue; left to museum. Exit Foothill Freeway [210] at Lake Avenue; south to Del Mar Boulevard; right to El Molino Avenue; left to museum.) (818) 449-9143. School-year schedule: Wednesday, 2–5 P.M.; weekends, noon–5 P.M. Summer schedule: Tuesday–Friday, 1–4 P.M.; weekends, noon–4:30 P.M. Tours scheduled at other hours with advance registration. Admission, adults and children ages 2 and up, $3; seniors and groups of 15 or more with advance registration, $2.50; under 2, free. Children must be accompanied by an adult.

NORTON SIMON MUSEUM, 411 West Colorado Boulevard, Pasadena. (Exit Ventura Freeway [134] at San Rafael Avenue/Linda Vista Avenue; south to Colorado Boulevard; east to museum.) (818) 449-6840. Open Thursday–Sunday, noon–6 P.M. Admission, adults, $3; seniors and students, $1.50; under 13, free.

PACIFIC ASIA MUSEUM, 46 North Los Robles Avenue, Pasadena. (Follow Pasadena Freeway [State 110] to the end; continue north on Arroyo Parkway to Colorado Boulevard; right to Los Robles Avenue; left to museum. Exit Foothill Freeway [210] at Lake Avenue; south to Colorado Boulevard; right to Los Robles Avenue; right to museum.) (818) 449-2742. Open Wednesday–Sunday, noon–5 P.M. Adults, $3; seniors and students with valid I.D., $1.50; under 13, free.

ROSE BOWL, 9911 Rosemont Boulevard, Pasadena. (Exit Ventura Freeway [134] at San Rafael Avenue/Linda Vista Avenue; north on Linda Vista Avenue to Seco Street; right to Arroyo Boulevard; left to bowl. Exit Foothill Freeway [210] at Seco Street; east to Rosemont Boulevard; north to bowl.) (818) 577-3100. Gate B and Tunnel 28 open Monday–Friday, 9 A.M.–4 P.M. Free.

ROSE CITY DINER, 45 South Fair Oaks Avenue, Pasadena. (Exit Ventura Freeway [134] at San Rafael Avenue/Linda Vista Avenue; south to Colorado Boulevard; east to Fair Oaks Avenue; south to restaurant.) (818) 793-8282. Open daily, 6:30 A.M.–2 A.M. Live music Thursday night and Sunday afternoon.

ROSEMONT PAVILION, 700 Seco Street, Pasadena. (Exit Foothill Freeway [210] at Seco Street; east to Pavilion on corner of Rosemont Avenue.) Open December 28–31 for float-decoration viewing, 9 A.M.–9 P.M.

ROSE PALACE, 835 South Raymond Avenue, Pasadena. (Exit Pasadena Freeway [State 110] northbound at Fair Oaks Avenue; north to Glenarm Street; right to Raymond; left to palace.) Open December 28–31 for float-decoration viewing, 9 A.M.–9 P.M.

SOUTHWEST MUSEUM, 234 Museum Drive, Highland Park. (Exit Pasadena Freeway [State 110] at Avenue 43; west to Figueroa; right to Avenue 45; left to Marmion Way; right to Museum Drive; left to museum.) (213) 221-2163. Open Tuesday–Sunday, 11 A.M.–5 P.M. Adults, $3; students and seniors, $1.50; ages 7–18, $1; under 7 and school groups, free.

• *Casa de Adobe,* 4603 North Figueroa Street, Highland Park. (Below the Southwest Museum.) (213) 225-8653. Open Tuesday–Sunday, 11 A.M.–5 P.M. Free.
• *Lummis House,* 200 East Avenue 43, Highland Park. (Exit Pasadena Freeway [State 110] at Avenue 43; follow signs to house.) (213) 222-0546. Open Wednesday–Sunday, 1–4 P.M. Free.

SHARP SEATING COMPANY, Box 68, Pasadena, CA 91102-0068. (818) 795-4171. Call for Tournament of Roses Parade grandstand seats.

STOTTLEMYER'S THEATRICAL DELICATESSEN, 712 East Colorado, Pasadena. (Exit Foothill Freeway [210] at Lake Avenue; south to Colorado Boulevard; right to restaurant.) (818) 792-5351. Open Monday–Friday, 10 A.M.–6:30 P.M.; Saturday and Sunday, 10 A.M.–7:30 P.M.

TOURNAMENT OF ROSES PARADE, from Del Mar Boulevard, runs north on Orange Grove Boulevard; east on Colorado Boulevard; north on Sierra Madre Boulevard. January 1 (unless January 1 is a Sunday, then parade is held on January 2). Parade starts at 8:20 A.M.

VROMANS BOOK STORE, 695 East Colorado Boulevard, Pasadena. (Exit Foothill Freeway [210] at Lake Avenue; south to Colorado Boulevard; right to store.) (818) 448-5320. Open Monday–Thursday and Saturday, 9:30 A.M.–6 P.M.; Friday, 9:30 A.M.–9 P.M.; Sunday, 12–5 P.M.

For More Information

Pasadena Convention and Visitors Bureau, 171 South Los Robles Avenue, Pasadena, CA 91101; (818) 795-9311.

EAST SAN GABRIEL VALLEY
Hikes, Bikes, and Races

Wedged between downtown Los Angeles and the San Gabriel Mountains, San Gabriel Valley boasts some of Southern California's oldest communities. Once a ranch and citrus-growing region, the valley east of Pasadena has sprouted several dozen adjoining suburbs in recent years. On a visit to the valley, kids can learn about its history and play in some of the area's outstanding parks. They'll see racing cars and thoroughbreds, an eighteenth-century mission and a twentieth-century set for a TV show. To visit the spots recommended for children in this section, you'll have to do some driving, because the attractions are far-flung in this spread-out valley.

East of Pasadena in Arcadia, the **Los Angeles State and County Arboretum** is a real oasis in the middle of the suburbs. The 127-acre garden displays more than thirty thousand plants from around the world in areas that correspond to their geographic origins. There are forests, deserts, lakes, and meadows in the garden, plus a historical center with furnished homes.

For kids, the most interesting area of the garden is to the left (southwest) of the entrance. Follow the path from the entrance past the fountains to the Prehistoric and Jungle Garden. Children love to play in the junglelike atmosphere near the lagoon. This area has been the setting for many films and TV shows, including *Fantasy Island*. A path takes you close to the lagoon where you can feed the ducks or peacocks that roam throughout the park. Buy a handful of corn at one of the dispensers, and watch as the birds gather around to beg for food.

Follow the ring road to the left around the lagoon. You'll come to several structures that recapture the history of the San Gabriel Valley. At the 1839 Hugo Reed Adobe, steps placed below the windows allow little children to climb up and peer into the rooms. Walk over to the Gabrielino Indian village in the next yard. Dome-shaped grass wickiups contain stone grinding tools and fire pits, just as they did when Indians lived in similar houses near the spring-fed lagoon three hundred years ago. Nearby, go into the Victorian Coach Barn to see a well-maintained collection of old coaches and fire wagons. Look for the doghouse in front that was built in the same architectural style as the barn. Next, visit the red- and white-striped Queen Anne Cottage built by E. J. ("Lucky") Baldwin in 1885. Baldwin made his millions in silver mining and started the arboretum as a garden on his property. Look through low windows to see how the home was furnished in Baldwin's day. Kids may be most astonished by the bathroom, which has an iron bathtub and a wooden toilet.

Stop by the Santa Anita Depot, a classic brick train station built in 1890, where you'll see a station agent's office with a telegraph key and upstairs family living quarters. One of the arboretum's most scenic walks starts nearby, leading to a waterfall and aquatic garden. The Peacock Pavilion Coffee Shop near the arboretum entrance serves drinks and snacks. You can't picnic in the arboretum, but there are tables outside the entrance.

Across the street from the arboretum, you'll find another monument to Lucky Baldwin's legacy, **Santa Anita Park.** Built in 1934, the park has a racetrack, beautifully landscaped gardens, picnic areas, and children's playgrounds. You can take the kids to see the horses' morning workouts daily during race season—from the end of December to the end of April—between 7 A.M. and 9:30 A.M. The thoroughbreds are impressive as they go through their paces around the track. On Saturday and Sunday mornings during the season, climb aboard a tram for a free 20-minute ride through the grounds. Your guide points out famous horses and stops to let children off the tram to pet the barnyard animals.

If you decide to take the kids with you to the races, they'll be admitted free (under age 17). There's a picnic area in the infield, and a supervised playground for little ones nearby. When older kids tire of watching the races, they'll find more fun at Anita Chiquita, a covered patio with video games.

A few miles southeast of the racetrack in San Gabriel, you can visit one of the most important historical sites in the Los Angeles area, **Mission San Gabriel Archangel.** The adobe wall-enclosed complex was founded in 1771. The fourth California mission to be built, San Gabriel Archangel was once one of the most important political and social centers in Southern California. Indians from throughout the L.A. basin were taken by the Spanish from their villages to this mission. As a result, their descendents are now known as Gabrielinos. Indians helped build the Moorish-style church with its narrow vaulted sanctuary and buttressed walls. Today, the mission church and the adjacent museum are closed due to damage sustained during an earthquake in 1987. The church's original tower was destroyed in an earthquake in 1812.

There's still plenty for kids to see in the mission's gardens and in the areas featuring archaeological exhibits. Among treelike cactuses and flowering plants in the garden are remains of candle and soap factories and vats used for tanning hides. You can go inside a replica of an old kitchen to see the wood-burning stove and stone food-grinding tools. Be sure to visit the Court of the Missions at the back of the garden. Models of each of the 21 California missions sit side by side in this exhibit. Children who have visited other missions will enjoy finding them among the models.

A good place to let the kids play or to have a picnic after visiting the mission is nearby **Vincent Lugo Park.** Formerly called San Gabriel Municipal Park, it has a Kiddie Korral for children 6 years old or younger with pony swings and scaled-down climbing equipment. Children a little bit older will enjoy the fanciful cement sea animals in the Laguna de San Gabriel Nautical Playground located in the southeast corner of the park behind the baseball diamond. Kids crawl under parts of an arched sea serpent or scramble over a bright blue octopus. They climb up a big blue whale and slide out his open mouth or roll down the shell of a huge brown-and-yellow snail. There are shaded benches around the outside of the play area and covered tables nearby for picnics or birthday parties.

Another San Gabriel Valley history lesson awaits at the **El Monte Historical Museum** in the town of El Monte southeast of San Gabriel. Housed in a Spanish-style building, formerly the city library, the museum is full of memorabilia from El Monte's pioneer past. Once the end of the Santa Fe Trail, El Monte was populated by farmers who in 1851 began coming west in wagon trains. You can see some of these wagons and others in the museum's courtyard. Children especially like the museum's room settings, such as a dress shop, a two-room home, a schoolhouse, and a country store, which recreate the nineteenth century. Youngsters can walk into the settings, even sit at a desk in the school, to experience life in those days. Children also are able to compare their lifestyles with those of kids a century ago in Child's World, which displays toys, furniture, and clothes.

Next door to the museum is the El Monte Pool, where you can stop for a cool dip. The pool is open daily on summer afternoons. Across the street is **Tony Arceo Park.** The one-block-square park has wide grassy areas to play on and picnic tables near a children's playground.

Kids lured by speed won't want to miss the **Penske Racing Museum,** a mile east of the park in El Monte. This small museum displays a collection of race cars owned by former race-car driver Roger Penske. Cars on exhibit have won the Indianapolis 500 or were pace cars used for the races. The museum is located one floor below the main showroom of the Longo Toyota dealership, also owned by Penske. The collection is open only by appointment for groups of ten or more, but there are plans for expanded hours and a larger staff to handle more visitors.

Two miles north is **Peck Road Water Conservation Park,** a grassy strip bordering a reservoir where you can picnic or fish for bluegill, catfish, and rainbow trout. Bring your bikes to this park if you want to enjoy a scenic, safe ride with kids. The bike path follows the Rio Hondo Wash south past several parks to Whittier Narrows Recreation Area. Farther south it joins a bike path that follows the Los Angeles River all the way to Long Beach. From Peck Road Water Conservation Park, you'll ride south on the east levee of the Rio Hondo Wash, a paved riverbed. Less than a mile from the park the trail parallels the runway at El Monte Airport. From a rest area, youngsters have a close-up vantage point for watching planes land and take off.

Ride south another mile to **Pioneer Park,** where you'll find restrooms, play equipment, and picnic tables under tall shade trees. There's a drinking fountain at the adjacent RTD bus terminal. If the kids are older and good riders, continue south another two miles to **Whittier Narrows Recreation Area.** This 1,100-acre park offers a wide variety of recreational opportunities. At Legg Lake you can fish for trout or rent pedalboats and rowboats. A three-mile bike path circles the lake. Elsewhere there are 16 lighted tennis courts, 6 soccer fields and 7 baseball diamonds, an archery range, a trap- and skeet-shooting range, and miles of hiking and equestrian trails. Kids with radio-controlled or U-controlled planes practice on a model-plane airfield in the park, while others put model cars through their paces on a track, or race radio-controlled boats on the south lake.

On the northeast side of the park is the **American Heritage Park/Military Museum.** This outdoor exhibit displays the largest collection in the nation of military equipment from all branches of the service: Army, Navy, Marine Corps, and Air Force. More than a hundred pieces of equipment are on display at any one time, including jeeps, tanks, trucks, and cannons, mostly from World War II and the Korean and Vietnam wars. When you enter, pick up a directory that explains each of the numbered exhibits. Foreign equipment includes German tanks and guns and a Vietnamese riverboat that was used for laying mines. Kids who have watched M.A.S.H. on TV will enjoy seeing a replica of the set, which includes the hospital, tent camp, jeeps, ambulance, and a helicopter.

At the southeast end of the park, the **Whittier Narrows Nature Center** is a 320-acre sanctuary for a wide variety of plants and animals. Thousands of birds use its four lakes and network of streams. You can walk along ten miles of scenic trails through the park. Visit the park on the weekend to go on a guided nature hike near the center. Call for a schedule.

A few miles east in the town of La Puente, **The Donut Hole** is a famous monument to Southern California kitsch. This drive-through snack shop, built in 1946, is shaped like two giant chocolate doughnuts connected by a bread box. Kids love to ride through the holes in the 26-foot-diameter doughnuts to place and collect their orders. The one-of-a-kind structure is a popular location for television and movie shoots.

Attractions

THE DONUT HOLE, 15300 East Almar Road, La Puente. (Exit Pomona Freeway [60] at Hacienda Boulevard [39]; north to Almar Road; left to shop.) (818) 968-2912. Open 24 hours.

EL MONTE HISTORICAL MUSEUM, 3150 North Tyler Avenue, El Monte. (Exit San Bernardino Freeway [10] at Santa Anita Avenue; south to Mildred Street; left to Tyler Avenue; museum is on the corner.) (818) 444-3813. Open Tuesday–Friday, 10 A.M.–5 P.M.; Saturday, 10 A.M.–4 P.M. Free, but donations are accepted.

• *Tony Arceo Park* is across the street. Open daily. Free.

LOS ANGELES STATE AND COUNTY ARBORETUM, 301 North Baldwin Avenue, Arcadia. (Exit Foothill Freeway [210] at Baldwin Avenue; south about one quarter mile to entrance.) (818) 446-8251. Open daily, 9 A.M.–5 P.M. Adults, $3; ages 13 and over and seniors, $1.50; ages 5–12, 75 cents; under 5, free. Tram tours, Monday–Friday, 12:15, 1, 2:15, and 3 P.M.; Saturday and Sunday, every 45 minutes between 10 A.M. and 4 P.M. Tickets, $1.50 per person.

MISSION SAN GABRIEL ARCHANGEL, 537 West Mission Drive, San Gabriel. (Exit San Bernardino Freeway [10] at Del Mar Avenue; north to Mission Drive; left to Junipero Serra Drive; right to entrance.) (818) 282-5191. Open daily, 9:30 A.M.–4:15 P.M. Adults, $1; ages 5–12, 50 cents; under 5, free.

PENSKE RACING MUSEUM, 3534 North Peck Road, El Monte. (Exit San Bernardino Freeway [10] at Peck Road; north to Longo Toyota dealership; race cars are in museum one floor below dealership showroom.) (818) 442-1011 or (818) 448-6249. Open Monday–Friday, noon–4 P.M. Free.

SANTA ANITA PARK, 285 West Huntington Drive, Arcadia. (Exit Foothill Freeway [210] at Baldwin Avenue; south to Gate 8 on Baldwin Avenue to see morning workouts.) (818) 574-7223. See workouts during racing season, December 26–end of April; 7–9:30 A.M. Free. Tram rides, Saturday and Sunday during racing season, 8–9:30 A.M. Free. Children under 17 admitted to races free with an adult. Races: Wednesday–Sunday. Gate opens at 10 A.M.

VINCENT LUGO PARK, on Wells Street at Ramona Street. (Exit San Bernardino Freeway [10] at Del Mar Avenue; north to Wells Street; left to park.) (818) 308-2875. Open daily, 7:30 A.M.–10 P.M.

WHITTIER NARROWS RECREATION AREA, east and west of Rosemead Boulevard and north and south of Pomona Freeway (60), South El Monte. (Exit Pomona Freeway [60] at Rosemead Boulevard [19]; north or south to park.) (818) 444-9305. Open daily, 5 A.M.–10 P.M.

• *American Heritage Park/Military Museum*, 1918 North Rosemead Boulevard, South El Monte. (Exit Pomona Freeway [60] at Rosemead Avenue; north to entrance.) (818) 442-1776. Open Saturday and Sunday, noon–4:30 P.M. Closed if it rains. Adults, $2; ages 10 and older, $1; under 10, 50 cents.
• *Whittier Narrows Nature Center*, 1000 North Durfee Avenue, South El Monte. (Exit Pomona Freeway [60] at Rosemead Boulevard; south to Durfee Avenue; left to center.) (818) 444-1872. Open daily, 9 A.M.–5 P.M. Free.

For More Information

Pasadena Convention and Visitors Bureau, 171 South Los Robles Avenue, Pasadena, CA 91101; (818) 795-9311

SAN GABRIEL MOUNTAINS
Wilderness and Waterfalls

Rising above Pasadena, the San Gabriel Mountains are most familiar to a nation of TV viewers as the purple backdrop for the Tournament of Roses

Parade. Local residents, however, know these mountains for the wealth of recreational activities they provide for families, only an hour's drive from Los Angeles. With a number of peaks over six thousand feet, the slopes offer sledding and skiing in winter. In summer, when mountain temperatures are as much as 20 degrees cooler than in the valley below, you can go hiking, horseback riding, mountain biking, fishing, and camping.

The San Gabriel Mountains run east and west between Interstate Highways 5 and 15 and are bordered by Interstate Highway 210 on the south and State Highway 138 on the north. Much of this vast area is part of the **Angeles National Forest,** a 693,000-acre preserve. You can approach the mountains from all sides, but this section suggests places to go with children in the southwestern San Gabriels, closest to Pasadena and Los Angeles. (For San Gabriel Mountain skiing information, see the Skiing with Kids section in chapter 8.)

A good introduction to the mountain environment for young children is **Eaton Canyon Park,** nestled in the foothills of Pasadena and Altadena. You'll reach it along Altadena Drive in Pasadena. This 184-acre park has a museum, an interpretive center, and easy hiking trails through chaparral and oak woodlands. Take the kids first to the **Nature Center** near the parking lot. A babbling brook runs through the courtyard of this pleasant building, which exhibits canyon wildlife. In the Naturalist's Room, open on Saturday from 10 A.M. to 3 P.M., kids can touch live native animals such as rabbits, turtles, and bullfrogs. Exhibit rooms around the courtyard display insects and skeletons of animals in lifelike poses, even a little brown bat suspended in flight. One interesting case shows how animals use their teeth to tear, grind, and pound, along with a display of modern tools that perform the same functions. In the courtyard there's a small gift shop with children's books and toys.

If you have preschool-age children, walk the short nature-trail loop behind the center that is especially designed for such youngsters. On other trails, naturalists conduct short, informative hikes every Saturday morning at 9 A.M. Monthly workshops teach children about the natural environment. If your kids are up to it, take a three-mile hike along the canyon to 40-foot Eaton Falls. Along the hike, look for rabbits, lizards, and acorn woodpeckers who may be poking their harvests into holes in the trees for safekeeping.

Nearby in the San Gabriel Mountain foothills, **Descanso Gardens** preserves not only native California plants, but flora from around the world. A favorite stop in the 165-acre garden for young children is the duck pond near the fountain at the entrance. Buy a cup of food from dispensers near the pond to feed the friendly birds. Easy walking trails in the gardens lead through flowering displays and wooded areas. In spring, be sure to walk through the camellia garden, which displays more than six hundred colorful varieties. Some plants are so tall they form a forest along the trail that kids love to use for imaginary play. A good place to rest is the tranquil Japanese Tea House, where you can eat cookies and sip tea or punch between 11 A.M. and 4 P.M. daily.

East of the gardens, starting at Foothill Freeway (210) in La Canada, Angeles Crest Highway (2) winds up into the mountains. The scenic highway is dotted with picnic spots, easy hiking trails, and snow play areas that are especially fun for kids. You may want to stop at **Clear Creek Information Station** less than ten miles up the road from Foothill Freeway to pick up maps and trail guides for the area.

A short way east of the station on Angeles Crest Highway, you'll see signs for **Switzer Picnic Area,** a scenic spot to spend a day with children. You enter down a steep winding road that leads to a parking lot. Walk over the footbridge to an inviting picnic area where tables are set under tall trees along a rocky stream. There are restrooms and a drinking fountain near the bridge. Kids love to play on the rocky outcrops along a trail that follows the stream. At some places, the rocks dam up the stream, creating little pools that are perfect for youngsters to splash in on a hot day.

Perhaps the best-known spot in the San Gabriels is **Mount Wilson.** You'll reach it via Mount Wilson Road, a few miles farther up Angeles Crest Highway from Switzer Picnic Area. Turn right at Red Box Junction to take the winding road five miles to Mount Wilson's 5,710-foot peak. You'll see a forest of TV and radio transmitter antennas as you near the parking lot. Mount Wilson Observatory, built between 1904 and 1919, sits atop the mountain. Through its 100-inch reflecting telescope, scientists discovered that there is more than one galaxy in the universe. While the observatory still is used for research, the public galleries have been closed. But you're welcome to walk on the observatory grounds, where a small museum features photographs of the heavens and displays machinery from one of the telescopes. Walk around the observatory to the east side and continue out to Echo Point, about a quarter of a mile. From there, you'll be able to see 10,000-foot Mount Baldy to the east, and on a clear day, peaks as far as 90 miles away. Every Sunday during daylight savings time (between April and October), docents conduct walking tours of the observatory grounds.

Mount Wilson Skyline Park is a good place to picnic. From the park on clear days, you'll have a panoramic view of Los Angeles stretching all the way to the Pacific Ocean. Steep trails lead down to the valley below. You can buy drinks and snacks at the pavilion near the parking lot. This lot as well as Mount Wilson Road are plowed in winter, making the park a good spot for snow play.

Continuing north on Angeles Crest Highway, you'll come to **Charlton Flats Picnic Area.** This pretty spot is on the edge of a pine forest. From the west end of the picnic area near the bridge, take the Wolf Tree Nature Trail, a one-mile loop. You'll walk along a trail dotted with Coulter pines. Look for their huge, fragrant pine cones along the trail. You're not allowed to remove them, but kids can pick up the giant cones and smell them.

If the children are good hikers, try an easy trail that leaves from the picnic area. You'll hike less than two miles each way. The trail traverses a pine forest and flowering meadows as it heads up to a Forest Service fire lookout, where you'll have an uninterrupted view of the mountains in all directions.

Chilao Visitor Center, about 27 miles northeast of Foothill Freeway on Angeles Crest Highway, offers picnic areas, campgrounds, and hiking trails in addition to the center's displays on the wildlife and history of the San Gabriel Mountains. Four one-mile nature trails start from this area. Two are wheelchair accessible, so for very young children you can use a stroller on these trails. Get self-guided trail brochures from the center. On your hikes you'll learn about plant life, forest management, and the Indians who once lived in the mountains.

During summer months, join a forest naturalist for a hike or attend a campfire program at the Chilao Amphitheater. Every weekend during the summer the Visitor Center offers family nature walks and one-hour programs for children. Pick up a weekly schedule at the center. Plan to picnic at the Upper Chilao Picnic Area, which has tables and barbecues. If you didn't bring picnic supplies, you can eat at Newcomb's Ranch Café around the corner from the Visitor Center. It's the only restaurant in this part of the mountains, serving moderately priced food such as chili and hamburgers. In winter, Upper Chilao Picnic Area is good place for snow play. Its moderate slopes have been cleared of vegetation, making it a safe place for sledding.

Angeles Crest Highway isn't the only route into the mountains from San Gabriel Valley. Santa Anita Avenue, north of Arcadia, takes you about six miles north of Foothill Freeway to **Chantry Flat,** another pleasant place to spend the day. The Forest Service picnic ground here is shaded by tall oak trees. If the kids are old enough, take a scenic 3½-mile round-trip hike from Chantry Flat to Sturtevant Falls. Along a creekside trail, you'll encounter unusual sights for these dry mountains—large ferns and moss-covered rocks. You'll hear the falls before you reach them. They drop more than fifty feet into a natural rock pool. Keep the kids from climbing on the dangerous wet rocks near the falls.

If you head up State Highway 39 from Azuza, you'll come to the **San Gabriel Information Station,** a good place to get maps and trail guides for this part of the mountains. Drive on to **Crystal Lake Recreation Area** at the end of the road, about 27 miles from Azuza. Start your visit here at the small visitor center, which is open on weekends year round. It has displays of the area's animal and plant life. On weekends during summer, rangers lead nature hikes near the center and conduct programs for children. Recent programs included making plaster casts of animal tracks and creating ink leaf prints.

Take one of the four self-guided nature trails that leave from this area. On the Tototngna Trail, you'll find an earthquake fault and many large boulders. (*Tototngna* is a Gabrielino Indian word for "place of the stones.") On the Golden Cup Trail you'll learn about the area's live oak trees. In late spring and early summer, try fishing in tiny Crystal Lake (adults need a license). You may have a good chance of catching some of the rainbow trout that are stocked there each year. Nearby there's a campground and a picnic area with tables under huge oaks.

Attractions

ANGELES NATIONAL FOREST: Day-use picnic areas are open from 6 A.M.–10 P.M. unless otherwise posted. Parking is free. Camping is available on a first-come/first-served basis. Roads are subject to closure with ice and snow. Call Angeles National Forest, (818) 574-5200 or Caltrans, (213) 626-7231 for road conditions.

CHANTRY FLAT, at the end of Santa Anita Avenue. (Exit Foothill Freeway [210] at Santa Anita Avenue; north to the end of the road, about six miles.) Information station: (818) 355-0712. Open daily.

CHARLTON FLATS PICNIC AREA. (Exit Foothill Freeway [210] on Angeles Crest Highway [2]; north about 24 miles.) Open daily.

CHILAO VISITOR CENTER. (Exit Foothill Freeway [210] at Angeles Crest Highway [2]; north about 27 miles.) (818) 796-5541. Open daily.

CLEAR CREEK INFORMATION STATION, at the junction of Angeles Crest Highway (2) and Angeles Forest Highway (N3). (Exit Foothill Freeway [210] at Angeles Crest Highway [2]; north to station.) (818) 797-9959. Summer hours: daily, 8 A.M.–4:30 P.M. Winter hours: Friday–Sunday, 8 A.M.–4:30 P.M.

CRYSTAL LAKE RECREATION AREA. (Exit Foothill Freeway [210] at State Highway 39; north about 27 miles.) (818) 910-1149. Visitor Center summer hours: daily, 8 A.M.–4:30 P.M. Winter hours: Friday–Sunday, 8 A.M.–4:30 P.M.

DESCANSO GARDENS, 1418 Descanso Drive, La Canada. (Exit Foothill Freeway [210] at Angeles Crest Highway [2]; south to Foothill Boulevard; right to Verdugo Boulevard; left to Descanso Drive; left to gardens.) (818) 790-5571. Open daily, 9 A.M.–4:30 P.M. Adults, $1.50; seniors and ages 5–17, 75 cents; under 5, free.

EATON CANYON PARK AND NATURE CENTER, 1750 North Altadena Drive, Pasadena. (Exit Foothill Freeway [210] at Sierra Madre Boulevard; follow signs to Altadena Drive; north 1½ miles to park.) (818) 794-1866. Park is open 7 A.M.–10 P.M. Nature Center is open daily, 9:30 A.M.–5 P.M. Family nature hikes on Saturday at 9 A.M. Free.

MOUNT WILSON, end of Mount Wilson Road. (Exit Foothill Freeway [210] at Angeles Crest Highway [2]; north to Red Box Junction; right on Mount Wilson Road to end.) (818) 449-4163. Open daily, weather permitting.

SAN GABRIEL INFORMATION CENTER. (Exit Foothill Freeway [210] at State Highway 39; north about three miles.) (818) 969-1012. Open Friday–Sunday, 8 A.M.–4:30 P.M. year round.

SWITZER PICNIC AREA. (Exit Foothill Freeway [210] at Angeles Crest Highway [2]; north past Clear Creek Information Station to sign at entrance road.) (818) 790-1151. Open daily.

For More Information

Angeles National Forest, 701 North Santa Anita Avenue, Arcadia, CA 91006; (818) 574-5200.

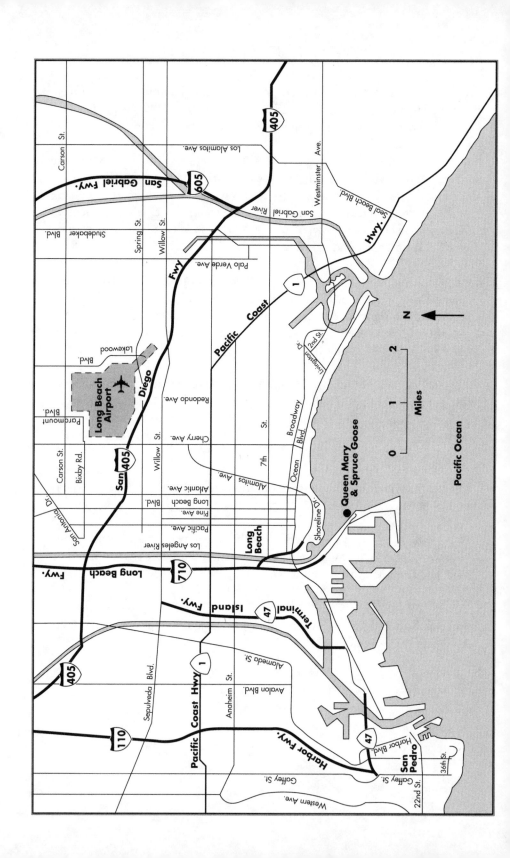

4

Southbay and Catalina Island

South of Los Angeles where the city meets the sea, the waterfront communities of Long Beach and San Pedro combine to form one of the nation's busiest port areas. This Southbay region's rich history and wealth of resources also make it a popular spot for family recreation.

Without question, the Southbay's "biggest" attractions are the *Queen Mary* and *Spruce Goose*. But a trip to the venerable ocean liner and mysterious flying boat is only the first of many itineraries in the area that will amuse and educate the kids. Marine museums, merry-go-rounds, harbor cruises, tide pools, historic buildings, nature walks, and bike paths make up a variety of diversions from which families can fashion a day's activities.

Just offshore two more "big" attractions await. The annual migration of the Pacific gray whale connects youngsters with one of nature's great pageants, while a visit to Catalina Island puts them in touch with a unique seaside resort and a special slice of California history. Although there are whale-watch trips available from ports up and down the Southern California coast, a large percentage of them leave from Southbay harbors. For that reason, this chapter contains a section that details what youngsters can expect on any of the whale-watch cruises.

QUEEN MARY AND SPRUCE GOOSE

BIG Attractions in Long Beach

The world's largest ocean liner, the *Queen Mary,* and the world's largest airplane, the *Spruce Goose,* sit side by side in Long Beach Harbor. Now permanently moored to terra firma, the two giant attractions offer kids a view of the past that is sure to make a BIG impression.

You'll explore the 1,000-foot-long *Queen Mary* on a self-guided walking tour that shows you shipboard life as it was in the 1930s and 1940s. Under the adjacent geodesic dome you will gasp at the size of Howard Hughes's wooden flying boat and climb into its cargo hold. One ticket pays for both attractions. It takes about four hours of walking to see them both, so you'll want to make sure your kids are old enough to keep going. They won't be bored, though, because there's plenty for them to explore, plus lots of places to rest and buy snacks.

It's best to begin your tour of the twin attractions early in the day at the *Spruce Goose* because the lines can be quite long, especially on weekends or during the summer. When kids enter the darkened clear-span aluminum dome where the wooden giant dramatically awaits, they will be most impressed by the plane's immense size. The fact that it's the world's largest airplane really comes home to them when they learn that a wide-bodied DC-10 can fit under each wing of the *Spruce Goose.*

Walk around the reflection pond and climb up the steps into the plane's cavernous cargo bay. Long lines form at the bottom of the steps later in the day, so climb aboard early and see other displays under the dome later. You'll see the gaping inside of the plane and then walk along a platform that gives you a good view of the 1940s-era flight deck. In the cockpit there's a life-size model of Howard Hughes sitting in the pilot's seat ready for takeoff, giving kids a good idea of how he looked when he flew the plane briefly on November 2, 1947. Back on the ground, take your time viewing the videos and exhibits surrounding the plane which explain the controversial story of Hughes's life, his affiliation with the movies, and, of course, his 200-ton wooden experiment. You'll see footage of the plane's one-minute flight and learn about the secrecy that kept it hidden in a hangar for thirty years.

There's a gift shop and a snack bar under the dome, but if it's a nice day, you may prefer to eat lunch or snacks out on one of the *Queen Mary*'s decks, where you will have a good view of the harbor. There is often a band playing outside.

To reach the *Queen Mary*, walk across the courtyard and go up escalators to the upper decks. The huge ship, pride of Cunard's fleet, was once the fastest in the world. Before the onset of transatlantic jet crossings, the *Queen Mary* ferried wealthy passengers across the ocean in luxurious style. The liner attracted such well-known passengers as the Duke and Duchess of Windsor, Fred Astaire, Greta Garbo, and Winston Churchill.

Today the ship houses a 390-suite hotel and a whole boatload of shops, restaurants, and historical exhibits. It's a masterpiece of art-deco design. On the lower decks, visit the first-class passenger lounges, the print shop, and a multi-image show that tells the history of the *Queen Mary*. Take older kids to the sound and light presentation in the engine room that brings to life a fictitious near-collision at sea (preschoolers might be frightened by the show's loud soundtrack). Children and adults alike are dwarfed by the pumps and machinery in the room.

Take an escalator or walk up to the upper decks to see the first-class staterooms and wood-paneled dining rooms. Kids find that the 1940s barbershop, children's play room, and exercise gym look quite primitive. Crowded bunk quarters and a mess hall recreate the time during World War II when the ship was used to carry more than 750,000 American troops overseas. Each evening during the summer there is entertainment on the upper decks, ending with fireworks at 9 P.M.

After touring the stationary ship, you may be yearning for an actual sea cruise. At the bow of the *Queen Mary* you can climb aboard a **Catalina Cruises** boat for a 45-minute narrated tour of Long Beach Harbor and its scenic bay. You'll see freighters, U.S. Navy ships, and pleasure craft in this, one of America's busiest harbors. You can buy tickets that combine the cost of the harbor tour and the *Queen Mary/Spruce Goose* tour in one package. Cruises run daily during summer, departing on weekends and holidays during the rest of the year.

If you don't want such a long cruise, take a ten-minute hop on a **Bay Shuttle Water Taxi** across Queensway Bay to **Shoreline Village.** From the water taxi, which leaves every half hour from the bow of the *Queen Mary,* you'll have a good vantage point for taking photos of the huge ocean liner.

Shoreline Village contains more than thirty specialty shops, restaurants, and, for young children, a Charles Looff–designed merry-go-round built in 1906. Grab on to a brass pole and take a turn on one of the carousel's 62 carefully restored horses, giraffes, camels, lions, or sheep. It's a small reminder of the famed Pike Amusement Park that used to attract tourists to the shores of Long Beach.

Adjacent to the village is **Shoreline Aquatic Park,** with picnic areas and grassy lawns for flying kites and relaxing. Stroll along the park's bayside paths and continue along Downtown Long Beach Marina's scenic walkway to view hundreds of moored yachts. Take the water taxi back to your car in the parking lot at the *Queen Mary.* The kids will be tired after a full day in the ocean air.

Attractions

BAY SHUTTLE WATER TAXI, Long Beach. (Travels between bow of *Queen Mary* and Shoreline Village.) (213) 514-3838. Open daily, ten-minute trips every half hour: Sunday–Thursday, 12:10–7:40 P.M.; Friday and Saturday, 12:10–10:40 P.M. Adults, $2; children, $1; under 2, free.

CATALINA CRUISES SCENIC BAY CRUISE, Long Beach. (Leaves from bow of *Queen Mary* and Shoreline Village.) Ticket booth in Shoreline Village, next to Mardi Gras restaurant. (213) 514-3838. 45-minute cruises daily in summer and weekends in winter, 11 A.M.–5 P.M. Adults, $5.95; children 5–11, $3.95; under 5, free. You can purchase a combo ticket with *Queen Mary/Spruce Goose* tour.

QUEEN MARY AND SPRUCE GOOSE, Long Beach Harbor at end of Long Beach Freeway (710), Long Beach. (Follow Long Beach Freeway [710] south to its end; follow signs to the *Queen Mary.*) (213) 435-3511. Open daily, 10 A.M.–6 P.M.; during summer (July 4–Labor Day), entertainment and fireworks on upper decks until 9 P.M. All-day pass: adults, $14.95; seniors, $11.95; children 5–11, $8.95; under 5, free. Parking, $3.

SHORELINE VILLAGE, 407 Shoreline Village Drive, Long Beach. (Exit Long Beach Freeway [710] at Shoreline Drive; follow signs to village.) (213) 590-8427. Shops, restaurants, and carousel. Summer hours: daily, 10 A.M.–10 P.M. Winter hours: daily, 10 A.M.–9 P.M. Free parking.

For More Information

Long Beach Area Convention and Visitors Council, One World Trade Center, Suite 300, Long Beach, CA 90831; (213) 436-3645, (800) 234-3645.

LONG BEACH POTPOURRI
Fire Trucks and Sailboats

All along the extended stretch of sand that gives Long Beach its name, you'll find dozens of activities that children will enjoy. In addition to the *Queen Mary* and *Spruce Goose* (see preceding section), Long Beach offers enough to keep you in the area for several days.

One of the city's most appealing attractions is its shoreline. In all, there are 5½ miles of beaches, marinas, and bays in Long Beach that provide a wide array of recreational opportunities for kids. Locals will tell you that the safest beach in the area for young children is **Marina Beach,** located on the west side of Marine Stadium just north of 2nd Street in Naples. With its gently lapping bay water, the beach is appropriately nicknamed "Mother's Beach." You can rent umbrellas, boogie boards, chairs, and aqua bikes on the sand.

Another quiet beach in the area is the **Bayshore Aquatic Playground** in **Alamitos Bay,** which has a park with children's play equipment. The City of Long Beach Parks and Recreation Department gives sabot (8-foot boats) sailing instruction to kids at the **Leeway Sailing Center** in a nearby area of Alamitos Bay.

Fishing is another water sport readily available in Long Beach. You can fish at lakes in **El Dorado Regional Park** or from the **Belmont Pier** at Ocean Boulevard and Termino Avenue. For a half-day or full-day ocean-fishing experience, take the kids out from the pier by shuttle to **Annie's Barge,** a 150-foot all-steel platform that accommodates 300 ocean sportfishermen. The barge has indoor and outdoor eating areas, a lounge area with color TV, and video games.

The three-mile-long **Long Beach Shoreline Bicycle/Pedestrian Path** runs along the entire length of the beach from the Los Angeles River and Shoreline Village to the San Gabriel River at the east end of the Long Beach city limits. The shoreline bike path connects the Los Angeles River and San Gabriel River bike paths, creating a 60-mile loop. This 17-foot-wide paved path has two 6-foot-wide bike lanes and a pedestrian lane, making it a safe place for kids to ride. The bike path is best in winter when there are fewer crowds at the beach. You can rent bikes at a small kiosk on the beach just east of the Downtown Shoreline Marina.

Inland from the shore, Long Beach has nearly forty parks where children can play. The largest is **El Dorado Regional Park,** an 800-acre recreational complex divided into east and west sections, with lakes, playgrounds, and bike paths. A favorite spot for kids is **El Dorado Nature Center,** an 85-acre wildlife preserve located in El Dorado East Regional Park. Framed by the San Gabriel River channel and San Gabriel Freeway (605) south of Spring Street, the nature center is a surprisingly quiet and wild oasis. It has three miles of trails through a woods and along a lake and stream. On the trail, look for foxes, opossums, and swimming turtles. Walk across a wooden bridge to visit the nature-center building on an island in the lake. Inside, kids can explore "touch and feel" exhibits. The center offers programs for children throughout the year, including naturalist-led hikes, workshops, and evening concerts.

The east park also has several lakes where you can fish, rent paddle-boats, or try out remote-control model boats. There's a model-glider area too, as well as playgrounds, picnic areas, and an archery range (used for the 1984 Olympics). The park is encircled by a bike and roller-skating path. At El Dorado West Regional Park (west of the San Gabriel River), you'll find a duck pond, a playground, baseball diamonds, tennis courts, and a golf course.

If you're looking for less active pursuits, there's a handful of museums to choose from in Long Beach that children of varying ages will find interesting.

The city has its own museum for kids, the **Long Beach Children's Museum,** adjacent to the Long Beach Plaza shopping mall. This small museum offers hands-on experiences that delight young children. At the Art Café, kids turn out creations made of string, paint, paper, and glue. In Granny's Attic, they try on firefighter suits and fancy dresses. Another area lets kids spend their time using screwdrivers to disassemble typewriters and toasters. There's a Grand Prix car to "drive" and a rowboat surrounded by fabric fish to allow kids to "go fishing." You may never get your child out of the Lego corner, which features more than thirty thousand of the plastic interlocking blocks.

Drive directly to the museum or add a little more adventure to the day by parking at Long Beach Marina's Shoreline Village and taking a free tram along the six-block-long Promenade from the village to the mall near the museum. This plan works out well for small children because Shoreline Village has a merry-go-round and snack bars.

To catch the tram from the village, walk up steps to the tram stop near the white gazebo on a bridge above Shoreline Drive. Open-air trams run about every ten minutes between the village and Long Beach Plaza. Along the bricked Promenade you'll pass the **Long Beach Visitors Center,** where you can get off the tram to pick up maps and city information. The tram also stops at an outdoor amphitheater where you can catch a concert some days during the lunch hour. To reach the children's museum, get off the tram at the Long Beach Plaza mall entrance on 3rd Street, walk one-half block east to Long Beach Boulevard, turn left, and continue one-half block north to the museum.

Along Long Beach Boulevard, you'll find one of the city's largest bookstores, **Acres of Books.** A large children's-book section is in the front of the store.

The **Long Beach Firefighters Museum** is about two miles northeast of the children's museum. Housed in the city's old Station No. 10, the museum features motorized fire engines, horse-drawn steamers and hand-drawn carts dating from the 1890s. The equipment has been lovingly restored by retired Long Beach firefighters who explain how various pieces work to interested visitors. In the captain's office, you'll see boots and uniforms laid out, ready for a fire call. The old dormitory has hundreds of firefighters' hats and badges hanging on the walls, donated from all over the world. Ask to see the scrapbook of "Sam the cat," a famous Long Beach feline who slid down poles and rode on engines with firefighters in the 1960s.

For a step much further back in time, visit the **London Brass Rubbing Center** at St. Luke's Episcopal Church less than a mile away at Atlantic Avenue and 7th Street. Open during October and November each year, the center provides forty medieval brass engravings for making rubbings. You can buy wax and paper for a small fee. Kids produce professional-looking rubbings with minimal instruction.

On the east side of town at **Rancho los Alamitos** you'll see Long Beach as it was when the first European settlers came. Now located on 7½ acres in a residential area near California State University at Long Beach, the adobe ranch house was built in 1806 on a 300,000-acre Spanish land grant.

Kids will enjoy exploring the Rancho's well-kept gardens, barns, and blacksmith's shop, and they probably won't recognize an old gasoline pump near the house. To see the interior of the house, you need to go on a one-hour guided tour, which would be most interesting to older children who have studied a bit of history. Within the cool, four-foot-thick adobe walls, you get a feel for old California. Look for fine Indian baskets and blankets throughout the house. In the game room, make sure the kids see the cabinet full of nineteenth-century games, including some they'll recognize, such as dominoes and Parcheesi. The children's room has a chamber pot under the bed.

At the west end of town near Long Beach Freeway (710), **Rancho los Cerritos** re-creates sheep-ranching life of the 1870s. The home once sat on 27,000 acres. Surrounded by serene gardens and huge shade trees today, the two-story Spanish-colonial hacienda gives you a strong sense of entering that earlier era. On a one-hour guided tour, you'll see a blacksmith shop, a loom room where fleece was made into cloth, and a children's room that displays Victorian antique toys and dolls. There are shaded picnic tables on the grounds.

The **Long Beach Museum of Art,** housed in a 1911 Craftsman-style house on a bluff overlooking the beach, specializes in contemporary and video art. Exhibits change frequently, and some are more interesting to children than others. A good time to visit with kids is December, when the museum presents its annual Magical Mystery Tour. This exhibit is created each year to introduce children and adults to the fantasy and playful use of imagination in contemporary art. At any time of year, kids enjoy the outdoor sculpture garden and the bookshop that carries children's art books.

If you are planning a day for ten or more children, consider touring two of Long Beach's well-known institutions. The **Press-Telegram** tour lets kids see how a newspaper is put together. They will view the entire operation, from reporters writing at their computers to the copy being printed on giant presses. The minimum age for this tour is third grade.

On Saturdays at the **Long Beach Naval Station,** groups of ten or more with kids over the age of 8 can tour one of the Navy ships moored in Long Beach Harbor. A variety of ships are used throughout the year for the free tours. Uniformed personnel guide groups through the vessel and explain its operation.

Attractions

ACRES OF BOOKS, 240 Long Beach Boulevard, Long Beach. (Exit Long Beach Freeway [710] at 7th Street; east to Long Beach Boulevard; right to store.) (213) 437-6980. Tuesday–Friday, 9:15 A.M.–5 P.M.

ANNIE'S BARGE, INC., Box 26, Seal Beach. (213) 434-6781. Shuttle boat departs Belmont Pier in Long Beach every other hour. (See directions to Belmont Pier, below.) Summer hours: daily, between 6:30 A.M. and 4:30 P.M. Winter hours: Friday–Sunday, 6:30 A.M.–5:30 P.M.

BEACHES

• *Bayshore Aquatic Playground*, 14 54th Place, Long Beach. (Exit Long Beach Freeway [710] at Pacific Coast Highway [1]; east to Redondo Avenue; right to Ocean Boulevard; left to 54th Place; left to beach.) (213) 429-6301 or (213) 425-4712. Open daily.

• *Marina Beach*, in Marine Stadium south of the 2nd Street Bridge in Naples. (Exit San Diego Freeway [405] at Bellflower Boulevard; south to Pacific Coast Highway [1]; left to Westminster Avenue; right over bridge to Appian Way; right to beach.) Open daily.

BELMONT PIER, Ocean Boulevard and Termino Avenue. (Exit San Diego Freeway [405] at Cherry Avenue; south to Ocean Boulevard; left to pier at south end of 39th Place.) Fish for free. Pole rental: $5.

EL DORADO REGIONAL PARK AND NATURE CENTER, 7550 East Spring Street, Long Beach. (Exit San Gabriel Freeway [605] at Willow Street/Katella Avenue; west on Willow Street; follow signs to park.) (213) 425-8569. Nature Center hours: Monday–Friday, 10 A.M.–4 P.M.; Saturday and Sunday, 8 A.M.–4 P.M. East Park hours: 8 A.M.–4 P.M. West Park hours: 6 A.M.–10 P.M. Free.

LEEWAY SAILING CENTER, 5437 East Ocean Boulevard, Long Beach. (Exit Long Beach Freeway [710] at Pacific Coast Highway [1]; east to Redondo Avenue; right to Ocean Boulevard; left to center.) (213) 439-5427. Call for class schedules. Sail rentals: $50.

LONDON BRASS RUBBING CENTER, St. Luke's Episcopal Church, 7th Street and Atlantic Avenue, Long Beach. (Exit San Diego Freeway [710] at Atlantic Avenue; south to 7th Street.) (213) 437-1584. Open October and November. Call for schedule. Materials fee: $2.50–$15.

LONG BEACH CHILDREN'S MUSEUM, 445 Long Beach Boulevard, Long Beach. (Exit Long Beach Freeway [710] at 6th Street; east to Long Beach Boulevard; right to museum.) (213) 495-1163. Open Thursday–Saturday, 11 A.M.–4 P.M.; Sunday, noon–4 P.M. Admission: $2.50; under 3, free. Field trips Wednesday–Friday mornings for groups of 30 or more, $1.25 per person. Free parking in mall structure.

LONG BEACH FIREFIGHTERS MUSEUM, 1445 Peterson Avenue, Long Beach. (Exit Long Beach Freeway [710] at Anaheim Street; east to Peterson Avenue; left one block to the museum.) (213) 597-0351. Open to the public on the second Saturday of each month, 10 A.M.–3 P.M., or by appointment for groups. Free.

LONG BEACH MUSEUM OF ART, 2300 East Ocean Avenue, Long Beach. (Exit San Diego Freeway [405] at Cherry Avenue; south to Ocean Boulevard; left to museum.) (213) 439-2119. Open Wednesday–Sunday, noon to 5 P.M. Donation: $1.

LONG BEACH NAVAL STATION, NAVAL SHIP TOUR, Public Affairs Office, Naval Surface Group Long Beach, Long Beach. (Exit Long Beach Freeway [710] at Willow Street; west to Terminal Island Freeway [47]; left to Ocean Boulevard; right to Navy Way; left to entrance.) Group tours on Saturday, 9 A.M. and 1 P.M. Call at least one week in advance. Minimum age: 8. Free.

LONG BEACH SHORELINE BICYCLE/PEDESTRIAN PATH, runs along the beach between the Los Angeles River and Shoreline Village on the west and the San Gabriel River on the east.

PRESS-TELEGRAM TOURS, 604 Pine Avenue, Long Beach. (Exit Long Beach Freeway [710] at 7th Street; east to Pine Avenue; right to office.) Group tours for ten or more: Monday–Friday, 10 A.M. and 2 or 4 P.M. Make reservations one month in advance. Minimum age: 8.

RANCHO LOS ALAMITOS, 6400 Bixby Hill Road, Long Beach. (Exit San Diego Freeway [405] at Palo Verde Avenue; south to security gate to get pass; continue on Palo Verde Avenue to Bixby Hill Road; left to entrance.) (213) 431-3541. Open Wednesday–Sunday, 1–5 P.M. Free.

RANCHO LOS CERRITOS, 4600 Virginia Road, Long Beach. (Exit San Diego Freeway [405] at Long Beach Boulevard; north to San Antonio Drive; left to Virginia Road; right to ranch at end of street.) (213) 424-9423. Open Wednesday–Sunday, 1–5 P.M. Free.

For More Information

Long Beach Area Convention and Visitors Council, One World Trade Center, Suite 300, Long Beach, CA 90831; (213) 436-3645, (800) 234-3645.

LOS ANGELES HARBOR AREA
Whale Watches and Tide Pools

From the end of December through March, Southern Californians are treated to the amazing spectacle of thousands of Pacific gray whales swimming along the coast. These gentle giants pass by on their annual migration from Alaska to the quiet bays of Baja California, where they bear their young.

The chance to see the huge mammals on their 10,000-mile round-trip journey is a remarkable experience for both children and adults. Atop bluffs along the coast or aboard boats at sea, you can see the whales' spouts and tails, and if you get close enough, their barnacle-encrusted bodies.

To see whales from land, you'll need binoculars to spot their telltale spouts offshore. Any bluff top such as the one at **Point Fermin Park** in San Pedro will give you a good view. Some parks and museums with a view, such as the **Point Vicente Interpretive Center** on the Palos Verdes Peninsula, have knowledgeable staffs who help you see the whales.

At sea, you'll get a closer look as captains steer their vessels as close to migrating groups of whales as possible without harming or frightening them. Most cruises are staffed by well-versed docents who point out the whales and tell you about their habits. Kids will leave the trip knowing that whales are mammals, not fish. They'll also have a new vocabulary of such words as "flukes" (whale's tails) and "baleen" (the hundreds of thin plates these whales have instead of teeth).

Whale-watch cruises depart from more than a dozen places along the Southern California coast between San Diego and Santa Barbara. Cruises closest to Los Angeles depart from Long Beach or San Pedro at Los Angeles Harbor. You can choose from about a dozen cruises in that area (see the listing at the end of this section). Most cruises last 2½ to 3 hours and cost about $10 to $12 for adults and $6 to $8 for children.

A few tips for your whale-watching cruise: Make your reservations in advance, because the trips are quite popular and are offered only between December and April, the whale migration season. Be sure to dress warmly, wear sunscreen, and bring binoculars and a camera (preferably with a tele-photo lens). Most of the boats sell snacks on board.

While most boats offer indoor and outdoor viewing, you generally have a better vantage point outside, and it's better for taking photos. Most captains, if they can, will try to keep the whales between their ship and the shore, so you'll probably do best to stake out a place facing the shore before the whales are spotted. Remember, though, there are no guarantees where the whales will surface, so be patient and your chance to see them will come.

After your whale-watch trip, plan to stay in the area to learn more about the whales, the sea, and the harbor. There's a handful of museums and seaside parks nearby to entice you.

Visit **Ports o' Call,** a re-creation of a nineteenth-century seaport town, located on the main channel of Los Angeles Harbor. Stroll along its cob-blestoned streets and browse through some of the 75 shops that sell toys, kites, and clothing. Or dine at harborside in one of the village's 15 inter-national restaurants.

Ports o' Call sits on the very site where the harbor was established in the 1880s. You still can see the six-mile-long breakwater that was crucial in the creation of Los Angeles Harbor from the ten-foot-deep estuary that origi-nally existed there. Today, Los Angeles Harbor is the second largest man-made harbor in the world (Amsterdam is larger). You will have a good view from Ports o' Call of the cargo cranes, cruise boats, and container ships that make up the waterfront skyline.

Just north of Ports o' Call, at the end of 6th Street, is the **Los Angeles Maritime Museum.** You'll easily find the large white museum, housed in the old Ferry Building, with a clock on its tower and a tall mast out in front flying nautical flags. The museum contains models of ships, full-size boats, and nautical memorabilia. You'll see the ship model used for filming *The Poseidon Adventure* and an 18-foot replica of the *Titanic*, with one side cut away to show the interior. A full-size ship's wheelhouse looks out over the harbor. Walk up the curving ramp past full-size craft to the second floor. Be sure to stop at the knot display near the top of the ramp. There's a pole below the display with ropes tied on to it so kids can practice knot tying. Upstairs you can listen in as a ham radio operator talks to people from around the world. Downstairs, a gift shop sells model shipbuilding kits, games, and books.

To find out more about whales and other creatures who live in the sea, drive south on Pacific Avenue and turn east on Stephen White Drive to the **Cabrillo Marine Museum.** Exhibits at the museum interpret Southern California's marine environment. In more than thirty aquariums, you'll be able to look at fascinating animals up close, such as toothy moray eels, several species of octopus, and bright-colored lobsters.

Children especially enjoy the touch tanks at the back of the museum, filled with tide-pool creatures, including prickly sea urchins, squishy sea anemones, and crusty starfish. A museum staff member explains tide-pool life and encourages youngsters to touch the animals. In a camouflage tank nearby, see how many animals the kids can spot. At the shark exhibit, look for a shark jaw that has five sets of formidable teeth. A life-size model of a killer whale "swims" above the courtyard. Below, you can examine huge whalebones up close and measure yourself against a full-size outline of a Pacific gray whale. A multimedia show on marine life is presented in the auditorium.

The museum sponsors whale-watch trips from January through March, a grunion program from March to July, and tide-pool tours at other times during the year. There are tide pools and a beach with play equipment, picnic areas, and barbecues across the street from the museum. You can fish from adjacent Cabrillo Fishing Pier without a license.

South of the museum is **Point Fermin Park,** a 37-acre bluff-top reserve where you can picnic on the grass and look for whales and ships on the sea that stretches out on three sides. The old white clapboard Point Fermin lighthouse (now a private residence) still sits out on the point with a beacon in its rooftop cupola. You can reach tide pools below the bluff by walking about a quarter of a mile west on Paseo del Mar to a metal stairway that leads to the ocean. A sign shows the way to this Point Fermin Annex tide-pool trail. You'll find dozens of interesting creatures living in the rocky pools; but remember, it's illegal to remove them.

One block up the hill on Gaffey Street is **Angels Gate Park,** a high grassy knoll topped with the **Korean Friendship Bell,** the biggest bell in the country, given to the people of the United States during our bicentennial in 1976. The 17-ton bell, which is rung on special occasions during the year, sits in a traditional Korean-style pagoda, painted with multicolor designs. From the steps of the pagoda, there's an expansive view of the ocean, Catalina Island, and the coastline. This windy, treeless park is an ideal place to fly a kite.

Angels Gate Park and the surrounding land were once a part of the coastal defense system. You can go down into the bunkers that housed weapons and ammunition during World Wars I and II at the **Osgood Farley Military Museum.** To reach the museum, turn east into the park on 37th Street from

Gaffey Street, and follow the directional signs. Inside the cool underground museum, you'll see guns, cannons, a jeep, and other wartime memorabilia. Visit the plotting room where World War II generals planned the defense of Los Angeles Harbor. Children like exploring an underground tunnel to see where the guns were secretly placed. They learn that the weapons were never fired and are now obsolete because of technological advancements in airplanes, missiles, and submarines.

North of the park on Gaffey Street near 34th Street, the observation point at the top of the hill also was once part of the coastal defense system. From this turnout, you'll have a bird's-eye view of Los Angeles Harbor. Telescopes let you see it up close.

To the west of Point Fermin, on the Palos Verdes Peninsula, the **Point Vicente Interpretive Center** sits on a bluff overlooking the coast from another vantage point. Walk up to the second-floor viewing area to look for whales. Exhibits inside the well-lit museum focus on marine life, geology, and the cultural history of the peninsula. There are picnic facilities adjacent to the center and a walking path along the coast.

To learn why Los Angeles Harbor is located where it is, visit the **General Phineas Banning Residence Museum,** north of the harbor off Pacific Coast Highway in Wilmington. This 23-room Greek Revival home was built in 1864 by Banning, who was instrumental in having the harbor dredged and a rail line built to connect it with the City of Los Angeles. Conducted tours of the house, which take about ninety minutes, start on the trellis-covered patio on the east side of the house. On the tour you'll see a multimedia presentation about Banning's important role in the early years of Los Angeles and a photo exhibit of the building of the harbor. Among the carefully refurbished rooms in the house, the Victorian kitchen, children's rooms with antique toys, and the one-room schoolhouse will be of greatest interest to kids. A tree-filled park surrounding the home has children's play equipment and picnic area.

Attractions

ANGELS GATE PARK AND KOREAN FRIENDSHIP BELL, 3601 South Gaffey Street, San Pedro. (Follow Harbor Freeway [110] south to the end where it joins Gaffey Street; south to entrance between 32nd Street and Paseo del Mar.) (213) 548-7705. Open daily, 8 A.M.–6 P.M. Free.

CABRILLO MARINE MUSEUM, 3720 Stephen White Drive, San Pedro. (Follow Harbor Freeway [110] south to the end where it joins Gaffey

Street; south to 22nd Street; left to Pacific Avenue; right to 36th, which becomes Stephen White Drive; left to museum.) (213) 548-7562. Open Tuesday–Friday, noon to 5 P.M.; Saturday and Sunday, 10 A.M.–5 P.M. Free. Parking, $4.

GENERAL PHINEAS BANNING RESIDENCE MUSEUM, 401 East M Street, Wilmington. (Exit Harbor Freeway [110] at Pacific Coast Highway [1]; east one mile to Avalon Boulevard; right to M Street; left to museum.) (213) 548-7777. Docent-led tours on Tuesday, Wednesday, Thursday, Saturday, and Sunday at 12:30, 1:30, 2:30 and 3:30 P.M. Donations: adults, $2; children under 12, free. Park open daily, 6 A.M.–10 P.M.

LOS ANGELES MARITIME MUSEUM, Berth 84, San Pedro. (Exit Harbor Freeway [110] to Terminal Island Freeway [47]; exit at Harbor Boulevard; south to 6th Street; left to museum.) (213) 548-7618. Open Tuesday–Sunday, 10 A.M.–5 P.M. Free.

OSGOOD FARLEY MILITARY MUSEUM, Angels Gate Park, 3601 South Gaffey Street, San Pedro. (Follow Harbor Freeway [110] south to the end where it joins with Gaffey Street; south to entrance between 32nd Street and Paseo del Mar.) (213) 548-7705. Open Saturday and Sunday, noon–5 P.M. Free.

POINT FERMIN PARK, 805 Paseo del Mar, San Pedro. (Follow Harbor Freeway [110] south to the end where it joins Gaffey Street; south to end.) Open daily, 5:30 A.M.–10:30 P.M. Free.

POINT VICENTE INTERPRETIVE CENTER, 31501 Palos Verdes Drive West, Rancho Palos Verdes. (Follow Harbor Freeway [110] to end where it joins Gaffey Street; south to 25th Street, which becomes Palos Verdes Drive South; right to center.) (213) 377-5370. Open daily. Winter hours: 10 A.M.–5 P.M. Summer hours: 10 A.M.–7 P.M. Adults, $1; ages 4–14 and seniors, 50 cents.

PORTS O' CALL VILLAGE, San Pedro. (Follow Harbor Freeway [110] to Terminal Island Freeway [47]; exit at Harbor Boulevard; south to 6th Street; left into the parking lot.) (213) 831-0287. Open daily. Admission and parking: free.

WHALE-WATCH CRUISES

(End of December to beginning of April only. Most three-hour cruises cost about $12 for adults and $9 for children.)

• *Belmont Pier Whale-Watch Cruises,* end of Belmont Pier. Box 14686, Long Beach, CA 90814. (213) 434-6781. Three-hour cruises Monday–Friday, 10 A.M.; Saturday and Sunday, 9 A.M.–1 P.M.
• *Catalina Cruises,* 330 Golden Shore Boulevard, Long Beach. (213) 755-6111, (213) 514-3838, or (714) 527-7111. Three-hour cruises on weekdays, 10 A.M.; weekends and holidays, 11:30 A.M. and 3:30 P.M.
• *Long Beach Sportfishing,* Berth 55 off Pico Avenue, in the Port of Long Beach. (213) 432-8993. Cruises daily, 10 A.M. and 1 P.M.
• *Los Angeles Harbor Sportfishing,* Berth 79, Ports o' Call Village, San Pedro. (213) 547-9916. Cruises depart daily, weekdays at 10 A.M. and 1 P.M.; weekends, 9 A.M., 11:30 A.M., 2 P.M.
• *Pilgrim Sailing Cruises,* Berth 76, Ports o' Call Village, San Pedro. (213) 547-0941. Two-masted sailing ship departs Saturday and Sunday, 10:30 A.M. and 1 P.M.
• *Skippers 22nd Street Landing,* 141 West 22nd Street, San Pedro. (213) 832-8304. Cruises depart on weekdays, 10 A.M. and 1 P.M.; and weekends, 9 A.M., 11:30 A.M., and 2 P.M.
• *Spirit Adventures,* Berth 75, Ports o' Call Village, San Pedro. (213) 831-1073. Cruises aboard powerboat *The Adventure:* weekdays, 11 A.M.; weekends, 10 A.M. and 12:30 P.M. Aboard the two-masted sailing boat *The Spirit:* weekends, 9 A.M., noon, and 2:45 P.M. Guaranteed to see a whale or you get another cruise for free.

CATALINA ISLAND
An Offshore Playground

Just 22 miles off the Southern California coast, Santa Catalina Island "is awaitin' " for your kids with sand, surf, and miles of unspoiled parkland to explore. The old song touts the romance of this Mediterranean-like island, but today's visitors, especially the young ones, are looking for the active pursuits available there: swimming, snorkeling, hiking, biking, and horseback riding, just for starters.

While these pleasures are also available on the mainland, the 76-square-mile island offers them in an isolated, unspoiled environment. California's only offshore resort is a quiet, old-fashioned microcosm of what the crowded mainland used to be. It's easily accessible by boat or plane for a day trip. And if you want to stay awhile, there are more than forty hotels or vacation rental units, plus several campgrounds, on the island.

Most activity on the 21-mile-long island centers around its only town, Avalon. Set in a picturesque crescent-shaped cove, Avalon is an ideal place for families because it is small and safe to explore on foot. There are few cars on the island and none are allowed on the city's bay-shore street, Crescent Avenue (called Front Street by the locals). You can stroll from Cabrillo Mole, where cross-channel boats dock, to the circular, colonnaded Casino at the other side of the bay without encountering a single stoplight or hurried motorist.

There's a surprising variety of activities for children to enjoy within Avalon's square-mile boundary. Number one on the list during summer is Catalina's clear ocean water. If you have small children, head for Crescent Beach, which runs along the bay in front of the town. Gently lapping waves at this roped-off harbor beach are perfect for the little ones. On busy weekends you'll want to stake out a place for your towels on this small strip of sand early in the day. You can rent lockers, beach chairs, and inflatable rafts on the green Pleasure Pier adjacent to the beach.

If the kids are good swimmers and want to snorkel, walk over to the marine preserve at Lovers Cove along Pebbly Beach Road at the south end of town. There, kelp beds and rocks near shore provide a safe harbor for sea life. You'll see a variety of colorful marine creatures, including California's state fish, the bright orange garibaldi. Several tour companies with offices on the green Pleasure Pier or in town rent snorkel equipment, offer classes or guided snorkeling trips, and even rent underwater cameras. The same companies offer scuba instruction and dive trips to adults and children 12 and older.

To see the underwater scene without getting wet, take a glass-bottom boat cruise. Through windows in the flat-bottom boat, you will see waving forests of kelp and schools of fish up close. At night, there's a flying-fish boat tour that uses brilliant searchlights to attract the fish. You'll watch the fish use winglike fins to fly across the water, sometimes right into your boat.

You can rent boats too, on Pleasure Pier or on the Cabrillo Mole boat transportation dock. Available between May and October are pedalboats, rowboats, motor boats, and paddleboards. Kids who are good swimmers can rent windsurfing equipment and take lessons on how to use it. If the kids want to fish, they can rent poles and fish on the pier for free. There are also sportfishing charter boats for more serious anglers.

On land there's plenty for kids to explore, too. Walk over to Catalina's famous landmark, the Casino. Built in 1929, it was well known during the big-band era of the 1930s for its huge ballroom. The Casino, which ironically was never the scene of any gambling, has two attractions for today's kids. One is a small museum in the basement that features artifacts made by Indians who lived on the island for several thousand years before the Europeans discovered it in 1542. Be sure to notice the finely carved effigies of whales and other sea creatures the Indians carved from soapstone (steatite) quarried on the island. A topographical map of Catalina gives kids a good idea of its rugged terrain.

Upstairs is a movie theater that shows first-run features. Colorful murals depicting fanciful scenes of ocean life decorate the walls of this classic theater. If you're spending the night in Avalon, you can walk over to see a movie with the kids, or if they are old enough, send them to a film while you enjoy a leisurely dinner nearby. Kids love the independence of exploring this safe little town on their own.

If your children are between the ages of 5 and 12, and you're visiting the island in the summer, stop by the **Marine Interpretive Center** under blue canopies on Crescent Avenue at Metropole Street. The Catalina Island Marine Institute (CIMI) runs a free program there for kids during the summer. Staffed by CIMI biologists and high school students from Southern California who are interested in marine science, the center displays local sea creatures in touch tanks and 30-gallon aquariums. Kids who attend three days of demonstrations and lessons at the center earn a Junior Marine Biologist card. The institute also runs one-week and three-week programs at its Catalina Sea Camp on Toyon Bay for students ages 8 to 17.

Avalon is a stroller's town, with no dearth of specialty shops and casual restaurants. For the kids, there are game arcades, ice-cream shops, and stores that sell an island specialty, saltwater taffy. When young children need a break from shopping, walk to the community park at the south end of Crescent Avenue, which has play equipment and barbecue pits.

As an alternate mode of transportation, rent bikes on Crescent Avenue. Ride on flat roads around the harbor (except on Crescent Avenue in the middle of town, which becomes a pedestrians-only street). If the kids are older and you're in good shape, tackle the roads on the steep hills around town. Bike-rental shops also rent strollers and wheelchairs. Licensed drivers 21 or older can rent gas- or electric-powered golf carts to take the kids for an open-air spin around town.

There's horseback riding, too, in the canyons and hills behind town. At **Catalina Stables** on Avalon Canyon Road, children must be at least 8 years old to take a 1½-hour guided trail ride through five miles of canyon and hillside terrain. Out on the trail you'll see plenty of cactus and low chaparral, and if you're lucky you might spot an island fox or a wild goat.

Near the stables, the **Catalina Island Golf Club** has a pleasant nine-hole golf course open to the public. It's a good place to introduce your kids to the game because the course is not difficult. You can rent golf clubs, balls, and tees at the pro shop. There are two tennis courts at the club with rental equipment available, or you can play tennis on the courts at the high school nearby when it's not in session.

If a full-size golf course is too challenging for the kids, try a shorter game at the **Miniature Golf Gardens.** These old-fashioned links are quite entertaining and, in addition, boast a large family of cats who call the course home. A fat black cat snoozes on the windowsill where you get your clubs, and others lounge in the flowery rough around the holes. Young children may be more fascinated with the cats than the game, and the feline interference gives your game a noncompetitive, casual air.

The best way to see more of the island with kids (older than preschool) is on a bus tour. Make reservations for these tours at the **Island Plaza,** located a few blocks back from the beach on Metropole Avenue, or at the Information Center on Crescent Avenue.

On a tour of the island's interior, you'll travel on dirt roads over unspoiled terrain owned and protected by the Santa Catalina Island Conservancy. You may see some of the five hundred buffalo that roam freely, descendents of the herd of 14 that were brought to the island in 1924 for the filming of a silent movie, *The Vanishing American.* You might also see wild boar, goats, and the reintroduced bald eagle.

Tours vary in length and theme, but you'll be sure to visit Catalina's quaint, red-tile-roofed **Airport-in-the-Sky.** There, the kids will enjoy the Santa Catalina Island Conservancy's new **Nature Center,** which features exhibits on island Indians, rarely seen native animals, and local plants. At the **Runway Café** you may want to try a buffalo burger (made from nonlocal animals). Other stops on the tour include Little Harbor, to see the remains of an ancient Indian village; Middle Ranch, where kids can feed and touch farm animals; and El Rancho Escondido, for an Arabian horse performance.

Hiking in the interior is strenuous and exciting for older kids. You need to get a free hiking permit from the Santa Catalina Island Conservancy offices in Avalon, at the airport, or in Two Harbors near the northwest end of the island. A good plan for day hiking is to take a shuttle bus (not a tour) from Avalon to either the airport or Two Harbors, and use one of those places as a base. Both have food and water. The island's terrain is rugged and steep, but the scenery is worth the trip. Be sure to carry water. Four campgrounds are available for backpackers in the interior of the island, three of them near beaches.

An enjoyable place to spend a day with older kids is Two Harbors. This little community can be reached by hiking trails, shuttle bus, or boat from either Avalon or the mainland. The beach at Two Harbors is actually wider than the one at Avalon and less crowded. There are beach volleyball courts and a park with swings. Stroll the short distance across the isthmus past the Civil War barracks to Catalina Harbor on the other side of the island. Or rent snorkel and scuba equipment or boats and surfboards on the pier. Tourist facilities are limited, but one bed and breakfast inn, a market, and snack stands are near the pier.

Summer is Catalina's busiest season, so be sure to book your channel crossing and make hotel reservations several months in advance. Fall and spring bring excellent weather and fewer crowds. If you go over between January and March, you'll have a bonus on your cruise, a chance to see migrating Pacific gray whales.

Cross-channel boats leave from Long Beach, San Pedro, Newport Beach, and San Diego. What used to be a long crossing is getting shorter, with new boats such as the *Catalina Flier*, which makes the trip from Newport Beach to Avalon is just 75 minutes. Crossing on any of the boats can be rough, so be prepared if you or the kids are prone to seasickness. You can also reach the island by plane, flying boat, or helicopter. Whatever way you travel to the island, remember that for kids, getting there is likely to be half the fun.

Attractions

AIRPORT-IN-THE-SKY, 1 Airport Road, Avalon. (213) 510-0143. Open, 8 A.M.–7 P.M., April 15–October 15; 8 A.M.–5 P.M., October 16– April 14.

• *Nature Center.* (213) 510-1421. Open same hours as airport. Free.
• *Runway Café.* (213) 510-0143. Open, Monday–Friday, 8 A.M.–4 P.M.; Saturday and Sunday, 8 A.M.–4:30 P.M.

AVALON BOATSTAND/JOE'S RENT-A-BOAT on green Pleasure Pier. (213) 510-0455. Open daily, April–October, 7 A.M.–7 P.M. Rent motorboats, rowboats, pedalboats, paddleboards, and fishing tackle.

BROWN'S BIKES, 107 Pebbly Beach Road (at the south end of town near Cabrillo Mole). (213) 510-0986. Daily. 9 A.M.–5 P.M. year round. Rent mountain bikes, tandems, single speeds, five speeds, and strollers. Rates start at $4 per hour.

CATALINA ADVENTURE TOURS, Avalon. (213) 510-2888. Ticket booth on green Pleasure Pier. Tours of Avalon and the interior leave from Cabrillo Mole. Glass Bottom Boat tour leaves from green Pleasure Pier. Call for schedule.

CATALINA ISLAND GOLF CLUB, 1 Country Club Drive (3 blocks from beach). (213) 510-0530. Open to the public daily. Summer hours: 7 A.M.–7 P.M. Winter hours: 8 A.M.–5 P.M. Nine holes, par 32. Greens fees: $8.50. Tennis courts. Rental equipment.

CATALINA ISLAND MUSEUM, in Casino at end of Crescent Avenue. (213) 510-2414. Open April–mid-November: Tuesday, Wednesday, and Saturday, 10:30 A.M.–4 P.M.; other days, noon–4 P.M. and 7–9 P.M. Free.

CATALINA SAFARI BUS, Two Harbors. (213) 510-0303 or (213) 510-2800. Shuttle bus between Avalon and Two Harbors makes three stops in between these destinations. Bus leaves from Island Tour Plaza in Avalon and near pier in Two Harbors. Summer hours: daily 7 A.M.–midnight. Winter hours vary. One-way trip: adults, $12.50; children, $9.25.

CATALINA SAFARI TOURS, Two Harbors. (213) 510-0303. Naturalist-led tours from Two Harbors include nature walks, interior bus tours, and snorkeling trips. Open daily.

CATALINA STABLES, Avalon Canyon Road (three blocks from beach). (213) 510-0478. Summer hours: daily, 8 A.M.–4 P.M. Winter hours: Friday–Wednesday, 9 A.M.–3:30 P.M. Trail rides (1½ hours): $18 per person. Minimum age: 8. Rent horses at office; no phone reservations taken.

HIKING PERMITS issued free by the Santa Catalina Island Conservancy at: **Los Angeles County Department of Parks and Recreation**, Island Plaza, Avalon, (213) 510-0688; **Airport-in-the-Sky**, (213) 510-0143; **Catalina Cove and Camp Agency**, at the end of the pier, Two Harbors, (213) 510-0303.

MARINE INTERPRETIVE CENTER, Crescent Avenue at Metropole Street, Avalon. (213) 510-1622. Open daily, mid-June–Labor Day, 10 A.M.–3:30 P.M. Free.

MINIATURE GOLF GARDENS, Sumner Avenue, Avalon (one block west of beach in the Island Plaza). (213) 510-1200. Open daily, April–October, 9 A.M.–11 P.M. Winter hours: weekends, holidays only, 10 A.M.–sundown. Adults, $5; children under 48 inches tall, $3.

SANTA CATALINA ISLAND COMPANY, Avalon. (213) 510-2000. Tours include: Avalon Scenic Tour, Inland Motor Tour, Glass Bottom Boat Tour, and Flying Fish Boat Tour. Motor tours leave from Island Tour Plaza. Boat tours leave from green Pleasure Pier.

BOAT SERVICE TO CATALINA ISLAND

From Long Beach:

• *Catalina Cruises*, Catalina Landing, 330 Golden Shore Boulevard, Long Beach. (213) 514-3838. Daily service to Avalon year round; to Two Harbors, March–October.

From San Pedro:

• *Catalina Cruises*, Catalina Passenger Terminal, Berths 95 and 96 at end of Harbor Boulevard, San Pedro. (213) 514-3838. Daily service to Avalon (weekends only, October–April); to Two Harbors, March–October.
• *Catalina Express*, Catalina Passenger Terminal, Berth 95, San Pedro. (213) 519-1212. Daily service to Avalon and Two Harbors year round.

From Balboa Pavilion, Newport Beach:

• *Catalina Flyer*, Catalina Passenger Service, 400 Main Street, Balboa. (714) 673-5245. Daily service to Avalon. Large catamaran makes crossing in 75 minutes.

From San Diego:

• *California Cruisin'*, B Street Terminal in San Diego Harbor. (619) 235-8600. Daily service to Avalon between May and November.

AIR SERVICE TO CATALINA ISLAND

• *Allied Air Charter,* Avalon. (213) 510-1163. Daily flights to Catalina Airport from Southern California airports in six-seater planes.

• *Catalina Vegas Airlines,* 3760 Glenn Curtiss Road, San Diego. (619) 292-7311. Daily flights on four ten-seater planes to Catalina Airport from Montgomery Field in San Diego.

• *Helitrans,* 3501 Lakewood Boulevard, Long Beach. (213) 548-1314. Daily helicopter service to Avalon from Catalina Passenger Terminal, Berth 95, San Pedro.

• *Island Express,* 900 Queensway Drive, Long Beach. (213) 510-1163. Daily helicopter service to Avalon from near the *Queen Mary* in Long Beach or Catalina Passenger Terminal, Berth 95, San Pedro.

For More Information

Catalina Island Visitor's Information Center, Box 737, Avalon, CA 90704; (800) 4-AVALON or (213) 510-2000. Office open daily on Pleasure Pier.

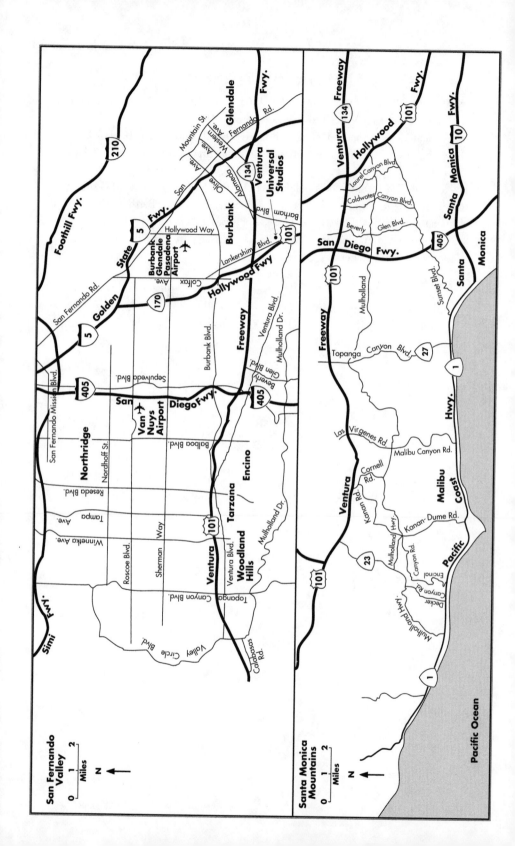

5

San Fernando Valley and the Santa Monica Mountains

You can find just about everything in San Fernando Valley. From antique cars to studio tours to pony rides, the valley has it all. This onetime bedroom community, 20 miles northwest of downtown Los Angeles, is a sprawling resource of family activities.

San Fernando Valley presents two distinct faces, east and west. The east valley has more attractions, museums, and historic sites, while the west valley sports a rural image with its parks, pony rides, and agriculture. The wide variety of these activities makes it impractical to suggest specific itineraries for the valley. Instead, you'll want to pick from among these attractions to put together a day exploring your own family's interests.

To the south, the Santa Monica Mountains separate the valley from

L.A.'s westside communities and beaches. Although both the westside and valley share the Santa Monicas, these mountain parklands are included in this chapter because most of them are easily reached from the valley.

While housing tracts have encroached upon many of the Santa Monicas' foothills and reach well into the canyon passes, much of the mountains' natural beauty is being protected through a growing network of parks that make up the Santa Monica Mountains National Recreation Area. Programs in these mountain parks introduce toddlers to the out-of-doors, youngsters to Indian ways, and everyone to the serenity of nature. Best of all, this wilderness resource is only minutes away from Southern California's largest population center.

EAST SAN FERNANDO VALLEY
Movie Lots and Lots of Fun

Two of the east valley's most popular attractions revolve around the entertainment industry, which long ago moved into the area from Hollywood. **Universal Studios** in Universal City (right next door to Hollywood) is the best place for kids to learn what goes on behind the scenes in movie making. More like a movie theme park than a working studio, the Universal tour experience is far more entertaining than the real thing. Plan to spend most of a day at this 420-acre site, touring its huge backlot, watching live-action shows, and shopping for movie memorabilia. Universal is one of the world's largest and busiest movie and TV studios, but it is rare to see actual filming taking place during your visit. What you will see on a narrated tour through backlot streets are outdoor movie and TV sets, a sound-stage demonstration of special effects, and encounters with King Kong and the shark from *Jaws*. You'll also have a chance to experience a major earthquake.

After the tour, visit the 4½-acre Entertainment Center, with its selection of restaurants, snack stands, and souvenir shops. Don't be surprised to see some look-alikes of famous stars wandering about, and don't be shy about getting your picture taken with them. Live-action shows feature cowboy stuntmen, performing animals, and fast-paced productions that amaze audiences even as they reveal the technology behind the trickery. For youngsters raised on TV fare, the true novelty is seeing the action live. Stage-struck kids even get a chance to get into the act in some of these productions.

A few tips on visiting Universal. It is most crowded in the summer, especially on weekends, so plan to arrive early to be able to take it all in without having to rush. Summer days can get quite hot, and you are likely to be in the sun more than you realize. Hats are helpful and sunscreen lotion is a must, especially for youngsters with fair skin.

If a visit to Universal Studios whets your appetite for the movies, you need step only a few hundred paces east of the studios' entrance to satisfy your hunger. The Cineplex Odeon complex of movie theaters has 18 screens that should provide ample variety for any family's film tastes. If your hunger pangs have more to do with food, the area near the studios' entrance features several fine restaurants. They don't necessarily cater to children, however, and they are not inexpensive.

Another popular studio tour, though not as extensive as Universal's, can be found a few miles east in the city of Burbank. **NBC Studios Tours** takes you through the network's large complex of television studios and offers some behind-the-scenes glimpses of its own. The tour starts with a brief video history of the NBC network, then kids get a chance to see themselves on TV during a demonstration of video special effects in a simulated control room. Most of the 75-minute tour walks you through several sound stages. Tours vary depending on studio use and other activity. Most groups are able to visit a newscast set and the studio set for *The Tonight Show Starring Johnny Carson*. You're also likely to glimpse some of the wardrobe area, watch a video presentation on makeup, and see the props studio. But you won't see any shows actually being shot. For youngsters, the real tour highlights come at the end, when your guide creates a radio quiz show out of sound effects and gives a few members of the tour group a chance to be weather reporters with the aid of video special effects. Your tour ends by the Peacock Garden Café. A small shop nearby sells NBC mementos.

By the way, to see a show, you will need to get tickets in the office where you bought your tour tickets. Be sure to check the minimum age limit for the show you want to see. It can vary depending on the type of show.

A third well-known movie facility in the area offers tours to the public, but **Burbank Studios** is decidedly uncommercial in its approach. The two-hour tour of this movie-making complex, once headquarters for Warner Bros. and Columbia Pictures, is more a technical and educational experience than an entertaining one. Children need to be at least 10 years old to go on the tour. The guided walking tour includes the backlot, sound stages, arts and crafts shops, and other departments, depending on the day's activities.

Not far from the studios, on Olive Street in downtown Burbank, the **Burbank Historical Society/Gordon R. Howard Museum** fills a small complex of buildings with mementos of the city's past and other historical treasures. Enter the museum through a restored 1887 Eastlake Victorian home that faces Olive. Be sure to see the child's room with its small-scale furniture and dolls.

Walk through the home to get to the rest of the museum's buildings. One holds a small selection of antique cars, dating back to a 1904 Franklin and a 1949 fire engine that is a hit with most kids. Other favorite collections include an aviation exhibit of large-scale model planes and displays from NBC and the Walt Disney Studios, the latter also located in Burbank. Children especially enjoy the museum's vignettes of earlier days that come alive with music, sound effects, and recorded conversations. Youngsters listen on old black telephones to the two-minute slices of history that take place in such spots as a doctor's office and a country store. Because of its small staff the museum can open only a few hours on Sunday afternoons, but the historical society will put together tours at other times for groups of ten or more.

Just east of Burbank in the city of Glendale, **Brand Park** offers acres of open space for recreation and picnics. You'll find a children's play area on the east side of the park. A large mansion, inspired by East Indian architecture, dominates the park from its place of honor atop a small hill. The mansion was built in 1904 by Leslie C. Brand and today contains the Brand Library, whose collection is devoted to art and music. A new gallery wing exhibits local artists. The ornate interior of the library and the gallery exhibits are likely to appeal more to adults than children, but just behind the library there is a small picnic area with barbecues and plenty of grass to play on.

Just a short ride up Golden State Freeway (5) north of Burbank takes you into the valley's distant past. **Mission San Fernando,** on San Fernando Mission Road in Mission Hills, was founded in 1797. Rebuilt after a damaging quake in 1971, the mission is open daily for self-guided tours. After entering through the gift shop, kids see restored living quarters and workshops, as well as the church. A small museum displays artifacts from mission days. The old mission's gardens are across the street and are now part of a public park (a different Brand Park) that features plants from each of the other 20 California missions and, ironically, a statue of Father Junipero Serra. Mission San Fernando was founded by Father Fermin Lausen 13 years after Father Serra's death.

From the park, walk or drive about a half mile south of the mission, where Brand Boulevard runs into Sepulveda Boulevard, to find **Andres Pico Adobe.** This fine old two-story house was built by the mission Indians in 1834 and was bought in 1853 by General Andres Pico, the brother of California's last

Mexican governor, Pio Pico. The house has been restored with nineteenth-century furnishings but not with the usual Do Not Touch signs. Youngsters are welcome, even encouraged, to sit on chairs, grind corn with old Indian implements, and even to try out the 1880s piano. Families are welcome to picnic anywhere on the lawn, but bring a blanket because there are no tables.

A few miles farther north, in the city of Sylmar, is one of the valley's most unusual museums, the **Merle Norman Classic Beauty Collection at San Sylmar.** Lovers of antique automobiles come here to view one of the most extensive and thoroughly restored collections of classic cars to be found anywhere in the world. Only about 30 of the museum's total collection of 100 antique cars are on display at any one time in a neoclassic, marble floor galleria. Led by a docent, you will work your way through the museum up to the third-floor collection of fully restored mechanical musical instruments. The antique equipment ranges from player pianos to complete mechanical orchestras. You will leave this exhibit with your ears ringing from the awe-inspiring sounds of "The Mighty Wurlitzer" theater organ. A few tips for visiting the Merle Norman Museum: children must be at least 13 years old to tour the galleries, and you must make tour reservations months in advance. The experience is well worth the wait.

A few miles from the museum, in the mountains to the east, the **Wildlife Waystation** is a popular stop for youngsters who love animals. The facility, in Little Tujunga Canyon, cares for injured and abandoned animals. You can tour the center on the first and third Sundays of the month at 4 P.M.

Attractions

ANDRES PICO ADOBE, 10940 Sepulveda Boulevard, Mission Hills. (Exit San Diego Freeway [405] at San Fernando Mission Boulevard; east to Sepulveda Boulevard; right to adobe.) (818) 365-7810. Open Wednesday–Sunday, 1 P.M.–4 P.M. Free.

BRAND PARK, 1601 West Mountain Street, Glendale. (Exit Golden State Freeway [5] at Western Avenue; north to Mountain Street; right to park. Exit Ventura Freeway [134] at Riverside Drive; north to Western Avenue; right to Mountain Street; right to park.) (818) 243-8177. Open daily, 8 A.M.–10 P.M. Free.

BURBANK HISTORICAL SOCIETY/GORDON R. HOWARD MU-SEUM, 1015 West Olive Avenue, Burbank. (Exit Ventura Freeway [134] westbound at Alameda Avenue; east to Olive Avenue: left to museum. Exit

Ventura Freeway [134] eastbound at Pass Avenue; south to Alameda Avenue; left to Olive Avenue; left to museum.) (818) 841-6333. Open Sunday, 1 P.M.–4 P.M. Free, but donations appreciated.

BURBANK STUDIOS, 4000 Warner Boulevard, Burbank. (Exit Hollywood Freeway [101] at Barham Boulevard; north and continue after road becomes Olive Avenue to intersection with Warner Boulevard and studios. Exit Ventura Freeway [134] eastbound at Pass Avenue; south to Warner Boulevard; left to studios. Exit Ventura Freeway [134] westbound at Alameda Avenue; left to Pass Avenue; left to Warner Boulevard; left to studios.) (818) 954-1008. Must call to make reservation. Tours Monday–Friday, 10 A.M. and 2 P.M. All ages, $20 (must be 10 years old or older). For live audience information, call (818) 506-0067.

MERLE NORMAN CLASSIC BEAUTY COLLECTION AT SAN SYLMAR, 15180 Bledsoe Street, Sylmar. (Exit Golden State Freeway [5] at Roxford Street; north to San Fernando Road; right to Bledsoe Street; left to museum.) (213) 641-3000. Must call to make reservation. Open Tuesday–Saturday, tours at 10 A.M. and 1:30 P.M. Free. Children must be 13 or older to tour museum.

MISSION SAN FERNANDO, 15151 San Fernando Mission Boulevard, Mission Hills. (Exit San Diego Freeway [405] at San Fernando Mission Road; east to mission. Exit Golden State Freeway [5] at San Fernando Mission Road; west to mission.) (818) 361-0186. Open Monday–Saturday, 9 A.M.–5 P.M.; Sunday, 10 A.M.–5 P.M. Adults, $1; ages 7–15, 50 cents.

NBC STUDIOS TOUR, 3000 West Alameda Boulevard, Burbank. (Exit Ventura Freeway [134] westbound at Buena Vista Street; north to Alameda Avenue; left to studios. Exit Ventura Freeway [134] eastbound at Pass Avenue; south to Alameda Avenue; left to studios.) (818) 840-3537. Open Monday–Friday, 8:30 A.M.–4 P.M.; Saturday, 10 A.M.–4 P.M.; Sunday, 10 A.M.–2 P.M. Adults, $6.50; ages 5–14, $4.50; under 5, free with adult. For tickets to shows, call (818) 840-3539 or (818) 840-3538. Each show has its own age limit.

UNIVERSAL STUDIOS, 3900 Lankershim Boulevard, Universal City. (Exit Hollywood Freeway [101] at Universal Center Drive; north to studios.) (818) 508-9600. Open daily, 9:30 A.M.–9 P.M. Adults, $21; ages 3–11 and seniors, $15.50; under 3, free.

WILDLIFE WAYSTATION, 14831 Little Tujunga Road, Lake View Terrace. (Exit Foothill Freeway [210] at Osborne Street; northeast and continue as road becomes Little Tujunga Road to facility.) (818) 899-5201. Open, first and third Sunday of each month. 4 P.M. Free.

For More Information

Greater Los Angeles Visitors and Convention Bureau, 515 South Figueroa Street, 11th Floor, Los Angeles, CA 90071; (213) 689-8822.

Greater Burbank Visitor and Convention Bureau, 425-A South Victory Boulevard, Burbank, CA 91502; (818) 845-4266.

WEST SAN FERNANDO VALLEY
Down on the Farm; Up on the Stage

Like a mighty concrete river, San Diego Freeway (405) divides San Fernando Valley into eastern and western halves. West of the freeway, the valley's attractions become more recreational and rural than those of its eastern half. As a result, a typical west-valley itinerary combines hiking or biking with a visit to a historic site, the airport, or a local live theater performance for kids.

West valley parks are numerous and offer a variety of experiences for youngsters. The largest by far is the 2,000-acre **Sepulveda Dam Recreation Area.** Adjacent is the 80-acre **Balboa Park.** Together, the two facilities offer a laundry list of activities for families. The two parks are located not far from the junction of the San Diego (405) and Ventura (101) freeways at the intersection of Balboa and Burbank boulevards. In the smaller Balboa Park you will find athletic fields, tennis and basketball courts, a children's sandy play area, skate and bike paths, and a picnic area (though there are no facilities for cooking). A paved seven-mile bike path that is separated from automobile traffic circles the entire recreation area and its two 18-hole golf courses. At the model-airplane field off Woodley Avenue on the eastern side of the park, the kids will enjoy watching hobbyists prepare and fly their miniature planes.

To see the real thing, head north up Woodley about a mile to **Van Nuys Airport.** More than nine hundred aircraft are based at Van Nuys, making it the busiest noncommercial airport in the world. Kids who love planes will enjoy the 90-minute guided tour of the sprawling airport, but they must be at least 6 years old, and you will need to make reservations several weeks in advance. The free tours are scheduled at 9:30 and 11:30 weekday mornings and one Saturday a month, based on demand.

On the tour, kids will go inside an Air National Guard hangar and climb aboard a huge, green C-130 military transport plane. The tour continues along the airport's flight line, giving youngsters a close-up look at sleek corporate jets, single-engine private planes, and large cargo jetliners. Several companies based at Van Nuys do aircraft maintenance and custom remodeling, giving kids a chance to see how an airplane is put together. On Wednesday, the tour includes a stop at the Crash Unit and Airport Fire Department for a look at special firefighting equipment and techniques.

The tour isn't the only way to see airplanes. For a ringside view of the arrival and departure of all kinds of aircraft, try the airport's public observation site on Waterman Drive off Woodley Avenue between Saticoy Street and Roscoe Boulevard. The parklike area, with picnic tables and palm trees, is fenced off near the main runway. Parking is limited but the area is open from 8 A.M. to 8 P.M.

Long before the Wright Brothers, San Fernando Valley was a peaceful place of large ranchos and small farms, and you can still find evidence of both here. At **Los Encinos State Historic Park** you'll catch the faint echoes of early California. The 5-acre park, located just off Ventura Boulevard near Balboa Boulevard, is all that's left of a Gabrielino Indian village and the 4,500-acre de la Ossa cattle ranch. This calm oasis of historic buildings, tall trees, and a small reservoir fed by an underground spring is ideal for picnics. The reservoir is a popular stop for migratory birds and its resident ducks always enjoy a handout.

The nine-room adobe ranch house, built in 1849, has been restored and filled with furnishings of the period. The Garnier Building, a two-story limestone structure nearby, was built in 1874 but is not open to the public. Artifacts from the rancho era are displayed in the visitors center, while other exhibits at the park include a blacksmith shop and a kitchen garden. To complete the picture, park docents dressed in period costumes re-create an 1870s picnic on Living History days. Call the park for a schedule.

Another popular park in the west valley is **Orcutt Ranch Horticultural Center,** just south of Chatsworth in Canoga Park. The estate, now a historical monument, is two parks in one. It was once the vacation home of William Orcutt, a geologist who was among the first to excavate the La Brea Tar Pits (see Beverly Hills/Mid-Wilshire District section in chapter 2). You can visit the ranch house on a docent-led history tour the last Sunday of every month from 2 P.M. to 5 P.M. The house remains furnished much as it was when built in the 1920s. Kids will enjoy poking around the display of antique farm machinery near the parking lot. The grounds include a rose garden, herb garden, and fern grotto.

The ranch also serves as a horticultural center. Much of the 24-acre park is covered with fruit orchards, and once a year in late spring or early summer they are opened to families for picking. You'll need to bring your own grocery bags and ladder, but you can rent a long-handled fruit picker to go after ripe oranges and grapefruit at the top of the trees. Pick as much fruit as you want; the park charges only $1 per grocery bag. You can picnic in several locations on the grounds, but one of the nicest spots is a small grove of trees on the south side of a stream that runs through the park.

For a more complete agricultural experience take the kids to **Los Angeles Pierce College** in Woodland Hills. The college maintains a working farm as part of its agricultural sciences studies and children are welcome to tour the facility with a guide or with their own families. (You'll need to make reservations for the guided tour.) At any given time the kids are liable to see students plowing, planting, or harvesting the crops, or tending to the livestock that includes cattle, dairy cows, sheep, goats, chickens, and pigs. After the tour, you can buy some of the fruits of all this labor at a small market on the northwest corner of the campus.

A few miles west of Pierce College in the community of Calabasas, the **Leonis Adobe** has been restored to its former 1880 glory days. Be sure to notice the windmill bringing water up from a well on one side of the house and on the other, a corral with longhorn cattle. Young children will like visiting the chickens and ducks in pens out back. Older kids may be more interested in the contents of the barn, which include old farm equipment such as wagons and a buggy, and a blacksmith shop.

In an odd twist of fate, the adobe's visitors center is in the Plummer House, an 1870s structure that was moved to its present location from West Hollywood in 1983 to save it from destruction. A century ago, the Leonis and Plummer families were acquainted and visited each other on journeys that would take several hours. The center contains a small museum of photographs, mementos, and clothing.

If all this history gets the kids wondering about what it was like to sit tall in the saddle, take them to **Rent-a-Pony** in the mid-valley community of Reseda near the intersection of Tampa Avenue and Roscoe Boulevard. Kids as young as six months old can circle the corral on docile ponies. The inside track is reserved for youngsters who want to have their parents walk alongside, while the faster ponies take the outside track. Youngsters have to weight less than 100 pounds to be allowed to ride. Children also play on old tractors or feed a menagerie of farmyard animals. Cups of feed cost 50 cents.

Chickens, ducks, geese, goats, peacocks, and turkeys roam the yard in search of a handout and try to avoid being cuddled by enthusiastic toddlers. Rent-a-Pony does not sell food for humans, but does have tables for families who want to bring a picnic.

In contrast to its many rural attractions, the west valley is home to several theater groups whose productions either are aimed at kids or involve kids or do both. **California State University at Northridge** and **Los Angeles Pierce College** both have theater arts programs that usually manage one or more productions a year for children, often around the holidays.

At **The Enchanted Forest** in Woodland Hills, kids can enroll in a variety of classes that allow them to explore the arts in various forms. With classes like Dinosaurs and Spacemen, Spaceships and Outer Space, kids tap their imaginations to work on different creative projects. Classes cover puppetry, magic, clowning, dramatics, dance, and music. Every Saturday and Sunday, marionettes perform at 11:30 A.M. and 1 P.M., while Sunday evening at 6 and 7:30 children appear in productions for kids. Most of the performers and members of the audience are 10 years old or younger. One of the Enchanted Forest's unique features is its toy shop, which sells toys from around the world that stimulate creative play for youngsters, and all without batteries.

Stimulating young imaginations also is on the bill of fare at **Pages Books for Children and Young Adults.** At this bookstore on Ventura Boulevard in Tarzana, you'll find titles for readers from preschool to high school and even a section on parenting. The store sells audio tapes, puppets, and stuffed animals, too. At 11 A.M. Saturday story hours, aimed at 3- to 8-year olds, youngsters hear a story, then handcraft an object related to the book. The store also holds frequent free programs for children that feature authors, entertainers, or concerts. Call the bookstore for a newsletter calendar of events.

About 15 miles west of the San Fernando Valley, in the community of Thousand Oaks, **California Lutheran University** draws children from far and wide for its day-long workshops in science and art, held on selected Saturdays during the school year. Kids might learn about electricity or animation in a variety of classes. The workshops are very popular and fill up quickly.

Attractions

BALBOA PARK, 17015 Burbank Boulevard, Encino. (Exit Ventura Freeway [101] at Balboa Boulevard; north to Burbank Boulevard; left to park.) (818) 343-4143. Open daily. Free.

CALIFORNIA LUTHERAN UNIVERSITY, 60 West Olsen Road, Thousand Oaks. (Exit Ventura Freeway [101] at Lynn Road; north to Olsen Road; right to university.) (805) 493-3130. Call university for workshop schedules and registration form.

CALIFORNIA STATE UNIVERSITY AT NORTHRIDGE THE-ATER, 18111 Nordhoff Street, Northridge. (Exit Ventura Freeway [101] at Reseda Boulevard; north to Nordhoff Street; right to campus. Exit San Diego Freeway [405] at Nordhoff Street; west to campus.) Speech Drama Ticket Office, (818) 885-3093. Call box office for productions and ticket prices.

THE ENCHANTED FOREST, 20929 Ventura Boulevard, Woodland Hills. (Exit Ventura Freeway [101] at De Soto Avenue; south to Ventura Boulevard; right to theater.) (818) 716-7202. Toy shop open daily, 10 A.M.–5 P.M. Marionette Theater, Saturday and Sunday, call for schedule. Children's performances, Sunday, 6 and 7:30 P.M. All tickets for Marionette Theater: $5. Evening performances: adults, $7.50; 12 and under, $6.50.

LEONIS ADOBE, 23537 Calabasas Road, Calabasas. (Exit Ventura Free-way [101] at Calabasas Parkway; south to Calabasas Road; left to adobe.) (818) 712-0734. Open Wednesday–Sunday, 1 P.M.–4 P.M. Group tours may be arranged at other times. Free, but donations accepted.

LOS ANGELES PIERCE COLLEGE, 6201 Winnetka Avenue, Wood-land Hills. (Exit Ventura Freeway [101] at Winnetka Avenue; north to campus.) (818) 719-6425 for farm tour reservations. Tours Saturday at 10 A.M., noon and 2 P.M. for families and groups. 50 cents per person. (818) 347-0551 for theater productions, schedules, and performance times.

LOS ENCINOS STATE HISTORIC PARK, 16756 Moorpark Street, Encino. (Exit Ventura Freeway [101] at Balboa Boulevard; south to Moor-park Street; left to park.) (818) 784-4849. Open Wednesday–Sunday, 10 A.M.–6 P.M. Docent tours Wednesday–Sunday, 1 P.M.–4 P.M. Free. Tours: $1 per person.

ORCUTT RANCH HORTICULTURAL CENTER, 23600 Roscoe Bou-levard, Canoga Park. (Exit Ventura Freeway [101] at Topanga Canyon Boulevard; north to Roscoe Boulevard; left to park.) (818) 883-6641. Open daily. Docent tours last Sunday of month, 2 P.M.–5 P.M. Free.

PAGES BOOKS FOR CHILDREN AND YOUNG ADULTS, 18399 Ventura Boulevard, Tarzana. (Exit Ventura Freeway [101] at Reseda Boulevard; south to Ventura Boulevard; left to store.) (818) 342-6657. Open Monday–Saturday, 10 A.M.–5 P.M. Story hour, Saturday at 11 A.M. Free.

RENT-A-PONY, 8701 Tampa Avenue, Reseda. (Exit Ventura Freeway [101] at Tampa Avenue; north to pony corral.) (818) 341-2770. Open Saturday and Sunday, 10 A.M.–6 P.M. $2.25 per person; under 1, free.

SEPULVEDA BASIN RECREATION AREA, 17017 Burbank Boulevard, Encino. (Exit Ventura Freeway [101] at Balboa Boulevard; north to Burbank Boulevard, right to park.) (818) 893-3700. Open daily. Free.

VAN NUYS AIRPORT, 16461 Sherman Way, Van Nuys. (Exit San Diego Freeway [405] at Sherman Way; west to airport.) (818) 785-8838 for airport tours. Open daily. Tour hours: Monday–Friday, 9:30 A.M. and 11:30 A.M.; one Saturday a month depending on demand. Call to confirm the date and time. Free.

For More Information:

Greater Los Angeles Visitors and Convention Bureau, 515 South Figueroa Street, 11th Floor, Los Angeles, CA 90071; (213) 689-8822.

SANTA MONICA MOUNTAINS
A Natural Playground in L.A.'s Backyard

The Santa Monica Mountains stretch almost fifty miles from near the heart of Los Angeles all the way to Point Mugu State Park on the Pacific Coast in Malibu. Of this vast area, 150,000 acres are parklands, undeveloped pockets amid encroaching housing tracts and commercial projects. The meadows of wild grasses, chaparral-lined trails, and shady streams offer a quiet, scenic play yard for both kids and adults to enjoy. And best of all, these oases are within a short drive for most of the 11 million people who live in the area.

The Santa Monica Mountains National Recreation Area was formed in 1978 to preserve and manage the use of this land. Today, national, state, and county agencies administer more than twenty parks in the area. While kids would enjoy a visit to any of these mountain parks, those listed in this section have special activities or facilities for children.

Rangers or docents lead easy hikes every day of the week at one or more of these parks. These hikes and interpretive programs have themes that range from geology to edible plants. On a plant-foraging hike, you might learn how the Indians lived in these mountains or, on a starlight walk, how to identify constellations. If you're lucky, you'll see some of the animals that live in the mountains—red-tailed hawks, mule deer, and raccoons.

This section suggests regularly scheduled activities and hikes, along with information on each park. Some schedules change throughout the year and topics change every week. For a quarterly calendar of daily events at each of the parks, write to Santa Monica Mountains National Recreation Area, or call the park Information Center (see listing, page 115). At park headquarters you'll find a selection of books and maps about the national parks for the whole family.

There are two groups that offer programs in the mountains for children 6 years old and younger. **Nursery Nature Walks,** sponsored by the Palisades-Malibu YMCA, is a program that introduces families with infants and preschoolers to the parklands. Docents lead walks with many stops for touching, smelling, and learning about the outdoor environment. These activities are held several times a week at various Santa Monica Mountains parks. Call for a schedule of events and to reserve a place on one of the hikes.

Another nonprofit group that presents programs for children is the William O. Douglas Outdoor Classroom (WODOC). Docents give these programs at either Franklin Canyon Ranch or Malibu Lagoon State Beach. Babes in the Woods and Babes at the Beach introduce children ages 3 months to 3 years to the sights and smells of the outdoors. Tykes on Hikes is for 4- to 6-year-olds. Tales in the Woods features nature stories and Native American legends for children of all ages. Call WODOC for more information and to reserve a space in one of these programs.

Before you visit any of the following parks, keep these tips in mind: Cool days in the winter months are ideal for exploring the inland parks. During summer the parks can be quite hot, so plan to go early or late in the day. Whenever you go, pack some extra water and food before you head out to explore the wilderness with children.

The parks are listed in approximate order from east to west, starting with those closest to downtown Los Angeles.

Franklin Canyon Ranch is a 600-acre natural oasis in the middle of Beverly Hills. Steep trails march up and down the narrow canyon in both the Upper Franklin Reservoir area and the lower ranch section. Take kids to the William O. Douglas Outdoor Classroom's recently built Nature Center near the reservoir. Interactive displays in the center's four main galleries explain the importance of water in the canyon and the park's chaparral, animals, and early Native American residents. Kids touch live and stuffed animals in one area; in another, they try their hand at grinding acorns with Indian tools. WODOC sponsors after-school hikes on Thursday at 4 P.M., as well as programs for disabled children and walks for adults with preschoolers. These programs are free, but reservations are required.

A short Discovery Trail winds around the parking lot in the lower canyon area. Fifth- and sixth-grade students from nearby Warner Avenue Elementary School wrote and illustrated a trail guide that corresponds to numbered posts on this trail. Pick up a copy of the guide at National Park headquarters in the old Doheny ranch house nearby. You'll learn about oak trees, poison oak, and animals that inhabit this area. Children also enjoy the scavenger hunt suggested in the guide.

Across Coldwater Canyon Drive at the upper end of Franklin Canyon you'll find **Coldwater Canyon Park,** headquarters for TreePeople, an organization dedicated to encouraging Southern Californians to care for and improve their environment. The park has a nature trail, an Education Center, gardens, orchards, and a retail nursery. Take the kids first to the Education Center, to the right of the parking lot as you enter, to see exhibits relating to trees. You'll find a fine pine-cone collection and exhibits of animals who rely on trees to live. Kids like to count the rings on a cross section of a redwood tree, and when they open a narrow red door on the wall nearby, they encounter the Tree Monster. Outside, there's a miniature urban forest planted in the Children's Garden.

Next, stop at the information booth in the middle of the bark-covered parking lot and pick up a self-guided nature-trail brochure, then head down the Magic Forest Nature Trail to the left of the lot. On a leisurely paced hike you'll learn about the plants and animals in the forest. Near the end of the trail you'll encounter the Elfin Forest, a kid-size woods of chaparral. On Sunday from 10 A.M. to 4 P.M. docents lead one-hour guided tours of the entire complex. The retail nursery is open Saturday and Sunday from noon to 5 P.M.

West of Beverly Hills in Pacific Palisades, **Will Rogers State Historic Park** is a good place to spend a weekend day with kids. This 186-acre park formerly was the ranch of the famous humorist. Children in elementary school or older enjoy touring the 31-room ranch house and the grounds, even if the don't know anything about Will Rogers and haven't seen any of his sixty movies. Start with a self-guided audio tour of the grounds that begins at the Visitor Center. Through a hand-held wand you'll hear 1920s music and other sound effects as you walk past Rogers's 1928 Buick, his stables, and the practice roping arena. Then tour the comfortable ranch home that is maintained as it was when the Rogers family lived there in the 1920s and 1930s. You'll see Rogers's collection of Indian baskets and rugs. Look for the place where the roof was raised so the "Cowboy Philosopher" could practice roping a mounted calf indoors. At the Visitor Center you'll see a 12-minute film of Rogers's life, followed by *Ropin' Fool,* a film that shows his skill with a lasso.

Bring a picnic to enjoy in the picnic area at the far end of the parking lot or on the broad lawn near the house. At the polo field, where Will used to play with friends Walt Disney and Spencer Tracy, you can still see polo matches on some weekends. With young children, try the one-mile-long nature trail, using the self-guided brochure available at the visitors center to learn about native plants and animals. If the kids are older, take the two-mile loop hike that ascends to Inspiration Point, where you'll have a spectacular view of the ocean. A scenic nine-mile trail leads to Trippet Ranch in Topanga State Park.

Topanga State Park is the world's largest wildland situated within the boundaries of a major city. The 9,000-acre park has 32 miles of hiking trails that stretch from Mulholland Drive overlooking San Fernando Valley almost to the ocean in Pacific Palisades. For kids, the main interest centers on the park's headquarters at Trippet Ranch. At the end of the parking lot there's a picnic area shaded by towering oak trees. You'll see lots of water birds at a small pond nearby. Look for tracks in the mud to identify animals that have made a recent visit. Help yourself to a nature-trail pamphlet from a box near the pond and take a self-guided one-mile walk along a pretty trail up the hill through the woods. You'll learn about native plants and animals and the effects of fire in the area. A small nature center is open on weekends in the lodge you pass along the trail. From the fire road at the highest point of the nature trail, walk through a meadow to an overlook where you'll have a view of the ocean in the distance. Older kids may enjoy hiking from this point about 1½ miles to a waterfall or to Eagle Rock, which looks like its namesake. Rangers and docents lead short, informative hikes in the park on most weekends.

About 5 miles west of Topanga is **Malibu Creek State Park.** This 8,000-acre park has 15 miles of hiking and horseback riding trails through meadows, along streams, and into rugged canyons. Rangers and docents lead short hikes in this area nearly every weekend. However, there's plenty for kids to see within about a mile of the parking lot. From the lot, walk along the level fire road over a low bridge and through a meadow to a picnic area shaded by eucalyptus trees. From here it's a short walk to the visitors center,

housed in a gracious white ranch home near the bridge. The newly renovated center, open on weekends from noon to 4 P.M., offers hands-on exhibits such as stuffed and mounted animals for kids to touch and manos and
metates (Native American grinding implements) that children can use to
grind acorns. At the small gift shop you can buy maps, books, and cold soft
drinks.

From the center, walk over the bridge and bear left on a short path to the
rock pool. This picturesque pond, which has served as a background for
many films and TV productions, is fed by a waterfall. An adjacent stream has
rocky islands that kids love to explore. Older children may enjoy walking
1½ miles to Century Lake, created by the dammed up Malibu Creek which
runs through the park. Bring a fishing pole (and a license for adults) to catch
trout in the well-stocked lake in spring and early summer. A 2½-mile hike
leads to the site where the TV series *M.A.S.H.* was filmed. All that remains
of the set after a brushfire in 1982 is a burned-out jeep and ambulance, but
the scenic buttes in the background are easy to recognize.

You can park for a small fee at the park's main entrance off Las Virgenes
Road or for free at the northwest end of the park on the corner of Cornell
Road and Mulholland Highway. A trail from the latter leads through
the foothills. There are a few shaded picnic tables along the trail, but a
meadow adjacent to the trail's beginning is also a good place to spread out
a tablecloth.

Less than a mile south of Malibu Creek State Park's main entrance you'll
come to a shady gem, **Tapia Natural Area Park.** Situated in a grove of
huge oak trees, this park has dozens of picnic tables and barbecues with
adjacent parking spots. It's a good place to picnic with very young children
because you don't have to walk far from your car to a table. Nearby there
are rocks to climb on, meadows to run in, and a rocky stream to walk
along. Bring a bat and ball to use on the park's diamond if the kids like
sports.

Northwest of Malibu Creek State Park you'll find **Paramount Ranch.**
Owned by Paramount Pictures Corporation from the mid-1920s to the mid-
1940s, the ranch was used as a setting for dozens of motion pictures. TV
westerns such as *The Cisco Kid, Bat Masterson,* and *Have Gun Will Travel*
were filmed here during the heyday of the television cowboy. Take a walk
with the kids down the town's dusty streets and amble along its boardwalks
past the feed store and the Wells Fargo Office. You may recognize these
buildings in a present-day film or TV commercial, because the ranch is still
in demand with production companies. Don't let kids enter the buildings—
they are unsafe.

Rising behind the town is Sugarloaf Peak, a rugged basalt mountain that dominates the park's skyline. At the base of the peak is a large grassy area with picnic tables. At the small bridge nearby, pick up a copy of the Coyote Canyon Nature Trail guide and walk the one-mile loop to learn about plants used by the Indians and how nature copes with fire and drought. After the hike, try the scavenger hunt suggested in the guide. Rangers and docents lead nature walks and present a variety of programs for kids nearly every weekend and on some weekdays.

Nearby on Mulholland Highway is **Peter Strauss Ranch,** a 65-acre spread once owned by the actor. Leave your car in the free parking lot and walk across the creek to the ranch. A 250-seat, tree-shaded outdoor amphitheater is the site of many musical and theatrical productions throughout the year. The Theater Arts Festival for Youth (TAFFY) takes place at the ranch in October each year, with music, storytelling, and art workshops for kids. On the first Sunday of the month between May and September, Sunday concerts in the Park are held at 2 P.M. Many of the featured artists, such as bluegrass groups and international folk dancers, appeal to children as well as adults. If you visit the park on a day when there isn't a scheduled show, your children may want to put on their own performance in the inviting amphitheater. Have a picnic on the tree-shaded lawn nearby and hike along the foothill nature trail through chaparral and oak trees.

Rocky Oaks, near the corner of Kanan Road and Mulholland Highway, is a pleasant park for picnics and easy walks with children. Dotted with oak trees as the name implies, this small park has a wide meadow surrounded by shaded picnic tables. Near the parking lot is a small outdoor amphitheater where kids may enjoy telling stories or putting on skits. At the other end of the meadow, walk along an easy hiking trail to the pond, where you'll see birds and other wildlife.

Charmlee County Natural Area overlooks Pacific Coast Highway in Malibu. Trails through the park afford scenic views of the blue Pacific and Point Dume below. Stop first with kids at the Nature Center near the parking lot to see exhibits on wildlife, geology, and the history of the area. There are picnic tables nearby. Walk along a wide road or narrow Botany Trail, which features native plants, down to a wide meadow. In spring, the meadow erupts in color from thousands of wildflowers. Any time of year, westerly winds off the ocean make the meadow and its wide trails an ideal place to fly a kite. Follow the trail south through the meadow to find the bluff-top Ocean Vista Trail. Rangers lead hikes through the park on most weekends.

Farther west on Pacific Coast Highway is the 15,000-acre **Point Mugu**

State Park. Extending three miles along the ocean and nearly six miles back into the Santa Monica Mountains, the park includes three beaches, a campground, and a giant sand dune (see Westside Beaches section in chapter 2). Inland, the park has more than fifty miles of hiking trails through rugged hillsides and forested valleys. You'll find a more moderate hike along Overlook Trail, which also affords spectacular ocean views. From the parking lot, walk past Big Sycamore Canyon Campground and around a locked gate to head up the fire road along the creek. Half a mile from the campground bear left at the sign for Overlook Trail and continue up the ridge where you'll have bird's-eye views of the ocean and coast below. You can return the way you came or continue on a longer loop. There are picnic tables near the campground. Rangers lead nature walks from the campground every Saturday at 9 A.M.

At the north end of Point Mugu State Park near the town of Thousand Oaks, **Rancho Sierra Vista/Satwiwa** offers a different nature experience. The park has interpretative programs that explain two phases of its history: as a home for the Chumash Indians and as a working horse ranch. To learn about the Chumash, visit the new Cultural Center in the Satwiwa Native American Indian Natural Area on Sunday from 9 A.M.–5 P.M. *Satwiwa* means "the bluffs" in the Chumash language, and indeed, the area is dominated by a huge bluff, 3,000-foot Boney Mountain. To reach the center from the parking lot, walk along the paved road toward Boney Mountain, about a quarter of a mile. Inside the center, you'll see exhibits of Chumash Indian tools and decorative objects, as well as photographs of the Indians' colorful rock paintings. After visiting the center, walk along the 1½-mile loop trail that skirts a pond and a Native American assembly area with a standing frame of a Chumash home. Indians and rangers lead interpretative programs from the center on some weekends, featuring such topics as edible plants and Native American crafts.

Near the parking lot you can learn about the area's more recent history as a horse ranch. The Moorpark College Equine Management and Training Programs puts the horses through their paces every Saturday at 2 P.M. If the kids want to see the horses up close, tour the ranch on a Saturday or Sunday at 2 P.M.

The Parks

CHARMLEE COUNTY NATURAL AREA. (Follow Santa Monica Freeway [10] to its western end; continue north and west on Pacific Coast Highway [1] to Encinal Canyon Road; right four miles to park entrance.) (213) 457-7247. Open daily, 9 A.M.–5 P.M.

COLDWATER CANYON PARK. (Exit Ventura Freeway [101] at Cold-water Canyon Boulevard; south to intersection with Mulholland Drive; left at entrance on east side of intersection.) (818) 769-2663 or (213) 273-8733. TreePeople Park is open daily, 9 A.M.–dusk. Nursery is open Saturday and Sunday, noon to 5 P.M. One-hour docent tours, Sunday, 11 A.M.

FRANKLIN CANYON RANCH. (Exit Ventura Freeway [101] at Cold-water Canyon Drive; south to intersection with Mulholland Drive and Franklin Canyon Drive; right on Franklin Canyon Drive; continue a seventh of a mile through gate to parking lot. Exit San Diego Freeway [405] at Sunset Boulevard; west to Beverly Drive; north and follow signs "to Coldwater Canyon Drive" to stoplight at Beverly Hills Fire Station #2; left approximately one mile to Franklin Canyon Drive; right 1½ miles to Lake Drive; follow signs to the park.) (213) 858-3834. Park open daily from dawn to dusk. Nature Center open Monday–Friday, 9 A.M.–5 P.M. Free.

MALIBU CREEK STATE PARK. (Exit Ventura Freeway [101] at Las Virgenes Road; south three miles to Mulholland Highway intersection [traffic light]; continue straight to park entrance a quarter of a mile south of the intersection on Las Virgenes/Malibu Canyon Road. Follow Santa Monica Freeway [10] to its western end and continue north and west on Pacific Coast Highway to Malibu Canyon Road; right to park entrance.) (818) 706-8809 or (818) 706-1310. Park open daily, 8 A.M.–7 P.M. Visitors center open Saturday and Sunday, noon–4 P.M. Parking: $3. Reagan Ranch Street parking at corner of Cornell Road and Mulholland Highway is free.

PARAMOUNT RANCH. (Exit Ventura Freeway [101] at Kanan Road; south three quarters of a mile to Sidway; left to Cornell Road; south 2½ miles to entrance on right side of road.) (818) 597-9192. Open daily from dawn to dusk.

PETER STRAUSS RANCH (LAKE ENCHANTO). (Exit Ventura Freeway [101] at Kanan Road; south 2.8 miles to Troutdale Road; left to Mulholland Highway; left, then right under arch into parking lot. Walk back across the bridge on Mulholland and enter the gate into the ranch.) (818) 597-9192. Open daily from dawn to dusk.

POINT MUGU STATE PARK. (Follow Santa Monica Freeway [10] to its western end and continue north and west on Pacific Coast Highway to park entrance at Sycamore Canyon Campground.) (818) 706-1310 or (805)

987-3303. Open daily, dawn to dusk. Ranger-led walks, Saturday, 9 A.M. Day-use parking: $4.

RANCHO SIERRA VISTA/SATWIWA. (Exit Ventura Freeway [101] at Wendy Drive in Newbury Park; south to Potrero Road; right to park entrance at intersection of Potrero Road and Pinehill Road.) (818) 597-9192. Park open from dawn to dusk. Rancho Sierra Vista horse demonstration on Saturday, 2 P.M. Tours of horse ranch on Saturday and Sunday, 2 P.M. Satwiwa, Native American Culture Center, open Sunday, 9 A.M.–5 P.M.

ROCKY OAKS. (Exit Ventura Freeway [101] at Kanan Road; south to Mulholland Highway; right on Mulholland to parking lot on right. Follow Santa Monica Freeway [10] to its western end and continue north and west on Pacific Coast Highway to Kanan-Dume Road; right to Mulholland Highway; left to parking lot on right.) (818) 597-9192 or (818) 789-3456. Park open daily from dawn to dusk.

TAPIA NATURAL AREA PARK, 884 North Las Virgenes Road, Calabasas. (Exit Ventura Freeway [101] at Las Virgenes Road; south five miles to park entrance. Follow Santa Monica Freeway [10] to its western end and continue north and west on Pacific Coast Highway to Malibu Canyon Road [becomes Las Virgenes Canyon]; right three miles to park entrance.) (818) 348-0279. Open daily. 8 A.M.–sunset.

TOPANGA STATE PARK. (Exit Ventura Freeway [101] at Topanga Canyon Boulevard; south to Entrada Road; east and make two left turns to stay on Entrada to park entrance.) (213) 455-2465 or (818) 706-1310. Park open daily, 8 A.M.–7 P.M. Parking: $3.

WILL ROGERS STATE HISTORIC PARK, 14253 Sunset Boulevard, Pacific Palisades. (Follow Santa Monica Freeway [10] to its western end and continue north and west on Pacific Coast Highway [1] to Sunset Boulevard; east eight miles to entrance on left. Exit San Diego Freeway [405] at Sunset; west to park entrance on right.) (213) 454-8212. Park open daily, 8 A.M.–6 P.M. Film and tour of ranch house, daily, 10 A.M.–5 P.M. Polo matches on most Saturdays at 2 P.M. and Sundays at 10 A.M., weather permitting. For polo information, call (213) 459-7322. Parking: $3.

For More Information

Santa Monica Mountains National Recreation Area, National Park Service Visitor Information Center, 30401 Agoura Road, Suite 102, Agoura Hills, CA 91301; (818) 597-9192. Open Monday–Saturday, 8 A.M.–5 P.M.

Nursery Nature Walks, Box 250, 12021 Wilshire Boulevard, Los Angeles, CA 90025; (213) 454-5591 or (213) 472-5100.

William O. Douglas Outdoor Classroom (WODOC), Tykes on Hikes and Babes in the Woods, 3960 Laurel Canyon Boulevard, Suite 344, Studio City, CA 91604; (213) 858-3834.

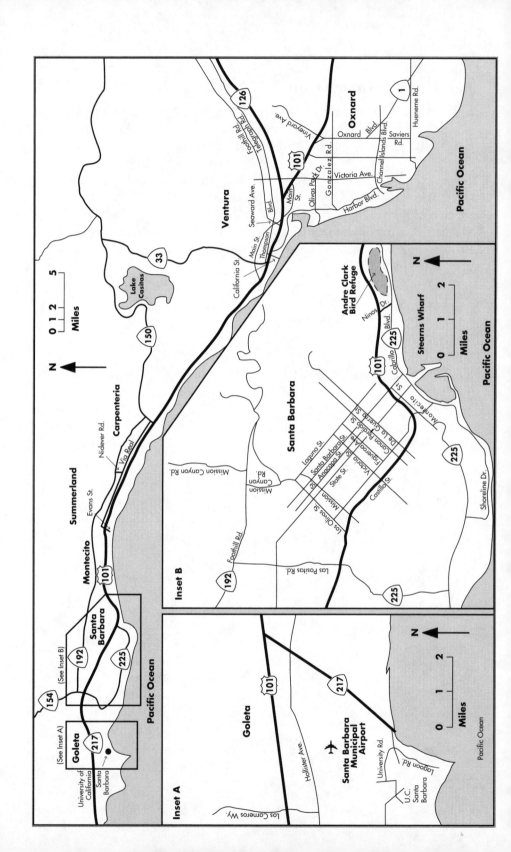

6

Ventura County and Santa Barbara

The Santa Barbara–Ventura region northwest of Los Angeles County boasts some unique family attractions: island nature preserves; a state park with vast, shifting sand dunes; and historic Spanish cities. While you're sampling the area's points of interest, you'll appreciate the sweeping beauty of the coastline and mountain ranges, as well as the balmy climate they engender.

The two destinations, Ventura County and Santa Barbara, are an exercise in contrasts. Ventura remains largely rural and solidly middle class in its values, while the City of Santa Barbara justifiably retains its image of an upscale resort community. Its working-class elements, such as the fishing fleet, only add to the community's picturesque qualities.

Either destination can be reached by car in less than two hours from downtown Los Angeles. Santa Barbara is accessible by train from Los Angeles, too, and it has a very convenient public transport system that allows you to get around the city easily without a car. Ventura's trolleys also enable you to park your car and ride between the beaches and the historic city.

The sections that follow suggest two itineraries for Santa Barbara—a one-day highlights tour and a summary of all the city's other attractions for families. You could easily spend several days here. The Ventura/Oxnard section describes things for kids to do, beginning in the town of Ventura and moving south along the coast. This area, too, will take more than a day to see.

S ANTA   B ARBARA
Museums, Monkeys, and a Mission

Santa Barbara, with its red-tiled roofs and air of gentility, is often pictured as a haven of the privileged classes. But for all its casual elegance, the city is filled with sites and attractions that appeal to youngsters.

Santa Barbara is 90 miles northwest of Los Angeles on U.S. Highway 101. You can make it by car in less than two hours. For a change of pace, try the train. Amtrak schedules two trains a day between Los Angeles and Santa Barbara along some of the most beautiful coastal right-of-way in Southern California. The train is usually crowded, so make your reservations well in advance.

You can visit Santa Barbara in a day, but there is more than enough to see and do to warrant an overnight stay or more than one trip. The following itinerary covers the city's basic highlights for kids. If you only have one day to spend in the area, these are the places to be sure to visit.

Without doubt, the city's most venerable landmark is **Mission Santa Barbara,** aptly called the Queen of the Missions. No, it doesn't have push-button displays or re-enactments of famous battles, and admittedly, younger children might be ready to leave after only a half hour. But the mission is a must see. Once they've been there, the kids will recognize pictures of the mission in almost every book or travel article about California.

Founded in 1786, the mission was completed in 1820 and still serves as a parish church. Children will be impressed by its sheer size and intrigued with the bubbling fountain in front of the colonnaded entrance. Once you pass through the gift shop, you can follow a self-guided tour through the old padres' former living quarters. Displays of frontier furniture, clothing, tools, and cooking utensils attest to the rugged life in early California. The long, narrow sanctuary is colorful and cool, even on the hottest days. You'll see how the walls were painted to simulate materials, such as marble, that were unavailable to the Franciscans, and to suggest architectural features not actually part of the building. Just outside the door, mausoleums and markers in the mission's high-walled cemetery date back to the 1850s. Some four thousand Indians are reportedly buried here. Across the street from the mission, a large grassy expanse is just right for kite flying, Frisbee tossing, or simply running off steam.

Two blocks north of the mission, off Mission Canyon Road at Puesta del Sol Road, is another Santa Barbara treasure, the **Museum of Natural History.** You'll know you've arrived when you spot the stark white skeleton of a 72-foot-long blue whale in front of the museum's Spanish-style buildings. Housed in the many buildings are an excellent Indian Hall, with dioramas of Chumash Indian life (the area's last inhabitants before the Europeans); geological exhibits; displays of local birds and animals; and a planetarium. Kids will like pushing a button to shake a rattlesnake rattle and startle passersby. A live beehive, safely behind glass, allows youngsters an inside look at this hard-working insect community. A working seismograph gives vivid evidence of earthquake activity in the area. Out back, shaded tables are available for picnics.

From the museum, head back down to the beach for a chance to see some more animals at the **Santa Barbara Zoological Gardens.** Located just off the beachfront Cabrillo Boulevard at Niños Drive, this zoo is tailored to a child's scale. Though smaller than many metropolitan zoos, the facility has most of the animals youngsters want to see—lions, elephants, sea lions, otters, and a variety of monkeys. There's a children's petting zoo of barnyard animals near the entrance. If the animals aren't enough, there's a playground with rocks, tunnels, and climbing equipment; a picnic area; and a miniature train that circles the grounds.

The zoo also affords a great vantage point to overlook the **Andree Clark Bird Refuge.** This freshwater lagoon is just east of the zoo and is surrounded by lush gardens. The watercourse plays host to more than two hundred varieties of birds that are free to come and go as they choose. If you want a closer look, the refuge is rimmed by a walkway and bike path. Be sure to take some bread along to feed the ducks that always seem to be waiting for a handout.

Just a few long blocks from the zoo on Cabrillo Boulevard is another Santa

Barbara landmark—**Stearns Wharf.** Built in 1872 and restored in 1981 following a fire, the wharf juts into the Pacific Ocean from the foot of State Street. Be sure to notice the "Dolphin Fountain" at the wharf entrance (actually the Bicentennial Friendship Fountain, built in 1982 to commemorate the city's 200th birthday).

You can walk or drive onto the pier, where there are restaurants, curio stores, and snack shops. It's a great place to pause for a custom-blended ice-cream cone at Hobsons, to let the kids fish (a full-service tackle shop can meet your needs), or to sign up for a harbor cruise.

One of the wharf's newer attractions is the **Sea Center,** operated by the Santa Barbara Museum of Natural History. The center focuses on the marine life and environment of the Santa Barbara Channel with a computer learning center, dioramas, and models. In the center's aquariums, you can see tiny fish embryos in their egg sacs, or try to spot the fish that bury themselves in the sand. Dominating the interior of this two-story, open structure is an awe-inspiring, life-size model of a gray whale.

If you have time before heading home, go west on Cabrillo from Stearns Wharf one block to Chapala Street, turn right and go three blocks. There you will meet one of Santa Barbara's oldest and best-known residents, the Moreton Bay Fig Tree. This native of Australia was planted in 1874 and is the largest tree of its kind in the nation. Its branches span 160 feet, and the kids will love to scramble over its huge roots.

Attractions

AMTRAK. Two trains daily from Los Angeles to Santa Barbara. $38 round-trip for adults, $19 round-trip for children, ages 2–11. Call (800) 872-7245 for times and more information.

ANDREE CLARK BIRD REFUGE, 1400 East Cabrillo Boulevard, Santa Barbara. (Exit U.S. Highway 101 at Cabrillo Boulevard [225]; south half a mile. Refuge is in lagoon on right.) Open daily during daylight hours. Free.

MISSION SANTA BARBARA, upper end of Laguna Street, Santa Barbara. (Exit U.S. Highway 101 at Mission Street; north to Laguna Street; left to mission.) (805) 682-4713. Open daily, 9 A.M.–5 P.M. Adults, $1; under 17, free.

SANTA BARBARA MUSEUM OF NATURAL HISTORY, 2559 Puesta del Sol Road, Santa Barbara. (Exit U.S. Highway 101 at Mission Street; north to Laguna Street; left to Los Olivos Street; right to Mission Canyon Street; left to Puesta del Sol Road and museum.) (805) 682-4711. Open daily, 9 A.M.–5 P.M. (Sunday and holidays from 10 A.M.) Free.

SANTA BARBARA ZOOLOGICAL GARDENS (Santa Barbara Zoo), 500 Niños Drive, Santa Barbara. (Exit U.S. Highway 101 at Cabrillo Boulevard [225]; south to Niños Drive; right to zoo.) (805) 962-6310. Open daily, 10 A.M.–5 P.M. Adults, $4; ages 2–12, $2; under 2, free.

SEA CENTER, Stearns Wharf, Santa Barbara. (Exit U.S. Highway 101 at State Street; south to wharf.) (805) 963-1067. Open Memorial Day–Labor Day, daily, 10 A.M.–9 P.M.; Labor Day–Memorial Day, Sunday–Thursday, noon–5 P.M.; Friday–Saturday, 10 A.M.–9 P.M. Adults, $1; ages 2–12, 50 cents; under 2, free. School tours Tuesday and Thursday morning, reservation required. (805) 682-4711.

STEARNS WHARF, Santa Barbara (see directions to Sea Center). (805) 963-2633.

For More Information

Santa Barbara Conference and Visitors Bureau, 22 East Anapamu Street, Santa Barbara, CA 93101; (805) 966-9222.

IN AND AROUND SANTA BARBARA
Surf, Sand, and Santa Claus

After you've visited Santa Barbara's highlights for kids, described in the preceding section, you'll know there is plenty more to do in the area. Second-day experiences can range from a walk in the woods to a romp in the surf or a step back in time. You won't be able to cover all these activities in only one more day, but you are sure to structure an enjoyable stay from the following suggestions.

Start out in the cool, quiet of the morning at the **Botanic Garden,** a few blocks from the Museum of Natural History on Mission Canyon Road. Just wandering along some of the garden's three miles of trails will give the kids an appreciation of the variety of California plant life. There are plenty of cacti and wildflowers, and there's even a stand of redwood trees at the north end of the garden. The trail that goes past the redwoods will take you down into a canyon to a dam built by the Indians during the mission period. Kids also will like walking across the high bridges that cross the garden's babbling stream. There are plenty of benches and drinking fountains if you decide to take a break during your stroll.

Down from the foothills, the city of Santa Barbara holds a number of surprises for kids, some historic and some contemporary. If the youngsters are up for the walk, take the self-guided Red-Tile Walking Tour along a 12-block downtown area. The tour includes old adobes, the remnants of a fortress, museums, shops, and the city's famed courthouse. Get a walking-tour map from the **Santa Barbara Visitors Center** at 1 Santa Barbara Street. Even if you don't do the complete tour, you can take the youngsters to see the area's best-known attractions.

Tops on the list is the **Santa Barbara County Courthouse.** This imposing white structure, like so many of the city's Spanish-Moorish–inspired buildings, was built following a disastrous 1925 earthquake. Take the elevator to the top of its 70-foot-tall clock tower to get a panoramic view of Santa Barbara's beautiful setting and its red-tile roofs. The tower's wrought-iron balconies provide a safe barrier for older youngsters, but you'll want to hold your toddler's hand.

Downstairs, the courthouse is a delight of colorful imported tiles, hand-carved balconies and doors, open beam ceilings, and wrought-iron chandeliers. Make sure the kids see the ornate Board of Supervisors hall on the second floor. The two-story walls are covered with paintings, reminiscent of N. C. Wyeth, that depict historical events in Santa Barbara's development. At the Santa Barbara Street entrance the kids will find a more tangible element of history—the last stagecoach to carry mail and passengers over the San Marcos Pass, north of the city. The huge L-shaped building shares an entire city block at Anacapa and Anapamu streets with spacious green lawns and a central sunken garden that seems to invite youngsters to come and play.

For a glimpse of early Santa Barbara, stop at **El Cuartel,** three blocks south of the courthouse in the State Historic Park. This building once served as the soldiers' barracks in the royal fortress (Presidio Real) built in 1782. On display is a scale model of the original Presidio that will help youngsters put into perspective the remnants of walls and foundations that now remain.

A block farther south, at De la Guerra Street, the **Santa Barbara His-torical Society Museum** affords a broader view of Santa Barbara history. Kids will see early Indian, Spanish, Mexican, and American mementos, especially costumes and items used in everyday life. Also featured are maps, paintings, dolls and other toys, and equestrian paraphernalia.

Two blocks west of the museum is State Street, Santa Barbara's main retail thoroughfare, planned with pedestrians in mind. The wide sidewalks are shaded by jacaranda trees and there are plenty of conveniently placed benches. The street offers a wide selection of shops, galleries, and gift stores as well as a variety of fast food stands, snack shops, and restaurants.

Head three blocks north on State Street and you will find the **Santa Barbara Museum of Art,** which houses impressive collections of ancient sculpture, Oriental art, and American and European paintings. Kids will be interested in the collection of dolls dating from ancient Egypt to eighteenth-century Europe. The museum's bright, airy atmosphere will strike most children as quite welcoming.

One block north, at Victoria Street, is the **Earthling Bookstore** with well-stacked aisles of books on almost every subject imaginable and a huge children's section that carries titles for all age groups. Browsers are more than welcome at this store, which provides music, oversize reading chairs, and a central fireplace.

If you're still looking for just the right book, **Another Bookshop,** half a block west on Victoria, is almost entirely devoted to children's books. Other items on sale include educational workbooks, flash cards, cassettes, and puzzles. The shop's windows are lined with benches and there is a small table for drawing and for assembling puzzles.

By early afternoon, you may be ready to spread your towel on Santa Barbara's wide, white crescent beach and let the kids play in the surf. The beach can be quite crowded on summer weekends, so be prepared to spend a little time finding a parking place.

East of Stearns Wharf the wide stretch of sand called East Beach often is the focus of volleyball games. You'll find picnic tables in Chase Palm Park, a wide, palm-shaded strip of grass that runs nearly half the length of East Beach and separates it from Cabrillo Boulevard. At the end of the park, the Cabrillo Bathhouse has showers, bathrooms, a snack bar, and beach-equipment rentals. Next to the bathhouse and right on the beach, a complex of children's play equipment includes swings, rings, and climbing apparatus.

West of Stearns Wharf is West Beach, smaller than East Beach and better suited to younger children because it is protected by both the wharf and the harbor breakwater. And west of the harbor and breakwater is Ledbetter Beach, where the surf is more lively. Shoreline Park at the west end of Ledbetter has picnic facilities and great views of the coast and the city.

The harbor is the place to see more than a thousand boats, from pleasure craft to commercial fishing boats. At the end of West Beach you can stroll a half mile past the fishing fleet's Navy Pier and out the flag-lined breakwater. The hand-made flags snapping in an afternoon breeze represent the city's 26 community services organizations, and they are flown every Wednesday through Sunday, unless the weather is stormy. You can rent boats at the breakwater or from the Sea Landing pier halfway down West Beach. (See Sailing Rentals and Tours listing in the Attractions section.) Depending on your and your youngsters' skills, you can skipper your own sail or motor boat, sign on for sailing lessons, or charter yachts for luncheon or dinner cruises. Between February and May, whale-watch cruises leave from both places. (See the Whale Watching listing at the end of the Attractions.)

If you and the kids aren't so nautically inclined, Santa Barbara's beach-front has a bikeway that runs along West and East Beach and around the Clark Bird Refuge (see listing, page 120). You can rent bikes, roller skates, or four-wheel Pedalinas, family-size surreys that offer side-by-side pedaling with seating in front for smaller children. **Beach Rentals** at State and Cabrillo has a wide selection of rentals (for this and others see Bike Rentals listing in the Attractions section) and will even provide a bike tour map, or you can get maps of bike routes from the visitors center on Santa Barbara Street.

Sundays are special at the beach. Beginning at 10 A.M. until sunset, hundreds of painters, sculptors, potters, weavers, jewelers, photographers, and other artisans display their work along Cabrillo Boulevard in Chase Palm Park. Most children will find something to fascinate them among the stalls, but be careful. Everything is for sale.

Up Castillo Street near the west end of West Beach, you'll find three attractions, open from 2 P.M. to 4 P.M. on Sunday only. The **Carriage Museum** in Pershing Park, off Castillo, houses more than forty horsedrawn carts and carriages from Santa Barbara's pioneering days. There are early Army wagons, a big black hearse, and a bright red steam pumper used by nineteenth-century firefighters. Each year during Santa Barbara's Old Spanish Days the carriages are paraded along the city's streets.

Nearby on West Montecito Street are two of the city's better-preserved early homes—**Fernald House** (built in 1862) and **Trussel-Winchester Adobe** (built in 1854). Both were restored and fully furnished by the Santa Barbara Historical Society, and they are open only for escorted tours. The 14-room Fernald House is a Victorian masterpiece inside and out, and will show the youngsters what nineteenth-century life was like for the well-to-do. The kids may be interested to learn that the Trussel-Winchester Adobe next door was built with timbers taken from the wreck of a ship off Anacapa Island in the channel.

There's more history waiting in Goleta, a few minutes west of Santa Barbara on U.S. Highway 101. Exit 101 at Los Carneros Road and head north a half mile to a rambling, two-story Victorian structure built in the 1870s by the Stow family. **Stow House** has been fully restored and furnished with period furniture, clothing, and toys. The house sits in a 13-acre park where you can picnic in the shade of a redwood grove.

Nearby is a distinctive yellow wooden building that served as Goleta's railroad depot beginning in 1901. Moved to its present site in 1981, the building is now the home of the **Goleta Depot Railroad Museum,** with a collection of railroading artifacts, photographs, and exhibits. Sure to please most youngsters is the 400-square-foot model railroad layout, which is being built on Saturdays by community volunteers. You should note, however, that this museum is closed on Sunday.

On your way back to Los Angeles along U.S. Highway 101, there are a few additional stops you can consider. In Summerland, five miles south of Santa Barbara, **The Big Yellow House** is a local fixture as a family restaurant. Big and yellow as its name implies, the restaurant is easy to spot from the highway and makes a convenient dinner stop on the way home. This multistory Victorian structure has six dining rooms, but it's still best to arrive early or call ahead for reservations. The kids will enjoy weighing in on a big old-fashioned scale, which will determine the price of their dinner.

A few miles farther south, the **Santa Barbara Polo & Racquet Club** welcomes visitors to the polo matches on Sundays between April and November. World-class players have competed on this field, which is actually in the seaside community of Carpinteria. Children who love horses or sports are likely to find a polo match different and exciting . . . at least for a little while.

Another site the kids are sure to spot from the highway is the 30-foot statue of Frosty the Snowman, who beckons travelers to stop off at Santa

Claus Lane. This is a community that only exists for tourists. There's a large toy shop, a store featuring Christmas baked goods, and restaurants offering the usual fare. You may want to take advantage of a unique feature in town and mail a card or letter to a friend or relative, just to have it postmarked "Santa Claus Lane, CA." Where else but in California?

Attractions

ANOTHER BOOKSHOP, 11 West Victoria Street, #17, Santa Barbara. (Exit U.S. Highway 101 at State Street; north to Victoria Street; left to shop.) (805) 962-3992. Open Monday–Thursday, 9:30 A.M.–6 P.M.; Friday and Saturday, 9:30 A.M.–9 P.M.; Sunday, noon–5 P.M.

THE BIG YELLOW HOUSE, 108 Pierpont Avenue, Summerland. (Exit U.S. Highway 101 northbound at Evans. Exit U.S. Highway 101 southbound at Summerland. Restaurant is visible from highway exits.) (805) 969-4140. Open Monday–Friday, 7:30 A.M.–9 P.M.; Saturday, 7:30 A.M.–12:30 A.M.; Sunday, 7:30 A.M.–12:30 P.M. and 2 P.M.–8:30 P.M.

BIKE RENTALS
• *Beach Rentals,* 8 West Cabrillo Boulevard, Santa Barbara. (Exit U.S. Highway 101 at State Street; south to Cabrillo Boulevard; right to store.) (805) 963-2524. Open daily, 8 A.M.–7 P.M. Call for rental prices.
• *Open Air Bicycles,* 224 Chapala Street, Santa Barbara. (Exit U.S. Highway 101 at Chapala Street; south to store.) (805) 963-3717. Open daily, 9 A.M.–8 P.M. Call for rental prices.
• *Pacific Traveller's Supply,* 529 State Street, Santa Barbara. (Exit U.S. Highway 101 at State Street; north to store.) (805) 963-4438. Open Monday–Saturday, 10 A.M.–6 P.M.; Sunday, noon–5 P.M.

BOTANIC GARDEN, 1212 Mission Canyon Road, Santa Barbara. (Exit U.S. Highway 101 at Mission Street; north to Laguna Street; left to Los Olivos Street; right to Mission Canyon Road; left to garden.) (805) 682-4726. Open daily, 8 A.M.–sunset. Free.

CARRIAGE MUSEUM, 129 Castillo Street, Santa Barbara. (Exit U.S. Highway 101 at State Street; south (a few yards) to Montecito Street; right to Castillo Street; left to museum at rear of ball park.) (805) 569-2077. Open Sunday, 2 P.M.–4 P.M. Admission by donation.

EARTHLING BOOKSTORE, 1236 State Street, Santa Barbara. (Exit U.S. Highway 101 at State Street; north to store.) (805) 965-0926. Open Sunday–Thursday, 10 A.M.–10 P.M.; Friday and Saturday, 10 A.M.–11 P.M.

EL CUARTEL, 123 East Canon Perdido Street, Santa Barbara. (Exit U.S. Highway 101 at Santa Barbara Street; north to Canon Perdido Street at El Presidio de Santa Barbara State Historic Park.) (805) 966-9719. Open Monday–Friday, 10:30 A.M.–4:30 P.M.; Saturday and Sunday, noon–4 P.M. Free.

FERNALD HOUSE AND TRUSSELL-WINCHESTER ADOBE, 414 West Montecito Street, Santa Barbara. (Exit U.S. Highway 101 at State Street; south (a few yards) to Montecito; right to museums.) (805) 966-6639. Open Sunday, 2 P.M.–4 P.M. Admission, $1.

GOLETA DEPOT RAILROAD MUSEUM, 300 Los Carneros Road, Goleta. (Exit U.S. Highway 101 at Los Carneros Road; north to museum.) (805) 964-3540. Open Wednesday–Sunday, 1 P.M.–4 P.M. Admission by donation. Train rides, $1.

SAILING RENTALS AND TOURS

• *Captain Don's Harbor Cruises*, Stearns Wharf, Santa Barbara. (Exit U.S. Highway 101 at State Street; south to wharf.) (805) 969-5217. Open June 15–Labor Day, daily departures on the hour, 11 A.M.–4 P.M.; Labor Day–June 15, weekend and holiday departures only, 11 A.M.–4 P.M. Adults, $6; ages 3–12, $4; under 3, free.
• *Santa Barbara Boat Rentals/Sailing Association*, Breakwater, Santa Barbara. (Exit U.S. Highway 101 at State Street; south to Cabrillo Boulevard; right to end of West Beach; walk to breakwater.) (805) 962-2826 or (800) 248-1244, ext. 7245. Open daily for boat rentals, cocktail cruises, island charters. Call for prices.
• *Sea Landing Aquatic Center*, Santa Barbara Harbor, Santa Barbara. (Exit U.S. Highway 101 at State Street; south to Cabrillo Boulevard; right one half mile to Sea Landing pier.) (805) 963-3564. Open daily for coastal and island charters, cocktail or dinner cruises. Call for prices.

SANTA BARBARA COUNTY COURTHOUSE, 1100 block of Anacapa Street, Santa Barbara. (Exit U.S. Highway 101 at Santa Barbara Street; north to Figueroa Street; left to Anacapa Street and courthouse.) (805) 681-4200, or (805) 962-6464. Open Monday–Friday, 8 A.M.–5 P.M.; Saturday and Sunday, 9 A.M.–5 P.M. Free.

SANTA BARBARA HISTORICAL SOCIETY MUSEUM, 136 East De la Guerra Street, Santa Barbara. (Exit U.S. Highway 101 at Santa Barbara Street; north to De la Guerra Street and museum.) (805) 966-1601. Open Tuesday–Friday, noon–5 P.M.; Saturday and Sunday, 1 P.M.–5 P.M. Free.

SANTA BARBARA MUSEUM OF ART, 1130 State Street, Santa Barbara. (Exit U.S. Highway 101 at State Street; north to museum.) (805) 963-4364. Open Tuesday–Saturday, 11 A.M.–5 P.M. (Thursday to 9 P.M.); Sunday, noon–5 P.M. Admission by donation.

SANTA BARBARA POLO & RACQUET CLUB, U.S. Highway 101 at Nidever Road, Carpineria. (Exit U.S. Highway 101 southbound at Padaro Lane; north to Via Real; right to entrance. Exit highway northbound at Santa Claus Lane; north on Via Real to Nidever Road; left to entrance.) (805) 684-6683. Matches April–November, Sunday, 1 P.M.–3 P.M. Adults, $5; under 12, free.

SANTA BARBARA VISITORS CENTER, 1 Santa Barbara Street, Santa Barbara. (Exit U.S. Highway 101 at Anacapa Street; south to Cabrillo Boulevard; left to Santa Barbara Street and center.) (805) 965-3021. Open Monday–Friday, 10 A.M.–4 P.M.; Saturday and Sunday, 9 A.M.–5 P.M.

STOW HOUSE, 304 Los Carneros Road, Goleta. (Exit U.S. Highway 101 at Los Carneros Road; north to house.) (805) 964-4407. Open Memorial Day–Labor Day, Saturday and Sunday, 2 P.M.–4 P.M.; Labor Day–Memorial Day, Sunday, 2 P.M.–4 P.M. Free, but donations accepted.

WHALE WATCHING

• *Condor, Sea Landing, Santa Barbara Harbor, Santa Barbara.* (805) 963-3564. Call for availability and prices.
• *Santa Barbara Museum of Natural History:* (805) 682-4711. Call for arrangements, availability, and prices.
• *Santa Barbara Sailing Association, Breakwater, Santa Barbara.* (805) 962-2826. Call for arrangements, availability, and prices.

For More Information

Santa Barbara Conference and Visitors Bureau, 22 East Anapamu Street, Santa Barbara, CA 93101; (805) 966-9222.

VENTURA AND OXNARD

Island Excursions and Mainland Diversions

One hour north of Los Angeles along U.S. Highway 101, historic Ventura and pastoral Oxnard combine seaside recreation with inland attractions. The area's harbors and beaches rival those of its more famous neighbors, Santa Barbara and Malibu. Mainland attractions include a mission, an archaeological site, and some of the best strawberries in the world. Beyond the shoreline, kids can visit the islands comprising Southern California's only national park.

When Father Junipero Serra founded the ninth of California's 21 missions in 1782, he named it San Buenaventura, which means "good fortune." Although its name has been shortened to Ventura, the city still reflects its good fortune at being established along this picturesque crescent of Southern California coastline.

You give the kids an interesting history lesson by making a one-block loop tour of the **Ventura Downtown Historic Area.** Start this walking tour into the city's past at the site where it all began, an Indian village that has been uncovered by archaeologists. You'll find the excavation site and a small exhibit building at the **Albinger Archaeological Museum** on Main Street. Climb up onto the platform at the north end of the dig to let kids have a good overview of what an archaeological excavation looks like. During 1974–75, archaeologists unearthed more than 30,000 artifacts from this area, covering a span of 3,500 years, from the time of the Indians to more recent settlers. You'll see the foundations of mission barracks used from 1804–1834, the low walls of a mission church that was abandoned in 1790, and an earth oven that dates from 300 B.C.

Outside the adjacent exhibit building, notice the replica of a *tomol*, a wood-plank canoe like those used by the Chumash Indians to greet Juan Rodriguez Cabrillo in 1542 when he became the first European to sail up the Southern California coast. Look for the seams where the planks were tied together and caulked with tar. Inside the museum you'll see excavated evidence of the five different cultures that once lived in the area. There are stone bowls and thousands of shell trade beads made by the Indians; pottery and glass beads from the eighteenth-century Spanish occupation; spurs and roofing tiles left by the Mexicans in the 1820s; glass bottles and buttons used by Americans in the 1870s; and Chinese coins and soy sauce jars from the early 1900s. An audiovisual presentation in the theater shows the dig in progress and explains the significance of the finds.

Walk a block east of the dig to **Mission San Buenaventura.** You are welcome to tour the nearly 200-year-old stone and adobe church when it is not in use for religious services. Worn steps and floor tiles in the dark church will help kids understand how old it is. Stop near the fountain in the garden outside to see the olive press, once an important piece of machinery. Next door to the mission there's a small museum that displays the mission's two original wooden bells and Spanish books and clothes brought to California by the padres.

Across the street from the mission is Figueroa Plaza, formerly the city's Chinatown, now a pedestrian mall with tile fountains and broad sidewalks. Next to the plaza is Mission Park. This appealing stretch of grass is dominated by the spreading branches of a 100-year-old Morton Bay fig tree. It's a good place to rest and let the kids run. It's also a quiet spot for a picnic.

Next door to the park is the **Ventura County Museum of History and Art.** This pleasant Spanish-styled stucco museum is just the right size for kids—small enough so they can see it all without fatigue, yet full of interesting exhibits. You'll see finely woven baskets made by the Chumash, a replica of an Indian pictograph painted on a rock wall, and Spanish and Mexican costumes and dolls. Chinese items include embroidered shoes and clothing from their native land. To learn about a more recent period of history, kids like to push a button to activate the working parts of a miniature oil well. Nearby, there's a scale model of the San Buenaventura Mission and the surrounding town as it looked in the 1880s.

A darkened room with well-lit cases displays doll-size, intricately detailed likenesses of famous historical personalities, created by Ojai artist George S. Stuart. Kids who have studied some history are interested in seeing what various U.S. presidents and European royalty looked like. Outdoors, a display of early farm equipment usually attracts younger children. Time your visit for a Sunday at 2 P.M., when you can take a docent-led tour of the museum.

The streets south and east of the museum are filled with restaurants and antique shops in renovated historic buildings. If you walk east along Main Street, you'll discover several family restaurants. At the **Busy Bee Café,** two blocks east of the mission, you can relive Ventura in the 1950s. Kids like eating at the restaurant's red booths, which have juke box selectors mounted on the wall. The soda fountain serves sundaes and root-beer floats to go with hamburgers and a wide selection of sandwiches.

A number of children's events are held in **Plaza Park,** two blocks south of Main Street at Chestnut. At the Children's Celebration of the Arts, held every year on the Saturday before Mother's Day, elementary-school–age kids attend free art and music workshops. In October, preschoolers dabble in the arts at the park's Little People's Festival. Throughout the year, the park hosts an arts and crafts festival on the first Sunday of each month.

If you want to see more of Ventura after this downtown tour, you can drive or leave your car where it is and take a **Buenaventura Trolley Company** trolley. Kids love riding these trolleys on wheels, which run daily on regularly scheduled routes. The trolley connects downtown Ventura with the beaches, the harbor, and other attractions in town.

From downtown, it's a short drive or trolley ride to **San Buenaventura State Beach** on the other side of U.S. Highway 101. This wide sandy beach has picnic areas amid gnarled trees, children's play equipment, and a snack bar. Ventura Pier at the north end of the beach is a good place to fish. If the kids want to surf, you can rent boards or boogie boards by the hour or the day at the **Pipeline Surf Shop** on Seaward Avenue near the south end of the beach.

A few blocks east of the beach on Telegraph Road, there's a special children's book store, **Adventures for Kids.** The store has one of the biggest inventories in Southern California, with more than 16,000 titles for sale. Selections range from picture books to novels for teens. A wide selection of nonfiction books for all ages is arranged by subject, as in a library. In one corner of the store a sailboat made of benches and large blocks attracts kids. Stop by the store with preschoolers for a storytime held every Tuesday at 10:30 A.M. from October to July.

A special treat awaits kids a few blocks away at the **City Bakery.** This old-fashioned bakery sells breads, sandwiches, soup, chocolate-chip cookies, and their specialty, scones. The baking area is in the center of the shop so children can see the bakers mixing dough and taking baked goods out of the oven. It's impossible to smell the aroma without buying something. Every Saturday at 10 A.M. there's a children's story hour in the shop, and on Thursday night at 7 P.M. kids who like to play games can join in Pizza and Pictionary.

Two miles south near the harbor, visit the **Olivas Adobe** to show the kids what ranch life was like in Southern California nearly 150 years ago. The two-story home was built in 1847 on 6,600 acres that were part of a Mexican land grant given to two faithful soldiers in the Mexican army. Start your visit at the Exhibit Building, where the kids can look at photos of the 22 children who were raised in the house. On a tour through the home, look for the large bedroom where all the girls slept and the balcony used as a sleeping porch for the boys. Down the hall there's the family chapel where a mission priest led services once a month. The gardens that surround the adobe were planted by the Olivas family.

Ventura Harbor is just west of the adobe. Outdoor cafés and shops line the waters around this man-made bay. For kids, there's a video arcade and bright yellow pedalboats to rent. A paddle-wheel boat, the **Bay Queen,** takes visitors around the harbor on 40-minute cruises.

The most interesting place at the harbor for children is the **Visitor Center** for the **Channel Islands National Park.** To get there, you don't have to board a boat. Just drive to the end of Spinnaker Drive on the west side of the harbor. This cheery waterside building is the mainland focal point of Southern California's only national park, which encompasses five of the eight Channel Islands off the coast. Climb or ride the elevator up to the center's third-floor observation tower on a clear day and you'll see one or more of the islands: Anacapa, Santa Cruz, Santa Rosa, San Miguel, and Santa Barbara.

Start your tour of the center in the downstairs auditorium, where you'll see a 25-minute film that describes the islands and their unique resources. Enter the main gallery next, where open exhibit areas are low enough for young children to reach. Displayed are plants, animals, and Indian artifacts from the islands. An indoor tide pool has sea anemones and shellfish that kids can touch. Nearby, a sign on an exhibit of Indian grinding stones reads Please Touch. Another exhibit displays *caliche* (kah-LEE-chee), calcium-carbonate sand castings of the ancient trees found on San Miguel Island. Pick up maps and information about the islands from National Park Service rangers at the desk in this room.

If you'd like to visit one of the islands, walk next door to **Island Packers** to make reservations. This outfit makes regularly scheduled trips to each of the five islands. Most trips are one day long, although you can camp overnight on Anacapa and Santa Barbara, or spend the night in a refurbished ranch house on Santa Cruz. The rugged islands are protected as nature sanctuaries with restricted recreational use. For some excursions you stay on the boat and look at the wildlife. Others involve some hiking and occasional wet landings on the islands. A visit to one of the islands is an exciting and memorable experience for kids old enough to handle these adventures.

The best island to visit with children is the closest one, Anacapa, which is only an 11-mile, 90-minute boat ride away. Anacapa is actually composed of three islets, and is easily identified by Arch Rock, an outcrop at the east end with an opening in the middle that has been cut out by waves. On the ride across the channel, look for dolphins swimming alongside the boat and sea lions barking from rocks near the island. At the east end landing, you'll climb 153 steps up to a plateau where there are a picnic area, a nature center, and two miles of nature trails to explore. A National Park Service ranger leads groups on an informative hike along the bluff, from which you'll have a panoramic view of the other islands and the mainland.

Sign up for a trip to Anacapa on weekends between June and September if your kids are good swimmers and like to snorkel. You'll land at Frenchy's Cove and spend your time examining the sea life swimming in rich kelp beds near the shore. In the winter, you'll explore tide pools in this same area. Whale-watch trips, which are scheduled during the whale-migration period from the end of December through March, cruise the channel near Anacapa. You'll not only see whales, but other marine mammals, such as seals and sea lions, that live near the islands.

On a trip to Santa Cruz Island you'll visit Indian sites and learn about the native plant and animal life. Trips to the other three islands involve boat crossings of about three hours and rough landings best suited for adults and teenagers.

For a mainland play experience by the sea, spend some time at **McGrath State Beach** two miles south of Ventura Harbor. McGrath is a two-mile stretch of broad beach with sand dunes. You can camp at this beach, although it's very crowded in summer. There are picnic areas, lifeguards, and restrooms near the campground. Stop by the small visitors center near the entrance to learn about the area's plants and wildlife. You'll see plenty of bird life if you walk along a nature trail that leads away from the beach, through the Santa Clara River Estuary.

Less than five miles south, **Channel Islands Harbor** in Oxnard is another bustling marina. Stop by the **Visitor Center** on South Harbor Boulevard for maps and information on how to enjoy the harbor. You can rent 14-foot to 27-foot sailboats for day sailing at **Channel Islands Landing** on Victoria Avenue.

The most noticeable feature of the harbor is **Fisherman's Wharf** at the corner of Channel Islands Boulevard and Victoria Avenue. This collection of brightly painted Cape Cod–style buildings surrounds a cobblestoned courtyard where there is live musical entertainment on weekends. You can eat at one of the restaurants around the courtyard or buy a picnic to eat at one of the tables overlooking the water. Walk over to the dock where commercial fishermen unload their catch each day. Hiking and biking trails wind through the grassy park areas around the marina, where you'll also find a children's playground.

Down the street, **Cisco's Sportfishing** at Captain Jack's Landing offers sportfishing trips daily. On three-quarter-day or all-day fishing trips you'll catch rock cod, blue perch, or halibut, if you're lucky. Cisco's does whale-watch trips too, during the whale-migration season from the end of December through March.

Every year in late April or early May, the harbor plays host to the **California Strawberry Festival,** showcasing Oxnard's most famous agricultural crop. Clown acts, puppet shows, and shortcake-eating contests are a few of the activities that make this annual event so festive. A children's fun center entertains kids with arts and crafts projects.

Throughout spring and early summer you can buy strawberries at one of the many produce stands along back roads between Highway 101 and State Highway 1 west of Lewis Road. At other times of the year, stop at the stands and let the kids help you select farm-fresh produce: corn, oranges, lettuce, and pumpkins. Urban youngsters may be interested in seeing the crops growing in fields near the stands.

On the coast south of this agricultural plain, Port Hueneme has an interesting attraction, the **Civil Engineer Corps/Seabee Museum.** The museum showcases projects built by the U.S. Navy Seabees around the world, and also displays cultural items from the countries where they have served. You'll see dioramas of such efforts as an amphibious landing and construction of a Pacific island beach camp in World War II. Kids will especially enjoy seeing the Kodiak bearskin surrounded by artifacts made by Alaskan natives and the cases of dolls and miniature boats collected from many countries.

Attractions in the Ventura Area

ADVENTURES FOR KIDS, 3457 Telegraph Road, Ventura. (Exit U.S. Highway 101 northbound at Main Street; north to Mills Road; right to Telegraph; left to store [across from the Buenaventura Shopping Center.] Exit U.S. Highway 101 southbound on Seaward Exit; south on Harbor Boulevard to Seaward Avenue; north to Thompson Road; left to Telegraph Avenue.) (805) 650-9688. Open Monday–Saturday, 10 A.M.–5 P.M.

BUENAVENTURA TROLLEY COMPANY, 21 South California Street, #402, Ventura. (805) 643-4724 for tour information. Trolley runs daily (except Monday) on regularly scheduled routes. Adults $2; seniors, $1; under 5, free.

BUSY BEE CAFÉ, 478 East Main Street, Ventura. (Exit U.S. Highway

101 at California Street; north to Main Street. Café is near corner.) (805) 643-4864. Open daily. 6 A.M.–9 P.M.

CITY BAKERY, 2358 East Main Street, Ventura. (Exit U.S. Highway 101 at Seaward Avenue; north to Main Street; right to bakery.) (805) 643-0861. Open Monday–Friday, 7 A.M.–7 P.M.; Saturday, 8 A.M.–3 P.M. Children's storytime, Saturday 10 A.M. Pizza and Pictionary, Thursday, 7 P.M.

OLIVAS ADOBE, 4200 Olivas Park Drive, Ventura. (Exit U.S. Highway 101 at Victoria Avenue; south to Olivas Park Drive; right to adobe.) (805) 644-4346. Adobe open Saturday and Sunday, 10 A.M.–4 P.M.; grounds open daily, 9 A.M.–4 P.M. Free, but donations are accepted.

PIPELINE SURF SHOP, 1124 South Seaward Avenue, Ventura. (Exit U.S. Highway 101 at Seaward Avenue; west to beach.) Open Tuesday–Friday, 10 A.M.–5:30 P.M.; Saturday, Sunday, and Monday, 10 A.M.–5 P.M.

PLAZA PARK, between Chestnut Street and Fir Street, and between Thompson Boulevard and Chestnut Street, Ventura. (Exit U.S. Highway 101 at California Street; north to Thompson Boulevard; right to park.)

SAN BUENAVENTURA STATE BEACH, west of Harbor Boulevard, south of California Street. (Exit U.S. Highway 101 at Seaward Avenue; west to Harbor Boulevard; right to park headquarters.) (805) 654-4611.

VENTURA DOWNTOWN HISTORIC AREA

(To reach the following listings, exit U.S. Highway 101 at California Street; north to Main Street; left to attractions.)

• *Albinger Archaeological Museum*, 113 East Main Street, Ventura. (805) 648-5823. Open Tuesday–Sunday, 10 A.M.–4 P.M.
• *Mission San Buenaventura*, 211 East Main Street, Ventura. (805) 643-4318. Museum and gift shop: open, Monday–Saturday, 10 A.M.–5 P.M.; Sunday, 10 A.M.–4 P.M. Museum admission: Adults, 50 cents; under 17, 25 cents.
• *Ventura County Museum of History and Art*, 100 East Main Street, Ventura. (805) 653-0323. Open Tuesday–Sunday, 10 A.M.–5 P.M. Suggested donation: Adults, $1; under 13, 50 cents.

VENTURA HARBOR

(To reach the following listings, exit U.S. Highway 101 at Victoria Avenue; south to Olivas Park Drive; right to Ventura Harbor entrance at Harbor Boulevard; continue straight onto Spinnaker Drive.)

• *Channel Islands National Park Visitor Center*, 1901 Spinnaker Drive, Ventura. (805) 644-8262. Open daily, 8 A.M.–5:30 P.M. Free.
• *Island Packers*, 1867 Spinnaker Drive, Ventura. (805) 642-1393. Trips to all five islands in the Channel Islands National Park. Schedules vary, call for reservations: (805) 642-1393. Information: (805) 642-7688. Whale-watch trips, December 26–April.

Attractions in the Oxnard Area

CHANNEL ISLANDS HARBOR

(Exit U.S. Highway 101 at Victoria Avenue; south to harbor at intersection of Channel Islands Boulevard.)

• *Visitor Center at Channel Islands Harbor*, 3600 South Harbor Boulevard, Suite 215, Oxnard. (West on Channel Islands Boulevard to South Harbor Boulevard; left to center.) (805) 985-4852. Open Tuesday–Sunday, 10 A.M.–3 P.M.
• *Channel Islands Landing*, 3821 South Victoria Avenue, Oxnard. (805) 985-6059. Open Monday–Friday, 8 A.M.–6:30 P.M.; Saturday and Sunday, 8:30 A.M.–5:30 P.M. Sailboat rentals, 14-foot to 27-foot boats, start at $10 an hour.
• *Cisco's Sportfishing*, 4151 South Victoria Avenue, Oxnard. (805) 985-8511. Full-day sportfishing trips leave at 2 A.M. Adults, $45; 11 and under, $29.50. Three-quarter-day trips leave at 6 A.M. and 7 A.M. Adults, $25; 11 and under, $12.50. Whale-watch trips between December 26 and April, 9 A.M. and 2 P.M. $15 per person.
• *Fisherman's Wharf*, corner of Channel Islands Boulevard and Victoria Avenue.

CIVIL ENGINEER CORPS/SEABEE MUSEUM, Naval Construction Battalion Center, Port Hueneme. (Exit U.S. Highway 101 at Vinyard Avenue; south to Oxnard Boulevard; left to Gonzales Road; right to Ventura Road; left to museum south of Channel Islands Boulevard.) (805) 982-4493. Open Monday–Friday, 8 A.M.–4:30 P.M.; Saturday, 9 A.M.–4:30 P.M.; Sunday, 12:30 P.M.–4:30 P.M. Free.

McGRATH STATE BEACH, 2211 Harbor Boulevard, Oxnard. (Exit U.S. Highway 101 at Victoria Avenue; south to Gonzales Road; right to

Harbor Boulevard; left to entrance.) (805) 654-4611. Open daily. Day-use fee, $3.

For More Information

Oxnard Convention and Visitors Bureau, 400 Esplanade Drive, Suite 100, Oxnard, CA 93030; (805) 485-8833.

Ventura Visitors and Convention Bureau, 785 South Seaward Avenue, Ventura, CA 93001; (805) 648-2075.

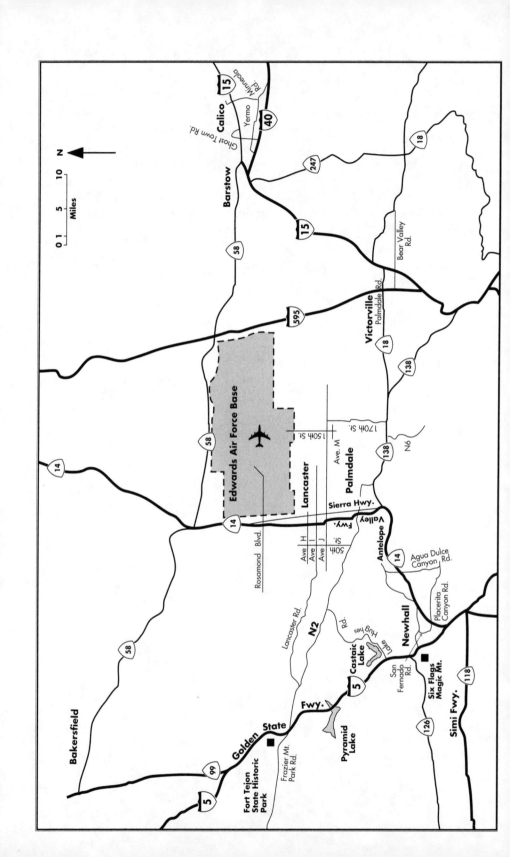

7

North of Los Angeles

Most people think of Los Angeles County and its 11 million residents as one huge urban landscape. But wide-open spaces still do exist at the north end of the county in the Santa Clarita and Antelope valleys. Together with the desert communities of Barstow and Victorville in San Bernardino County, the region north of Los Angeles holds many surprises for family outings.

This high desert terrain is largely arid and can be downright hot during summer months. Climate aside, the landscape is harshly beautiful. Its parks offer all forms of recreation and will fascinate youngsters with unique geological formations and breathtaking displays of beauty when wildflowers bloom in spring.

Man-made attractions north of Los Angeles include such varied destinations as spaceflight facilities, two historic cowboy museums, and one of Southern California's most popular theme parks.

This chapter is divided into three sections, each requiring at least a day to see its highlights. The relatively long distances between attractions means you will need a car and several days to cover them all. If you decide to spend a night, you'll find ample accommodations at reasonable prices in each of the three areas. Whether you make a series of weekend visits or one extended stay, the region north of Los Angeles will prove to be a hidden treasure of family recreation resources.

SANTA CLARITA VALLEY AND THE TEHACHAPI MOUNTAINS
From the "Revolution" to the Civil War

As any child from Southern California can tell you, the "Revolution" in Santa Clarita Valley has nothing to do with a political crisis. It's the loop-the-loop roller coaster at Magic Mountain amusement park. Families visiting this valley area in northern Los Angeles County will find more than a revolution waiting for them. Aside from the rugged, rocky beauty of many of its mountainous parks, you'll see the spot where gold was first discovered in California, the ranch-house estate of a silent-screen cowboy star, and a Civil War–era fort where volunteers reenact battles. It all adds up to several days of family fun.

Six Flags Magic Mountain has carved out its place among Southern California's amusement parks by offering an array of dizzying, spine-tingling roller coasters. With ride names like Colossus, Shock Wave, and Ninja, you begin to get the picture. For Southern California kids, being able to say you rode them is like earning a badge of courage. On Ninja you streak by on sleek, black trains suspended from an overhead track, on Shock Wave you stand up through the loops, and Colossus is just what it says, the world's largest dual-track wooden roller coaster. Tidal Wave combines a roller coaster with white-water thrills that will leave you very wet. Height requirements for passengers are posted in front of all ride lines and at the main ticket booth. Make sure the kids are tall enough to go on a ride (generally 42–48 inches) before you wait in line.

Not all Magic Mountain's thrills come on roller coasters. With FreeFall, you ride in a cage down a ten-story drop, while Z-Force lets you experience an upside-down stall in a Navy fighter jet. Water adventures at Roaring Rapids, Log Jammer, and Jet Stream help you cool off on a hot day. In all, there are more than a hundred rides, shows, and attractions within the park's 260 well-landscaped acres.

When it's time to rest, visit the dolphin and sea lion shows at the Aqua Theatre or see one of the park's changing performances. There's a fireworks show nightly during summer. You'll find food concessions and shady resting spots throughout the park.

Take younger children to Bugs Bunny World, a six-acre section of the park designed for kids under 54 inches tall. Scaled-down rides and adventures include Baron Von Fudd's mini prop planes, Road Runner racer cars, and a pint-size thrill ride called the Wile E. Coyote Coaster. Next door at Foghorn Leghorn's Animal Farm and Petting Zoo, kids get to touch barnyard animals, miniature horses, and birds. More exotic animals perform in "Animal Chatter," a touch and see show held nearby at the Valencia Falls Pavilion. A big attraction for younger children, too, is the Grand Carousel near the park's entrance. A ride on the restored 1912 merry-go-round reminds you how tame amusement parks used to be.

Three unique parks in the southern Santa Clarita Valley offer quieter, less expensive adventures. You'll find each one off Antelope Valley Freeway (14) as it heads east from Interstate 5.

At **Placerita Canyon State and County Park** you'll see the "Oak of the Golden Dream." Legend has it that this is the spot where a hungry sheepherder awoke from dreaming of finding gold and discovered gold flakes clinging to the roots of a wild onion he dug up nearby. That 1842 discovery brought hundreds of prospectors to the area, but the gold soon played out. Today, few Californians realize, as they drive through the foothills of the San Gabriel Mountains near the southern end of Highway 14, that this was the spot where gold was first discovered in California.

Now the site is in a pleasant canyon park with picnic tables under spreading oak trees and eight hiking trails, one of which is paved for wheel chair and stroller access. Many television shows and movies have been shot in the park, going all the way back to *The Adventures of Robin Hood* with Errol Flynn. Visit the Nature Center on the west side of the park, where there are exhibits of local animals, rocks, and plants. In low glass cases, kids come eye to eye with a live rattlesnake, fuzzy tarantulas, and lizards. A small gift shop in the center sells books and inexpensive nature-related items. Every Saturday and Sunday at 1 P.M., rangers present live animal shows in the center's classroom or patio. Kids will learn about such animals as hawks, rabbits, and snakes at the free shows.

From the Nature Center, walk the half-mile Heritage Trail to see the oak near where gold was discovered. Where the trail passes under a nearby road, murals on the tunnel wall depict the area's history from the Alliklik Indians to the missionaries and gold prospectors. After winter rains, you'll find pollywogs in the stream nearby. Another favorite is the half-mile Ecology Trail, which features the park's plants and animals, while the short Hillside Trail gives a good view of the park. Ask for self-guided trail brochures at the center.

William S. Hart Park a few miles west of Placerita Canyon enshrines the memory of the movies' first cowboy superstar. Hart, a silent screen star, built the home in 1925 when he retired from making westerns. Today the house is a museum and the 250 acres that surround it are a county park. Near the park entrance there's a shaded picnic area, restrooms, and a small ranch house filled with Hart's movie memorabilia. Pick up a nature trail guide and walk up the winding path to the house. On the way you'll pass the dog graveyard and you may spot some of the buffalo herd that roams the grounds.

Take a guided tour of the Spanish-revival–style mansion to see Hart's original furnishings, including Indian artifacts and a fine collection of western art by Hart's friends, Charles Russell and Frederic Remington. For kids, one of the most interesting stops on the tour is the upstairs living room where a huge buffalo head ("Clyde") hangs over the fireplace and a Kodiak bearskin rug with a gaping toothy mouth lies on the floor. The "dogs' bedroom" fascinates children too with its two sofa dog beds and photos of the Great Danes that lived there. Outside, kids are most interested in the animals that live in corrals. Children can feed any of the animals (horses, goats, mules, ducks, and deer) that come to the fence. You can buy food for the animals in the gift shop.

If you visit Hart Park on a Sunday afternoon, walk over to the **Saugus Train Station** next door. The little depot was a busy Southern Pacific train station in Saugus at the turn of the century, and was moved to this site by the Santa Clarita Valley Historical Society in 1980 to save it from demolition. The station agent's office is furnished as it was in the early 1900s, with a telegraph key, kerosene lanterns, and a crank telephone. A separate baggage room has a freight cart with luggage on it that kids can try picking up to see how heavy bags used to be. Elsewhere in the small museum, children can pound acorns with Indian grinding tools, ring a bell from a steam engine, and look through a window into a diorama that depicts gold-mining techniques used in the valley a hundred years ago. A steam engine and tender sit on the tracks outside the station. Nearby, the Santa Clarita Historical Society is developing a heritage park that will include a schoolhouse, chapel, and several early-twentieth-century homes when it is completed.

Vasquez Rocks County Park, a few miles to the east along Highway 14, is best saved for another day of picnicking and hiking, preferably during the cool months. Giant slabs of sandstone that have been compressed and thrust up by earthquakes dominate the park. Rising 150 feet and tilted at 60-degree angles, the dramatic rock outcrops have formed the background for dozens of western movies. The rocks were named after Mexican bandit Tiburcio Vasquez, who is said to have hidden in their caves from the law in the 1870s. Kids today like to explore these caves, but be careful not to let them climb too high. Along the Geology Trail, you'll be able to scramble over a number of low caves and sedimentary rocks that are some 8 million to 15 million years old. Keep young children off the high rocks where on weekends you'll often see climbers descending by ropes. There are unshaded picnic tables near the parking lot, but you should be able to find more interesting rock tables along the trails.

Back along Golden State Freeway (5), family activities take on a nautical flavor at two large reservoirs less than an hour from Los Angeles.

Castaic Lake is Los Angeles County's largest recreation area with 9,000 acres and two lakes. The main reservoir has two arms; the east arm is open to boats with a 20-mph speed limit, and the west arm is for waterskiing and power boating. You can rent fishing boats at the dock. At the adjacent Afterbay Lagoon, you'll be able to swim, use nonpowered boats, and fish from the shoreline. You can rent sail-, row-, and paddle boats, as well as canoes and sailboards at the lagoon. Both lakes are stocked with trout during winter. Around the lagoon is a green carpet of grass with picnic tables under large wooden canopies. Food concessions in the park sell snacks and you'll find fast food restaurants along Castaic Road between the lake and the freeway.

Pyramid Lake sits like a bright blue jewel, nestled in a valley in the Tehachapi Mountains a few miles north along Golden State Freeway. The lake gets its name from the 250-foot pyramid-shaped rock south of the dam that was cut from a ridge during construction of old Highway 99 during the 1930s. You'll need to bring or rent a boat to enjoy this lake because much of its 21-mile shoreline is inaccessible by foot or by car. There are boat-in picnic sites and swimming beaches around the lake, but you can drive to the campgrounds. Rent boats for skiing, fishing, or cruising at the marina. The lake is stocked with fish throughout the year and is known as a prime striped bass fishing area.

While you'll want to visit the lakes during the warm months, **Mount Pinos,** a few miles north, is good for hiking any time of year and is especially fun for kids in winter. Between mid-December and April, this area is a favorite snow-play site for families from Los Angeles because it's only an hour away and doesn't involve mountain driving. All you have to do to reach snow is drive north on Golden State Freeway to Frazier Park Road, then head west on mostly straight, gently rising roads to a parking lot on Mount Pinos at the mountain's 8,000-foot elevation level. At the Chula Vista Campground the kids can sled and make a snowman. If the parking lot is full, as quickly happens after a fresh snowfall, park along the road (on the downhill side only) and walk back to Chula Vista or to either McGill or Mount Pinos, the other two roadside campgrounds. If you can't get to one of these campgrounds on a crowded day and have to find a place to sled along the road, keep in mind that most of the area is private property and you will need to respect owners' fences. Bring your own sleds because there is no place to rent them nearby.

Cross-country skiing is popular in this area, where there are more than 25 miles of ski trails. You can rent skis, boots, and poles, and also buy sleds, toboggans, and snow accessories at **Frazier Ski and Pack** in the town of Frazier Park. The store offers ski instruction on weekends and holidays with classes for beginners through advanced. Children and adults learn together.

In summer, visit Mount Pinos to hike, picnic, fish, or camp. Stop at **Chuchupate Ranger Station** on Lockwood Valley Road in Frazier Park for maps and information about the area. Bring a picnic to Chula Vista Campground for dining under tall pine trees. You can buy sandwiches and other picnic supplies in Frazier Park on the way up the mountain. McGill Campground nearby has good hiking trails and a short nature trail. Bring a fishing pole or rent equipment to fish for trout in Cuddy Creek. The creek has been dammed just west of Frazier Park by Frazier Ski and Pack, which stocks the waters and charges a small fishing fee. You also can buy bait and tackle from the store.

A short drive farther north on Golden State Freeway brings you to **Fort Tejon State Historic Park.** The park is about seventy miles north of Los Angeles in the high Tejon Pass that cuts through the Tehachapi Mountains to the huge San Joaquin Valley in the north. Fort Tejon once guarded the northern supply routes to Los Angeles. In the 1850s, it held more than twenty buildings and two hundred men, mostly members of the First U.S. Dragoons, plus a camel corps. The trusty dromedaries were used to transport supplies through the dry valleys below the fort.

To help bring history alive for the kids, visit the fort on the first Sunday of any month from 10 A.M. to 4 P.M. Docents dress in period costumes and reenact fort life in the 1850s. Men in dragoon uniforms march with their polished muskets, while others make adobe bricks or work as blacksmiths. Women churn butter and bake bread on an open hearth to share with visitors. You can tour the fort's restored buildings and picnic at tables on the grassy grounds.

For a different kind of living history, visit the fort on the third Sunday of any month between April and October to see Civil War battles reenacted. Some 250 to 500 Civil War buffs, clothed in authentic blue and gray uniforms, use muskets and cannons to re-create historic battles. Bring chairs and blankets to sit behind barriers along the parade grounds. An announcer gives a blow-by-blow description of the action. Between battles, go on a one-hour living-history tour of the Union and Confederate camps. The link between Fort Tejon and the Civil War is an authentic one. Fifteen officers who served at Fort Tejon later became generals in the Civil War on both sides of the conflict. The fort arranges interpretive tours on other days for schools and other groups.

Attractions

CASTAIC LAKE STATE RECREATION AREA, 32132 Ridge Route Road, Castaic. (Exit Golden State Freeway [5] at Lake Hughes Road; east to Ridge Route Road; left to entrance.) (805) 257-4050. Open daily, dawn to dusk. Parking: $3.

FORT TEJON STATE HISTORIC PARK, Lebec. (Exit Golden State Freeway [5] at Fort Tejon Road; cross freeway west to entrance.) (818) 248-6692. Open daily, 10 A.M.–4 P.M. Adults, $1; children, 50 cents. Daily life historical reenactments, first Sunday of the month, year round, 10 A.M.–4 P.M. Civil War battle reenactments, third Sunday of the month, April–October, 10 A.M.–4 P.M. To arrange interpretive tours for groups, call (805) 265-5004.

MOUNT PINOS and FRAZIER PARK, about seventy miles north of Los Angeles in the Tehachapi Mountains. (Exit Golden State Freeway [5] at Frazier Mountain Park Road; west to attractions.)

• Chuchupate Ranger Station, 34580 Lockwood Valley Road, Frazier Park. (Exit Golden State Freeway [5] at Frazier Mountain Park Road; west to Lockwood Valley Road; left to station.) (805) 245-3731. Open daily, 8 A.M.–4:30 P.M.
• Frazier Ski and Pack, 3620 Mount Pinos Way, Frazier Park. (Exit Golden State Freeway [5] at Frazier Mountain Park Road; west to Monterey Trail; right one block

to Mount Pinos Way.) (805) 245-3438. Open Monday–Friday, 9 A.M.–6 P.M.; weekends and holidays (with snow), 7 A.M.–6 P.M. Cross-country ski lessons, winter weekends and holidays, 9 A.M. and 1 P.M. From $25 to $35.

PLACERITA CANYON COUNTY AND STATE PARK (PLACERITA NATURE CENTER), 19152 Placerita Canyon Road, Newhall. (Exit Antelope Valley Freeway [14] at Placerita Canyon Road; east to entrance.) (805) 259-7721. Park open daily, 9 A.M.–5 P.M. Free.

PYRAMID LAKE RECREATION AREA, about 55 miles north of Los Angeles. (Exit Golden State Freeway [5] at Hungry Valley Road; follow signs to lake.) Marina: (805) 257-2790. Open daily. Free.

SAUGUS TRAIN STATION, 24107 San Fernando Road, Newhall. (Exit Antelope Valley Freeway [14] at San Fernando Road; north to entrance.) (805) 254-1275. Open Sunday, 2–4 P.M. Free.

SIX FLAGS MAGIC MOUNTAIN, 26101 Magic Mountain Parkway, Valencia. (Exit Golden State Freeway [5] at Magic Mountain Parkway; west to entrance.) (805) 255-4100 or (818) 367-5965. Open daily from Memorial Day to Labor Day; weekends and holidays during rest of the year. Closing hours vary, but park always opens at 10 A.M. One-price unlimited-use ticket: adults, $21; children under 48 inches tall and seniors, $10; under age 2, free. Parking, $4.

VASQUEZ ROCKS COUNTY PARK, 10701 West Escondido Canyon Road, Saugus. (Exit Antelope Valley Freeway [14] at Agua Dulce Canyon Road; north to Escondido Canyon Road; right to entrance.) Open daily. Free.

WILLIAM S. HART REGIONAL PARK, 24151 San Fernando Road, Newhall. (Exit Antelope Valley Freeway [14] at San Fernando Road; north to entrance.) (805) 254-4584. Park hours: daily, 9:30 A.M.–sunset. Guided tours of museum every half hour. Summer tour hours: Wednesday–Sunday, 10 A.M.–3:30 P.M. Winter tour hours: (mid-September–mid-June) Wednesday–Friday, 10 A.M.–12:30 P.M.; Saturday and Sunday, 11 A.M.–3:30 P.M. Free.

For More Information

Santa Clarita Valley Chamber of Commerce, 24275 Walnut Street, Newhall, CA 91321; (805) 259-4787.

ANTELOPE VALLEY
Space Adventures and Earthly Pleasures

Named for the large herds of prong-horned antelope that once roamed the area, Antelope Valley in northern Los Angeles County now claims aerospace and agriculture as its predominant attributes. Children who visit Antelope Valley and its principal town of Lancaster are able to learn firsthand about these industries. Whether it's touring NASA's flight research facility or learning to pick fresh fruit, kids have fun exploring the valley's wideranging attractions.

For a unique Antelope Valley experience, bring the kids between March and May to see the surrounding valley floor carpeted with colorful desert wildflowers. There are more than a dozen wildflower preserves near the city. You can picnic and hike in most of the sanctuaries.

To locate the best blooms, stop by Lancaster's **Wildflower Center** in the City of Lancaster Museum and Art Gallery, where you can pick up maps and see displays of labeled flowers. Hosted by the Lancaster Woman's Club, the Wildflower Center is open for a few weeks each April when the wildflowers are in bloom. The center has a telephone (number changes each year) so you also can call to find out where the flowers are in bloom.

The best place to see California's state flower is the **Antelope Valley-California Poppy Reserve** about 15 miles west of Lancaster. During April, the poppy's prime flowering time, the preserve is open daily between 9 A.M. and 4 P.M. Kids are intrigued by the Interpretive Center, which is built into a hill for better insulation from summer desert heat. Inside you'll see displays of desert flowers and paintings. Pick up a map at the center and walk along the flower-lined trails in the 1,760-acre park. You can't pick the flowers, of course, but kids like finding as many different kinds as possible. Some blooms are called belly flowers because they are so small you have to bend down close to appreciate them. Young beginning photographers have good success shooting these bright, stationary targets.

If your children like to fish, try to combine your visit to the preserve with the Kid's Fishing Derby, held annually on a Saturday in late April or early May in **Apollo Park** on West Avenue G in Lancaster. The park has three lakes, named after the Apollo 11 astronauts who first landed on the moon: Armstrong, Aldrin, and Collins. On Derby day, kids under the age of 15 bring their own fishing tackle and bait to try their luck between 7 A.M. and 11 A.M. Prizes are awarded to different age groups at this free event. Of course, you can fish at the park any time of year. Bring a picnic to enjoy

SOUTHERN CALIFORNIA FOR KIDS

under the pine trees. There are barbecues and children's play areas nearby. A paved biking and hiking trail leads through the park. Be sure to see the Apollo space capsule on display that was loaned to the park by the Smithsonian Institution.

On the other side of town, the **Antelope Valley Indian Museum** interests youngsters as much with its architecture as its collections. It is built around huge boulders whose surfaces form some interior elements of the museum. One part of a butte serves as a natural stone floor for an upper-level room. The exterior of the Swiss-chaletlike building is decorated with paintings of Indians and Indian symbols.

The museum was the former home of Howard Arden Edwards, a Hollywood set designer and artist who was fascinated by Indians. He painted the ceilings throughout the home, most notably in the living room, where there are large paintings of kachina dolls. Called Kachina Hall, this room contains a collection of kachina dolls, as well as Indian baskets, pottery, and blankets. Kids like climbing up steps between boulders to the upper-level California Hall, where they can hold on to tree branch handrails to circle the uneven, rock-floored room. Artifacts in the room's cases include stone tools, arrowheads, and shell-bead jewelry.

Be sure to visit Joshua Cottage on the museum grounds, which has a table of artifacts for kids to touch. They can grind acorns into meal with stone tools and try their hand at starting a fire by twirling a wooden stick. An Indian artist usually displays and sells Southwestern Indian jewelry in another room in the cottage. You can buy Indian art at the gift shop, too, along with soft drinks. A half-mile nature trail that leaves from the parking lot points out desert plants used by the Indians. Because of limited funds, the museum is open only one weekend each month.

Combine your trip to the museum with a visit to **Saddleback Butte State Park,** less than five miles east. The 3,000-acre park was established to preserve the Joshua trees and other native plants and animals in the area. Picnic among the spikey trees and hike along the half-mile Joshua Trail. A printed trail guide explains how the trees adapt to changes in the desert environment. Along the trail you may be lucky enough to see some high desert fauna too, such as road runners, desert tortoises, and kit foxes. There's a campground in the park with 50 sites. From there, you can hike along a clearly marked 1½-mile trail to the top of 3,651-foot Saddleback Peak, east of the saddle. You'll have a good view east to the Mojave Desert, south to the San Gabriel Mountains, and north to Edwards Air Force Base.

Well known as the landing site of America's space shuttles, **Edwards Air Force Base** has two attractions that visitors can tour free, both more suited for older children. NASA's **Ames-Dryden Flight Research Facility** conducts 90-minute tours twice a day on weekdays. No reservations are required for groups fewer than ten people. The center is the nation's main flight-test facility. You'll start the guided tour with a 25-minute film on the history of flight research, then walk through hangars housing aircraft used in current testing. You may view the X-29 forward-swept-wing aircraft or Mission Adaptive Wing aircraft, which varies its wing angle during flight. You'll also see some "hangar queens," retired aircraft that once were used for experimental flights. Among these is a leggy lunar-landing module used to train Apollo astronauts. At the visitors center, a small aeronautics museum displays aircraft models. Kids like to pick up phones at the displays to listen to the history of each plane. A gift shop near the entrance sells astronaut ice cream, shuttle patches, and other space memorabilia.

The Air Force base offers group tours once a month by reservation to visitors ages 13 and over. Teenagers enjoy this varied, guided tour, which lasts from 9 A.M. to 3 P.M. It includes a bus tour of the flight line to see operational jet fighters such as the F-111 and F-4, and a walking tour to see new planes such as the B-1 bomber and the F-16. A pilot or navigator accompanies the group to explain the characteristics of each plane. You'll eat lunch at the Officer's Club or the NCO Club, and then visit the altitude chamber where volunteers sit in the pilot's seat to demonstrate how the chamber is used. Kids are interested in examining pressure suits used by pilots over the last forty years, including those worn by astronauts today and a suit similar to one used by Chuck Yeager when he broke the sound barrier at Edwards in 1947. The tour ends with a demonstration of military working dogs used by the security police force.

For more earthbound experiences, head a few miles south of Lancaster along the Pearblossom Highway (138). Some of Southern California's finest fruit grows in orchards near the town of Littlerock. You'll find stands that sell this produce on both sides of the highway near town. In fall you can buy fresh apples, pears, and pumpkins; in spring and summer, it's peaches, apricots, and cherries.

Try picking your own fruit to add more adventure to the outing. Kids love climbing ladders to choose the ripest produce, and they'll never forget how fruit grows once they've actually picked it. You'll see lots of signs along Highway 138 directing you to **Littlerock U-Pick Orchards.** You may want to stop at the Littlerock Chamber of Commerce for a map that locates the more established farms. Wherever you pick, you will need to bring containers to take your fruit home. Farms provide ladders and buckets for picking. As an added bonus, you're allowed to eat all you want while you pick.

When you're finished, take your fruit along for a picnic in a pine forest at **Devil's Punchbowl Natural Area Park,** a few miles southeast of Littlerock. The park's most interesting feature is the deep bowllike depression piled with pink, tan, and white slabs of rock, the result of two earthquake fault lines that meet there and move in opposite directions. Exhibits at the Interpretive Center near the parking lot explain this geological phenomenon and describe the natural history of the area. Low display cases allow young children to see and hear live exhibits such as a rattlesnake, lizards, and a tiny deer mouse in his tunneled house. Shelves hold marine fossils, evidence of the sea that once covered this inland park.

From the Interpretive Center, walk a short way to the rim of the bowl. Take the one-mile loop trail that leads 300 feet down from the rim to the bottom of the punchbowl. A stream with waterfalls and tall sycamores awaits you at the bottom. Or walk a shorter, flatter trail, called the Piñon Pathway, through a pine forest to see other views of the punchbowl from above. There are picnic tables among the pines near the rim.

A few miles east in Valyermo, St. Andrew's Priory opens its doors during the last weekend in October each year for the Valyermo Fall Festival. There's entertainment for the entire family at the 500-acre Benedictine monastery, including Irish folk music and drama productions in the 400-seat outdoor theater. For youngsters, the festival's Children's World features a petting zoo, face painting, and art projects. Clowns entertain the crowds throughout the grounds. There's plenty of food, including a favorite with most kids: Belgian waffles.

Attractions

AMES-DRYDEN FLIGHT RESEARCH FACILITY, Edwards Air Force Base, Edwards. (Exit Antelope Valley Freeway [14] at Rosamond Boulevard; east 19 miles to Lilly Avenue at Edwards Air Force Base; right and follow signs to center.) (805) 258-3460. Tours on weekdays, 10:15 A.M. and 1:15 P.M., except on shuttle-landing days and federal holidays. No reservations required for fewer than ten people. Free.

ANTELOPE VALLEY-CALIFORNIA POPPY RESERVE, 15101 West Lancaster Road, Lancaster. (Exit Antelope Valley Freeway [14] at Avenue I; west and continue when Avenue I becomes Lancaster Road to reserve at 151st Street.) (805) 724-1180 (only during bloom season). Open only during bloom season, approximately between March 15 and May 15, daily, 9 A.M.–4 P.M. $3 per car.

ANTELOPE VALLEY INDIAN MUSEUM, 15701 East Avenue M, Lancaster. (Exit Antelope Valley Freeway [14] southbound at Avenue J; east 17 miles to 150th Street; right to Avenue M; left to museum. Exit Antelope Valley Freeway [14] northbound at 20th Street; north to Avenue J: follow directions above.) (805) 942-0662. Open October–July, the second weekend of the month, 10 A.M.–3 P.M. $3 per car.

APOLLO PARK, 4555 West Avenue G, Lancaster. (Exit Antelope Valley Freeway [14] at Avenue H; west to 50th Street; right and follow road around General William J. Fox Airport to park at end of road.) (805) 945-8290 or (805) 259-7721. Open daily. Free. Kid's Fishing Derby, first Saturday in May or last Saturday in April, 7–11 A.M. Free.

DEVIL'S PUNCHBOWL NATURAL AREA PARK, 28000 Devil's Punchbowl Road, Pearblossom. (Exit Antelope Valley Freeway [14] at Pearblossom Highway [138]; east to Longview Road [N6]; right seven miles following N6 through several jogs to parking lot.) (805) 944-2743 or (805) 944-9151. Open daily, dawn to dusk. Free.

EDWARDS AIR FORCE BASE, Edwards. (Exit Antelope Valley Freeway [14] at Rosamond Boulevard; east to entrance.) (805) 277-5517. Tours for ages 13 and over given one day each month only, 9 A.M.–3 P.M. Call for reservations. Free.

LITTLEROCK U-PICK ORCHARDS, along Pearblossom Highway (138), Littlerock. (Exit Antelope Valley Freeway [14] at Pearblossom Highway [138]; continue about nine miles to Littlerock.) Open daily.

SADDLEBACK BUTTE STATE PARK, at 170th Street East and Avenue J., Lancaster. (Exit Antelope Valley Freeway [14] southbound at Avenue J; east 19 miles to park. Exit Antelope Valley Freeway [14] northbound at 20th Street; north to Avenue J; right to park.) Open daily, dawn to dusk. $3 day-use fee.

WILDFLOWER CENTER, at City of Lancaster Museum and Art Gallery, 44811 Sierra Highway, Lancaster. (Exit Antelope Valley Freeway [14] at Avenue I; east to Sierra Highway; right to museum.) New telephone number issued each year for operational period in April. Open during wildflower-bloom season in April only, daily, 9 A.M.–3 P.M. Free.

For More Information

Lancaster Chamber of Commerce, 44943 North 10th Street West, Lancaster CA 93534, (805) 948-4518.

Littlerock Chamber of Commerce, 7317 Pearblossom Highway, Littlerock, CA 93543, (805) 944-3333.

VICTORVILLE AND BARSTOW
Cowboys and Indians

For many Southern Californians and visitors, the communities of Victorville and Barstow in the sunbaked Mojave Desert are places to drive by on the way to somewhere else. But those who stop to spend a little time in and around these communities will discover a wealth of family activities. There's a ghost town, museums that bring to life the era of Indians and cowboys, and acres of parkland to explore, all within an hour's drive northeast of Los Angeles.

The best time to visit these two communities is between October and May when the weather is mild and sunny. By contrast, summer temperatures hover above 100 degrees most days. No matter what time of year you go, it's always a good idea to carry water in your car when you head for the desert.

The main attraction for families in Victorville is the **Roy Rogers–Dale Evans Museum.** You can't miss the large brown fortlike building as you drive along Interstate 15. Adults who remember when Roy Rogers was the country's top box-office star will appreciate this museum in a different way than will kids who have never heard of the singing cowboy and his leading lady. Rogers made ninety movies before he started his long television career. The museum is full of photographs, trophies, and mementos of the couple's professional and personal lives. You'll see Roy's horse Trigger and Dale's horse Buttermilk mounted and displayed along with the family dog, Bullet. There are cases of costumes, guns, arrowheads, and scale-model western vehicles. Stuffed and mounted animals (even a rare albino raccoon) are displayed in habitat exhibits. Young children enjoy trying to identify all the animals. Older kids like seeing Roy's speedboats and cars, including a white Pontiac parade car with cow horns on the hood, guns for door handles, and silver dollars embedded in the dash. At the Happy Trails gift shop you'll find western-theme gifts and Roy Rogers and Dale Evans souvenirs.

After walking through the museum, you may want to make your own "happy trails" over to **Mojave Narrows Regional Park,** on the southeast side of Victorville. If you plan to picnic there, you can buy the makings at fast food restaurants or markets near the museum along I-15. This 860-acre preserve is located along the Mojave River, which once served as a trail through the high desert for Indians, explorers, and settlers. Today the desert park offers plenty of watery pleasures at two lakes surrounded by tall cottonwood trees. Picnic tables with barbecues are near the lakes. Fish for trout in stocked Horseshoe Lake or rent pedalboats and aqua cycles at the boathouse to take out to the island. Rent horses or go on a hayride at the park's equestrian center. A network of trails winds through the park. Every Father's Day weekend, the park hosts its Huck Finn Jubilee, a family festival with country and bluegrass entertainment, a raft-building contest, and a crafts fair.

A 40-minute drive north on I-15 brings you to Barstow, the largest town in the Mojave Desert. Three highways head out through the desert from the city. Barstow is also a major railroad hub, for many years the crossroads of the Union Pacific and Santa Fe railways.

A good place to start exploring the area is at the **California Desert Information Center.** Managed cooperatively by the Bureau of Land Management and the Barstow Area Chamber of Commerce, it is located on Barstow Road in a buff-colored building called the Barstow Way Station. The center distributes maps and information about recreation, sight-seeing, and the ecology of the Mojave Desert region.

Interactive exhibits at the center interpret the desert environment. You can touch Old Woman Meteorite, a 6,070-pound hunk of iron that fell out of the sky into the desert. You'll find desert plants the Indians used for food and medicine on a low table nearby. Kids can touch and taste these plants, including mesquite, sagebrush, and chia. A push-button display informs you about such desert hazards as poisonous snakes, and you can test your Desert IQ at another interactive display. Near the entrance there's a small shop with desert books for sale.

Two blocks up the street is the **Mojave River Valley Museum,** where you'll see artifacts created by prehistoric travelers and historic settlers along the Mojave River Valley. There's a fine collection of Indian baskets and arrowheads. One case features stone artifacts from the Calico Early Man site located near Barstow. Kids can pound acorns with an array of Indian grinding tools on the floor. Children are also fascinated by the exhibit of a human skeleton of a desert "scout," lying in a dirt grave just as an archaeologist might find him. More recent artifacts include models of space-tracking equipment from the Goldstone Tracking Station north of Barstow. A gem collection shows desert minerals such as agates and turquoise, both polished and in their natural state. A small gift shop carries educational toys and books for kids. Outside, notice the small jail, once used to transport prisoners by wagon.

Across the street at the intersection of Barstow Road and Virginia Way, recently refurbished **Centennial Park** contains some outdoor exhibits from the city's past. Kids can climb on the back of a red Sante Fe caboose, scramble over a World War II tank, and examine rocks in a mining exhibit.

On a third corner of this same intersection, **Dana Park** has more shade trees, plus picnic tables, barbecues, and an area with play equipment. Centerpiece of the park is the Al Vigil Community Swim Center, an indoor swimming pool open to the public year round.

From the museum, go back to I-15 and head north to Barstow's Main Street exit, where you'll find a popular stop for traveling families, **Barstow Station.** This collection of restaurants and shops is housed in a group of old railroad cars. A McDonald's restaurant uses converted train cars for its dining room, and a bakery in another railroad car sells sandwiches and fresh-baked pastries. A large gift shop in a building that connects the cars sells candy and inexpensive souvenirs. The station makes a good lunch stop, with food and a bit of entertainment combined in a 1900s train depot atmosphere.

Once you're fortified, head about ten miles northeast of town to **Calico Ghost Town,** a thriving silver-mining camp in the 1800s. Today the town still boasts many of its original buildings, whose restoration was begun in 1951 by Walter Knott, founder of Knott's Berry Farm. He later turned the town over to San Bernardino County, which now administers it as a regional park.

Walk along the wooden sidewalks on Main Street and you'll get a real feeling for the Old West. The street is lined with shops, many of them in original buildings, that re-create nineteenth-century enterprises. Children are particularly interested in the general store which sells candy in bins, and the bottle shop that is actually made of bottles. Visit the town's small museum to see life-size dioramas of a barbershop, blacksmith's workshop, and other Calico enterprises as they used to be. At the top of the street, look in on the old schoolhouse and try out its schoolyard play equipment. Next door there is an ice-cream parlor and snack shop. If you're really hungry, Calico House at the other end of town serves such hearty western specialties as Old Miner's Stew.

Head over to the Maggie Mine for a walking tour of the played-out mine, and take a short ride on the Calico & Odessa Railroad. You can buy a combination ticket for these attractions. Stop at the Calikage Playhouse for an old-fashioned melodrama where you'll boo the villain and cheer on the hero. There's a campground and picnic area in a shady canyon next to the town.

For an even more authentic 1880s experience, rent horses from a nearby stable and ride up to Calico. Guides at **Pan McCue Ranch** will lead you on a three-hour ride that includes a free half-hour look at the Ghost Town. The ranch also offers hayrides and shorter trail rides through scenic high desert open country.

You'll go much further back in time at the **Calico Early Man Archaeological Site.** Archaeologists and volunteers have been excavating this site since 1964, hoping to find some of the earliest traces of humans in the Western Hemisphere. They have found more than 11,000 chipped rocks buried deep in alluvial soil that may have been tools made 200,000 years ago. Their findings are controversial because the earliest evidence of humans found by archaeologists working at most other American sites suggests that people first came to this continent from Asia between 10,000 and 20,000 years ago. No skeletal remains have been found at Calico. On either a guided or self-guided tour of the site, you'll see excavated trenches and pits, some of them more than 25 feet deep. See if your budding archaeologists can spot some of the rocks—believed to be ancient tools—that are visible in the walls and unexcavated columns in the pits.

On the first weekend of every month you can learn to dig at the site. Kids must be teenagers, old enough to carefully wield the dental picks and paint brushes required to do the painstaking work. Even if you don't plan to dig, you can learn more about the site at a small museum in a miner's shack that displays some of the finds and compares them with artifacts found in other parts of the world. Exhibits also explain how stone tools were made.

A fun place for children to eat in the area while learning about more recent history is **Peggy Sue's Nifty 50s Diner,** near the corner of Ghost Town Road and Yermo Road. The menu gets you right into the swing of things, offering such items as Buddy Holly bacon cheeseburgers, Mickey Mouse club sandwiches, and Ozzie and Harriet apple pie. You can sit at a booth or at the counter to order root-beer floats and milk shakes made the old-fashioned way. A jukebox plays Elvis tunes and the walls are covered with black and white photos of 1950s movie stars, including Ronald Reagan. If this restaurant seems more authentic than some fifties diners, it's because the building has housed similar restaurants under different names since 1954. A sign on the door as you leave states: Sorry, Back to the Future.

Instead, you may choose to go further into the past at **Rainbow Basin Natural Area.** The area's multicolored cliffs and twisted rock formations were formed in sedentary layers along ancient lake beds more than 10 million years ago. Paleontologists have found well-preserved fossils of mammals in these layers, such as the oldest North American mastodon, small camels, and saber-toothed tigers. To see the area today, you'll drive through the spectacular striped hills along a narrow four-mile loop road. You can park at turnouts and walk along marked foot trails through some of the colorful canyons. See if you can spot fossils in the layered rocks. Owl Canyon Campground, one mile east, is a convenient place to picnic or spend the night.

Attractions in the Victorville Area

MOJAVE NARROWS REGIONAL PARK, 18000 Yates Road, Victorville. (Exit I-15 two miles south of Victorville at Bear Valley Road; east to Ridge Crest; left to park.) (619) 245-2226. Open daily, 7:30 A.M.–dusk. Parking: $3 per car. Fishing fees: $3 per person 6 and older.

ROY ROGERS–DALE EVANS MUSEUM, 15650 Seneca Road, Victorville. (Exit I-15 at Palmdale Road; west to Kentwood Boulevard; right to Civic Drive; right to corner of Seneca Road and museum.) (619) 243-4547. Open daily, 9 A.M.–5 P.M. Adults, $3; ages 13–16 and seniors, $2; ages 6–12, $1; under 6, free.

Attractions in the Barstow Area

BARSTOW STATION, 1611 East Main Street, Barstow. (Exit I-15 at Main Street; east to station.) (619) 256-8282. Shops open daily, 9 A.M.–10 P.M.; McDonald's open Sunday–Thursday, 6 A.M.–11 P.M.; Friday and Saturday, 6 A.M.–midnight.

CALICO EARLY MAN ARCHAEOLOGICAL SITE, 15 miles northeast of Barstow, Yermo. (Exit I-15 at Minneola Road; follow signs north about 2½ miles on graded dirt roads to entrance.) Open Wednesday, noon–4:30 P.M.; Thursday–Sunday, 8:30 A.M.–4:30 P.M. Guided tours, Wednesday, 1:30 and 3:30 P.M.; Thursday–Sunday, 9:30 and 11:30 A.M., 1:30 and 3:30 P.M. Free. To make reservations for digging on the first weekend of the month, September–May (ages 14 and older), call (818) 355-9884.

CALICO GHOST TOWN, eight miles northeast of Barstow, Yermo. (Exit I-15 at Ghost Town Road; north about three miles to park.) (619) 254-2122. Open daily, 7 A.M.–dusk. Shops open, 9 A.M.–5 P.M. Parking: $3 per car.

CALIFORNIA DESERT INFORMATION CENTER, Barstow Way Station, 831 Barstow Road, Barstow. (Exit I-15 at Barstow Road; north two blocks to center. (619) 256-8617. Open daily, 9 A.M.–5 P.M. Free.

MOJAVE RIVER VALLEY MUSEUM, 270 East Virginia Way, Barstow. (Exit I-15 at Barstow Road; north one block to Virginia Way; left to museum.) (619) 256-5452. Open daily, 11 A.M.–4 P.M. Free. Across the street: **Centennial Park** and **Dana Park.**

PAN McCUE RANCH, 7 miles northeast of Barstow, Box 541, Barstow. (Exit I-15 at Ghost Town Road; north 1.2 miles and follow signs to ranch.) (619) 254-2184. Open, 8 A.M.–one hour before dark. Guided horseback rides: $8 per hour. Children under 3 ride with adult.

PEGGY SUE'S NIFTY 50s DINER, 35654 Yermo Road, Yermo. (Exit I-15 at Ghost Town Road; east half a block to Yermo Road; left to restaurant.) (619) 254-3370. Open Monday–Friday, 5:30 A.M.–9 P.M. (Friday until 10 P.M.); Saturday, 6 A.M.–10 P.M.; Sunday, 6 A.M.–9 P.M.

RAINBOW BASIN NATURAL AREA, 10 miles north of Barstow. (Exit I-15 at State Road 58; west to Fort Irwin Road; north 5½ miles to Fossil Bed Road; follow signs 3 miles to entrance.) Open daily. Free.

For More Information

Barstow Area Chamber of Commerce, 831 Barstow Road, Barstow, CA 92311; (619) 256-8617.

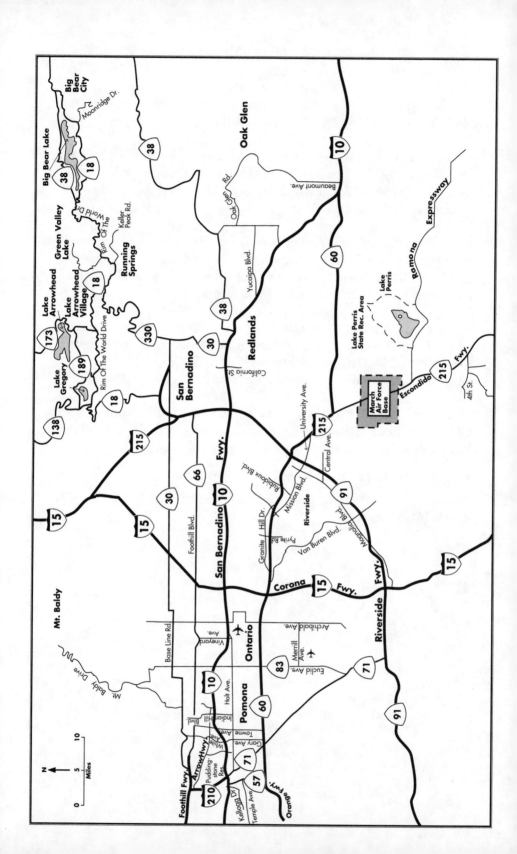

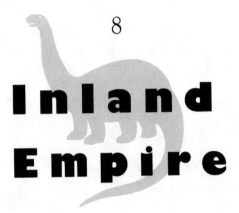

8

Inland Empire

Below the imposing San Bernardino Mountains, Southern California's Inland Empire embraces dozens of communities that have grown up on the wealth of agriculture. From Pomona to Riverside, however, many of the orange groves and lettuce fields have given way to a new crop—suburban homes. With the homes have come families, and with the families have come an increasing variety of things to see and do. From modern planes to vintage trains, from dinosaur digs to living fossils, Inland Empire attractions educate and fascinate kids.

Recreation comes in many different forms in the Inland Empire. Its large regional parks allow families to enjoy boating, fishing, and swimming in several man-made lakes. Above the valley floor, the San Bernardino Mountains present a rich recreational resource throughout the year. Hiking, camping, horseback riding, and biking in the summer give way to downhill and cross-country skiing, snowmobiling, and sledding in the winter.

The Inland Empire is served by several major freeways as well as an international airport, so that travel to and from the area is easy. Public transit within the region is comprehensive, but you will find it easier to maintain your own itinerary with an automobile because so many attractions are widely scattered throughout the region.

In addition to sections on Claremont and Pomona, Riverside, the east Inland Empire, and the San Bernardino Mountains, a separate section covers skiing with kids. Here, you'll discover which ski resorts in the area have special programs for kids and find a few tips on appropriate clothing and travel arrangements. The section includes both downhill and cross-country ski areas in the San Gabriel and San Bernardino mountains.

CLAREMONT AND POMONA
Airplanes and Animals Past and Present

At the west end of the Inland Empire, a grouping of five communities offers a diverse set of hands-on experiences for kids. In the towns of Chino, Ontario, Pomona, Claremont, and San Dimas, children are able to climb into historic and modern airplanes, touch dinosaur bones and live Arabian horses, and tackle some of the most exciting water slides in Southern California. You can easily spend half a day at many of these attractions. They are grouped in this section by location to help you organize the most convenient itinerary for your family.

Start your day in Chino as early as 9 A.M. at the **Planes of Fame Museum** where the kids can see and touch a large collection of historic aircraft. Located outdoors and in hangars at the Chino Airport, the museum displays aircraft spanning the air age from an 1896 Chanute hang glider to jets used in the Vietnam War. World War II aircraft include the only flyable Japanese Zero fighter still in existence and a German jet fighter. Also displayed is a buzz bomb like those that terrified London during the Blitz.

Inside one hangar, kids climb into a Sabre jet cockpit to try out the controls. On weekends they can go inside *Piccadilly Lilly*, a World War II B-17 bomber parked outside the museum. Once inside the aircraft, you'll walk from the tail to the cockpit to see the gunners' turrets and the bomb bay. This plane was featured in the 1960s TV series *Twelve O'Clock High*. Veterans who actually flew B-17s during the war provide the most interesting history lesson at the museum for kids. They tell what it was like to fly the aircraft and they share their scrapbooks of those war years. Every May the museum hosts an air show that features these historic planes. A souvenir shop near the entrance sells model-airplane kits, posters, books, and video cassettes of the air show.

When you leave the museum, turn right from the parking lot and drive to the end of the divided street. From a small parking lot there, you'll be able to see planes taking off and landing at the Chino airport.

For a good place to eat with kids before or after seeing the museum, try **Flo's Airport Café,** a few blocks east of the museum. Since 1963, people from all over California have flown or driven in to enjoy Flo's "down-home cooking." You'll find such specialties as biscuits and gravy, hot beef sandwiches, and homemade cobbler served at reasonable prices.

There's a small grassy park a block north of Flo's that has barbecues, a few small picnic tables, and restrooms. For a whole day's worth of park activities, head one mile south on Euclid to **Prado Regional Park.** The main feature at this pleasant 2,000-acre recreation area is a 60-acre lake that is stocked with trout and channel catfish. You can rent rowboats, pedalboats, and aqua cycles during summer months, or launch your own boat. You'll find picnic shelters around the edges of the lake as well as children's play equipment, a snack bar, and restrooms. One finger of the lake is reserved just for radio control boats. Elsewhere there are soccer and softball fields, a 75-site campground, and an equestrian trail. You can't rent horses, but children can ride ponies in a small corral near the center.

North of Chino, in Ontario, another airport gives kids an educational experience. **Ontario International Airport** is California's fourth-largest airport, and it offers tours to groups of 15 or more. You'll need to make reservations months in advance because the tours are very popular with scout and school groups. On the one-hour walking portion of the tour, kids enter the gate area as if they were taking a flight and learn about metal detectors, ticket counters, and skycaps. They board an airplane too, if one is available. When groups have their own buses, they take a second part of the tour, driving around the perimeter of the airport to see the runways, and by request, the in-flight kitchen and the fire station.

If you aren't taking a tour, it's still possible to see planes taking off and landing. Park along Haven Avenue at the east end of the runway and you'll be right under the flight path for landing jet liners. If the kids get hungry, there's a cafeteria and a snack bar in the main terminal.

There are no picnic facilities at the airport, but less than two miles north is **Cucamonga-Guasti Regional Park.** This 22-acre park has picnic tables, barbecues, and a snack bar. During summer, take the kids to the swim complex where you'll find two water slides and a three-quarter–acre shallow swimming lagoon that is ideal for young children. The park also has a lake where you can fish or rent pedalboats for an afternoon of fun.

For a more down-to-earth tour, visit the **Graber Olive House.** Located on a residential Ontario street, this pleasant complex has an olive-packing factory that dates from 1894, two gift shops, and picnic tables on a spacious lawn. Take a 30-minute guided tour of the historic factory during olive season (mid-October to Christmas). You'll see the vat room where olives are cured in salt brine and watch workers grading the olives by sizes before filling cans. Kids can get up close to see this process. You'll follow the cans as they move along a conveyer belt through the canning machine, and then watch as they are sterilized and labels are applied. There's a small museum adjacent to the factory with antique equipment. You can taste and buy the delicious tree-ripened olives in the gourmet shop, which also sells almonds, candies, and other gift items.

Northeast of Ontario, the picture-postcard university town of Claremont holds several special attractions for families. The **Raymond M. Alf Museum** is a must for kids who like dinosaurs and fossils. Located on the campus of the Webb Schools in Claremont, the museum features fossils collected from around the world, many by high school students. On the main floor in the Hall of Life, you'll discover the scope of life on earth as it's found in fossilized remains. Starting with 3.5-billion-year-old rocks that contain evidence of single-cell life, you'll see ancient plants preserved in stone, dinosaur bones, and skull casts of human ancestors. At a table labeled Please Touch, kids feel dinosaur bones, a mastodon tusk, and compare the weight of heavy fossilized bones with newer bones that haven't absorbed minerals. A fossil pine tree trunk stretches across the floor nearby. Continue around the circular museum to find Egyptian and American Indian artifacts. Kids can grind corn in this area as the Indians did, with stone mortars and pestles.

Downstairs in the Hall of Footprints you'll find slabs of rock imprinted with tracks left behind by animals and insects when the rock was soft mud. Busy rodents, reptiles, camels, horses, elephants, and even spiders left their marks on these slabs. Kids can relate to the size of a brontosaur by sitting in a cast of its huge footprint that is propped upright like a deep chair. Many of the prints are from California, including 15-million-year-old camel and scorpion tracks from Barstow and 10-million-year-old horse hoofprints from Death Valley. A small gift shop near the entrance on the main floor sells dinosaur models, rock jewelry, and science-related toys. The museum is open only during the school year, on weekdays and one Sunday each month. Call for a schedule.

Griswold's Claremont Center, another local institution, is a good place to take hungry kids. The family restaurant offers a Swedish smorgasbord for breakfast, lunch, and dinner daily. Children like being able to choose their own meal from the many selections of salads, meat balls, egg dishes, and desserts. Guests can return for more food as many times as they wish. If the kids get bored, they can watch chefs decorating elaborate cakes through a large window in the adjacent bakery. The Griswold's complex, which was once a high school, also includes a hotel, gift shops, and the Candlelight Pavilion, a dinner theater with family-oriented Broadway musical productions and holiday shows. On weekends between 9 A.M. and 5 P.M. you can browse at a crafts fair on the lawn in front of the complex.

Less than a mile away, the **Rancho Santa Ana Botanic Garden** houses the largest display of native California plants in the world. The collection of more than 1,500 species is used for research and education as well as public enjoyment. If your children are willing to walk a bit, they'll see a microcosm of California landscapes in an hour-and-a-half stroll along paved walkways and dirt trails in the 40-acre park. In the coastal garden they'll see sand dune and island plants. The woodland trail is shaded by oaks and walnut trees, the riparian trail follows a stream with tall deciduous trees, and a pleasant-smelling pine forest marks the conifer collection. The desert garden, which contains nearly all of the state's cactus species, is best when it blooms between mid-April and late May.

If you're in Claremont on a weekday afternoon, plan to visit the **George G. Stone Center for Children's Books,** a few blocks south of the garden. Housed in a cozy California bungalow, the library has more than 18,000 children's books and adult reference books about children's literature. The collection ranges from nineteenth-century literature to contemporary books. The library is part of the Claremont Graduate School, but it's open to children and adults who want to read quality literature. On a visit, you'll see children quietly reading at tables or next to the stone fireplace. To check out books you need to be a teacher, an associate of one of the Claremont colleges, or a Friend of Stone Library. The center publishes two annotated lists annually of the best in children's literature. In March, the center sponsors its annual Young People's Reading Conference, an all-day fair where children in second through eighth grades can meet with authors and learn about creative writing.

A few blocks farther south on Yale Street, you'll find the **Folk Music**

Center, a hands-on museum of ethnic instruments. Museum pieces and instruments for sale mingle in this eclectic store. Children are welcome to play any of the instruments, which include such diverse pieces as a 100-year-old African log drum, an Australian digeridoo, and Brazilian rain sticks. Started more than thirty years ago by Charles and Dorothy Chase, the store also sells tapes, records, children's books, and puppets. Charles Chase delights in taking school groups and other interested children on a 45-minute trip around the world with instruments, and Dorothy Chase teaches music.

East of Claremont, the town of Pomona sports one of the area's oldest attractions—the **Adobe de Polamares.** A rambling home built in 1854, the gracious hacienda gives kids an idea of life in old California. Children are surprised to see that outdoor hallways connect the rooms. Period furnishings inside have been collected from all over California. Some, such as the English piano in the living room, were brought across the country in covered wagons. Youngsters will notice a cradle, small chairs, and a carriage near the fireplace in the master bedroom. In the children's rooms, toys and chamber pots sit beside the beds. Stop to see the outdoor oven and the blacksmith shop near the garden and the cobbled ditch that once brought water to the rancho from San Antonio Canyon at the base of Mount Baldy.

West of the adobe on Arrow Highway is the **L.A. County Fair and Exposition Complex,** otherwise known as **Fairplex.** This is the site of the L.A. County Fair, which runs for 18 days every year between mid-September and the beginning of October. The fair is always crowded, but exciting and educational for children. There are animal exhibits, shows, and a midway with amusement rides. You'll see demonstrations of horse shoeing, cow milking, and cake decorating. Ganesha Junction, an elaborate model railroad, attracts kids with its trains speeding over bridges and through well-landscaped neighborhoods with tiny model trucks and cars driving on the streets alongside.

Fairplex hosts a number of trade shows during the rest of the year. Many of these are open to the public, with such displays as antique cars, model trains, and computers. Call Fairplex for a schedule of events.

During summer, plan to spend most of a day with kids at **Raging Waters,** a water recreation park with slides, chutes, and lagoons located west of Fairplex. You'll find the 44-acre attraction in the northwest corner of **Frank G. Bonelli County Regional Park.** Take young children to the Li'l Dipper pool where the water is shallow and there are small slides. Older kids prefer slides with names like Demon's Drop, Rampage Sled Chute, and Thunder

Run. On Adventure Island, youngsters climb over water on a ropes course. If they can't make it across, relief is only a refreshing plunge away. There's also a wave cove for bobbing in inner tubes and a white water river for more exciting tubing. Restaurants and picnic facilities provide a respite from the park's activities.

The rest of Frank G. Bonelli Park offers nearly 2,000 acres of recreational activities centered around Puddingstone Reservoir. The 250-acre lake has approximately five miles of shoreline and is divided into separate areas for sailing, water skiing, and shoreline fishing. At a swimming beach at the south shore of the lake, lifeguards are on duty from 10 A.M. to 6 P.M. You can rent aqua cycles, boats, and fishing equipment nearby. Picnic Valley on the south shore area has tables, barbecues, a snack bar, and bicycle rentals. Elsewhere in the park, kids can hike through natural areas on 14 miles of trails where they may spot raccoons, rabbits, and many different kinds of birds.

About a mile southwest of the park, you'll see a more noble breed of animal at **Kellogg's Arabian Horse Farm** on the campus of California State Polytechnic University in Pomona. The beautiful Arabians are raised and trained by students at the university. Families are welcome to visit daily between 8:30 A.M. and 4:30 P.M. You can wander the grounds and go into the stable area to see and pet the Arabians. On the last Sunday of every month between October and June, the farm hosts an hour-long horse show. You'll see western and English riding, plus a special treat for kids, trick horses. These trained horses demonstrate their intelligence with such tricks as placing a doll in a buggy and rocking it, and opening a cash register to deposit money.

Overlooking Pomona and the other Inland Empire communities is the rounded granite peak of **Mount Baldy.** Officially named Mount San Antonio, the 10,064-foot bare promontory is visible from much of Los Angeles. It is especially noticeable in winter when the summit gleams with a mantle of white snow. During winter you can ski at Mount Baldy Ski Resort (see Skiing with Kids section at end of chapter). In summer, Mount Baldy is a cool place to hike and have a picnic. Ride Chairlift Number 1 up the mountain on weekends and holidays during the off-season for a scenic ride. At the top you can walk along trails and find a picnic spot. Another good place to hike with kids is the one-mile round-trip trail from Manker Flat, below the ski lifts, to San Antonio Falls. You can picnic at Manker Flat campground nearby. This campground is an ideal spot for sledding and snow play in winter, but parking is limited.

Attractions

ADOBE DE PALOMARES, 491 East Arrow Highway, Pomona. (Exit San Bernardino Freeway [10] at Towne Avenue; north to Arrow Highway; left to adobe.) (714) 623-2198. Open Tuesday–Sunday, 2–5 P.M. Free.

CUCAMONGA-GUASTI REGIONAL PARK, 800 North Archibald Avenue, Ontario. (Exit San Bernardino Freeway [10] at Archibald Avenue; north one block to park.) (714) 945-4321. Open daily, 7 A.M.–dusk. Day-use fee: $3. Fishing fee for ages 6 and older: $3.

FLO'S AIRPORT CAFÉ, Chino Airport, 7000 Merrill Avenue, Chino. (Exit San Bernardino Freeway [10] or Pomona Freeway [60] at Euclid Avenue [83]; south to Merrill Avenue; left to restaurant.) (714) 597-3416. Open daily, 5:30 A.M.–7 P.M.

FOLK MUSIC CENTER, 220 North Yale Avenue, Claremont. (Exit San Bernardino Freeway [10] at Indian Hill Boulevard; north to 2nd Street; right to Yale Avenue; left to center.) (714) 624-2928. Open Tuesday–Saturday, 9:30 A.M.–5:30 P.M. Free.

FRANK G. BONELLI REGIONAL COUNTY PARK, Puddingstone Reservoir, San Dimas. (Exit 210 Freeway at Via Verde Drive; east to park. Exit San Bernardino Freeway [10] at Ganesha Boulevard; north to Via Verde Drive; left to entrance.) (714) 599-8411. Open daily, 7:30 A.M.–dusk. Day parking, $3. Fishing fee, $3.

GEORGE G. STONE CENTER FOR CHILDREN'S BOOKS, 131 East 10th Street, Claremont. (Exit San Bernardino Freeway [10] at Indian Hill Boulevard; north to 10th Street; right to center.) (714) 621-8000, ext. 3670. Public hours: Monday–Thursday, 1:30–5:30 P.M. Free.

GRABER OLIVE HOUSE, 315 East 4th Street, Ontario. (Exit San Bernardino Freeway [10] at Euclid Avenue; south to 4th Street; left to entrance.) (714) 983-1761. Open daily, Monday–Saturday, 9 A.M.–5:30 P.M.; Sunday, 9:30 A.M.–6 P.M. Free tours every 15–20 minutes.

GRISWOLD'S CLAREMONT CENTER, 555 West Foothill Boulevard, Claremont. (Exit San Bernardino Freeway [10] at Indian Hill Boulevard; north to Foothill Boulevard; left to Griswold's.) (714) 621-9360. Open daily, 6:30 A.M.–11 A.M.; 11:30 A.M.–4 P.M.; and 5–8 P.M. Call for Candlelight Pavilion dinner-theater schedule.

KELLOGG'S ARABIAN HORSE FARM, Kellogg Campus, California State Polytechnic University, Pomona. (Exit San Bernardino Freeway [10] at Kellogg Drive; south and follow signs to farm. Exit Orange Freeway [57] at Temple Avenue; west to South Campus Drive; right and follow signs to farm.) (714) 869-2224. Open daily, 8:30 A.M.–4:30 P.M. Free. Horse shows held on first Sunday of the month, October–June. Adults, $1.50; seniors, $1; ages 6–17, 50 cents; under 6, free.

L.A. COUNTY FAIR AND EXPOSITION COMPLEX (FAIR-PLEX), Pomona. (Exit San Bernardino Freeway [10] eastbound at White Avenue; north to McKinley Avenue; left to Fairgrounds. Exit 210 Freeway at Bonita Avenue; east to White Avenue; right to McKinley Avenue; right to Fairgrounds.) (714) 623-3111. Call for schedule of shows.

MOUNT BALDY, San Gabriel Mountains. (Exit San Bernardino Freeway [10] at Euclid Avenue [83]; north and continue after road becomes Mountain Avenue to Mount Baldy Drive; right to Mount Baldy ski area.) Open daily.

ONTARIO INTERNATIONAL AIRPORT, Ontario. (Exit San Bernardino Freeway [10] at Vineyard Avenue; south to airport. Exit Pomona Freeway [60] at Grove Avenue; north to Airport Drive; right to airport.) (714) 983-8282. Reserved tour hours: Monday–Friday, 9 A.M.–noon or other hours by request. Free.

PLANES OF FAME AIR MUSEUM, Chino Airport, 7000 Merrill Avenue, Chino. (Exit San Bernardino Freeway [10] or Pomona Freeway [60] at Euclid Avenue [83]; south to Merrill Avenue; left to museum.) (714) 597-3722. Open daily, 9 A.M.–5 P.M. Adults, $4.95; ages 5–12, $1.95; under 5, free.

PRADO REGIONAL PARK, 16700 South Euclid Avenue, Chino. (Exit San Bernardino Freeway [10] or Pomona Freeway [60] at Euclid Avenue [83]; south to park.) Open daily, 7:30 A.M.–dusk. Day-use fee: $3. Fishing, ages 6 and older: $3.

RAGING WATERS, 111 Raging Waters Drive, San Dimas. (Exit 210 Freeway at Raging Waters Drive; follow signs to park.) (714) 592-6453 or (714) 592-8181. Open daily during summer-school vacation; open weekends only, beginning of May to mid-June and beginning of September to mid-October; 10 A.M.–9 P.M. Adults, $14.95; children 42–48 inches tall, $8.50; under 42 inches, free.

RANCHO SANTA ANA BOTANIC GARDEN, 1500 North College Avenue, Claremont. ʏ(Exit San Bernardino Freeway [10] at Indian Hill Boulevard; north to Foothill Boulevard; right to College Avenue; left to entrance.) (714) 625-8767. Open daily, 8 A.M.–5 P.M. Free.

RAYMOND M. ALF MUSEUM, 1175 West Base Line Road, Claremont. (Exit San Bernardino Freeway [10] at Towne Avenue; north to Base Line Road; left to entrance of Webb School campus.) (714) 624-2798. Open from September to May, Monday–Thursday, 1–4 P.M.; one Sunday a month, 1–4 P.M. Closed on school holidays. Free, but $1 donation is suggested. Group tours scheduled by appointment.

For More Information

Greater Ontario Visitor and Convention Bureau of Southern California, Box 31, Ontario, CA 91762-8031; (714) 984-2450.

R I V E R S I D E
Dinosaurs, Puppets, and Hula Hoops

Many family activities in the eastern end of the Inland Empire center around the community of Riverside. Whether it's digging up dinosaur bones, learning to juggle, or discovering how photography works, youngsters will have fun exploring a variety of attractions on both sides of the Santa Ana River that gives the town its name.

Every Saturday is Dinosaur Day at the **Jurupa Mountains Cultural Center.** Located along Highway 60 on the northwestern edge of Riverside, the learning facility offers natural history and science classes to children and adults. Included in the 104-acre complex are the Earth Science Museum, a warehouse museum and shop, nature trails, and a dinosaurland with seven giant models measuring from 47 feet to 90 feet long. On any Saturday at 9 A.M. you can participate in Collecting Rocks with the Dinosaurs. The weekly program takes youngsters on a nature walk up the hill to hunt for fossils and minerals in an area near the dinosaurs that is seeded with specimens. If you arrive too late for that program, kids 6 years and up can attend the Kid's Fossil Shack class at 10:30 A.M. Here you'll learn how to identify, clean, prepare, and label a fossil to take home.

On a guided tour through the Earth Science Museum, youngsters glimpse the remains of real dinosaurs, fossils preserved in stone. There's even a large orange-colored egg with the dinosaur embryo still inside. Other well-organized displays present an extraordinary array of fossils, including petrified ferns, palms, fish, hard woods, insects, and mammals. The museum's large glass-windowed cases are low enough for young children to see into easily.

Bring a picnic if you wish, to enjoy in the sunken garden next to the museum. Plants growing in this area are the same as some of the fossilized specimens in the museum. You can buy fossils, inexpensive gem stones, and used books in the warehouse museum gift shop. This museum also displays a collection of miniature buildings with detailed interiors that kids find interesting, including models of a mission, theater, and toy shop. During the week, the center offers programs for school groups on geology, nature study, and Indian life, and it has developed special programs for disabled students.

A few miles south of the center along Riverside's Santa Ana River, kids can explore a nature center, hiking trails, and pleasant picnic spots shaded by sycamores and poplars. All are available at several small parks within **Santa Ana River Regional Park.** At Rancho Jurupa Park, south of Mission Boulevard, you'll find 80 camping spots and a lake stocked with fish. For maps and information, stop at county park headquarters, located in a colonial-styled 1950s home near the park entrance. Weeping willows shade the lawn around the lake. A half-mile trail leads from the lake past playing fields to the Louis Rubidoux Nature Center, where displays explain the area's animal and plant life. Outside, ducks near the lake are always looking for a handout and you can walk with the kids along a short nature trail to learn more about river ecology. There's a pecan grove nearby with nuts that ripen in the fall. You're allowed to pick a few, and children will enjoy cracking open and tasting the fresh pecans. Across the river at Martha McLean–Anza Narrows Park, there's a paved hiking trail which can accommodate wheelchairs and children's strollers.

From the parks, drive east on Mission Boulevard, which becomes University Avenue, into the center of Riverside. On the way you'll pass Riverside's prominent landmark, Mount Rubidoux. Kids like the adventure of going by car to the top of the rocky, 1,337-foot hill via winding Mount Rubidoux Drive. From the top near a memorial cross and peace tower, you'll have a 360-degree view of Riverside and the surrounding inland valley.

Drive to the restored city center, where you'll find a cluster of cultural attractions that interest children of varying ages. Park your car near 7th and Orange streets and walk through the historic city to visit the sights.

Downtown Riverside's most noticeable attraction is the **Mission Inn,** which takes up an entire block in the middle of the city. Its archways, balconies, and domes make it one of California's most distinctive buildings, and a national historic landmark. The Inn is due to open in the fall of 1990, after a four-year, multimillion-dollar expansion. Built between 1901 and 1930, the rambling Mission-Revival style inn has hosted many famous people, including several U.S. presidents.

You can take a 45-minute guided tour of the inn even if you're not staying there. Buy tickets in the lobby on the same day. The tour will mean most to older children who have studied some history. Popular curiosities with kids include former owner Frank Miller's bell collection and his granddaughters' antique doll collection, both of which are displayed throughout the hotel. In the St. Francis Chapel you'll see impressive Tiffany stained-glass windows and learn about the Hollywood stars such as Humphrey Bogart and Bette Davis, who were married there. The Famous Flyers Wall in the atrium off the chapel features copper wings signed by such well-known aviators as Amelia Earhart, John Glenn, and Chuck Yeager.

A small museum near the four-story rotunda houses more of Miller's collections including a seven-foot, gold-lacquer Buddha and a re-created Mission Inn barbershop from the 1900s. No reservations are required to visit this free museum. Of the inn's restaurants, the Spanish Dining Room and Patio are probably the best for kids, serving American cuisine and some southwestern specialties.

From the inn, cross the street at the corner of 7th and Orange streets, to the **Riverside Municipal Museum.** Children like this small museum, whose collections feature both local and natural history. The geology section displays fossils and minerals found near Riverside. Kids can push a button at one display case to see different colors in luminescent rocks. Nearby, low cases exhibit skeletons of ancient mammals that once roamed the area, such as a camel, dire wolf, and grazing ground sloth. A glass case on the floor in the center of the room allows little ones to come face to face with the skeleton of a saber-toothed cat. Dioramas illustrate local life from the time of the Indians to the days of the early explorers and settlers. Lifelike habitat displays feature mounted animals such as a California brown bear, desert bighorn sheep, and an owl feeding its chicks. In one corner, an impressive California mountain lion growls audibly from atop a rock outcrop. A gift shop near the entrance sells books, nature toys, and natural history-related items.

On the opposite corner, the **Riverside Central Library** has a children's room with more than 25,000 book titles. Stop by for the preschool storytime on Monday mornings at 11 if you have young children. In front of the library, a bright red, blue, and green Chinese pagoda commemorates the Chinese population that once worked the navel orange groves nearby. Notice the stone lion's clenched jaws that hold a ball that rotates but can't be removed.

Two blocks down 7th Street is the **Riverside Art Museum.** This private fine arts museum is housed in the former Riverside YWCA, designed by Hearst Castle–architect Julia Morgan. Exhibits in the 1929 building change every few months and spotlight modern and contemporary California artists. Children ages 3 to 15 can enroll in the museum's series of eight-week art classes, offered four times a year. The two-hour classes offer instruction in printmaking, drawing, painting, clay techniques, and puppetry. Kids who visit the museum may want to see the artwork created in these classes that is displayed in a gallery upstairs. As an added treat for the kids, you can eat lunch in the museum's outdoor courtyard, open between 11 A.M. and 2 P.M. The menu includes sandwiches, salads, soups, and desserts.

One block south, in the large brick Life Arts Building, **Kidstuff, The Children's Performing Arts Center of California** presents live performances every Saturday and Sunday afternoon at noon and 3 P.M. Shows feature magicians, mimes, jugglers, and puppeteers. Emphasis is on audience participation, with performers teaching kids how to do magic tricks or juggle. After each half-hour show, children join in a question-and-answer session with the performers. A small museum area in the theater displays special puppets, and there's a box of hand puppets nearby that kids can use to create their own shows. At other times of the week, the museum gives classes for parents and children together, so the learning can be reinforced at home. Topics include puppet making, mime, and juggling. School and club groups can schedule performances and workshops during the week.

If your children are interested in photography, head one block south of the Mission Inn to the **California Museum of Photography.** The museum occupies the 1929 Kress variety store on the Main Street Mall, Riverside's pedestrians-only commercial area. Galleries on three levels of the building display historical and contemporary prints from the museum's collection of more than ten thousand photographs. Don't miss the interactive gallery on the second floor. It features exhibits such as a camera obscura and a shadow wall that freezes the motion of people moving in front of it, to give kids a better understanding of how photography works. Another gallery explains photo technology, displaying cameras and related accessories. The museum offers workshops for both children and adults that teach about photography.

When the kids are hungry for a hearty meal, drive about two miles east on University Avenue to **Herbie K's.** This 1950s-style restaurant is well known to locals for its combination of good food and hula hoops. Dozens of the bright-colored rings hang from the restaurant's walls. You're welcome to take a hula hoop off the coat stand and demonstrate your swivel-hipped prowess in the restaurant's aisles. Small jukebox selectors at every booth allow kids to play their favorite rock and roll tunes. Waitresses sit down at your table to chat and help you choose from a menu that includes hamburgers, Swiss steak, and spaghetti.

A few blocks away, the University of California at Riverside's **Botanic Gardens** form a large outdoor classroom where youngsters can learn about plants from around the world. The gardens are popular for school trips. In the desert gardens kids see many varieties and shapes of cactus, and in the herb garden they smell plants with scents that range from lemon to peanut butter. A lath geodesic dome house contains cycads, plants that grew when dinosaurs still roamed the earth. Pick up a self-guided brochure at the entrance to the gardens and wander the hilly paths at your own pace. A paved pathway for wheelchairs and strollers traverses the gardens.

In the middle of the University of California campus, kids can get a more elevated view of the surrounding area by riding an elevator or climbing stairs to the top of the 161-foot **Carillon Tower.** From this vantage point, you'll not only have a good view of Riverside, but also a close-up look at the carillon, which plays each hour.

A few blocks south of the campus on Canyon Crest Drive, **Imagine That** sells books exclusively for children. The bookstore has a full range of fiction and nonfiction titles, from picture books to young adult literature. Brightly colored murals decorate the walls with storybook characters from classics such as *The Little Engine That Could* and *Alice in Wonderland.* Kids can sit at a table to peruse books before they buy. The store also sells stuffed animals, puzzles, cassettes, and records.

South of the center of town on Magnolia Street, the **Sherman Indian Museum** gives kids a young-person's view of North American Indian cultures. The museum is located in the original administration building of the Sherman Institute, a boarding school for Native American children that was founded in 1902. Native American high school students from the Southwest, Oregon, and California still attend the institute. The museum is open on weekday afternoons only and is closed during school vacations. It's worth a weekday trip, however, to see the items that have been donated by former students and other benefactors. You'll see Hopi kachina dolls, southwestern pottery, California tribal baskets, and ceremonial costumes. Dioramas illustrate the many different lifestyles found among America's diverse Indian cultures.

Attractions

CALIFORNIA MUSEUM OF PHOTOGRAPHY, 3824 Main Street Mall, Riverside. (Exit Pomona Freeway [60] at Market Street; south to parking lots between 7th and 9th streets; walk one block east to museum. Exit Riverside Freeway [91] southbound at 7th Street; west to parking on Market Street. Exit Riverside Freeway [91] northbound at University Avenue; west to parking on Market Street; walk to Main Street Mall.) (714) 784-FOTO or (714) 787-4787. Open Wednesday–Friday, 11 A.M.–6 P.M.; Saturday and Sunday, noon–5 P.M. Ages 12–adult, $2; under 12, $1; families, $5.

HERBIE K'S, 1201 University Avenue, Riverside. (Exit Riverside Freeway [91] at University Avenue; east to restaurant.) (714) 683-4833. Open daily, 24 hours.

IMAGINE THAT, 5225 Canyon Crest Drive, #13, Riverside. (Exit I-215 at Central Avenue; west to Canyon Crest Drive. Store is on corner of Canyon Crest and Central in the Canyon Crest Town Center.) (714) 784-0132. Open Monday, Wednesday, Thursday, and Saturday, 10 A.M.–6 P.M.; Tuesday and Friday, 10 A.M.–8 P.M.; Sunday, 12–5 P.M.

JURUPA MOUNTAINS CULTURAL CENTER, 7621 Granite Hill Drive, Riverside. (Exit Pomona Freeway [60] eastbound at Pyrite Street; north to Granite Hill Drive; right to center. Exit [60] westbound at Valley Way; south to Mission Road; right to Camino Real; right to center.) (714) 685-5818. Warehouse Museum open Tuesday–Saturday, 8:30 A.M.–5 P.M. Free. Earth Science Museum open Tuesday–Friday, 1–4 P.M.; Saturday, 12–4 P.M. Adults, $3; ages 3–18, $2. Drop-in field trips for families and individuals, Saturdays only: Collecting Rocks with the Dinosaurs, 9 A.M. Donation: $2.50. Kid's Fossil Shack, 10:30 A.M. Donation: $3.

KIDSTUFF, THE CHILDREN'S PERFORMING ARTS CENTER, 3475 University Avenue, Riverside. (Exit Riverside Freeway [91] southbound at 7th Street; turn immediately south on Lime Street to University Avenue; right to center in Life Arts Building. Exit [91] northbound at

University Avenue; west to center.) (714) 684-4555. Performances every Saturday and Sunday year round (except September), noon and 3 P.M. Tickets: $3 per person; under 2, free. Call for schedule of workshop classes.

MISSION INN MUSEUM AND OMNI MISSION INN, 3649   7th Street, Riverside. (Exit Riverside Freeway [91] southbound at 7th Street; west to Inn. Exit [91] northbound at University Avenue; north one block on off-ramp to 7th Street; west to Inn.) (714) 781-8241. Museum open, Tuesday–Saturday, 9 A.M.–4 P.M. Free. Guided tours of Inn, Tuesday–Sunday, 9:30 A.M. and 3:30 P.M. Adults, $7; ages 2–12, $3.50; under 2, free.

RIVERSIDE ART MUSEUM,   3475 7th Street, Riverside. (Exit Riverside Freeway [91] southbound at 7th Street; west to museum. Exit [91] northbound at University Avenue; north one block on off ramp to 7th Street; west to museum.) (714) 684-7111. Open Monday–Friday, 10 A.M.–5 P.M.; Saturday, 10 A.M.–4 P.M. Free.

RIVERSIDE CENTRAL LIBRARY, 3581 7th Street, Riverside. (Exit Riverside Freeway [91] southbound at 7th Street; west to library. Exit [91] northbound at University Avenue; north one block on off ramp to 7th Street; west to library.) (714) 782-5201. Open Monday–Wednesday, 10 A.M.–9 P.M.; Thursday–Saturday, 10 A.M.–6 P.M. Preschool storytime, Monday, 11 A.M.

RIVERSIDE MUNICIPAL MUSEUM, 3720 Orange Street, Riverside. (Exit Riverside Freeway [91] southbound at 7th Street; west to museum on corner of 7th and Orange streets. Exit [91] northbound at University Avenue; north one block on off ramp to 7th Street; west to museum.) (714) 787-7273. Open Tuesday–Friday, 9 A.M.–5 P.M.; Saturday and Sunday, 1 P.M.–5 P.M. Free.

SANTA ANA RIVER REGIONAL PARK, headquarters: 4600 Crestmore Road, Riverside. (Exit Pomona Freeway [60] at Rubidoux Boulevard; south to Mission Boulevard; left one mile to Crestmore Road; right to entrance.) (714) 787-2551. Open daily. Headquarters hours, Monday–Friday, 8 A.M.–5 P.M. Free.

SHERMAN INDIAN MUSEUM, 9010 Magnolia Avenue, Riverside. (Exit Riverside Freeway [91] at Van Buren Boulevard; north one block to

Andrew Street; right to museum entrance.) (714) 359-9434. Open
Monday–Friday (except during school holidays), 1–3 P.M. Free, but donation accepted.

UNIVERSITY OF CALIFORNIA AT RIVERSIDE

• *Botanic Gardens,* on east side of campus. (Exit I-215 at University Avenue; east to
campus; follow Campus Drive to parking lot 13; follow signs through lot up to
Botanic Gardens parking lot.) (714) 787-4650. Open daily, 8 A.M.–5 P.M. Free.
• *Carillon Tower,* in center of campus. (Exit I-215 at University Avenue; east to
campus gate for parking information and campus map.) Open Monday–Friday, 8
A.M.–5 P.M.

For More Information

Riverside Visitors and Convention Bureau, 3443 Orange Street, Riverside,
CA 92501; (714) 787-7950.

AT THE EAST END OF THE INLAND EMPIRE

Hands-on Experiences for Kids

South and east of Riverside, below the San Bernardino Mountains, you'll
find several fun places in scattered locations that offer hands-on activities for
families. By driving short distances between the communities of Perris,
Redlands, and Oak Glen, you can plan a day children will long remember
that includes activities such as riding vintage trolley cars, petting live wild
animals, and climbing a tree to pick apples.

Children interested in airplanes enjoy the **March Field Museum,** at March
Air Force Base a few miles south of Riverside on State Highway 215. You'll
need to get a visitor vehicle pass at the Main Gate Visitor Center to enter
the base and go to the museum. Inside the museum, which once served as
the base commissary, you'll see exhibits dating from 1918 and including
America's first jet, the Bell P-59. Throughout the museum, life-size models
depict uniformed Air Force personnel from different eras. One impressive
exhibit shows two men in a World War II German prisoner-of-war camp.

From a viewing platform beside a B-47 bomber exhibit that was used in
the 1955 filming of Paramount Pictures' *Strategic Air Command,* you'll see the
cockpit and seating arrangement for the crew. A gift shop near the entrance
sells astronaut ice cream, airplane models, and Air Force memorabilia. Plan

to visit the museum in the early afternoon when a free bus takes visitors out to the flight line to see more planes, primarily from the Korean and Vietnam wars. You'll be able to get off the bus and walk around to view the planes and helicopters.

South of the museum in the town of Perris, you can experience a different kind of historical transportation. The **Orange Empire Railway Museum** has the only collection of operating trolley equipment in Southern California. On weekends, trolley cars and vintage steam trains roll along nearly three miles of track to give visitors an old-fashioned rail travel experience. The collection includes Red Cars from the Pacific Electric system that once connected four counties in the Los Angeles area, and Yellow Cars from L.A.'s streetcar system. Conductors explain the history and use of each of the carefully restored cars before taking you on a ride down the tracks. Buy all-day tickets for unlimited train rides at the Pinacate Train Station. This restored depot also serves as a gift shop, selling books, models, striped engineer's caps, and other train-related items.

When you're not riding the rails, wander through the grounds to see the locomotives and railroad cars on display in the Pie Yard. Visit the Middleton Museum, a display of dozens of toy trains and early-twentieth-century memorabilia, located in two Rio Grande baggage cars nearby. You can picnic at tables behind the station.

Five miles north of the museum, **Lake Perris State Recreational Area** is a popular spot for families. Rocky mountains with hiking, biking, and equestrian trails surround the 2,200-acre lake. Rent fishing, sailing, and paddle boats at the marina or bring your own. A fun place to picnic is on Alessandro Island in the middle of the lake. There are two swimming beaches on the north side of the lake, one with a water slide.

Fifteen miles farther north in the city of Redlands, the **San Bernardino County Museum** offers educational, interactive experiences for kids. You'll notice the large geodesic-domed building from San Bernardino Freeway (10) as you approach. Exhibits at the museum feature the history and natural environment of the area. The extensive bird displays include the world's largest collection of bird's eggs. Kids can push buttons near the exhibits to learn about the birds and their songs. Children enjoy the dioramas of North American mammals too, especially the polar bear display. Historical artifacts include covered wagons, stagecoaches, and a large collection of fine baskets made by Indians in San Bernardino County. A new exhibit hall features changing educational displays designed for the entire family. Topics include Ice Age mammals and modern descendents of the dinosaurs.

Plan to visit the museum with young children during the afternoon, Friday through Sunday, to see Discovery Hall. Everything is touchable in this child-oriented learning center, which is in a separate building of the museum. Kids can pet live animals, such as guinea pigs, snakes, and frogs, and use microscopes to examine insects and plants. They hunt for dinosaur bones and other fossils in a sandy area of the fossil room at the back of the hall. At the anti-gravity mirror, participants appear to hover above ground. Outside, there are mining exhibits, a steam engine with caboose, and a picnic area.

Plan to attend one of the museum's special family programs. Sensational Saturdays programs, held on the second weekend of each month, feature movies and interactive instruction. A tea concert series provides a good introduction to classical music on the second Sunday of the month. On Friday mornings, there's a one-hour preschool class. Six-week summer programs are designed for older children.

Less than five miles from the museum, **The Frugal Frigate** is a children's bookstore that specializes in classics, with more than six thousand titles for children from infants up to teenagers. Owners Ben and Katherine Thomerson, college instructors in English and children's literature, are uniquely qualified to help you find just the right books. Visit the store on Saturday morning at 10 for a story hour or theatrical production designed for children ages 3 to 8.

At **Oak Glen,** in the foothills of the San Bernardino Mountains about 15 miles east of Redlands, you can pick apples and experience old-fashioned farm life with the kids. The rural area along Oak Glen Road, which loops between Yucaipa and Beaumont, is the largest apple growing region in Southern California. Between September and December, orchard owners sell apples and fresh cider at roadside stands and many open their farms to allow the public to pick apples. The whole family will enjoy the fun of climbing ladders to pick the tree-ripened fruit. Most of the farms have picnic tables, and some farmers keep animals such as goats, geese, horses, and llamas for the kids to pet. A few owners give wagon rides and tours of their ranches.

You can buy picnic provisions, apple pie, and handicrafts at Oak Tree Village, an area of shops and restaurants in Oak Glen. The village's Candy Kitchen sells mouth-watering chocolate dinosaurs. Visit the animal park behind the village to see native animals. At Mountain Town, an adjacent shopping area, kids encounter mounted wild animals from around the world in a small museum with cavelike displays. Live reindeer graze outside.

Stop at the **Oak Glen School Museum and Country Activities Center** in

Oak Glen to show the children what back-country life was like sixty years ago. The 1929 stone building was once a multigrade country schoolhouse. It is open in spring and fall on weekends. Old-fashioned lunch pails sit beside the desks and there's a wood-burning stove in the corner. Pictures of Presidents Hoover and Coolidge hang at the front of the room. A picnic area and playground are next to the school. There is usually an activity taking place on the grounds while the building is open. Kids can participate in these activities, which include making butter, bread, and pine-needle baskets or planting seeds and picking wild berries. These same kinds of subjects are offered in classes at the two-story Country Activities Center down the hill from the school.

The crisp air and changing colors of the leaves make Oak Glen an appealing place to visit in fall, but weekends in October can be especially crowded. It's a good idea to arrive early if you plan to visit in the fall. You can sled and make a snowman in winter at most of the farms that offer U-pick opportunities during other times of the year. In April, the apple trees are in bloom, and Oak Glen holds its Apple Blossom Festival. During summer you can pick raspberries, peaches, and other fruits.

In late spring, nearby **Cherry Valley** is the place to pick fruit. Farmers open their cherry orchards to the public for picking and provide buckets and ladders. The city of Beaumont celebrates with a Cherry Festival in June that features pie-eating contests, a parade, and amusement-park rides.

Attractions

CHERRY VALLEY/CHERRY PICKING, Cherry Valley. (Exit San Bernardino Freeway [10] at Beaumont Avenue; north to Cherry Valley.) Cherry-picking season, June–August.

LAKE PERRIS STATE RECREATIONAL AREA, 17801 Lake Perris Drive, Perris. (Exit State Highway 215 at Ramona Expressway; east to Lake Perris Drive; north to parking area.) Open daily. Day-use fee: $4 per car.

MARCH FIELD MUSEUM, March Air Force Base, Riverside. (Exit State Highway 215 at March Air Force Base exit; follow signs to Main Gate Visitor Center for a vehicle pass and directions to the museum.) (714) 655-3725. Open Monday–Friday, 10 A.M.–4 P.M.; Saturday and Sunday, noon–4 P.M. Free.

OAK GLEN/APPLE PICKING, Oak Glen Road, Oak Glen. (Exit San

Bernardino Freeway [10] at Yucaipa Boulevard; east to Bryant Street; left to Oak Glen Road; right up hill to orchards.) Apple-picking season, September–December.

OLD SCHOOL MUSEUM AND COUNTRY ACTIVITIES CENTER, 11911 South Oak Glen Road, Oak Glen. (Follow directions to Oak Glen above.) (714) 797-1691. Open February–June and September–December, weekends only, 10 A.M.–4 P.M. Museum and center will open for groups at other times. Call for reservations.

ORANGE EMPIRE RAILWAY MUSEUM, 2201 South A Street, Perris. (Exit State Highway 215 at 4th Street in Perris; west to A Street; left to museum.) (714) 657-2605. Grounds open daily, 9 A.M.–5 P.M. Free. Ride trains and trolleys on Saturday, Sunday, and holidays, 11 A.M.–5 P.M. All-day train pass: adults, $4; ages 6–11, $3; under 6, free.

SAN BERNARDINO COUNTY MUSEUM, 2024 Orange Tree Lane, Redlands. (Exit San Bernardino Freeway [10] at California Street; north to Orange Tree Lane; right to museum.) (714) 798-8570. Open Tuesday–Saturday, 9 A.M.–5 P.M.; Sunday, 1–4 P.M. Free. Discovery Hall hours: Friday–Sunday, 1–4 P.M. Adults, 50 cents; children, 25 cents.

THE FRUGAL FRIGATE, A CHILDREN'S BOOKSTORE, 9 North 6th Street, Redlands. (Exit San Bernardino Freeway [10] westbound at 6th Street; south to store. Exit [10] eastbound at Orange Street; continue east across Orange Street to 6th Street; right to store.) (714) 793-0740. Open daily, 10 A.M.–6 P.M.; Thursday until 9 P.M.

For More Information

Cherry Valley Chamber of Commerce, Beaumont Avenue, Box 536, Cherry Valley, CA 92223; (714) 845-8466.

Inland Empire Tourism Promotion Council, 421 North Euclid Avenue, Ontario, CA 91762; (714) 984-2450.

Oak Glen Apple Growers Association, 39610 Oak Glen Road, Yucaipa, CA 92399; (714) 797-1005.

Redlands Chamber of Commerce, 1 East Redlands Boulevard, Redlands, CA 92373; (714) 793-2546.

SAN BERNARDINO MOUNTAINS
Along the Rim of the World

Marching shoulder to shoulder for fifty miles from the Cajon Pass to Palm Springs, the peaks of the San Bernardino Mountains create a formidable barrier between Southern California's harsh upper deserts and the fertile valleys of the Inland Empire. Families come to these mountains year round to camp, hike, boat, fish, ride horses, bike, ski (see following section, Skiing with Kids), or simply to sight-see.

Many of these recreational opportunities are managed by the U.S. Forest Service as part of the San Bernardino National Forest. You can easily spend several days at any of the sixty campgrounds, both public and private, that dot this 800,000-acre preserve. The forest's campgrounds and hiking trails are too numerous to cover in detail here, but you can get more information by contacting the Forest Service (see page 187).

The principal road through this mountain kingdom is Rim of the World Drive (State Highway 18), one of the most spectacular byways in Southern California. Stretching for forty miles from Waterman Canyon in the west to Big Bear Lake in the east, the road links a string of mountain communities and attractions. Traveling west to east along Rim of the World Drive, you'll discover several days' worth of activities to interest the family. To do them all justice you'll need to spend a night or two in a campground or any of several towns along the way.

To reach Rim of the World Drive from the city of San Bernardino below, follow State Highway 18 as it snakes upward across the mountain's ridge lines. Along the way, you'll see a rocky outcropping shaped like an arrowhead on the mountainside to the east. No one is certain exactly how it got there, but an Indian legend tells of a flaming arrow whose point guided wandering tribes to the lush valley below.

The highway levels off at 4,700 feet elevation in the community of Crestline. A logging center a century ago, this mountain resort is now a popular place for hang gliding. See if the kids can spot any of these brightly colored delta-winged crafts riding the steady mountain breezes.

Next door to Crestline, explore **Lake Gregory Regional Park,** which is open year round for fishing (you'll need a state license for adults and kids 16 and over) and for swimming during summer months. The lake's **Boat House** rents rowboats and paddleboards from April to October and supplies anglers with bait and tackle. Youngsters with a sense of adventure will want to try the 300-foot-long water slide adjacent to the **Swim Beach.** You can picnic at tables near the beach.

Continue east on State Highway 189 through the town of Blue Jay, which takes its name from the birds (actually "Stellar Jays") that populate the mountains in great numbers. Head for the town's principal attraction, **Blue Jay Ice Castle,** an outdoor skating rink that is open year round. Surrounded by tall evergreen trees, this Olympic-size rink is the perfect place to strap on a pair of skates and introduce the kids to this slippery pastime. At another Blue Jay fixture, Jensen's Market, you'll find plenty of provisions for a mountain picnic. The market's old Country Bakery has gained a reputation for quality that approaches near legendary proportions with local residents.

Head another mile east on State Highway 189, past the Arrowhead Hilton Lodge, to reach Lake Arrowhead Village, the commercial center of this upscale resort community. The cobalt-blue lake was created with a dam on Little Bear Creek in the 1890s. Today, except for a public beach near the village and the marina, most of the lake's 12-mile shoreline is privately owned.

The village was intentionally burned to the ground in 1979 as part of a firefighting exercise to make way for a newer development with more modern facilities. One village landmark, the spire-topped Dance Pavilion, was spared from the flames and reconfigured to hold several small shops. While the new village may not be as quaint as the original, its 60 shops maintain Arrowhead's reputation for quality apparel, furnishings, and art. On the practical side for children, you will find a fast food restaurant, ice-cream emporiums, amusement arcade, and miniature golf course tucked in amid the boutiques.

Walk to the end of Village Point, just north of the village, to find a picnic area and public beach with a view of the lake and mountains. The **South Shore Marina,** on the eastern side of Village Point, rents boats year round, weather permitting. You can rent everything from a rowboat to a powerboat by the hour, half day, or day. Waterski boats require a $300 deposit. If you'd rather let someone else do the driving, the **Arrowhead Queen,** adjacent to the marina, will take you on a narrated, 45-minute paddle-wheeler excursion of the lake. On the cruise you'll get a good look at some of the spectacular homes that hug the shoreline. You'll want to plan ahead with kids, though, because the boat does not sell food or drinks on board and has no restrooms.

Follow State Highway 173 south out of the village to get back to Rim of the World Drive. For more information on hiking trails in the area, head west back to the Arrowhead District Ranger Station in Rimforest, just below Strawberry Peak.

You'll find several good picnic spots, all with spectacular views of the mountains and Inland Empire far below, perched along Rim of the World Drive. Baylis Park is a little more than a mile farther west of the ranger station. Crest Park is just opposite the junction of State Highways 173 and 18. Switzer Park is about half a mile east of the junction.

Another mile and a half east on Rim of the World Drive you'll find the mountain communities' only theme park—**Santa's Village.** Tailored for children 2 to 12 years old, the 15-acre park combines rides, attractions, animals, and shops. You can stake out a quiet, sunny spot while the kids take the Christmas Tree Ride and the Bumblebee Monorail nearby. Children can touch an icy North Pole, pet barnyard animals in a pen, and, of course, meet Santa Claus, whose house is in the middle of the park. Puppet shows are held throughout the day. The park also has a snack bar, bakery, and ice-cream parlor if the children get hungry.

Heading east along Rim of the World Drive another half mile brings you to **Heaps Park Arboretum.** Walk along the two-thirds-mile, self-guided trail to see varieties of mountain greenery that include sequoia trees, ponderosa pines, oaks, quaking aspens, and ferns. On a clear day from the peak's ridge, you'll be able to see San Bernardino to the south and well into the Mojave Desert to the north.

Drive east again another five miles along Highway 18 to reach the community of Running Springs. At the fire station in the middle of town, turn right onto Keller Peak Road for a six-and-one-half-mile trip to see the spectacular view from the Forest Service lookout 7,882 feet atop Keller Peak. The last two miles of this road are graded dirt. If you stay on the paved road instead of heading up to the peak, you'll find a dirt road that leads to the **National Children's Forest.** A self-guided nature trail acquaints you with a part of the forest that is reestablishing itself after a devastating fire several years ago destroyed 53,000 acres of brush and timber. The forest name comes from the fact that it is re-emerging for the "children of today and tomorrow." A paved trail accommodates strollers and wheelchairs, and signs along the trail are in braille for the benefit of blind visitors.

Back on Rim of the World Drive (18), continue east almost four miles to find the **Snowdrift Winter Playground.** When winter turns the mountains into a fantasyland, kids enjoy just getting out into the snow to throw snowballs and ride inner tubes down powdery hillsides. Snowplay is allowed anywhere in the National Forest where it is not specifically prohibited. You'll soon discover, however, that parking is limited along Highway 18. Snowdrift is one of the few areas, aside from the ski resorts, that has plenty of room to park and plenty of slopes to play on. From November to May, youngsters can rent "tube-boggins," large truck-tire inner tubes with handles, to slide down runs prepared for them. The runs are free of trees and rocks, and steps make the uphill climb easier.

The biggest of the San Bernardino Mountain lakes lies 18 miles east of Running Springs on Rim of the World Drive. Big Bear Lake is older, less exclusive, and more folksy than Lake Arrowhead. The lake was created in 1883 to provide irrigation for orange groves in the town of Redlands below. But the area's fame first blossomed in 1860 when William Holcomb discovered gold in the valley that now bears his name just north of the lake. Though it may be hard to believe, the city of Belleville, which sprang up briefly in the little valley, was at the time the second largest city in Southern California after Los Angeles.

You can still see the remnants of the town and gold mining activity in Holcomb Valley. Pick up a self-guided tour for Gold Fever Trail from the Big Bear District Ranger Station just off Highway 38 on the north side of the lake. The 11-mile driving tour is mostly over bumpy dirt roads and you should plan about three hours to complete it. In the ruins of Two-Gun Bill's Saloon, the Last Chance Placer mining site, and the Grasshopper Quartz Mill, kids will see the evidence of several enterprises that thrived briefly and faded quickly into oblivion.

While visiting the ranger station, pick up information about Big Bear's many hiking trails and learn the best ones for youngsters. Start with one of the most popular treks at the lake, to see the Champion Lodgepole Pine. To reach the trail, drive five miles along Forest Service Road 2N10 from the end of Tulip Lane off Highway 18 to road 2N11, and another mile to the parking area. From there a quarter-mile walk takes you to the largest lodgepole pine tree in California.

Not far from the Champion Lodgepole, off road 2N86, you'll find the trail to Castle Rock. This easy trek is about a mile and leads to the large rock, which is prominent in Bear Valley folklore. You can see the lake from the rock, and the foliage along the trail is especially colorful in the late summer and fall. A more strenuous route to Castle Rock climbs up from Highway 18, where the half-mile trail rises 500 feet.

In the town of Big Bear Lake on the southern shore, kids will enjoy discovering all the ways to go downhill at the **Alpine Slide at Magic Mountain.** On the Alpine Slide they ride a sled on wheels down a bare concrete track that resembles a toboggan run. Adjacent to the track, they can try out the **Water Slide,** which twists and turns before spilling riders into a 3½-foot-deep pool. At nearby **Snowplay Area,** they'll come down an icy slope on giant inner tubes. The **Alpine Slide** runs throughout the year, but the water slide operates from mid-June to mid-September only, and the snowplay area opens only when the weather is cold enough for natural snow conditions. When they tire of the downhill action, kids can take a break at the Alpine Slide's small video arcade. You can grab a quick bite at the snack bar or the barbecue on the sundeck.

Big Bear's biggest attraction is its lake. Seven miles long and a mile wide at its widest point, Big Bear Lake is a boater's paradise. The nine public marinas that ring the lake rent boats of every size and description. One of the largest facilities is **Pine Knot Landing and Marine** in the town of Big Bear Lake. Rowboats, canoes, powerboats, pontoon boats, jet skis, sailboards, even sailing lessons, are available at the landing.

You'll also bring the kids to Pine Knot Landing to catch the **Big Bear Lake Scenic Boat Tour.** This 80-minute narrated tour aboard the *Sierra* takes you near the lake's dam and other Big Bear sights, while affording one of the best views of Mount San Gorgonio and the surrounding peaks. The boat doesn't sell snacks and there are no restrooms on board, but both refreshments and bathrooms are available at the landing.

During the tour, youngsters always notice the stark white dome of **Big Bear Solar Observatory.** The solar observatory stands 200 yards off the north shore and is operated by Pasadena's California Institute of Technology. You can tour the observatory every Saturday afternoon in the summer. Cal Tech astronomy students talk about the telescope, the sun, and the work at the observatory. Kids enjoy watching the sun's activities on various TV monitors, which are equipped with different filters that help isolate various solar properties.

Big Bear also boasts a small zoo, **Moonridge Animal Park,** off Highway 18 at the east end of the town of Big Bear Lake. On a visit to the park, youngsters get acquainted with animals found in the surrounding forests. Black bears, bobcats, mountain lions, and timber wolves are all tucked away safely behind bars. The zoo is not open during winter months.

To get to know the area a little better, head up to the park in Big Bear City at the east end of the lake to visit the **Big Bear Museum.** Youngsters learn about the area's colorful history through exhibits on gold mining, cattle ranching, and lumbering. Historic photographs, mining artifacts, and movie-industry memorabilia all help bring these past days to life.

Attractions

(**Note:** All directions to attractions in this section start from the junction of State Highways 138 and 18 [Rim of the World Drive] in Crestline. To reach this junction, exit I-215 at Mountain Resorts [State Highway 30]; east to Waterman Avenue [18]; north to junction with State Highway 138.)

ALPINE SLIDE AT MAGIC MOUNTAIN, 800 Wild Rose Lane, Big Bear Lake. (East on Rim of the World Drive [18] and continue after road becomes Big Bear Boulevard [18] to corner of Wild Rose Lane.) (714) 866-4626.

• *Alpine Slide:* Open daily, mid-June–mid-September, 10 A.M.–6 P.M. (Saturday to 9 P.M.); mid-September–mid-June, Saturday–Sunday, holidays, 10 A.M.–dusk (daily hours during Christmas vacation). Adults, $3; ages 7–12, $2.50; under 7, free with adult.
• *Water Slide:* Open daily, mid-June–mid-September, 10 A.M.–6 P.M. All-day pass: adult, $10; ages 6–12, $8; under 6, free with adult.
• *Snowplay Area:* Open mid-November–mid-April (weather permitting), 10 A.M.– dusk. Day pass: $10 (includes rope tow inner tube); $3 (without tube); under 7, free with adult.

ARROWHEAD DISTRICT RANGER STATION, 26577 Highway 18, Rimforest. (East on Rim of the World Drive [18] to station.) (714) 337-2444. Open Monday–Friday, 8 A.M.–5 P.M.; Saturday, 8 A.M.–noon.

ARROWHEAD QUEEN, South Shore Marina, Lake Arrowhead Village, Lake Arrowhead. (East on Rim of the World Drive [18] to State Highway 173; left to Lake's Edge Road; left to village.) (714) 337-2553. Open Memorial Day–Labor Day, Monday–Friday, 11 A.M.–4 P.M.; Saturday and Sunday, 10 A.M.–4 P.M. Open Labor Day–Memorial Day, daily, noon–3 P.M. (weather permitting). Adults, $8.50; seniors, $6.50; ages 4–12, $5; under 4, free.

BIG BEAR MUSEUM, northeast corner of Big Bear City Park, Big Bear City. (East on Rim of the World Drive [18] and continue after road becomes Big Bear Boulevard [18] to Greenway Drive; left to Big Bear City Park and museum.) (714) 585-8100. Open mid-May–September, Saturday, 10 A.M.– 4 P.M.; Sunday, 1 P.M.–4 P.M. Free; donations accepted.

BIG BEAR DISTRICT RANGER STATION, State Highway 38, three miles east of Fawnskin. (East on Rim of the World Drive [18] to State Highway 38; left on North Shore Drive [38] to ranger station.) (714) 866-3437. Open Monday–Saturday, 8 A.M.–11:30 A.M., 12:30 P.M.–4:30 P.M.

BIG BEAR LAKE SCENIC BOAT TOURS, Pine Knot Landing and Marine, 439 Pine Knot Avenue, Big Bear Lake. (East on Rim of the World Drive [18] and continue after road becomes Big Bear Boulevard [18] to Pine Knot Avenue; left to landing.) (714) 866-2628. Open April–November, daily, 10 A.M.–6 P.M. Adults, $8.50; seniors, $6.50; ages 4–12, $5; under 4, free.

BIG BEAR SOLAR OBSERVATORY, 40386 North Shore Lane, Big Bear City. (East on Rim of the World Drive [18] to State Highway 38; left on North Shore Drive [38] to North Shore Lane; right to observatory.) (714) 866-5791. Open July 4–Labor Day, Saturday, 4 P.M.–6 P.M. Free; donations accepted.

BLUE JAY ICE CASTLE, corner of North Bay Road and State Highway 189, Blue Jay. (East on Rim of the World Drive [18] to junction with Lake Gregory Road and State Highway 189; east on State Highway 189 to North Bay Road and rink.) (714) 337-5283. Open daily (except Christmas). Call for hours. Adults, $5.50 for two hours (includes $1.50 skate-rental fee); ages 13–17, $5.25; under 13, $4.50.

HEAPS PARK ARBORETUM, Rim of the World Drive, 2.9 miles east of State Highway 173 junction, Sky Forest. (East on Rim of the World Drive [18] to arboretum.) (714) 337-2444. Open daily. Free.

LAKE GREGORY REGIONAL PARK, 24171 Lake Drive, Crestline. (North on State highway 138 to Lake Drive; right to park.) (714) 338-2233.

• *Lake Gregory Boat House:* Open late April–mid-October, daily, 7 A.M.–5 P.M. Call for boat rentals and prices.
• *Swim Beach:* Open Memorial Day–Labor Day, Monday–Friday, 10 A.M.–5 P.M.; Saturday and Sunday (July–August), 10 A.M.–6 P.M. $2 per person (must be at least 4 years old).
• *Waterslide:* Open (see Swim Beach). $3 per five-ride ticket; $6.95 swim-beach admission and all-day water-slide use.

MOONRIDGE ANIMAL PARK, 43285 Moonridge Road, Big Bear Lake. (East on Rim of the World Drive [18] and continue after road becomes Big Bear Boulevard [18] to Moonridge Road; right to park.) (714) 585-3656. Open Memorial Day–September, 8:30 A.M.–4 P.M. Free.

NATIONAL CHILDREN'S FOREST, Keller Peak Road, 4.3 miles east of Rim of the World Drive (18) turnoff, Arrowbear. (East on Rim of the World Drive [18] to Keller Peak Road; right to park.) (714) 337-2444. Open daily during months with no snow. Free.

PINE KNOT LANDING AND MARINE, 439 Pine Knot Avenue, Big Bear Lake. (See directions to Big Bear Scenic Boat Tours.) (714) 866-2628. Open April–Thanksgiving, daily, sunrise–sunset. Call for boat rentals and prices.

SANTA'S VILLAGE, State Highway 18, 1.7 miles east of State Highway 173 junction, Sky Forest. (East on Rim of the World Drive [18] to park.) (714) 337-2481. Open mid-June–mid-September and mid-November–early January, daily, 10 A.M.–5 P.M.; early January–March and Memorial Day–mid-June, Saturday–Sunday, 10 A.M.–5 P.M.; closed March–Memorial Day. Admission: ages 3–adult, $7.50; under 3, free.

SNOWDRIFT WINTER PLAYGROUND, State Highway 18, 4.8 miles east of junction with State Highway 330, Arrowbear. (East on Rim of the World Drive [18] to play area.) (714) 867-2640. Open November–May, daily, 9 A.M.–4 P.M. $4 per hour (includes tube-boggin rental).

SOUTH SHORE MARINA, Lake Arrowhead Village, Lake Arrowhead. (See directions for Arrowhead Queen.) (714) 337-2553. Open Memorial Day–Labor Day, daily 7 A.M.–5 P.M. Open Labor Day–Memorial Day, Monday–Friday, 10 A.M.–4 P.M.; Saturday and Sunday, 8 A.M.–4 P.M. Call for boat rentals and prices.

For More Information

Big Bear Chamber of Commerce, Box 2860, Big Bear Lake, CA 92315; (714) 866-4607.

Crestline Resorts Chamber of Commerce, Box 926, Crestline, CA 92325; (714) 338-2706.

Lake Arrowhead Resorts Chamber of Commerce, Box 155, Lake Arrowhead, CA 92352; (714) 337-3715.

Running Springs Area Chamber of Commerce, Box 96, Running Springs, CA 92382; (714) 867-2411.

San Bernardino National Forest, 144 North Mountain View Avenue, San Bernardino, CA 92408; (714) 383-5588.

S KIING   WITH   K IDS
More Than Bunny Slopes

Southern Californians like to boast that they can ski in snow and swim in the ocean all in the same day. Although most families wouldn't actually plan such a strenuous day, the fact is, quality ski areas are only a few hours' drive from most Southland beaches, thanks to the nearby San Gabriel and San Bernardino mountains. Some mountains in these ranges climb up to 7,000 feet, high enough to enjoy natural snowfall or the manmade variety for most of the winter.

Because of their proximity to Southern California's large population centers, the ski resorts in these mountains often are crowded, especially on weekends. Yet, with planning and a little patience, families can enjoy the local ski experience with a minimum of hassle. Here are a few tips to consider.

The most obvious way to avoid the crowds is to ski during the week rather than on weekends. As an added advantage, you'll find that midweek ski-rental rates are usually cheaper than on weekends. Even if your only ski opportunity is the weekend, you can make the trip a little easier by taking an extra day at either the beginning or end of your getaway. This will give you more time to enjoy the skiing and more flexibility on your departure time to avoid peak highway traffic. Be sure to check with the California Highway Patrol or the ski resort to determine road conditions before you go. In most cases, you should keep a set of chains in the car, even when they are not required. If you would rather not drive, check with local bus companies and airlines. Most of them expand their schedules to ski areas in the winter.

Skiing with children will be much more fun if you take the time to prepare them and yourself for the experience. Make sure the kids have the proper clothing to keep them both warm and dry. The best advice is to dress youngsters in layers, beginning with long underwear or ski pajamas, then a turtleneck. Outer clothing should be warm and water resistant. Avoid jeans and woolen mittens, which will absorb water and leave kids cold and miserable after the initial joy of being in the snow wears off. Two other essential items are a cap to keep the head warm and goggles or sunglasses to cut down the glare, even on hazy days.

If you don't own ski equipment, try to rent it before you go up to the mountains so you can avoid long lines at resort or local mountain rental shops. When renting before you go is impractical, call ahead to reserve equipment for children to ensure that you won't be left out in case the supply runs low.

Several Southern California ski resorts offer lessons and/or day-care programs for children. Check with your destination to find out about minimum and maximum ages they will take for instruction or day care, and what articles parents must provide (i.e., diapers and labeled bottles for infants) for day-care children.

Regardless of the levels of skiing accomplishment among family members, Southern California ski areas can accommodate everyone from novices to experts. You will find facilities for both downhill (Alpine) and cross-country (Nordic) skiing in the San Gabriel and San Bernardino mountains. Alpine is the more popular sport but is more difficult to master, while Nordic is easier to learn but requires greater stamina. In either case, children who learn to ski and who do it well will know the wonderful exhilaration of being in control as they glide through a quiet meadow or traverse a powdery slope.

The following are Southern California's most popular ski locations for families, beginning with those nearest to Los Angeles.

Heading up into the San Gabriel Mountains out of Glendale on Angeles Crest Highway (2), you will pass several good cross-country ski spots in Angeles National Forest. The closest is **Charlton Flats.** This 2½-mile loop is an ideal beginner's trail because it has mostly flat terrain and the trail is clearly marked and closed to traffic. There is a toilet at the trailhead, but no food services or equipment rentals at this stop.

Another good spot for Nordic skiing is three miles farther up the highway at **Chilao Flats.** The four-mile one-way trail follows plowed and unplowed Forest Service roads through the area's campground, though the trail is unmarked. A visitors center and toilets are located at the trailhead, and the area's only restaurant, Newcomb's Ranch Café, is nearby.

The closest Alpine ski facility to Los Angeles is another eight miles beyond Chilao Flats on Angeles Crest Highway. **Mount Waterman** lists its runs at about one-third each for novices, intermediates, and advanced skiers. Often overlooked because there are few accommodations nearby, the resort is not usually crowded and is ideal for a day or half day of skiing. Skiers take a chair lift to the top of the mountain where the beginner's runs are carved out of the slopes in a gentle saddle between two peaks. Here you will find a restaurant, restrooms, and a ski-rental shop. Mount Waterman provides ski lessons for all levels and kids under 13 ski free with a paying adult.

Two miles east on Angeles Crest Highway is **Snow Crest at Kratka Ridge.** Runs at Kratka are rated 30 percent novice, 30 percent intermediate, and 40 percent advanced. You can eat at the Terrace Lodge or a snack bar and rent equipment at Kratka's ski shop, all at the base of the mountain. Kratka offers ski lessons for all abilities, but there are no special programs for children.

Three miles west of Wrightwood on Angeles Crest Highway, **Mountain High Ski Area** has two mountains with 19 miles of ski runs: 25 percent each for novice and advanced skiers, and 50 percent for intermediates. You can rent or buy ski equipment at two shops on the mountains, and take a break from the slopes for a bite to eat at snack bars on top of Mountain High East, at Midway Lodge on the face of Mountain High West, or at the lodges at the base of both mountains. Kids under 11 ski free with a paying adult. The resort's Buckaroo program takes kids from 4 to 8 years old from 9 A.M. to 3 P.M. for lessons and lunch. Kids aged 9 to 13 join the Youth Beginners program for lessons from 9:30 A.M. to 11 A.M. and from 2 P.M. to 4 P.M.

Ski Sunrise, about six miles northwest of Wrightwood off Angeles Crest Highway, has 30 percent runs for novices, 45 percent for intermediates, and 25 percent for advanced skiers. Facilities include a cafeteria, restrooms, and a rental shop. The motto here is: "If at first you don't succeed, lessons are free until you ski." Novice skiers who have trouble mastering the skills at the "A" (beginner's) level can keep coming back for free "A" lessons until they feel comfortable. On weekends and holidays, you can enroll youngsters 5 to 8 years old in a Children's Ski School. This two-hour experience includes equipment, lift ticket, and lesson, beginning at 10:30 A.M. or 1:30 P.M. Another special program gives kids under 6 a one-hour private lesson, plus equipment, and an all-day lift ticket.

At the eastern end of the San Gabriels, the granite dome of **Mount Baldy** rises 8,600 feet above the Pomona Valley. The mountain is more for accomplished skiers, with only 20 percent of its runs for novices, and the remainder split between intermediate and advanced skiers. A lodge at Mount Baldy Notch, halfway up the mountain, has a cafeteria, snack shop, barbecue, restrooms, and a rental shop nearby. Mount Baldy does not offer special children's programs or day care, but lessons are available for all levels of skiers.

The closest ski area in the San Bernardino Mountains is in Green Valley, 12 miles east of lake Arrowhead off Rim of the World Drive (18). **Ski Green Valley** is well suited to skiers just getting started, with three quarters of its runs devoted to novice and intermediate levels. The small Alpine facility opens for weekends and holidays only, but will open up during the week for groups. A lodge at the base of the mountain has a restaurant, restrooms, and a ski-rental shop. Ski Green Valley's Ski School doesn't have special programs for kids, but its Beginners Hill is located away from the rest of the action so that novices are separated from the busy end-runs near the lodge.

At the east end of Green Valley you'll find the **Green Valley Lake Cross-Country Ski Center,** one of the largest such facilities in these mountains. The center rents Nordic ski equipment, or snowshoes and inner tubes. You can take a lesson in Nordic skiing or join a guided cross-country tour along the several miles of marked trails. For the really hardy skiers, the center offers snow camping.

Snow Valley is three miles east of the Green Valley turnoff on Rim of the World Drive. One of the biggest and busiest of the San Bernardino Mountains ski areas, runs at Snow Valley are rated 35 percent novice, 35 percent intermediate, and 30 percent advanced levels. You can sign the kids up for a special children's Snow School for 3- to 5-year-olds that runs from 10 A.M. to noon and 1 P.M. to 3 P.M. The program doesn't include lunch or a ski rental package. Snow Valley has a large rental shop, plus a restaurant, cafeteria, snack bar, and restrooms.

East of Snow Valley on Rim of the World Drive, the town of Big Bear Lake hosts three popular mountain ski areas. The smallest is **Snow Forest,** with 25 percent novice, 45 percent intermediate, and 30 percent advanced ski runs. You can rent ski equipment at Snow Forest, or pause for a bite at the restaurant, cafeteria, or snack bar. The ski school gives lessons for all levels of skiers but there are no special programs for children.

A mile east of Snow Forest is one of the most popular San Bernardino Mountains ski destinations, **Snow Summit.** Its 17 miles of ski runs are allocated 35 percent to novice, 35 percent to intermediate, and 30 percent to advanced skiers. Take a midday break from Snow Summit's slopes to eat lunch at the spectacular View Haus on top of the mountain, or try the fast food at the Bear Bottom Lodge at the bottom of the mountain. There is a ski-rental shop at the base area and the ski school offers lessons for all levels of skiers, with a beginners area completely separated from the faster runs.

You also will find one of the area's most complete programs for children at Snow Summit. The Little Bear Care Center entertains children as young as 2 years old for the day from 9 A.M. to 4 P.M., including a hot lunch and snacks. Youngsters 4 to 8 years old enroll in Little Bear Ski School for a half-day or full-day lesson. You'll need to make reservations if you plan to take advantage of either program on peak ski days.

East of the town of Big Bear Lake at the end of Moonridge Road, **Bear Mountain** offers some of the area's highest and most challenging terrain along with a large Learn-to-Ski Center. Runs at Bear Mountain are 30 percent novice, 40 percent intermediate, and 30 percent advanced. In the spacious lodge at the base of the mountain, you can rent ski equipment, eat at a variety of snack bars and cafeterias, or sit back and watch the activity on the slopes from a large deck.

Beginners receive instruction in a separate learners' area where slopes have been groomed to enhance rapid skill development. You will find the children's ski school (Powder Pandas), for youngsters 5 to 12 years old, in the same Learn-to-Ski Center. A daylong program runs from 9:45 A.M. to 3 P.M. You can sign up the youngsters for half-day programs from 10 A.M. to noon and from 1 P.M. to 3 P.M. The children's instruction is part of the nationwide SKIwee program, which involves standardized terminology and skills-evaluation. At the end of their lessons, youngsters pick up a progress card that tells a SKIwee instructor anywhere else in the country exactly what a child has accomplished and where to start the next lesson.

Skiing at Big Bear isn't all downhill. Visit the **Big Bear Ranger District Station** on the north side of the lake for information about several cross-country ski runs in the San Bernardino National Forest. Most of the trails follow Forest Service roads through the wilderness and are a short drive from the ranger station.

Attractions

BEAR MOUNTAIN, Box 6812, Big Bear Lake, CA 92315. (Exit I-215 at Mountain Resorts [30]; west to State Highway 330; left to Rim of the World Drive [18]; east and continue after road becomes Big Bear Boulevard [18] to Moonridge Drive; right to resort.) (714) 585-2519; for snow conditions, (714) 585-2517. Open, mid-November–mid-April, Monday–Friday, 8:30 A.M.–4 P.M.; Saturday and Sunday, 8 A.M.–4 P.M. All-day lift ticket, $32. Powder Pandas (ages 5–12), $35 for all-day program.

BIG BEAR DISTRICT RANGER STATION, State Highway 38, three miles east of Fawnskin. (Exit I-215 at Mountain Resorts [30]; west to State Highway 330; left to Rim of the World Drive [18]; east to State Highway 38; left on North Shore Drive [38] to ranger station.) (714) 866-3437. Open Monday–Saturday, 8 A.M.–11:30 A.M., 12:30 P.M.–4:30 P.M.

CHARLTON FLATS, 23 miles north of I-210 on Angeles Crest Highway

(2). (Exit Foothill Freeway [210] at Angeles Crest Highway [2]; north to flats.) (818) 796-5541. Open daily. Free.

CHILAO FLATS, 26 miles north of I-210 on Angeles Crest Highway (2). (See directions to Charlton Flats.) (818) 796-5541. Open daily. Free.

GREEN VALLEY LAKE CROSS-COUNTRY SKI CENTER, end of Green Valley Road, Green Valley. (Exit I-215 at Mountain Resorts [30]; east to State Highway 330; left to Rim of the World Drive [18]; east to Green Valley Road; left to center.) (714) 867-4505. Open daily, December–April. Call for prices.

MOUNT BALDY SKI LIFTS, Box 459, Mount Baldy, CA 91759. (Exit San Bernardino Freeway [10] at Euclid Avenue [83]; north and continue after road becomes Mountain Avenue to Mount Baldy Drive; right to ski area.) (714) 982-0800; for snow conditions, (714) 981-3344. Open Thanksgiving–Easter, Monday–Friday, 8 A.M.–4:30 P.M.; Saturday and Sunday, 7:30 A.M.–5 P.M. All-day lift ticket: $28; under 13, $17.

MOUNT WATERMAN SKI LIFTS, INC., 817 Lynnhaven Lane, La Canada Flintridge, CA 91011. (Exit Foothill Freeway [210] at Angeles Crest Highway [2]; north to ski area.) (818) 440-1041; for snow conditions, (818) 790-2002. Open November–April, daily, 8 A.M.–4:30 P.M. All-day lift ticket: $25.

MOUNTAIN HIGH SKI AREA, Box 428, Wrightwood, CA 92397. (Exit I-215 at State Highway 138; west to Wrightwood Highway [2]; left to ski area. Exit Antelope Valley Freeway [14] at Pearblossom Highway [138]; east to Wrightwood Highway [2]; right to ski area.) (619) 249-5471; for snow conditions, (213) 626-6911, (714) 972-9242, (818) 888-6911, (619) 294-8780. Open November 28–March 30, Monday–Thursday, 8 A.M.–10 P.M.; Friday–Sunday, 7:30 A.M.–10 P.M. All-day lift ticket: adults, $29.75; under 14, $13. Buckaroo program (ages 4–8), $30 all day. Youth Beginners program (ages 9–13), $21 all day.

SKI GREEN VALLEY, Box 438, Green Valley Lake, CA 92341. (See directions to Green Valley Lake Cross-Country Ski Center.) (714) 777-1783; for snow conditions, (714) 867-2338. Open November–March, Saturday and Sunday, 8 A.M.–4 P.M. All-day lift ticket: adults, $18; under 13, $14.

SKI SUNRISE, Box 645, Wrightwood, CA 92397. (See directions to Mountain High Ski Area.) (619) 249-6150. Open November–April, Monday–Friday, 8:30 A.M.–4:30 P.M.; Saturday and Sunday, 8 A.M.–4:30 P.M. All-day lift ticket: adults, Monday–Friday, $15, Saturday and Sunday, $24; ages 6–12, daily, $10; under 6, free.

SNOW CREST AT KRATKA RIDGE, Star Route, La Canada Flintridge, CA 91011. (See directions to Mount Waterman Ski Lifts, Inc.) (818) 440-9749; for snow conditions, (818) 449-1749. Open December–March, daily, 8 A.M.–4:30 P.M. All-day lift ticket: adults, $20; under 13, $10.

SNOW FOREST, Box 1711, Big Bear Lake, CA 92315. (Exit I-215 at Mountain Resorts [30]; west to State Highway 330; left to Rim of the World Drive [18]; east and continue after road becomes Big Bear Boulevard [18] to Pine Knot Avenue; right to Knickerbocker Road; left to Cherry Lane; right to ski area.) (714) 866-8891; for snow conditions, (714) 886-5503. Open late November–late April, daily, 8 A.M.–4:30 P.M. All-day lift ticket: Monday–Friday, adults, $21; under 13, $11; Saturday and Sunday, adults, $26; under 13, $13.

SNOW SUMMIT SKI AREA, Box 77, Big Bear Lake, CA 92315. (Exit I-215 at Mountain Resorts [30]; east to State Highway 330; left to Rim of the World Drive [18]; east and continue after road becomes Big Bear Boulevard [18] to Summit Boulevard; right to ski area.) (714) 866-5766; for snow conditions, (213) 613-0602, (818) 888-2233, (714) 972-0601, (619) 294-8786. Open mid-November–mid-April, daily, 7:30 A.M.–10 P.M. All-day lift ticket; adults, $29; under 13, $16. Children's Ski School (ages 9–12), $20 all day. Little Bear Ski School (ages 5–8), $30 all day. Little Bear Care (ages 2–6), $30 all day.

SNOW VALLEY SKI AREA, Box 8, Running Springs, CA 92382. (Exit I-215 at Mountain Resorts [30]; east to State Highway 330; left to Rim of the World Drive [18]; east to ski area.) (714) 867-2751; for snow conditions, (714) 867-5151, (714) 625-6511. Open Thanksgiving–mid-April, Monday and Tuesday, 8 A.M.–5 P.M.; Wednesday–Sunday, 8 A.M.–9 P.M. All-day lift ticket: adults, $29.50; under 13, $15. Children's Snow School (ages 3–5), $25 all day.

For More Information

Angeles National Forest, 701 North Santa Anita Avenue, Arcadia, CA 91006; (818) 574-5200.

Big Bear Chamber of Commerce, Box 2860, Big Bear Lake, CA 92315; (714) 866-4607.

San Bernardino National Forest, 144 North Mountain View Avenue, San Bernardino, CA 92408; (714) 383-5588.

Wrightwood Chamber of Commerce, Box 416, Wrightwood, CA 92397; (619) 249-4320.

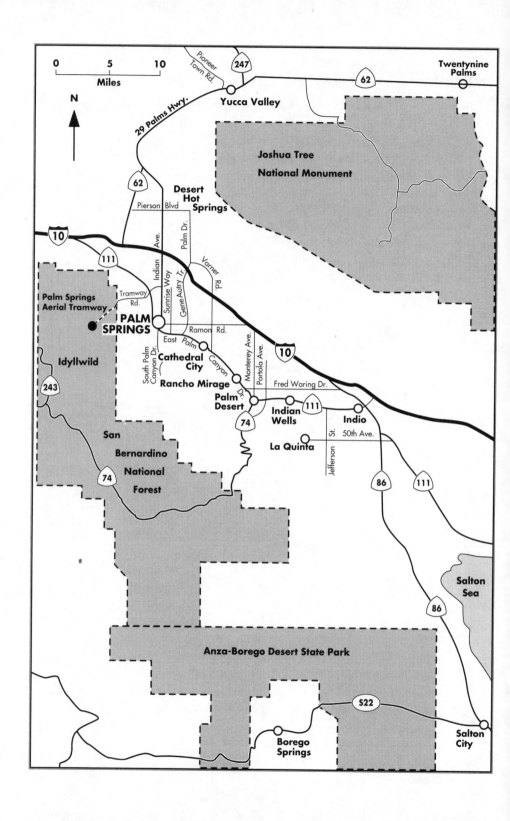

9

Palm Springs and Nearby Desert Communities

Made famous in the 1930s by Holly-wood's elite, the Palm Springs area still has that image of a glamorous *adult* playground. Palm Springs and the nearby desert communities that spread throughout the lower desert of the Coachella Valley boast some of the world's finest golf courses, elegant shops, and exciting nightlife—pursuits appreciated most by grown-ups.

Yet many families return year after year to enjoy a rich variety of activities with their children. There are horseback riding and bicycle trails, Indian canyons, and a desert zoo. And this is probably the only desert area in the world where you can snow ski, ice skate, and surf.

There are so many activities that kids will enjoy, and these sections suggest four different Palm Springs–area itineraries. The first two—one for the winter, the other for the resort's more-affordable summer season—cover ideas for fun within the city of Palm Springs itself. A third itinerary covers a variety of attractions in the desert resort communities southeast of Palm Springs, and the fourth offers a potpourri of easy day trips from any of these communities.

PALM SPRINGS IN WINTER
From Sand to Snow

Families flock to Palm Springs in the winter from all over North America. They plan to lie in the sun, dip into one of the area's eight thousand swimming pools, and play some golf or tennis—with the kids, if they are old enough. While adults may not tire of a daily diet of sun and relaxation, the kids will. Before long, they'll crave more variety. Lucky for you, there are plenty of activities right in Palm Springs that both adults and youngsters will enjoy.

The activities suggested here are geared to the winter months because some offer unique experiences in the cool weather, while others are open only in the winter.

A bike ride is a good way to start an active day in the desert. In the stillness of morning, the temperature is brisk and the air is crystal clear. The colors of the mountains around the city change from deep blue to purple to pink as the rising sun paints the desert in increasingly lighter hues. With the cool breeze on your face, you can appreciate this beauty before the streets get crowded.

Bring your own bikes or rent them at one of the shops listed at the end of this section.

Palm Springs has nearly forty miles of well-marked bicycle trails. Pick up a free bicycle trail map at the **Palm Springs Parks, Recreation and Library Department** located at Leisure Center in **Sunrise Park,** corner of Ramon Road and Sunrise Way. Or strike out on your own, looking for the blue and white bicycle signs to follow suggested trails.

A bikeway along uncrowded streets circles the center of Palm Springs in a flat three-mile Downtown Loop. Stop for a rest along the way at **Ruth Hardy Park,** a pleasant oasis along Avenida Caballeros with shaded picnic tables, restrooms, and children's play equipment. Or try the Coachella Valley Bikeway that stretches for 6½ miles from Palm Springs to Rancho Mirage. You can ride as far as you wish and return on the same path. Pick up the bikeway south of Sunrise Park and head east, where you'll ride along the Tahquitz Wash away from automobile traffic. A good place to rest along this bikeway is **Demuth Park,** which has a play area, restrooms, and a grassy area with picnic tables.

Another fun activity for a morning in Palm Springs with kids is a horse-back ride. **Smoke Tree Stables,** at the south end of Palm Springs on Toledo Avenue, rents horses to adults and children ages 4 and older. (Children under 4 ride double with an adult.)

A one-hour guided ride takes you through desert terrain along Palm Canyon Wash just outside the city. Children will enjoy looking for roadrunners and rabbits that dart among the desert chaparral and smoke trees along the trail. Two-hour guided rides go into **Andreas Canyon,** a lush oasis that was inhabited for centuries by the Cahuilla (ca-WE-ya) Indians. The trail through the canyon passes by groves of stately Washingtonia palms, unusual rock formations, and perennially cold Andreas Creek. Look for flat boulders with round depressions made by Indians who ground their food there long ago.

On a three-hour guided ride, you'll trot through either **Murray Canyon** or **Palm Canyon,** other lush oases on the Agua Caliente Indian Reservation. If you and your children are veteran riders, you can try full-day or overnight pack trips covering more of the 130 miles of riding trails near Palm Springs. For the less adventuresome, the stable offers popular hay rides.

You can also hike the Indian canyons, which are open to visitors from 8 A.M. to 5 P.M. daily, September through May. All three canyons on the reservation—Palm, Andreas, and Murray—are accessible, with well-marked hiking trails and picnic areas. Palm Canyon is best for younger children, with a moderately graded, paved footpath leading to picnic areas near the stream. Kids like scrambling over rocks and exploring the dense groves of fan palms that grow in the 15-mile-long gorge.

To reach the canyons, go south on South Palm Canyon Drive about three miles to the tollbooth on the Agua Caliente Indian Reservation. (Don't turn onto East Palm Canyon Drive when the road curves east.) At the Palm Canyon entrance there is a trading post where you can buy hiking maps, refreshments, and Indian art. Drive carefully down the narrow, winding road into Palm Canyon.

When you are entering or leaving the canyons on South Palm Canyon Drive, you'll pass **Moorten's Botanical Garden,** two blocks south of the junction with East Palm Canyon Drive. A visit to this unique garden will teach children more about the desert surrounding Palm Springs. Founded in 1938, the garden has nature trails that meander through a well-developed growth of cactus and succulents. Kids have fun looking at the crazy shapes of these plants, such as the boojum tree and beavertail cactus. There is more for children in this garden than plants. Be sure they see the live turtles, petrified logs, and real dinosaur footprints, too. In spring, ask owner Pat Moorten for a free map that shows where to find wildflowers in bloom in the Coachella Valley. She scouts the area for the best floral displays each year before making the map.

For a chance to study the desert's animals, its Indians, and the art inspired by its beauty, visit the **Palm Springs Desert Museum.** The pleasant split-level building is located on Museum Drive, west of Desert Fashion Plaza in the center of town.

Children especially enjoy the spacious museum's low eye-level cases of live desert animals such as scorpions, snakes, and the smallest rodent in the world, Coachella Valley's own little pocket mouse. A room-size diorama displays night and day in the desert with changing lights and an audiovisual presentation. The museum's collection of Cahuilla artifacts and baskets is particularly interesting to children who are studying Indians in school. You can tour the museum with a guide Tuesday through Saturday at 2 P.M. On Sunday there are afternoon concerts in the auditorium. A gift shop near the museum entrance sells books, Indian arts, and craft kits for children.

The museum offers natural history field trips each Friday and Saturday morning from October to May and will provide a schedule of destinations. The trips are best suited for older children because each involves hiking from two to ten miles. On the hikes you'll learn about desert ecology and geology. Bring water and be ready to leave from the museum's north parking lot with a full tank of gas in your car by 9 A.M.

Behind the north parking lot of the museum, a mile-long trail leads up into the foothills of the San Jacinto mountains. Markers along this nature trail describe plants and other features. The trail is fairly steep, but flattens out a bit when it meets the Lykken Trail at a picnic area above the museum. From there, you'll have a spectacular vista of the city and the entire Coach-ella Valley. A desert-trails map from the Palm Springs Parks, Recreation and Library Department gives information about this trail and others in the area.

From the museum, it's a short walk over to the **Village Green Heritage Center** on South Palm Canyon Drive where local history comes alive. You can tour three historic buildings on the Green. The **McCallum Adobe,** built from mud bricks in 1885, was the home of Palm Springs' first permanent non-Indian settlers, the John Guthrie McCallum family. On a self-guided tour, you'll see memorabilia of the early days of the city, furnished by the Palm Springs Historical Society. Included are antique dolls, children's toys, Indian artifacts, and clothing.

Next door at **Miss Cornelia White's House,** built from railroad ties for a Palm Springs pioneer in 1893, kids will be most intrigued by the old-fashioned appliances. See if they can guess the uses for such strange-looking machines as an apple corer, a toaster with removable sides, and a hand-crank telephone (the first phone in town).

You will find yourself back in the 1930s in **Ruddy's General Store Museum,** which features authentic showcases of products and advertising signs from that era. You'll hear radio commercials and period music in the background. Kids may notice the checkerboard set on a barrel ready for play.

When it's time for lunch, try one of the many restaurants along Palm Canyon Drive that serve cuisine that appeals to kids. You'll also find a variety of fast food shops at the Desert Fashion Plaza in the center of town.

Afternoon is a good time to leave the heat behind and head up Mount San Jacinto (hah-SIN-toe) on the **Palm Springs Aerial Tramway.** To reach the tramway, drive north on Palm Canyon Drive from downtown Palm Springs to the big T sign at Tramway Road. Turn left and continue to the tram's Valley Station. Bring jackets and other cold-weather gear because temperatures up on the mountain will be at least 40 degrees colder than in Palm Springs, with snow on the ground from November to May most years.

The tram ride takes you up the granite face of Mount San Jacinto to an altitude of 8,516 feet in just 15 minutes. Trams run every half hour starting at 8 A.M. weekends and holidays, and 10 A.M. on weekdays. There are plenty of big windows in the 80-passenger tram so children can see the expansive view of the valley below and the mountainside ahead. A recorded presentation describes the tram's construction, and it points out the mountain's changing plant life, from desert scrub to mountain-top pines, as you pass through five climate zones.

When you step off the tram at the Mountain Station, you'll immediately feel the cool difference. Inside the station, there's a restaurant and a gift counter, and a movie about the building of the tramway. From a terrace outside, you can gaze across the sprawling Coachella Valley, and the kids may want to use one of the pay-telescopes to pick out landmarks.

On the other side of the station is a paved walkway that leads down to Long Valley, a ten-minute walk. In this pine-studded meadow, you can walk along paths that connect with 54 miles of hiking trails in the **Mount San**

Jacinto State Park and Wilderness. Two short loop trails begin at the ranger station there, one a half-mile nature hike and the other a 1½-mile desert-view trail. Also near the ranger station, you can arrange to go on a mule-train ride through the valley. The 20-minute rides are a good length for small children. Mule rides are available year round unless the snow is too deep. Free wilderness permits are necessary if you plan to hike away from Long Valley. There are five overnight campgrounds in the 14,000-acre park.

Between November and May, you'll usually find enough snow in Long Valley to make a snowman or have a snowball fight. You can bring plastic disk sleds or inner tubes up on the tram with you for more snow fun (no metal runners are allowed). There's a good place to sled on a hill near the ranger station. At the Long Valley Nordic Ski Center, about a hundred yards from the ranger station, you can rent cross-country skis, boots and poles, or snowshoes. The center also offers ski classes.

If it is warm enough, eat outside under the pines at picnic tables in Long Valley or have a cup of hot chocolate and a snack inside the tram station. You also can eat dinner at the station's Alpine Restaurant. If you purchase a Ride 'n' Dine package when you buy your tram tickets after 2:30 P.M., you will get a complete meal at the Alpine Restaurant for a reduced rate. The last tram down the mountain in winter leaves at 9:15 P.M.

Attractions

(**Note:** All directions to attractions in this section start from the intersection of Palm Canyon Drive and Ramon Road. To reach this intersection, exit I-10 at State Highway 111, which becomes Palm Canyon Drive, and continue south to Ramon Road. In the center of Palm Springs, South Palm Canyon Drive becomes a one-way drive south and Indian Avenue, running parallel to it to the east, becomes a one-way drive north.)

BICYCLE RENTALS

At several Palm Springs–area bicycle shops and:

• *Burnett's Bicycle Barn,* 429 South Sunrise Way, Palm Springs. (East on Ramon Road to corner of Sunrise Way; shop is in Alpha Beta Shopping Center on corner across from Angel Stadium in Sunrise Park.) (619) 325-7844. Open Thursday–Monday, 8 A.M.–5 P.M.; Tuesday, 8 A.M.–noon; year round. Average price: $5 per hour.
• *Mac's Bike Rental,* 700 East Palm Canyon Drive, Palm Springs. (South on South Palm Canyon Drive to East Palm Canyon Drive; left to shop in front of Biltmore

Hotel.) (619) 327-5721. Hourly rental lot open daily, 9 A.M.–5 P.M., November–June. Bicycles delivered year round. Average price: $5 per hour.

MOORTEN'S BOTANICAL GARDEN, 1701 South Palm Canyon Drive, Palm Springs. (South on South Palm Canyon Drive to entrance two blocks south of junction with East Palm Canyon Drive.) (619) 327-6555. Open Monday–Saturday, 9 A.M.–4:30 P.M.; Sunday, 10 A.M.–4 P.M.; year round. Adults, $1.50; children 5–16, 50 cents; under 5, free.

MOUNT SAN JACINTO STATE PARK AND WILDERNESS, Long Valley Ranger Station at top of Palm Springs Aerial Tramway. (See directions to tramway below.) (619) 327-0222. Winter hours: 10 A.M.–6 P.M. Summer hours: 8 A.M.–8 P.M.

PALM, ANDREAS AND MURRAY CANYONS. (South on South Palm Canyon Drive to canyon entrance.) (619) 325-5673. Open daily September to May, 8:30 A.M.–4:30 P.M. Closed in summer. Adults, $3; seniors, $2; children, 75 cents.

PALM SPRINGS AERIAL TRAMWAY. (East on Ramon Road to Indian Avenue; north and follow signs to Palm Canyon Drive [111]; north on 111 to Tramway Drive; left 3½ miles to Tramway.) (619) 325-1391. Open weekdays, 10 A.M.; weekends, 8 A.M. (cars depart every half hour). Last car down at 9:15 P.M. in winter. Adults, $13.95; ages 3–12, $8.95. Alpine Restaurant Ride 'n' Dine package: adults, $17.95; children, $11.50.

PALM SPRINGS DESERT MUSEUM, 101 Museum Drive, Palm Springs. (East on Ramon Road to Indian Avenue; north to Tahquitz Way; west two blocks to Museum Drive; north to museum.) (619) 325-0189. Open September–May, Tuesday–Friday, 10 A.M.–4 P.M.; Saturday and Sunday, 10 A.M.–5 P.M. Closed in summer. Adults, $4; seniors, $3; ages 16 and under, $2; under 5, free.

PALM SPRINGS PARKS, RECREATION AND LIBRARY DEPART-MENT, 401 South Cerritos, Leisure Center, Sunrise Park, Palm Springs. (East on Ramon Road to park at corner of Sunrise Way and Ramon Road.) (619) 323-8277. Open Monday–Friday, 8 A.M.–5 P.M.

PARKS

• *Demuth Park*, 4365 Mesquite Avenue, Palm Springs. (East on Ramon Road to El Cielo Road; right to Mesquite Avenue; left to park.)
• *Ruth Hardy Park*, 700 Tamarisk Road, Palm Springs. (East on Ramon Road to Indian Avenue; north to Tamarisk Road; right to park.)
• *Sunrise Park*, corner of Ramon Road and Sunrise Way. (East on Ramon Road to park.)

SMOKE TREE STABLES, 2500 Toledo Avenue, Palm Springs. (East on Ramon Road to Sunrise Way; right and cross over East Palm Canyon Drive to Toledo Avenue; left three quarters of a mile to entrance on left side.) (619) 327-1372. Open daily, 8 A.M.–4 P.M., October–April; 8 A.M.–5 P.M. in summer. Adults and children, $15 per hour; ages 4 and under ride double with adult, $5.

VILLAGE GREEN HERITAGE CENTER, 221-223 South Palm Canyon Drive, Palm Springs. (East on Ramon Road one block to Indian Avenue; north to Tahquitz Way; left to Palm Canyon Drive; left one block to center.) (619) 323-8297. McCallum Adobe and Miss Cornelia White's House open mid-October–June: Thursday–Saturday, 10 A.M.–4 P.M.; Wednesday and Sunday, noon–3 P.M. Closed during summer. Admission: 50 cents per person; children with an adult, free.

• *Ruddy's General Store Museum*, 221 South Palm Canyon Drive, Palm Springs. (See directions above.) (619) 327-2156. Open October–June: Thursday–Sunday, 10 A.M.–4 P.M. Summer hours: Saturday and Sunday, 10 A.M.–4 P.M. Ages 12 and over, 50 cents; under 12, free.

For More Information

Greater Palm Springs Convention and Visitors Bureau, Airport Park Plaza, Suite 315, 255 North El Cielo Road, Palm Springs, CA 92262; (619) 327-8411.

PALM SPRINGS IN SUMMER
Playing It Cool

When it comes to summer family playgrounds, the desert is usually near the bottom of the list. That may have been a wise decision a few years ago, but on a summer visit to Palm Springs today, you'll find a wide variety of cool attractions. Sure, it's hot outside, but the warm, dry days are perfect for lounging by a pool, and Palm Springs has almost eight thousand of them, plus two water parks. Many air-conditioned attractions stay open during the summer, and there's a cool mountain playground easily accessible by tram. Perhaps most enticing of all, Palm Springs resort and hotel owners discount their room rates during the summer by 50 percent or more.

You'll find that some Palm Springs attractions are closed in summer, while others are open only at this time. The following itinerary suggests activities that are available only from late spring to early fall. Check the dates of operation also for activities listed in the Palm Springs in Winter section. Some of them are open year round.

One of the most refreshing ways to spend a summer day in Palm Springs with kids is at the 21-acre **Oasis Water Resort** on the west side of town. The park has water slides for kids with varying degrees of courage. There are two 400-foot-long speed slides and two 70-foot free-fall slides for daredevils. Less adventurous youngsters float on a wide white-water "river." Toddlers feel at home at Squirt City, where they play with giant, low-pressure squirt guns and ride down low water slides. Older kids tackle the one-acre wave pool, which generates four-foot surfing waves.

Adults can enjoy all the fun with the kids or just sit and watch the activity from semiprivate cabanas. If you want more exercise, try the European health club. Eat at one of the snack bars or at an outdoor restaurant that serves mesquite-broiled chicken and ribs.

You'll find another large waterside diversion at the **Palm Springs Swim Center** at Sunrise Park on Sunrise Way and Ramon Road. This complex features a 50-meter Olympic-size swimming pool with one- and three-meter diving boards. There's a separate, roped-off section for young children, and there are spacious lawns nearby to spread a towel on. Try night swimming in summer on Tuesday and Thursday evenings between 7:30 and 9:30 P.M.

Next door, the **Palm Springs Public Library** is a good place to enjoy a quiet break in a busy day. The city's library system has more than 18,000 children's books waiting in air-conditioned comfort for your family. The main branch is in Sunrise Park, and the Welwood Murray Branch is on South Palm Canyon Drive in the heart of town. There are weekly programs as well as toy loans for children.

If it's cool breezes you want, hop the **Palm Springs Aerial Tramway,** which you reach by driving north of the city on Palm Canyon Drive to Tramway Road. Trams climb up Mount San Jacinto every half hour, starting at 8 A.M. on weekdays and 10 A.M. on weekends. The last car down in summer is at 10:45 P.M. For a more complete description of the tram ride and

Mount San Jacinto State Park and Wilderness see the section Palm Springs in Winter.

At the top of the mountain you'll find plenty to keep kids busy for a whole day: explore some of the 54 miles of hiking trails, enjoy a picnic, or ride through the pine forest on a mule. Volunteers from the **Mount San Jacinto Natural History Association** lead guided nature hikes through the forest every Saturday and Sunday during summer between 1 and 4 P.M. Plan to go on a hike with the kids to learn about the plants, animals, and geology of these mountains. Groups set out from the base of the cement walkway in Long Valley, a ten-minute walk from the tram's Mountain Station. Association members also staff the visitors center in the station. Open in the afternoons, the Visitor Center sells trail maps and books about the area. There are five campgrounds in 14,000-acre Mount San Jacinto State Park and Wilderness. You'll need to get a free wilderness permit from the ranger station if you plan to hike out of Long Valley.

Back in Palm Springs, desert evenings are both enjoyable and economical. Take advantage of the early-bird specials offered by many of the city's fine restaurants in the summer. This will leave you plenty of time to buy an ice-cream cone and stroll along Palm Canyon Drive in the center of town, where art galleries and specialty shops stay open in the evening.

In fact, Palm Springs comes alive on summer evenings when the temperature cools. The **Palm Springs Angels,** a Class A baseball team, play more than seventy night games at Palm Springs Angel Stadium in Sunrise Park. Buy tickets at the box office before the 7:30 P.M. game time. Incidentally, the California Angels play about ten games at the stadium during their spring training in March. Call the box office for their schedule if you plan to be in town then.

Summer is also the time for other family entertainment in Sunrise Park. On Monday night, families gather on the lawn for free movies suitable for children. On Thursday night, there's a free pop or jazz concert under the stars. Bring a picnic and a blanket to sit on. Events start at 8:30 P.M. Call the **Parks, Recreation, and Library Development** for a schedule.

Attractions

(**Note:** All directions to attractions in this section start from the intersection of Palm Canyon Drive and Ramon Road. To reach this intersection see directions page 202 in the winter Attractions listings.)

MOUNT SAN JACINTO NATURAL HISTORY ASSOCIATION, 225 North El Cielo Road, Suite 141, Palm Springs. (For weekend nature hikes, meet volunteers at base of cement walkway in Long Valley at top of

Palm Springs Aerial Tramway. See directions below for tram.) (619) 323-3107. Free.

OASIS WATER RESORT, 1500 Gene Autry Trail, Palm Springs. (East on Ramon Road to Gene Autry Trail; right to park entrance.) (619) 325-SURF. Open daily, 10 A.M.–8 P.M., mid-June–Labor Day; weekends only, 11 A.M.–6 P.M., mid-March–mid-June and September–October. Adults, $13.95; children 4–11, $9.95; under 4, free.

PALM SPRINGS AERIAL TRAMWAY, (East on Ramon Road to Indian Avenue; north and follow signs to Palm Canyon Drive [111]; north on 111 to Tramway Drive; left 3½ miles to tramway.) (619) 325-1391. Open weekdays, 10 A.M.; weekends, 8 A.M. (cars depart every half hour). May–Labor Day. Last car down at 10:45 P.M. Adults, $13.95; ages 3–12, $8.95.

PALM SPRINGS ANGELS, Palm Springs Angel Stadium, corner of Sunrise Way and Baristo Road. (East on Ramon Road to Sunrise Way; left to corner of Baristo Road, across from the Palm Springs Library in Sunrise Park.) Box 1742, Palm Springs, CA 92263. (619) 325-HITS. Games start at 7:30 P.M. Call box office for schedule. Reserved seats, $3.50; general admission adults, $3; children, $1.50.

PALM SPRINGS PARKS, RECREATION AND LIBRARY DEPARTMENT, 401 South Cerritos, Leisure Center, Sunrise Park, Palm Springs. (East on Ramon Road to library at corner of Sunrise Way and Ramon Road.) (619) 323-8277. Open Monday–Friday, 8 A.M.–5 P.M. year round.

For More Information

Greater Palm Springs Convention and Visitors Bureau, Airport Park Plaza, Suite 315, 255 North El Cielo Road, Palm Springs, CA 92262; (619) 327-8411.

DESERT RESORT COMMUNITIES
Exploring near Palm Springs

East of Palm Springs, the desert communities of Cathedral City, Rancho Mirage, Palm Desert, Indian Wells, La Quinta, and Indio stretch like a string of pearls across the Coachella Valley along State Highway 111. Huge hotels and sprawling resorts dot the area. They have been so developed with lush flowers, manicured lawns, and bubbling fountains that your kids may be a little confused about just what a desert is.

A trip to the **Living Desert** in Palm Desert will answer their questions and spark new ones about this complex environment. When you enter the 1,200-acre botanical and wildlife sanctuary through the McManus Center, you'll immediately see plenty of desert activity. Kangaroo rats, fringe-toed lizards, deer mice, and other live animals invite close inspection in an exhibit darkened to simulate night. In another room, kids can examine small animals and insects in glass enclosed cases that are at low eye-level.

Outside, six miles of nature trails meander through botanical gardens of North American desert plants. You'll see displays of plants once used by the local Cahuilla Indians for medicine, food, and building houses. Rabbits, lizards, and roadrunners scamper freely among the plants. Coyotes, owls, and bighorn sheep live in large, outdoor natural-habitat enclosures. There are dozens of species of birds in a walk-through aviary. Be sure to see the sickbay for injured animals and the nursery for young ones. Both offer up-close viewing.

Preschool and elementary-school-age children may want to spend most of their time in the Discovery Room of the H. Earl Hoover Education Center. At this hands-on children's museum, kids (who must be accompanied by an adult) touch molted snakeskins and use metal casts to make animal tracks in sand boxes. They put their hands into feel-and-guess boxes that contain mysterious items such as tortoise shells, animal skulls, and rattlesnake rattles. They also have fun building a giant, green fabric Saguaro cactus by attaching removable branches to a trunk.

If the kids are warm after walking through the desert preserve, take a cool break at the **Ice Capades Chalet** in the Palm Desert Town Center less than five miles away. Surrounded by shops and food concessions in the air-conditioned shopping mall, the 160-foot-long ice-skating rink is a popular desert attraction. Rent some skates and enjoy the change of scenery for awhile. A disk jockey keeps the music lively. The rink holds classes to help novice skaters get started. You'll need to call for a schedule. In July, the rink holds a snowman-building contest for children, using ice scraped from the rink by grooming machines. When your ankles tire of skating, explore the mall's toy stores, book shops, and children's clothing boutiques.

Horseback riding is another active pursuit you can enjoy nearby. At the **Ranch of the 7th Range,** about ten miles east of Palm Desert in La Quinta, trails lead into the foothills of the Santa Rosa Mountains. On a guided trail ride, look for wildflowers, rabbits, and birds. You'll also see plenty of unusual

rock formations formed by the ancient Salton Sink. One of the most interesting rides is the Boo Hoff Trail that climbs to a panoramic view of the
Coachella Valley out toward the Salton Sea. The stables offer hay rides and
party facilities for groups, too.

Nearby at **Lake Cahuilla** you can swim, go boating (nonmotorized), or
fish. The inviting blue-green lake has a beach with a play area for children.
There are shaded picnic areas on the grass around the lake. Hiking trails lead
into the foothills of the Santa Rosa Mountains, and there's a campground
nearby. Bring along a fishing pole to try your luck with the trout, striped
bass, and bluegill that are stocked in the lake. Adults need a fishing license,
but children under 16 don't.

For a more passive experience with horses, spend some time at the **Eldorado Polo Club** in Indio. Families are welcome to visit the 140-acre property
to picnic and watch free polo matches. Stop by in the morning to see some
of the six hundred stabled horses being trained, between September and
May. You're allowed to wander through the stables with the kids to see the
horses up close and talk to trainers. On game days, spread a picnic tablecloth
on the grass under the trees beside the small lake, or have a tailgate picnic
at your car along the polo field sidelines.

Don't leave Indio without trying its most famous product, dates. The city
bills itself as the Date Capital of the World. Indeed, 95 percent of America's
date crop comes from the Coachella Valley, and you will see groves of
feathery date palms growing throughout the area, just as they have for nearly
a century.

At **Jensen's Date and Citrus Gardens** on State Highway 111 in Indio,
you can buy a thick date shake or a large cup of orange juice to sip while you
walk through a grove of date palms and citrus trees next to the gift shop.
Trees laden with unusual fruits are labeled and signs along the path explain
the process of growing dates. At **Shields Date Gardens** a few blocks west on
State Highway 111, you'll sit inside at booths or at an old-fashioned lunch
counter to taste date shakes and date ice cream. A free faded slide show (in
need of up-dating) illustrates "The Romance and Sex Life of the Date."
Indio hosts a National Date Festival and County Fair every February, an
extravaganza complete with camel and ostrich races and a free Arabian
Nights Pageant each evening.

For a different kind of evening with kids, check to see what is playing at
the **McCallum Theatre for Performing Arts** at the Bob Hope Cultural
Center in Palm Desert. On selected winter evenings, the theater presents a
series of family concerts. The shows change each year, but recent programs

have included such entertainments as folk dancers, circus performers, and magicians. Call the theater for a concert schedule.

Attractions

(**Note:** All directions to attractions in this section start from the intersection of Monterey Avenue and State Highway 111 in Palm Desert. To reach this intersection, exit I-10 at Monterey Avenue; south to State Highway 111.)

ELDORADO POLO CLUB, 50-950 Madison Street, Indio. (East on State Highway 111 to Jefferson Street; right to 50th Avenue; left to Madison Street; right half mile to entrance.) (619) 342-2223. Open mid-September–April, Tuesday–Sunday, all day. Games held, 10 A.M.–4 P.M. Free. Sunday admission to clubhouse: $5.

ICE CAPADES CHALET, Palm Desert Town Center, 72-840 State Highway 111, Palm Desert. (At the intersection of State Highway 111 and Monterey Avenue.) (619) 340-4412. Open Monday–Friday, 11 A.M.–5 P.M., and 7:30 P.M.–9:30 P.M.; Saturday, noon–10 P.M.; Sunday, 11 A.M.–5 P.M. Adults and children, $4.75; skate rental: $2.00.

JENSEN'S DATE AND CITRUS GARDENS, 80-653 State Highway 111, Indio. (East on State Highway 111 to gardens.) (619) 347-3897. Open daily, 8 A.M.–6 P.M. Free.

LAKE CAHUILLA COUNTY PARK, La Quinta. (East on State Highway 111 to Jefferson Street; right to 54th Avenue; left to Madison Street; right to 58th Avenue; right to park.) (714) 787-2553. Open daily, 6 A.M.–8 P.M., year round. Admission: $2 per vehicle, 50 cents for persons over 4 ($3 maximum.) Fishing fee: adults, $3; ages 10–17, $2.

LIVING DESERT, 47-9000 Portola Avenue, Palm Desert. (East on State Highway 111 to Portola Avenue; right 1½ miles to entrance.) (619) 346-5694. Open daily, 9 A.M.–5 P.M. Closed June–August. Adults, $3.50; ages 3–15, $1; 2 and under, free.

McCALLUM THEATRE FOR PERFORMING ARTS, Bob Hope Cultural Center, 73-000 Fred Waring Drive, Palm Desert. (North on Monterey Avenue one block to the corner of Fred Waring Drive.) (619) 340-ARTS. Call for schedule of performances.

RANCH OF THE 7TH RANGE, La Quinta. (East on State Highway 111 to Jefferson Street; right to 54th Avenue; left to Madison Street; right to 58th Avenue; right three quarters of a mile to entrance.) (619) 564-1414. Open October–April, 8 A.M.–5 P.M. Adults and children over 3, $18 per hour; children under 3 ride double with an adult, $6.

SHIELDS DATE GARDENS, 80-225 State Highway 111, Indio. (East on State Highway 111 to gardens.) (619) 347-0996. Open daily, 8 A.M.–6 P.M. Free.

For More Information

Desert Resorts Convention and Visitors Bureau, 44-100 Monterey Avenue, Suite 203, Palm Desert, CA 92260, or Box 280, Rancho Mirage, CA 92270; (619) 568-1886.

DAY TRIPS IN THE DESERT
Dates, Dinosaurs, and Dolls

With the Palm Springs area as your headquarters, you are in the midst of a number of attractions that make for convenient day trips with the kids. Each of the following five destinations is within a half-hour to two-hour drive from Palm Springs. Using these itineraries, you'll sample museums, hike among unusual rock formations, swim in salt water, or play in the snow. Pick one and tailor it to your children's interests.

Trip 1: Desert Hot Springs

For this trip, you can promise the kids dolls, Indians, fishing with an almost guaranteed catch, and dinosaurs, all within a few miles of Palm Springs. Start your day by driving north from Palm Springs on Gene Autry Trail, go over I-10, where the road becomes Palm Drive, and continue to Desert Hot Springs. Odorless mineral water bubbles up naturally all over this town. There are more than fifty spas and hotels where you can soak, some open to the public for a daily fee.

If the kids aren't interested in hot springs, you can grab their attention at **Cabot's Old Indian Pueblo Museum,** on Desert View Avenue just east of Palm Drive. This pseudo Hopi-style building was created single-handedly by one of the community's first European settlers, Cabot Yerxa. He built the four-story, 35-room structure over a 20-year period, without a blueprint, using secondhand lumber and old rusty nails. (Don't worry, it's quite sturdy.)

Take a guided tour through Yerxa's unusual living quarters and visit his personal museum to see curiosities such as Buffalo Bill's chair, a buffalo-leather war shield from Custer Battle Field, and Eskimo tools collected by Yerxa when he lived in Alaska during the gold rush. A courtyard art gallery displays contemporary and Native American art, and a trading post sells craft items and colorful rocks and minerals.

Just around the block on Pierson Street, the **Kingdom of the Dolls** is another testimony to single-handed craftsmanship. Here, Betty Hamilton has constructed an array of miniature dioramas that represent four thousand years of history. You'll see Cleopatra in her Egyptian palace, Vikings at sea in their ships, and Henry VIII in a castle with his six wives.

To create these scenes, Hamilton dressed small dolls in period costumes and surrounded them with backgrounds made of such common household materials as egg cartons, Popsicle sticks, and clay. Be sure to see the street of dollhouses dating from the 1800s to the 1940s, to give the kids an idea of how fashions have changed in interior design and architecture since their great-grandparents' time. The museum is an easy-to-take history lesson for children, and who knows, they might be inspired to create some dioramas of their own.

For lunch, eat at any of the small restaurants in town, or picnic at one of the following interesting spots a few miles away.

The **Morongo Wildlife Reserve** is on State Highway 62, less than ten miles north of Desert Hot Springs. Open from dawn to dusk, this pleasant park has a picnic area shaded by tall cottonwood trees. After your picnic, hike one of the reserve's seven trails. On an easy 1½-mile loop, part of which is a wheelchair access trail, you'll cross a year-round stream to find a desert garden filled with hundreds of plants that bloom in the spring and fall.

Another picnic option is at the **Whitewater Trout Company,** also known as **Rainbow Rancho.** From Desert Hot Springs, drive south on State Highway 62 to I-10, go west on I-10 one exit to the Whitewater turnoff and follow the road five miles to the end. Here, you catch your own lunch or dinner and grill it in a shaded picnic area near the lakes. Barbecues and charcoal are provided. For $2 you'll have the use of a fishing pole, a bucket, bait, towels, and someone to clean your fish. In addition, there's a reasonable charge for each fish per pound. Two lakes are virtually stuffed with rainbow trout, so children should have success in catching something, even if they aren't particularly patient fishermen. If you don't want to fish but would like to picnic on the grounds, the staff will net and clean some trout for you. Visit the hatchery to learn about raising fish.

About ten miles west of Whitewater on the north side of I-10 at Cabazon sit some eye-catching **Dinosaur** models. If you drove to Palm Springs from Los Angeles, the children probably noticed them. Located next to the **Wheel Inn Truck Stop and Café,** Dinney, a 45-foot-high brontosaurus, and Rex, a 55-foot-high tyrannosaurus, play a *big* part in bringing business to the place. Dinney, completed by designer Claude Bell in 1975, houses a small museum of southwestern memorabilia and a gift shop in its belly. Plans for Rex include a snack shop and a neck-long spiral staircase to allow children to walk into its mouth and look out at the world through its huge teeth. The dinosaurs are open to the public for a small admission fee, Friday through Sunday. You can buy dinner or snacks, including date shakes and ice cream, at the café.

Six miles farther west on I-10 near Banning is the **Malki Museum.** Take the Fields Road exit about one mile north to the museum entrance on the Morongo Indian Reservation. This small, Indian-run museum has a fine collection of Cahuilla Indian artifacts, including baskets, jewelry, and stone tools. Visit the ethnobotanic garden to learn how Indians used desert plants. The museum also has its own publishing company. Children studying Southern California Indians will find a good selection of Indian books here.

Attractions

CABOT'S OLD INDIAN PUEBLO MUSEUM, 67-616 East Desert View Avenue, Desert Hot Springs. (Exit I-10 at Palm Drive; north to Desert View Avenue; right to museum.) Open Wednesday–Monday, 9:30 A.M.– 4:30 P.M., year round. Adults, $2; seniors, $1.50; ages 6–16, $1.

DINOSAUR GARDENS AT THE WHEEL INN TRUCK STOP AND CAFÉ, Cabazon. (Exit I-10 at Cabazon.) (714) 849-8309. Open Friday–Sunday, 10 A.M.–5 P.M. Adults, 50 cents; ages 10–14, 25 cents; under 10, free.

KINGDOM OF THE DOLLS, 66-071 Pierson Boulevard, Desert Hot Springs. (Exit I-10 at Palm Avenue; north to Pierson Boulevard; left to museum.) (619) 329-5137. Open Tuesday–Sunday, noon–5 P.M. Summer hours by appointment. Adults, $2.50; children, 75 cents.

MALKI MUSEUM, 11-795 Fields Road, Morongo Indian Reservation, Banning. (Exit I-10 at Fields Road; north about one mile to entrance.) (714) 849-7289. Open Wednesday–Sunday, 10 A.M.–5 P.M. Free, but donation appreciated.

MORONGO WILDLIFE RESERVE, Morongo Valley, (Exit I-10 at Twentynine Palms State Highway [62]; north about ten miles to Morongo Valley.) (619) 363-7190. Open daily, 6:30 A.M.–dusk.

WHITEWATER TROUT COMPANY (RAINBOW RANCHO), Whitewater Canyon Road, Whitewater. (Exit I-10 at Whitewater Canyon Road; north five miles to the end.) (619) 325-5570. Open Tuesday–Sunday, 9 A.M.–5 P.M. Fishing fee: $2, plus $2.35 per pound for fish caught.

For More Information

Desert Hot Springs Chamber of Commerce, 13560 Palm Drive, Box 848, Desert Hot Springs, CA 92240; (619) 329-6403.

Trip 2: Joshua Tree National Monument

Plan to spend the whole day, or longer, on this trip, because there's plenty for the kids at **Joshua Tree National Monument.** From Palm Springs, the best way to enter the park is via Twentynine Palms Highway (62). There are two north entrances to the park off State Highway 62, at the towns of Joshua Tree and Twentynine Palms. Head for monument headquarters at the Twentynine Palms entrance for the best orientation to the area.

Pick up a free guide map and look at displays at the Visitors Center before starting off to see the 870-square-mile park. Ask about the ranger-guided activities available on weekends. If you only have a day to spend, explore the half-circle loop that meanders through the park between the two northern entrances. This will take you into some of the most scenic canyons and vistas in the park.

At White Tank Campground, walk the half-mile Arch Rock Nature Trail, which has signs explaining the geology of the area, evidenced in the intriguing rock formations. Climb on the boulders in Hidden Valley, but keep an eye on the children. Weathering loosens the rock surfaces and makes high climbing hazardous. You'll find a picnic area near the campground there, and an adjacent one-mile loop trail that takes you through rocky terrain to an old cattle rustler's hideout. Take a side trip down a paved road to Keys View for a panorama of rugged desert and stands of Joshua trees.

Incidentally, they really are not trees at all, but cousins of the yucca and the century plant. Mormon pioneers gave the tree its name because its tall shape and upraised branches reminded them of the prophet Joshua pointing the way to the Promised Land. Joshua trees grow almost exclusively in the Mojave Desert at elevations above 2,500 feet. Up close, look for birds' nests, insects, lizards, and other desert fauna around the plants.

If you have time, and especially if it's spring, when the desert is in bloom, drive through the entire park from north to south. It's only a 47-mile drive. As you descend to the lower desert, temperatures rise and plants become more sparse. You'll see fuzzy cholla and stick-branched ocotillo, as well as saltbush and other plants common to the lower desert. Stop at Cholla Cactus Garden to walk on paths along a thriving thicket of the prickly plants. Near the Cottonwood Visitor Center, stretch your legs on a short hike to the palm oasis. Exit the park at the southern entrance and return to Palm Springs via I-10.

If you spend your time exploring the northern part of the park only, you'll find a rewarding stop on the way home at the **Hi-Desert Nature Museum** in Yucca Valley. Located in the Community Center Complex off State Highway 62, this small museum houses nature collections from all over the world. You'll see large, well-lit exhibits of butterflies, insects, fossils, and birds' nests with eggs. Multicolored rocks and minerals are displayed with fluorescent lights.

Another unusual stop along State Highway 62 is **Pioneertown.** Located four miles northwest of Yucca Valley on Pioneertown Road, this western town was built in the early 1940s by Gene Autry and Roy Rogers to be used for filming cowboy movies. Today, the town has a small permanent population. Housed in its railroad-tie and adobe buildings are a post office, bowling alley, art gallery, and Pioneertown Palace, a family restaurant that features home-style food and live western entertainment.

Attractions

HI-DESERT NATURE MUSEUM, 5711 Twentynine Palms Highway, Yucca Valley. (Exit I-10 at Twentynine Palms Highway [62]; north to museum in the Community Center Complex in Yucca Valley.) (619) 365-9814. Open Wednesday–Sunday, 1–5 P.M. Free.

JOSHUA TREE NATIONAL MONUMENT, 74485 National Monument Drive, Twentynine Palms. (Exit I-10 at Twentynine Palms Highway [62]; north to park entrances in Twentynine Palms and Joshua Tree.) (619) 367-7511. Visitors center open daily, 8 A.M.–4:30 P.M. Free. Admission to Monument, $5 per vehicle.

PIONEERTOWN, Pioneertown Road. (Exit I-10 at Twentynine Palms Highway [62]; north to Pioneertown Road; left four miles to town.) Town open daily. Free. Pioneertown Palace: (619) 365-5956. Open Thursday–Sunday, 11 A.M.–midnight.

For More Information

Joshua Tree Chamber of Commerce, 61762 Twentynine Palms Highway, Joshua Tree, CA 92252; (619) 366-8011.

Trip 3: Salton Sea

Take the kids to the Salton Sea if you want to spend a day swimming, boating, or fishing at a most unusual inland desert lake. The 38-mile-long lake, located southeast of Palm Springs along State Highway 111, is California's largest. Its shimmering turquoise water stands in stark contrast to the parched, barren desert that surrounds it.

The Salton Sea is actually the result of an engineering accident. In 1905, the Imperial Valley irrigation system failed when a dam broke and the Colorado River flooded the old Salton Sink, a basin some 234 feet below sea level that once was part of the Gulf of California. Although fresh water flooded the basin, it absorbed minerals left by the prehistoric sea. Today the Salton Sea is slightly more salty than the Pacific Ocean.

The best place to enjoy the lake with children is the **Salton Sea State Recreation Area,** which stretches 14 miles along the northeast lakeshore. Stop at the visitors center to see a videotaped slide show about the history of the area and desert ecology. Young children will be fascinated by the displays of animal hides and skulls they can touch.

Swimming is best at Mecca Beach and at the beach near the headquarters. You'll float easily in the saline water. Watch the kids, though, because there are no lifeguards on duty. You can rent boats and waterskiing equipment just outside the park, near the headquarters entrance, and launch the boats at the park's harbor. If you want to fish, buy a day license at a convenience store in the nearby community of North Shore. Children under 16 don't need a fishing license. Four varieties of fish are abundant in the lake: corvina, sargo, gulf croaker, and talapia.

There are no food concessions in the park, so bring a picnic or pick up lunch at one of the stores or restaurants in North Shore. You can picnic at any of the park's five campgrounds.

Near the headquarters, there's a 1½-mile nature trail, and at a native plant garden and a pond by the ranger station, you'll see rare desert pupfish. The Salton Sea National Wildlife Refuge, near the south end of the lake, is a prime place for spotting some of the nearly four hundred species of birds that visit the area each year. Look for great blue herons and snow geese in the winter.

Attraction

SALTON SEA STATE RECREATION AREA, North Shore. (Follow State Highway 111 south from Palm Springs to the recreation area on the northeast shore of the lake.) (619) 393-3052. Open daily, year round. Admission, $3 per car.

Trip 4: Anza-Borrego Desert State Park

America's largest state park, Anza-Borrego, sits halfway between Palm Springs and San Diego. It's about ninety miles from either city to the park headquarters at Borrego Springs, a small community in the center of the 600,000-acre park.

The best time to visit is in the winter when cool temperatures make hiking pleasant, because hiking is the main activity in this desert park. If your kids don't like to hike, save this park for a time when they are old enough to appreciate it.

The **Anza-Borrego Desert State Park Visitors Center** is located at the west end of Palm Canyon Drive, northwest of Borrego Springs. Children find the center interesting because it's built underground, like the homes of many desert animals. In the cool interior, you'll find exhibits of Indian and pioneer artifacts. A slide show introduces you to the park and its wildlife. Near the center is the three-mile-loop Borrego Palm Canyon nature trail with signs pointing out the wildlife and plants that exist in this harsh environment. On the hike you'll learn about plants used for medicine and food by Indians who once lived here. Along this trail you'll also see an impressive stand of Washingtonia filifera, a native palm named in honor of the first U.S. president.

After the hike, buy a driving map at the visitors center for 50 cents and explore the park. Depending on the time you have to spend, you'll see rugged mountains, rainbow-colored badlands, and miles of desert lowlands with earthquake faults and odd-shaped rocks. Be on the lookout for bighorn sheep in the mountains and hundreds of varieties of birds. You can hike, drive, and if the kids are old enough, ride dirt bikes to explore the park. Rent bikes at the Agua Caliente General Store. Rangers lead nature programs and guided hikes on weekends between November and May.

Attraction

ANZA-BORREGO DESERT STATE PARK VISITORS CENTER, 200 Palm Canyon Drive, Borrego Springs. (Southeast on State Highway 111 to State Highway 86 at Coachella; south about thirty miles to Highway S22 at Salton City; left to Borrego Springs.) (619) 767-5311. Summer hours: Saturday and Sunday, 10 A.M.–3 P.M. Winter hours: daily, 9 A.M.–4 P.M. State park is open daily 24 hours, year round. Admission: $3 per car.

Trip 5: Idyllwild; From Palms to Pines

The aerial tramway isn't the only way to find snow near Palm Springs in the winter. You can drive there, too, on the scenic Pines to Palms State Highway (74) that winds up the mountain to the town of Idyllwild, or by a slightly shorter route, driving via I-10 to Banning, and south on State Highway 243 to Idyllwild. At 5,500 feet above sea level, Idyllwild usually has snow from November to April. Bring a sled for the kids and head for **Idyllwild County Park** to slide down some rolling hills and make a snowman. There are no sled or cross-country ski rentals in this fairly uncommercial town. During summer, the park offers hiking trails and picnic grounds. Idyllwild itself is a rustic village of redwood buildings and green roofs, with art galleries, gift shops, and restaurants to explore.

Just west of town is **Idyllwild School of Music and the Arts (ISO-MATA),** which offers weekend and weeklong classes to children in theater, dance, music, and the visual arts. Students present theater, music, and dance concerts that you can attend on most weekends throughout the summer. There are also weekly art gallery openings on campus. Call the school for schedules.

On the way back to Palm Springs along State Highway 74, stop at the **Living Free Animal Sanctuary** near Mountain Center. This animal refuge rehabilitates and cares for homeless or abused dogs and cats. Let the kids pick a dog to walk along the sanctuary's hiking trails, or play with the cats in the "cattery." Be careful, though; the refuge likes to arrange adoptions.

Attractions

IDYLLWILD COUNTRY PARK VISITOR CENTER, 54000 Route 243, Idyllwild. (Exit I-10 at State Highway 243; south to Idyllwild. Exit I-10 at Monterey Avenue; south past State Highway 111 and continue after road becomes State Highway 74; south and east to State Highway 243; right to Idyllwild. (714) 659-3850. Open Wednesday–Sunday, 9 A.M.–6 P.M. year round. Free.

IDYLLWILD SCHOOL OF MUSIC AND THE ARTS, Idyllwild. (Exit I-10 at State Highway 243; south to Tollgate Road; west into campus.) (714) 659-2171. Call for performance schedule.

LIVING FREE ANIMAL SANCTUARY, State Highway 74, Mountain Center. (Exit I-10 at Monterey Avenue; south past State Highway 111 and continue after road becomes State Highway 74 to sanctuary.) (714) 659-4684. Open Thursday–Monday, 10 A.M.–4 P.M. Free.

For More Information

Idyllwild Chamber of Commerce, 54274 North Circle (at Sugar Pine Shop), Box 304, Idyllwild, CA 92349; (714) 659-2810.

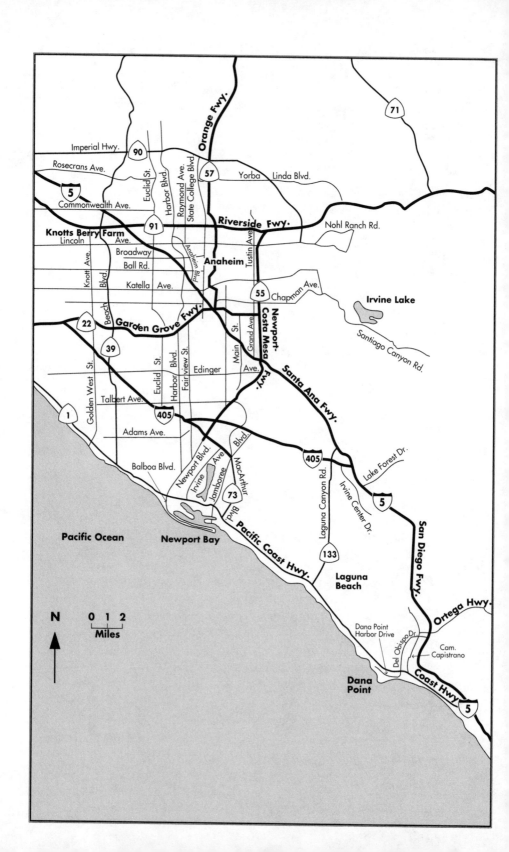

10

Orange County

For many kids, a trip to Orange County means visiting Disneyland and Knott's Berry Farm, and nothing more. It's too bad, because nearby those stellar theme parks are dozens of attractions that are designed especially for kids or have special children's programs.

Ever since Walt Disney opened his theme park in 1955, Orange County has been one of the fastest-growing regions in the nation. Two million people now live in houses that march in rows where citrus groves once stood. This burgeoning population in the county's 26 incorporated cities has spawned the need for children's museums, zoos, clean beaches, and wilderness parks throughout the county.

You'll find concentrations of these attractions in six areas described in this chapter. Typical of Southern California, few of these areas feature activities within walking distance of each other. Yet each area itinerary spotlights attractions within a short drive from one another. Many are connected by Orange County Transit District bus lines. Once you know which activities are near each other in a specific area, you can mix and match them to create a day that will appeal to you and your kids.

DISNEYLAND AND KNOTT'S BERRY FARM
Theme Parks for All Ages

For families with children, Disneyland and Knott's Berry Farm are the twin shrines of any Southern California amusement-park pilgrimage. They are the two most popular theme parks on the West Coast, and deservedly so. Both maintain immaculate facilities, take pride in their wholesome entertainment, and are constantly renewing and upgrading their attractions.

Each park requires at least a full day to see. Although they are barely ten miles apart, you should resist the temptation to visit Disneyland and Knott's Berry Farm on consecutive days. Each entails more walking and standing than you probably do in a month, and the exercise plus the stimulation will leave both you and the kids exhausted. As soon as you enter either park, plan a place to meet so that youngsters will know where to go if they get separated from you. Both parks have facilities for lost children, as well as stroller rentals and changing rooms for infants.

Disneyland is the number-one attraction for children and adults in Southern California and has been for several decades. Since the park opened in 1955, thousands of kids have danced down Main Street, walked in wonder over the bridge to Sleeping Beauty's Castle, and held their breath as hippos charged their jungle riverboat. Now a second generation is thrilling to rides that once excited their parents. And parents willingly come back.

Disneyland's biggest crowds arrive on summer weekends, so it's best to come on a weekday, or better yet, during the off season. Whenever you visit, try to arrive at the park when it opens, and head for the newest and most popular attractions first. Later in the day you may have to wait in line an hour or more for the same attraction. If you're staying in a hotel nearby during the summer, you'll avoid fatigue by seeing part of the park in the morning, then going back to the hotel to rest or swim, and returning in the evening to see the shows and the fireworks at closing time.

Disneyland has more than sixty attractions in seven themed "lands." If you have young children, head first to Fantasyland where the rides are calm and not too scary. There, you will fly with Peter Pan in a pirate ship over moonlit London; ride a caterpillar down a rabbit hole with Alice in Wonderland, and float in a boat through a fanciful setting of animated dolls who sing, "It's a Small World After All." On the whole, the Fantasyland rides are not frightening to small children, although some youngsters might be afraid of the special effects in Mr. Toad's Wild Ride or the huge open-mouthed whale that leads to the benign miniature world of Storybook Land.

Youngsters flock to Tom Sawyer's Island in the middle of Frontierland to explore forts, crawl through tunnels, and run across rope bridges. The island is open only during daylight hours and accessible only by raft. It's a place to let the kids run off some steam while adults grab a quiet cup of coffee in nearby New Orleans Square.

Older children may find the island too tame. They want to experience the park's "mountain" thrill rides. Since these rides are very popular and are scattered throughout the park, you will need to refer to the map you received at the entrance and head for the ride you want to see the most at the beginning of the day. Then work your way around the park in a circle, to avoid running back and forth.

Disneyland's "mountain" rides are the park's roller coasters, most popular with older kids. On Space Mountain, you whiz through darkness, while aboard the train at Big Thunder Mountain, you hurl over steep trails in the Wild West. You'll slide down a snowy peak in a bobsled on Matterhorn Mountain, and at Splash Mountain, you'll ride a hollowed-out log down a waterfall at a speed of 40 miles an hour. Splash Mountain, the centerpiece of an area renamed Critter Land, uses 105 animated characters such as Brer Rabbit and Brer Fox to re-create scenes from the 1946 Disney film, *Song of the South.*

This ride and several others make use of one of Disneyland's most outstanding innovations, Audio-Animatronics technology. With the aid of computers, figures with lifelike movements and synchronized sounds entertain you at some of the park's longest rides, such as the Haunted Mansion and the Pirates of the Caribbean near New Orleans Square.

Across the park in Tomorrowland, lines form early for Star Tours. This flight simulator makes you believe that you are having a bumpy ride aboard a StarSpeeder on the way to the Moon of Endor. Nearby, kids are fascinated with a 3-D musical space adventure film, *Captain EO*, in which Michael Jackson seems to dance right out of the screen while lasers shoot over the heads of the audience.

Be sure to make time to view a parade if one is scheduled while you're in the park. Costumes, musical groups, and lighting effects make these parades a special experience. When the kids are tired, there are plenty of places to rest and to eat, often with entertainment. If you're at the park at 9:30 P.M. in the summer, you'll be rewarded with a burst of fireworks that light up the sky over Sleeping Beauty's Castle.

Immediately west of Disneyland across West Street, the **Disneyland Hotel** is an attraction in itself. Linked directly to the Magic Kingdom by the Disneyland monorail, the hotel offers guests and visitors a variety of its own diversions. In the evenings at eight and nine o'clock, the Dancing Waters leap and cascade with the help of colored spotlights and musical accompaniment. You can rent pedalboats in a large lagoon, and a nearby "beach" features real sand and palm trees next to two swimming pools. Kids also enjoy the hotel's Video Adventure arcade, remote-controlled *Queen Mary* tugboats, and miniature off-road racing.

Ten miles from Disneyland, **Knott's Berry Farm** is Southern California's second-most popular family attraction. Ironically, it didn't start out to be a large amusement park. Long-time residents remember when Knott's offered only a few 25-cent rides and an Old West ghost town created by Walter Knott to entertain people waiting in line at a modest restaurant for his wife Cordilla's chicken dinners and berry pies.

Today, the 150-acre park has 165 rides, attractions, and live shows. Of the five themed areas, Camp Snoopy is the only one designed specifically for young children. The six-acre area features the Charles Schulz cartoon characters Snoopy and the *Peanuts* gang in a California Sierra Mountains campground setting. Kids explore a meandering stream with suspension bridges and play in attractions geared to kids under 12. Young children also like panning for real gold in the 1880s ghost town and riding on an authentic Butterfield stagecoach. Kids who like dinosaurs will be fascinated by the gigantic animated creatures they'll encounter on a seven-minute educational ride through the Kingdom of the Dinosaurs.

Other attractions have more appeal to older kids. Montezooma's Revenge hurls you through a loop-the-loop both frontwards and backwards at 55 mph. The Corkscrew, the very first roller coaster in the country to take riders upside down, snaps you through a series of 360-degree turns. If your kids like these kinds of rides, head for them early in the day because the lines get longer by afternoon.

One ride you'll want to save for the warmest hours of the day is Bigfoot Rapids, which takes you on a very wet white-knuckle ride down a man-made white-water river. This one obviously isn't for very young children.

Knott's also features live entertainment throughout the day. Kids especially enjoy the Wild West Stunt Show, and at the Birdcage Theater, they can hiss and boo the villain in an old-time melodrama. Of the several dozen eateries, Mrs. Knott's Chicken Dinner Restaurant still serves a quality meal at a reasonable price.

If you're here in the summer, and the kids are old enough, try to stay at the park until 9:45 P.M. to see Knott's Incredible Fireworks Machine, which choreographs fireworks with music above Reflection Lake.

Attractions

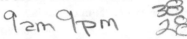

DISNEYLAND, 1313 Harbor Boulevard, Anaheim. (Exit Santa Ana Freeway [5] at Harbor Boulevard or Katella Avenue; follow signs to park.) (714) 999-4000 or (213) 626-8605. Open Memorial Day–Labor Day, daily, 8 A.M.–1 A.M. Labor Day–Memorial Day, Monday–Friday, 10 A.M.–6 P.M.; Saturday, 9 A.M.–midnight; Sunday, 9 A.M.–9 P.M. Adults, $25.50; seniors, $20.50; ages 3–11, $20.50; under 3, free (admission and unlimited use).

DISNEYLAND HOTEL, 1150 West Cerritos Avenue, Anaheim. (Exit Santa Ana Freeway [5] at Ball Road; west to West Street; left to Cerritos Avenue; right to hotel.) (714) 778-6600. Open daily.

KNOTT'S BERRY FARM, 8039 Beach Boulevard, Buena Park. (Exit Santa Ana Freeway [5] at Beach Boulevard [39]; south to park.) (714) 220-5200. Open Memorial Day–Labor Day, Sunday–Friday, 10 A.M.–midnight; Saturday, 10 A.M.–1 P.M. Labor Day–Memorial Day, Monday–Friday, 10 A.M.–6 P.M.; Saturday, 10 A.M.–10 P.M.; Sunday, 10 A.M.–7 P.M. Adults, $21; seniors, $14.95; ages 3–11, $15.95; under 3, free (admission and unlimited use).

For More Information

Anaheim Area Visitor and Convention Bureau, 800 West Katella Avenue, Anaheim, CA 92802; (714) 635-8900.

Buena Park Office of Tourism and Conventions, 7711 Beach Boulevard, Suite B, Box 5308, Buena Park, CA 90620; (714) 994-1511.

ANAHEIM AND BUENA PARK
Much More Than Theme Parks

Although Anaheim and Buena Park are best known for their family theme parks, Disneyland and Knott's Berry Farm, visitors are often surprised to find that these cities have other attractions that also appeal to kids. Some of these places were established in the area because of their successful neighbors. Others have been there since the turn of the century; and one even had its beginnings back in prehistoric times. It would take several days to see all the attractions in these two communities. You'll need to choose from among them to fit your family's interests.

Movieland Wax Museum capitalizes on the important role Southern California has played in the American film industry. Located a block north of Knott's Berry Farm on Beach Boulevard in Buena Park, this wax museum is the largest in the United States, with more than 240 stars portrayed in wax. Figures are placed in elaborate sets and costumes that duplicate the original movie or television productions. The tableaus span a period of seventy years. Kids will recognize many of the famous entertainers and sets, such as Michael Jackson, Superman, and characters from *The Wizard of Oz*. Blinking lights outline movie marquees in this well-lit museum, and musical scores or other sound effects highlight each exhibit. Rain falls on Gene Kelly as he poses on a set for *Singin' in the Rain* and noisy weapons flash with light as you walk through a gun battle on the *Delta Force* set with Chuck Norris.

The Chamber of Horrors has a separate entrance behind a souvenir and snack shop area. Through an archway draped with cobwebs, you'll enter a dark, scary world of thunder, lightning, and scenes from such films as *Alien*, *Creature from the Black Lagoon,* and *Frankenstein.* Younger children who would be frightened by this section can detour through the shop to calmer exhibits. In a gallery at the end of the tour, kids can hand-crank moving picture "flicks" on one of the antique Mutoscopes positioned at children's eye level.

Across the street from the museum, in a castle complete with towers, battlements, and a portcullis gate, **Medieval Times Dinner and Tournament** re-creates the year A.D. 1093. Brave knights joust on horseback and do battle with swords on the ground in a show planned to please children and adults alike. As guests enter the castle tower, they are given a color-coded crown that corresponds to the knight they will cheer during a show in the 1,040-seat arena. Children get a kick out of eating a four-course medieval dinner with their hands while they watch their knight do battle. A master of ceremonies makes the experience an educational one for kids. He explains the use of ancient weapons, tells the history of chivalry, and describes the equestrian events. The show runs every night of the week and there's a matinee on Sundays. Reservations are required. You also can tour the castle free, Monday through Saturday, to see the horses and the arena where the tournament takes place.

For a step much further back in time, drive north on Beach Boulevard to

Rosecrans Avenue and visit the **Ralph B. Clark Regional Park Interpretive Center.** This museum showcases the 70,000-year-old Pleistocene animal remains and the 1-million-year-old marine specimens found in rich fossil beds nearby. Six habitat groupings display ancient skeletons of animals such as a saber-toothed cat, tapir, and ground sloth, to teach kids how much times have changed in Orange County. Hands-on exhibits at the well-designed center allow children to manipulate models and push buttons to activate informative electronic displays. Youngsters shake plastic tubes to learn about sedimentary deposits and they measure themselves against silhouettes of ancient mammals painted on the museum walls. The center offers special programs for children on Saturday mornings that include such activities as sorting fossils in a lab and helping a paleontologist dig up some of the fossils in an excavation. The center also arranges tours for school and club groups.

Elsewhere in the park you'll find children's play areas, a sand volleyball court, picnic areas with barbecues, and a lake where you can fish or feed the ducks.

South of Buena Park in Anaheim, **Hobby City U.S.A.** is a good stop for children who have collections or who like to make craft items. The 23 craft and hobby shops that make up this complex specialize in such items as model trains, pets, teddy bears, educational toys, Indian crafts, and dolls. You can buy a supply of craft items here to keep kids happy on a long car trip or busy at home. On weekends, a miniature train takes youngsters for rides around a shady picnic area.

At the back of the parking lot you'll notice a half-scale replica of the White House, the site of the **Hobby City Doll and Toy Museum.** Displayed inside are nearly three thousand dolls and toys collected from around the world by Bea DeArmand and her husband, Jay, who started Hobby City in 1955 on an old chicken ranch. The exhibits date from 3,000-year-old Egyptian dolls to modern-day Barbie and Ken dolls. There are English beeswax dolls from the 1830s and German bisque dolls sitting on antique furniture. Hopi kachina dolls share a case with African tribal dolls. George and Martha Washington, who never lived in the real White House, are included in a group of dolls of famous historical figures, many of which older children will recognize. A replica of the Imperial Palace in Kyoto, Japan, houses finely costumed dolls that represent the Japanese royal court. Besides dolls, you'll see toy trains, cars, child-size sewing machines, and dollhouses. All displays are behind glass, so children can't touch. Yet kids will no doubt come away from a visit with a new appreciation for their dolls and toys, and they may become interested in collecting or making some of their own.

In downtown Anaheim, north of Disneyland, a cluster of places have special programs just for kids. At the **Anaheim Museum,** located in the restored Carnegie Library Building on South Anaheim Boulevard, there is a cheerful children's gallery downstairs. One of four galleries in the museum, the children's gallery has hands-on exhibits that correspond with the changing exhibits in two galleries upstairs. A fourth gallery features permanent displays on the history of Anaheim, detailing its beginnings in 1857 as a winemaking area for German settlers.

A few blocks west of the museum, the **Anaheim Central Library** on Broadway presents free children's films every Saturday at 1 P.M. and has storytimes for toddlers (under 3) every Wednesday morning, preschoolers (3–5) every Tuesday afternoon, and story hours for families every Tuesday night at 7 P.M. The library carries 45,000 titles for children. Plan to give your child some time to curl up with a good book in the gingerbread house in the children's library.

The museum administers one of Anaheim's cultural treasures, the **Mother Colony House,** a few blocks away on West Street. The first frame residence built in Anaheim, the 1857 structure is furnished with antiques from the period. On a self-guided tour, school-age kids will be most intrigued by the old-fashioned tools and appliances used in the kitchen and for winemaking, and by a pink and black plaid wedding dress on display.

Nearby, the **Anaheim Cultural Arts Center** offers several special programs for children. The **American Children's Theatre** presents plays every Saturday and Sunday at 2 P.M. All plays are musical versions of such classics as *Cinderella* or *Rumplestiltskin.* Buccaneer Ben greets children at the door and gives each one a pirate hat. The one-hour plays are presented in a theater in the round with two rows of seats, so young children are assured of a good view. An adjacent birthday party room is free.

Also at the Anaheim Cultural Arts Center, **Razzle Dazzle Fun Time Family Gatherings** showcase a variety of artists on Saturday at 4 P.M. Shows feature mimes, storytelling, and holiday themes. This same group presents family art and drama workshops at the center on Saturday mornings at 9 A.M.

If your children are interested in baseball and football, you'll have an opportunity to see both nearby at **Anaheim Stadium,** located east of Disneyland at the junction of the Santa Ana Freeway (5) and the Orange Freeway (57). This 70,000-seat stadium is the home of both the California Angels baseball club and the Los Angeles Rams football team. If you're in the area during the right season, you can catch a game. You also can tour the stadium daily on non-event days. On a one-hour tour you'll see locker rooms where players suit up, dugouts, press areas, and the Rams' suite where team owners watch the games. You'll also be able to walk out on the field. To join a tour, park free at Gate 1 and wait in the Gate 1 lobby until the next tour starts on the hour.

East of the city in Anaheim Hills, the **Oak Canyon Nature Center** has free drop-in family "Discovery" programs on Saturday at 10 A.M. Programs include slides, films, or live animal shows, and they usually conclude with a short walk through the canyon. Of course, you can hike along the park's six miles of trails on any day. On a walk through a chaparral and oak forest, you'll see a wide variety of birds, including quail and woodpeckers, and a shaded stream with pollywogs and water striders. The center also offers special nature tours by reservation for preschool groups and older children.

Attractions

ANAHEIM CENTRAL LIBRARY, 500 West Broadway, Anaheim, (Exit Santa Ana Freeway [5] at Harbor Boulevard; north to Broadway; left to library. Exit Riverside Freeway [91] at Harbor Boulevard; south to Broadway; right to library.) (714) 999-1880. Open Monday–Friday, 9 A.M.–9 P.M.; Saturday, 9 A.M.–6 P.M. Storytimes: ages 2 and under, Wednesday, 10 and 11 A.M.; ages 3–5, Tuesday, 3:30 P.M.; families with children ages 3–8, Tuesday, 7 P.M.; all ages, Saturday, 10 A.M. Free.

ANAHEIM CULTURAL ARTS CENTER, 931 North Harbor Boulevard, Anaheim. (Exit Santa Ana Freeway [5] at Harbor Boulevard; north to center. Exit Riverside Freeway [91] at Harbor Boulevard; south to center.)

• *American Children's Theatre*, (714) 533-3460. Plays presented on Saturday and Sunday, 2 P.M. Adults, $5; children, $4.
• *Razzle Dazzle Fun Time Family Gatherings*, (714) 533-3460. Workshops on Saturday at 9 A.M.; shows on Saturday at 4 P.M.

ANAHEIM MUSEUM, 241 South Anaheim Boulevard, Anaheim. (Exit southbound Santa Ana Freeway [5] at Euclid Street; south to Lincoln Avenue; east to Anaheim Boulevard; right to museum on corner of Broadway. Exit northbound Santa Ana Freeway [5] at Lincoln Avenue; east to Anaheim Boulevard; right to museum. Exit Riverside Freeway [91] at Harbor Boulevard; south to Broadway; left to museum on corner of Anaheim Boulevard.) (714) 778-3301. Wednesday–Friday, 10 A.M.–4 P.M.; Saturday and Sunday, noon–4 P.M. A donation of $1.50 is requested.

ANAHEIM STADIUM TOURS, 2000 State College Boulevard, Anaheim. (Exit Santa Ana Freeway [5] at State College Boulevard; north to stadium following signs for parking. Exit Orange Freeway [57] at Orange-wood or Katella avenues; follow signs to stadium parking.) (714) 937-6750. Box office open Monday–Friday, 9 A.M.–5 P.M.; Saturday, 9 A.M.–4 P.M. Call for game times and ticket prices. Hourly stadium tours on non-event days, October–April, 11 A.M.–2 P.M.; May–October, 10 A.M.–3 P.M. Tour admission: adults, $3; seniors and juniors under 16, $2; under 5, free. Meet at Gate 1 lobby.

HOBBY CITY U.S.A. AND DOLL AND TOY MUSEUM, 1238 South Beach Boulevard, Anaheim. (Exit Santa Ana Freeway [5] at Beach Boulevard; south about four miles.) (714) 527-2323. Open daily, 10 A.M.–6 P.M. Museum admission: adults, $1; children and seniors, 50 cents.

MEDIEVAL TIMES DINNER AND TOURNAMENT, 7662 Beach Boulevard, Buena Park. (Exit Santa Ana Freeway [5] or Riverside Freeway [91] at Beach Boulevard; south to castle.) (714) 521-4740, (800) 438-9911 (in CA), (800) 826-5358. (nationwide). Performances held nightly, and Sunday, 1 P.M. Performance times and admission costs vary during week. Admission includes dinner and show: adults, $27–$30; children 12 and under, $18–$19. Reservations required. Self-guided tours, Monday–Thursday, 9 A.M.–4 P.M. Free.

MOTHER COLONY HOUSE, 414 North West Street, Anaheim. (Exit Santa Ana Freeway [5] southbound at Euclid Street; south to Lincoln Avenue; left to West Street; left to house. Exit Santa Ana Freeway [5] northbound at Lincoln Avenue; east to West Street; left to house. Exit Riverside Freeway [91] at Harbor Boulevard; south to La Palma; right to West Street; left to house.) (714) 774-3840 or, to book tours, (714) 999-1850. Open Wednesday, 3–5 P.M.; Sunday, 1:30–4 P.M. Free.

MOVIELAND WAX MUSEUM, 7711 Beach Boulevard, Buena Park. (Exit Santa Ana Freeway [5] or Riverside Freeway [91] at Beach Boulevard; south to museum.) (714) 522-1154. Summer hours (Easter–Labor Day): daily, 9 A.M.–8 P.M. Winter hours (Labor Day–Easter): 10 A.M.–8 P.M. Museum closes 1½ hours after box office. Adults (12 and over), $9.95; children (4–11), $5.95; under 4, free.

OAK CANYON NATURE CENTER, 6700 Walnut Canyon Road, Anaheim Hills. (Exit Riverside Freeway [91] at Imperial Highway; south to Nohl Ranch Road; left to Walnut Canyon Road; left to park.) (714) 998-8380 or

(714) 999-5191. Daily, 9 A.M.–5 P.M. Discovery programs, Saturday, 10 A.M. Free.

RALPH B. CLARK REGIONAL PARK INTERPRETIVE CENTER, 8800 Rosecrans Avenue, Buena Park. (Exit Santa Ana Freeway [5] or Riverside Freeway [91] at Beach Boulevard; north to Rosecrans Avenue; right to park.) (714) 670-8045. Interpretive Center open, Tuesday–Sunday, 9 A.M.–3 P.M. Free. Park open daily. Winter hours: 7 A.M.–6 P.M. Summer hours: 7 A.M.–9 P.M. Free. Parking: $1.50 per car.

For More Information

Anaheim Area Visitor and Convention Bureau, Tourism Dept., Box 4270, Anaheim CA 92803; (714) 635-8900.

FULLERTON AND LA HABRA
Make Tracks to Children's Museums and More

Trains played a big part in the development of the Orange County cities of Fullerton and La Habra. These side-by-side communities are just two of several towns that grew in 1887 when the Santa Fe Railroad arrived. Fullerton was even named after George Fullerton, the agent who brought the train route to the area.

Today, you still can see the influence of railroads on these two communities. Kids who are fascinated with trains will be excited to know they can visit a children's museum in a train station, eat a spaghetti dinner in another historic depot, and even ride an Amtrak train to Fullerton to spend a day there.

The **Children's Museum at La Habra** is housed in La Habra's restored, red-tile-roofed Union Pacific Station. Old waiting rooms and depot offices are now full of interactive exhibits designed for kids. A sign near the entrance of the indoor Nature Walk sets the tone for the museum. It reads, "Please Touch the Animals." In this exhibit, kids walk among and pet mounted animals such as a skunk, mule deer, black bear, and an opossum hanging from a tree by his tail. A small adjacent room contains a live colony of bees making honey in a glass observatory. In another gallery, kids can push buttons to run a model railroad village, with two levels of trains moving over bridges, through tunnels and past houses with twinkling lights.

A red caboose filled with historic treasures from La Habra's early days sits outside on railroad tracks. The car's exhibits may be most interesting to adults, but kids enjoy seeing the inside of a caboose and they can climb up into the car's cupola observation tower. The museum's recent 8,000-square-foot expansion has a science station with participatory mini-exhibits and a theater equipped with costumes and props.

The museum sits at the edge of Portola Park, a flat, grassy area with picnic tables and play equipment. Adjacent to the museum is the **La Habra Depot Playhouse,** a theater in a railroad car. The La Habra Community Theater presents one children's production at the playhouse each season.

A few miles south of La Habra in Fullerton, there is another museum designed for children, the **Fullerton Youth Science Center.** Housed in Rooms 26 and 27 of Ladera Vista Junior High, this small museum has more than twenty hands-on science exhibits that encourage exploratory learning for kids. There are live animals and fossils to touch. A tesla coil generates visible sparks, while water mysteriously jumps out of a vibrating Chinese bowl. Kids love to ride the angular momentum carousel that changes speeds as users change their body angles. They whisper into large dishes to send secret messages across the room and crawl into a human-size kaleidoscope of mirrors. The museum is open for drop-in visits after school and on Saturday mornings, and at other times for prearranged groups. A full schedule of programs includes field trips and classes that require advance reservations. The **Hacienda Heights Youth Science Center,** a sister facility located less than ten miles north, features similar programs.

The **Fullerton Amtrak Station** sits in the middle of the city, a reminder of Fullerton's beginnings. Located in the renovated former Santa Fe station built in 1930, the station is the cornerstone of the Fullerton Transportation Center. In this pleasant plaza, you can catch trains and buses for more sightseeing. A fun day's outing with kids could begin with a train trip from either Los Angeles or San Diego to Fullerton. There are several attractions kids enjoy that are within walking distance of the station.

Next to the Amtrak station is **The Old Spaghetti Factory,** a restaurant popular with families. It is housed in the mission-style Union Pacific Depot which was built in 1923 and later moved to this site. There's plenty to look at in this bright, open restaurant, decorated with Victorian fringed lamps and colorful antiques. Kids keep busy making colorful cardboard train models while they wait for their spaghetti.

From the transportation center, walk a few blocks north on tree-lined Harbor Boulevard. You'll pass shops and art galleries housed in historic buildings. Older kids will be interested in shopping at the area's well-known (to local kids) comic book stores and baseball-card shops.

Turn right on Wilshire Avenue and walk one block to the **Fullerton**

Museum Center. This upgraded building, which once housed the city's main library, now offers science, history, and art exhibits, as well as educational activities for children. In three main galleries are traveling exhibitions from the Smithsonian Institution and other museums, plus shows originating from the museum's own collections. Docents who lead tours of the museum on weekends point out items of particular interest to youngsters in the group. Children's workshops accompany each show.

One block west of Harbor Boulevard on Wilshire Avenue is an unusual bookstore, **Lorson's Books & Prints,** which sells more than four thousand new titles for children, plus used books. Also for sale are collectibles such as old maps, botanical prints, and original art. A children's corner has a selection of books kids can look at and handle, such as pop-up books.

Another place where children are stimulated by books is the **Fullerton Public Library,** a few blocks west on Commonwealth Avenue. This pleasant, well-lit facility has a large children's section which offers preschool story times, puppet shows, and films for older children during the week. There are plenty of chairs and tables for quiet reading. Across the street, **Amerige Park** is a flat, shady place where you can picnic or the kids can play.

You'll need to drive or take the bus to other Fullerton destinations. A good place to spend several pleasant hours with kids is the **Fullerton Arboretum** at California State University, Fullerton. This 25-acre garden has flower-lined walking paths and a pond with ducks that children can feed. Tour the **Heritage House** near the arboretum entrance if it's open when you are there. Once the home of a local doctor, the Victorian house was built in the 1890s and has been furnished to re-create that period. On a docent-led tour you'll see a typical Victorian kitchen (with no refrigerator or cupboards) and a parlor with old-fashioned toys. In Dr. Clark's office, ask to see the forms once used for making pills, and the bleeder box with sharp protruding knives. Outside, walk through the labeled herb garden full of medicinal plants. The arboretum offers science adventure classes for children after school and on weekends. Reservations are required.

During summer, the Los Angeles Rams football team practices at the university. You can take the kids to watch them work out most days in July and August. If the kids wait patiently by the gate with pen and paper in hand, they might get an autograph of one of the well-known players.

Less than a mile north of the university is **Craig Regional Park.** This long strip of land has facilities for the entire family. Little ones like to feed the ducks at the lake in the center of the park. Ask for a trail brochure in the park office for the two-mile nature trail that starts near the park entrance. The trail passes children's play areas and a sports complex with volleyball, basketball, and racquetball courts. A visitors center features interpretive exhibits on native wildlife. You'll also find covered picnic tables and paved bicycle trails in the park.

If you want to interest kids in the performing arts, plan to see a Broadway musical presented by a cast of about forty children with the **Fullerton Children's Repertory Theater.** The shows, given during three weekends each January and July, are held at the Little Theater, behind Fullerton's Plummer Auditorium. Children who want to perform need to audition.

Attractions

CHILDREN'S MUSEUM AT LA HABRA, 301 South Euclid Street, La Habra. (Exit Riverside Freeway [91] at Euclid Street; north to the museum. Exit Orange Freeway [57] at Imperial Highway; west to Euclid; right to museum.) (213) 694-1011, ext. 271 or (714) 526-2227, ext. 271. Open Tuesday–Saturday, 10 A.M.–4 P.M. Closed Sunday, Monday, and national holidays. Adults, $1.50; children, $1; under 3, free.

CRAIG REGIONAL PARK, 3300 North State College Boulevard, Fullerton. (Exit Orange Freeway [57] at Imperial Highway [90]; west to State College Boulevard; left to park entrance.) (714) 990-0271. Open November 1–March 31, 7 A.M.–6 P.M.; April 1–October 31, 7 A.M.–9 P.M. Parking: $1.50 per auto per day.

FULLERTON AMTRAK STATION, 120 East Santa Fe Avenue, Fullerton. (Exit Riverside Freeway [91] at Harbor Boulevard; north about two miles to Santa Fe Avenue; right to station.) (714) 992-0530. Round-trip train fare, Los Angeles–Fullerton: adults, $12; children, $6.

FULLERTON ARBORETUM, California State University, Fullerton. (Exit Orange Freeway [57] at Yorba Linda Boulevard; west to Associated Road; left into university campus and follow signs to arboretum.) (714) 773-3579. Open daily, 8 A.M.–4:45 P.M. Free. Heritage House, open Sunday, 2–4 P.M. Adults, $1; children, 50 cents. Call for schedule of children's Science Adventure Classes.

FULLERTON CHILDREN'S REPERTORY THEATER, performances at The Little Theater, 201 East Chapman Avenue, Fullerton. (Exit Riverside Freeway [91] at Harbor Boulevard; north to Chapman Avenue; right to theater.) Children's Repertory phone: (714) 525-1726. Performances on weekends in January and July, $4 per seat.

FULLERTON MUSEUM CENTER, 301 North Pomona Avenue, Fullerton. (Exit Riverside Freeway [91] at Harbor Boulevard; north to Wilshire Avenue; right to corner of Pomona Avenue.) (714) 738-6545. Open Tuesday–Wednesday, 11 A.M.–4 P.M.; Thursday–Friday, 11 A.M.–9 P.M.; Saturday and Sunday, 11 A.M.–4 P.M. Closed Monday and major holidays. Adults, $2; seniors and students, $1; children under 12, free. Thursday, 6 P.M.–9 P.M., all ages, free.

FULLERTON PUBLIC LIBRARY, 353 West Commonwealth Avenue, Fullerton. (Exit Riverside Freeway [91] at Harbor Boulevard; north about two miles to Commonwealth Avenue; left to library.) (714) 738-6333. Open Monday–Thursday, 10 A.M.–9 P.M.; Friday, 10 A.M.–6 P.M.; Saturday, 10 A.M.–5 P.M.; Sunday, 1 P.M.–5 P.M. Free.

FULLERTON YOUTH SCIENCE CENTER, Rooms 26 and 27, Lindera Vista Junior High, 1700 Wilshire Avenue, Fullerton. (Exit Riverside Freeway [91] at Raymond Avenue; north to Commonwealth Avenue; right to Acacia Avenue; left to Wilshire Avenue; right to school.) (714) 526-1690. Open weekdays during the school year, 3–5 P.M.; Saturdays, 10 A.M.–noon. Summer hours: Monday–Saturday, 10 A.M.–noon.

HACIENDA HEIGHTS YOUTH SCIENCE CENTER, Room 8, Wedgeworth Elementary School, 16949 Wedgeworth Drive, Hacienda Heights. (Exit Pomona Freeway [60] at Azusa Avenue; south to Pepper Brook Way; right to Wedgeworth Drive; right to school.) (818) 968-2525. Open weekdays during school year, 3–5 P.M.; Saturday, 10 A.M.–2 P.M.

LA HABRA DEPOT PLAYHOUSE, 311 South Euclid Street, La Habra. (See directions to museum above.) (213) 905-9708 or (213) 691-8900.

LORSON'S BOOKS & PRINTS, 116 West Wilshire Avenue, Fullerton. (Exit Riverside Freeway [91] at Harbor Boulevard; north to Wilshire Avenue; left to store.) (714) 526-2523. Open Monday–Saturday, 10 A.M.–5:30 P.M.

THE OLD SPAGHETTI FACTORY, 110 East Santa Fe Avenue, Fullerton. (Exit Riverside Freeway [91] at Harbor Boulevard; north to Santa Fe Avenue; right to restaurant.) (714) 526-6801. Open Monday–Friday, 11:30 A.M.–2 P.M. and 5–10 P.M.; Saturday, 5–10:30 P.M.; Sunday, 4–10 P.M.

For More Information

Fullerton Chamber of Commerce, 219 East Commonwealth Avenue, Fullerton, CA 92632-0529; (714) 871-3100.

La Habra Chamber of Commerce, 321 East La Habra Boulevard, La Habra, CA 90631; (213) 697-1704.

SANTA ANA AND ORANGE
Taste Orange County as It Used to Be

Santa Ana and Orange, two proud old communities, sit at the heart of Orange County. Both cities have been sliced by a confluence of freeways and are surrounded by new housing tracts, yet each has preserved some of its colorful beginnings in a variety of attractions that teach children about the cultural history of the area. Two zoos and nearby wilderness areas also allow kids to discover the natural history of this region. You can combine a visit to one of the local museums with a trip to a zoo or park to make a pleasant day's outing for both adults and kids.

For a look at Orange County before these two communities were formed, take the kids to the **Bowers Museum** on Main Street in Santa Ana. The Spanish-mission–style museum, which is undergoing a renovation and expansion, specializes in the cultural arts of the Americas, the Pacific Rim, Africa, and Oceania. Kids usually are most interested in the American Indian gallery that displays artifacts such as bows and arrows, masks, clothing, and some of the museum's extensive collection of pre-Columbian baskets. Another gallery is devoted to Orange County early history. While most of the artifacts can't be touched, the museum holds hand-on classes for parents and children on weekends and some weekdays.

At the **Discovery Museum of Orange County,** on the west side of Santa Ana, you'll get a slightly more recent history lesson. It's an exploratory learning center for children, with the emphasis on participation and arts and crafts projects. The museum consists of four historic buildings and a citrus orchard located on an 11-acre site near the Santa Ana River in Santa Ana. Tour the H. Clay Kellogg House where exhibits show children what life was like in California at the turn of the century. Kids participate in churning cream into butter and tasting it, and washing clothes with a scrub board and wringer. They can try on period costumes if they wish. In the orchard, the children take a taste test to learn the difference between two varieties of the fruit for which the county is known: Valencia and navel oranges.

In the central area of Santa Ana, two attractions offer tours for school classes, scouts, and other groups. Visit the historic **Old Orange County Courthouse,** at the Santa Ana Civic Center Plaza, for a look at the law and order side of old Orange County. This red sandstone and granite 1901 building is a fine example of Richardson Romanesque architecture, with columns, archways, and gables. The museum is open to the public only on Tuesdays. On a self-guided tour you'll climb a grand staircase embellished with Corinthian columns to the historic courtroom on the third floor. You'll see the adjacent jury room and court reporter's office, as well as the judge's chamber. Older kids studying government or law can try out their courtroom skills in the historic room. Across the foyer, there's a gallery of exhibits documenting Orange County history.

You'll get an up-to-date view of Orange County at **The Register** in Santa Ana. The county's leading newspaper gives tours to groups of children by reservation only on weekdays. Kids see all aspects of newspaper production from the newsroom where reporters are busy writing stories on their computers, to the production area where paste-up artists assemble the paper, to the noisy, three-story-high presses that print seventy thousand copies an hour.

For a relaxing day outdoors, visit the **Santa Ana Zoo,** just off Santa Ana Freeway (5). The small zoo is undergoing an ambitious expansion program to create better housing for its collection of international animals. Start at the children's zoo near the entrance if you have small children in tow. Buy handfuls of pellets at food dispensers so the kids can feed sheep, goats, and other animals in the barnyard petting zoo. Go inside the barn to see baby chickens and pigs. Notice the educational exhibit under a tree nearby that poses questions about the animals and hides the answers in peepholes. Follow the path over the pond bridge to see South American llamas and Australian kangaroos. A wide walkway leads through a primate section that is lined with cages of monkeys and apes. Walk through the flight cage full of colorful birds. Nearby, kids get a thrill out of riding an elephant, a treat available on weekends between 11 A.M. and 3 P.M. There is a small snack stand and a children's playground inside the zoo. Outside, adjacent Prentice Park has picnic tables and play areas. The zoo offers several programs for kids including interactive zoology activities in the zoo laboratory and weekend family workshops on the natural history of local wilderness areas. Call the zoo for a program schedule.

A few miles east in the city of Orange, there are four parks with special attractions for kids. The **Irvine Zoo** at **Irvine Regional Park** exhibits animals only from the southwestern United States. Up close, you'll see local wildlife such as deer, coyotes, and many species of birds in fenced areas. Kids can touch docile animals in the petting zoo.

In the park that surrounds the zoo, there are pony rides, and stables where you can rent horses to ride along the park's equestrian trails. You can rent pedalboats during summer at the lagoon, or rent bikes to ride on the park's cement bike trails. Hike the scenic lookout trail in the natural area. It is short, but a little steep for young children. Plan to picnic at tables along Santiago Creek which bisects the park. **Nursery Nature Walks,** a nonprofit group of trained docents, offers guided hikes for toddlers and preschoolers in this park and other locations in Orange County. Administered by the South Coast YMCA, these nature walks encourage young children to look, listen, smell, and touch the plants and wildlife.

A few miles north is **Santiago Oaks Regional Park,** which also has hiking trails and picnic areas. The pleasant 125-acre park, formerly a ranch, is dotted with majestic coast live oaks and California sycamores. A 1938 ranch house has been converted into a nature center with exhibits and wildlife observation areas that allow you to see many different species of birds. If you plan to cook at the park, bring charcoal for the barbecues because no fire wood is allowed. There's a children's playground next to the picnic area.

South of these parks, on Santiago Canyon Road, is **Irvine Lake,** a private reservoir that is stocked with fish every week. You won't have much trouble catching catfish, bass or bluegill, although you'll have to pay to fish in the lake. There's no extra charge for the fish. Rent rowboats, powerboats, and fishing tackle at the dock.

Farther south on Modjeska Canyon Road is **Tucker Wildlife Sanctuary,** a 12-acre bird and animal refuge known for its hummingbirds. A viewing porch overlooks feeders that attract the tiny creatures. Hike the preserve's short loop trails and see how many more of the park's 170 species of birds and animals the kids can spot. Inside a small wildlife museum, look for live reptiles and rodents on display.

If you have doll lovers in the car, stop at **Doll City USA** in Orange, on the way back to the freeway. This huge store claims to be the world's largest doll shop, and you'll see why when you step in the door. Thousands of dolls line shelves along the walls. Doll City does not carry fad dolls for children, but specializes in collectibles and well-made specialty dolls.

Attractions

BOWERS MUSEUM, 2002 North Main Street, Santa Ana. (Exit Santa Ana Freeway [5] at Main Street; south to the museum.) (714) 972-1900. Tuesday–Saturday, 10 A.M.–5 P.M.; Sunday, noon–5 P.M. Free.

DISCOVERY MUSEUM OF ORANGE COUNTY, 3101 West Harvard Street, Santa Ana. (Exit Newport–Costa Mesa Freeway [55], at Edinger Avenue; east about three miles to Fairview Street at Centennial Regional Park; left to Harvard Street; right to museum.) (714) 540-0404. Saturday, 11 A.M.–3 P.M. Adults, $1; children, 50 cents.

DOLL CITY USA, 2040 North Tustin Avenue, Orange. (Exit Riverside Freeway [91] at Tustin Avenue; south to store on corner of Meats Avenue.) (714) 998-9384. Monday–Saturday, 10 A.M.–5 P.M.

IRVINE REGIONAL PARK and *IRVINE ZOO,* 21501 East Chapman Avenue, Orange. (Exit Newport–Costa Mesa Freeway [55] at Chapman Avenue; east approximately five miles to park entrance.) (714) 633-8072. Winter hours: 7 A.M.–6 P.M. Summer hours: 7 A.M.–9 P.M. Day-use fee: $2 per vehicle.

IRVINE LAKE, off Santiago Canyon Road. (Exit Newport–Costa Mesa Freeway [55] at Chapman Avenue; east approximately 5 miles to Santiago Canyon Road; right about 3½ miles.) (714) 649-2991. Open daily, 6 A.M.– 4 P.M. and 5 P.M.–11 P.M. Adults, $9; ages 12 and under, $7.

NURSERY NATURE WALKS, South Coast YMCA, 29831 Crown Valley Parkway, Laguna Niguel, CA 92677. (714) 643-1444. Call for a schedule of walks and directions to parks. Donation for walks: $3 per family.

OLD ORANGE COUNTY COURTHOUSE, corner of Santa Ana Boulevard and Broadway, Santa Ana. (Exit Santa Ana Freeway [5] at Main Street; south to Santa Ana Boulevard; right to courthouse.) (714) 834-4741. Open Tuesday, 9 A.M.–3 P.M. Free.

THE REGISTER, 625 North Grand Avenue, Santa Ana. (Exit Santa Ana Freeway [5] at Grand Avenue; south to entrance.) (714) 835-1234. Daily tours by reservation. Free.

SANTA ANA ZOO, 1801 East Chestnut, Santa Ana. (Exit Santa Ana Freeway [5] on 1st Street, west to Elk Lane along Prentice Park; left to Chestnut Avenue; left to zoo entrance.) (714) 835-7484. Open daily, 10 A.M.–6 P.M. Adults, $2; ages 3–13 and seniors, 75 cents; under 3, free.

SANTIAGO OAKS REGIONAL PARK, 2145 North Windes Drive, Orange. (Exit Newport–Costa Mesa Freeway [55] at Katella Avenue, which becomes Santiago Canyon Road; east three miles to Windes Drive; left to park at end of road.) (714) 538-4400. Open daily, 7 A.M.–sunset. Day-use fee: $2 per vehicle.

TUCKER WILDLIFE SANCTUARY, 29322 Modjeska Canyon Road, Orange. (Exit Newport–Costa Mesa Freeway [55] at Chapman Avenue; east to Santiago Canyon Road; south to Modjeska Canyon Road; left to sanctuary.) (714) 649-2760. Open daily, 9 A.M.–4 P.M. Wildlife museum donation: $1.50.

For More Information

Orange Chamber of Commerce, 80 Plaza Square, Orange, CA 92666; (714) 538-3581.

Santa Ana Community Events Center, 116A West Fourth Street #2, Box 1988-M86, Santa Ana, CA 92702; (714) 647-6561.

NEWPORT AND NEARBY BEACH COMMUNITIES
Sand Castles and Mud Pies

Water is the recurring theme of activities for kids in the Newport Beach area. This affluent Orange County community enjoys miles of wide beaches for surfing and fishing, calm harbor waters for boating and swimming, and a tidal estuary for shoreline hiking and biking. Inland there are museums and parks with children's programs.

A good place to begin a day in the area is at **Newport Pier,** where Newport itself began as a tiny fishing port in the 1880s. If you get up early, you can show the kids a bit of that 100-year-old fishing tradition on the beach next to the pier at the end of McFadden Place. Dory fishermen sell their catch there every morning between 7:30 and 11 A.M., just as they have since 1891. They leave Newport Harbor in small wooden fishing boats several hours before dawn to fish with hook and line in the open ocean. Kids are fascinated with the variety of strange-looking fish that the dorymen clean and sell alongside their boats on the beach. You may want to bring along an ice chest to buy dinner.

Across from the pier on McFadden Place is another Newport tradition, **Baldy's Tackle,** which has been selling fishing supplies since 1922. Rent a rod, reel, fly, and sinker at Baldy's and go out on the pier to try your luck. You can fish on the pier without a license. You can also rent surfboards at Baldy's.

Along the beach a bike path winds its way from 36th Street south to E Street near the end of the Balboa Peninsula. This is a scenic and safe place to ride bikes with kids since there is no automobile traffic. You do have to watch out for strolling pedestrians who ignore the bike path signs. **Baldy's Tackle** rents bikes too, as do several other shops nearby.

You could spend a whole day with kids in this area, but to explore the heart of Newport Beach, you'll need to ride bikes or drive south about a mile and a half on the Balboa Peninsula to **Balboa Pier.** If you drive, get there early because parking spaces in Newport are a rare commodity, as any local will tell you.

Out on the end of the pier is **Ruby's,** a 1940s-style diner that sells seafood and hamburgers at reasonable prices. Adjacent to the pier you can picnic or play on the grass at palm-tree-lined Peninsula Park. The bike path continues through the park along the beach. You can rent bikes or roller skates across the street from the pier at **Oceanfront Wheel Works.** The shop also rents boogie boards, beach chairs, and umbrellas to help you enjoy a day at the beach.

Walk or ride your bikes three short blocks from the pier along tree-lined Main Street to arrive at the symbol of Newport Beach, **Balboa Pavilion.** This California Historic Landmark was built in 1906 as the terminus for the Pacific Electric Car Line from Los Angeles. Looking much as it did when it was completed, the Victorian building with its flag-topped cupola still stands at the center of Newport's resort activities. Inside the building, the Tale of the Whale restaurant has a reasonably priced children's menu and an excellent view of the harbor.

To get a closer look at the harbor, take a harbor cruise aboard the *Pavilion Queen,* a Mississippi-style riverboat docked at the Pavilion. On 45- or 90-minute cruises, you'll see some of the bay's ten thousand pleasure boats and the waterside mansions owned by famous residents. You can board a whale watch cruise at the Pavilion also, between December and March, to see the giant mammals on their annual migration.

If the kids would rather pilot a boat themselves, you'll find rental concessions for sailboats or motorized boats, pedalboats, or kayaks along the Edgewater Avenue walkway west of the Pavilion. A stroll along this walkway leads you past snack shops and outdoor tables to a child-oriented attraction, the **Balboa Fun Zone.** This recently renovated area has a carousel, bumper cars, amusement-park rides, and arcade games.

To pry the kids out of the arcade, offer them a ride on one of Southern

California's last remaining ferryboats. The **Balboa Ferry** leaves from the end of Palm Street and takes you for a short trip across the bay to Balboa Island. Ferries carry walk-on passengers, bikes, and cars to the island every four minutes.

On the island, walk along the bayfront past narrow beaches, luxury yachts, and flower-decked resort homes to Marine Avenue near the east end of the island. There you'll find specialty stores and restaurants. Snack shops sell the island's favorite treat, Balboa Bars (known as Bal Bars), a slab of ice cream on a stick, dipped in chocolate and your choice of nuts, sprinkles, or other toppings. Frozen bananas are prepared the same way.

East of the harbor in Lower Newport Bay is **Newport Dunes,** a popular aquatic park that has day-use and overnight camping facilities. The park's sandy beaches ring a wide cove of calm water that seems designed for kids. There are diving rafts with water slides, floating blue-plastic whales to climb on, and shallow, roped-off swimming areas. When the kids are tired of swimming, rent pedalboats or aquacycles. Bring a picnic to enjoy at covered tables along the beach.

Upper Newport Bay, a mile north of the park, is Southern California's largest estuary, and an ecological reserve. You can hike or ride bikes on trails around the wetland, where you'll see some of the 200 species of migratory birds that stop there annually.

On the bluffs above the bay is a museum designed for kids, the **Natural History Museum of Orange County.** Housed in a former public school building in the middle of a residential district, this hands-on museum was started by concerned citizens who realized that a treasure trove of 200-million-year-old marine fossils and ancient sea-mammal skeletons was being dug up and scattered as houses were built on the cliffs. A number of these bones and fossils are on display for children to touch at the museum. Kids also can compare their own sizes to bones from mammoths and saber-toothed cats (the California state fossil) that once roamed the land in Newport Beach. Dioramas and touch tables of artifacts help children understand how Southern California Indians once lived along the ocean and the bay. The Insects up Close exhibit has a small insect zoo and enlarged photographs of crawly critters. The museum sponsors a full schedule of children's workshops and field trips.

Another museum in Newport that has programs for children is the **Newport Harbor Art Museum,** which displays contemporary art in changing exhibits. Workshops, classes, and school tours encourage kids to appreciate the art and create some of their own. Children especially like the sculpture garden and outdoor café behind the museum.

The **Children's Book Shop** on the other side of the bay has a large selection of hardback and paperback books for children and young adults. Through the shop's red door, children enter an attractive world filled with stuffed toys and small tables and chairs for quiet reading. The store offers a free story hour on Saturday morning for 5- to 8-year-olds that you can attend on a drop-in basis. For the 3- to 5-year-old's story hour held during the week, you need to make reservations well in advance.

When it's time for more exercise, try ice skating in nearby Costa Mesa at the **Ice Capades Chalet.** One of the last ice-skating rinks in the area, the Chalet is among the top training facilities for U.S. Olympic hopefuls. You can watch from a warming room as these graceful skaters practice their routines each morning between 8 and 10 A.M. The rink is open most afternoons and evenings for public skating.

You'll need at least another day to explore children's activities in the community of Huntington Beach, north of Newport. Head first for **Huntington Central Park,** a 300-acre recreational complex with several outstanding children's attractions. At the **Adventure Playground,** open during summer only, there is a muddy lake where kids can wallow and make mud pies, all supervised by park employees. Kids play Huck Finn as they pole across the lake on rafts and climb on a rope bridge. Dress the children for the playground in old clothes and closed-toed shoes. You'll need to bring a towel and clean clothes for them to change into after they shower near the exit. An adjacent area encourages kid-built constructions. Your children will use hammers, nails, and saws to add on to tree houses and clubhouses started by others, all under supervision.

The centerpiece of Central Park is the **Huntington Beach Public Library.** In the Children's Resource Center of this multilevel building, sixty thousand children's books and magazines, plus computers and toys wait for kids to enjoy. Story hours for elementary-school-age children are held every Saturday morning at 11 A.M., and preschool story hours are on Fridays.

Across the park on the northwest side is **Shipley Nature Center,** an 18-acre reserve with a small museum that is the hub of nature trails encircling Blackbird Pond and other wooded areas.

Huntington Beach is known as one of the surf capitals of California. The best spectator seats for watching expert surfers are on the beach near the Huntington Pier at the end of Main Street. You will find more gentle surf conditions for young surfers at **Bolsa Chica State Beach,** between the town of Huntington Beach and Huntington Harbor. This six-mile-long beach is a good place for children to do some ocean swimming too. Running the length of this beach and Huntington Beach is a safe bike path for kids which is closed to automobile traffic. You can also hike around the wetlands inland from the beach at the **Bolsa Chica Ecological Reserve.** Members of the Amigos de Bolsa Chica lead guided tours through the wetlands for adults and children on most weekends.

Attractions

BALBOA ISLAND. (Exit San Diego Freeway [405] at Jamboree Road; south to island.)

BALBOA PENINSULA. (Follow Newport–Costa Mesa Freeway [55] south until it ends; continue on Newport Boulevard to Balboa Boulevard; east to the following Balboa attractions.)

• *Balboa Ferry,* at north end of Palm Street, Balboa Peninsula. (Follow Balboa Boulevard east to Palm Street; north to bay.) (714) 673-1070. Runs every four minutes. Summer hours: daily, 24 hours. October–June: weekdays, 6:30 A.M.– midnight; weekends, 6:30 A.M.–2 A.M. Ages 12–adult, 25 cents; ages 5–11, 10 cents; under 5, free. Cars, 40 cents; motorcycles, 20 cents; bikes, 15 cents.
• *Balboa Fun Zone,* west of Balboa Pavilion, Balboa Peninsula. (See directions to Pavilion.)
• *Balboa Pavilion,* 400 Main Street, Balboa. (East on Balboa Boulevard to Main Street; north to Pavilion.)
• *Catalina Passenger Service:* (714) 673-1434. Offers the following:

• *Pavilion Queen.* Narrated cruises of Newport Harbor. Call for schedule. Daily 45-minute cruise: adults, $5; ages 6–12, 50 cents. Ninety-minute cruise: adults, $7; ages 6–12, $1.
• Whale Watch Cruises. Narrated 3-hour cruises between December and April. Call for schedule.

• *Balboa Pier,* at south end of Main Street, Balboa Peninsula.

• Oceanfront Wheel Works, at base of Balboa Pier. (714) 723-6510. Summer hours: daily, 9 A.M.–11 P.M. Winter hours: 10 A.M.–6 P.M. Rent bikes, skates, boogie boards, beach chairs, umbrellas.
• Ruby's Diner, at end of Balboa Pier. (714) 675-7829. Open Monday–Friday, 7 A.M.–9 P.M.; Saturday and Sunday, 7 A.M.–10 P.M.

BOLSA CHICA STATE BEACH AND ECOLOGICAL RESERVE, Huntington Beach. (Exit San Diego Freeway [405] at Golden West Street; south to Pacific Coast Highway [1]; north two miles to entrance.) (714)

848-1566. Day-use fee: $4 per car. For guided tours of wetlands, call Amigos de Bolsa Chica: (714) 897-7003.

CHILDREN'S BOOK SHOP, 1831 Westcliff Drive, Newport Beach. (Exit Corona del Mar Freeway [73] at Irvine Avenue; south to Westcliff Drive; left to store.) (714) 675-1424. Open Monday–Saturday, 10 A.M.–5 P.M. Story hour for 5- to 8-year-olds on Saturday, 10 A.M. Free.

HUNTINGTON BEACH CENTRAL PARK, Golden West Street and Talbert Avenue, Huntington Beach. (Exit San Diego Freeway [405] at Golden West Street; south about three miles to the park.)

• *Adventure Playground:* (714) 536-5486. Open Monday–Saturday, 10 A.M.–5 P.M., summer only. $1 per person. Reservations needed for ten or more children.
• *Huntington Central Public Library:* (714) 848-7813. Open Monday, 1–9 P.M.; Tuesday–Thursday, 9 A.M.–9 P.M.; Friday and Saturday, 9 A.M.–5 P.M. Storytimes: elementary ages, Saturday, 11 A.M.; preschoolers, Friday, 10 A.M. and 11 A.M.
• *Shipley Nature Center:* (714) 960-8847. (Follow yellow line from parking lot on west side of park.)

ICE CAPADES CHALET, 2701 Harbor Boulevard, Costa Mesa. (Exit San Diego Freeway [405] at Harbor Boulevard; south to Mesa Verde Drive Plaza, south of Adams Avenue.) (714) 979-8880. Viewing hours in mornings: Tuesday–Saturday. Public skating hours: Monday–Friday, 2–5 P.M.; Saturday and Sunday, 1–4 P.M. Evening hours: Tuesday–Thursday, 7:30–9:30 P.M.; Friday and Saturday, 8–10:30 P.M.

NATURAL HISTORY MUSEUM OF ORANGE COUNTY, 2627 Vista del Oro, Newport Beach. (Exit San Diego Freeway [405] at Jamboree Road; south to Eastbluff Drive; right to Vista del Sol; right to Vista del Oro; right to museum.) (714) 640-7120 or (714) 640-7121. Tuesday–Saturday, 10 A.M.–5 P.M.; Sunday, noon–5 P.M. Adults, $2; school-age children, $1; preschoolers, free.

NEWPORT DUNES, 1131 Backbay Drive, Newport Beach. (Exit San Diego Freeway [405] at Jamboree Boulevard; right to Backbay Drive; right to entrance.) (714) 644-0510. Open daily. Parking: $2 per car.

NEWPORT HARBOR ART MUSEUM, 850 San Clemente Drive, Newport Beach. (Exit San Diego Freeway [405] at Jamboree Boulevard; south to

Santa Barbara Drive; left to San Clemente Drive; left to museum.) (714) 759-1122. Open Tuesday–Friday, 10 A.M.–5 P.M.; Saturday, 10 A.M.–6 P.M.; Sunday, 12–6 P.M. Adults, $3; students and seniors, $2; under 6, free.

NEWPORT PIER, Newport Beach. (Follow Newport–Costa Mesa Freeway [55] until it ends; continue south on Newport Boulevard to McFadden Place [between 20th and 21st streets]; right to pier.)

• *Baldy's Tackle,* 100 McFadden Place, Newport Beach. (714) 673-4150. Rent fishing equipment, bikes, and surfboards. Summer hours: 6 A.M.–8 P.M. Winter hours: Monday–Friday, 7:30 A.M.–6 P.M.; Saturday and Sunday, 6 A.M.–6 P.M.

UPPER NEWPORT BAY. (Exit Corona del Mar Freeway [73] at Jamboree Boulevard; south to Backbay Drive; right to bay.)

For More Information

Huntington Beach Chamber of Commerce, 2213 Main Street, #32, Huntington Beach, CA 92648; (714) 536-8888.

Newport Beach Conference and Visitors Bureau, 3700 Newport Boulevard, Suite 107, Newport Beach, CA 92663; (714) 675-7040.

SOUTH ORANGE COUNTY
Swallows and Sea Life

South County, as the locals call it, stretches to the south and east of Newport–Costa Mesa Freeway (55). It's a vast area of wide beaches and coved inlets, of rolling hills and deep canyons. Much of this area from the ocean to the rugged Santa Ana Mountains appears to have been paved over recently by houses and shopping centers, but it also has sprouted new parklands, museums, and attractions for children.

You could spend a day with kids at each of South County's three main towns: Laguna Beach, Dana Point, and San Juan Capistrano. Or you can visit several areas on a day's expedition because they are not very far apart.

One of South County's most popular attractions is **Wild Rivers,** a water theme park with slides and pools for all ages to enjoy. Located just west of the junction of the 405 and 5 freeways, Wild Rivers occupies the former Lion Country Safari property. Remnants of that African-themed park are still around in Wild Rivers' watery attractions. Grab an inner tube near the entrance to slide down Congo River Rapids. Shoot down Sweitzer Falls or float on Safari River Expedition tubes for a quarter of a mile.

Monsoon Lagoon is good for bodysurfing and swimming. Pigmy Pond is the place for preschoolers, with a one-foot-deep pool and an elephant slide. Lifeguards are on duty throughout the park, but children still need to be accompanied by adults. You can spend a whole day in the park or come to cool off at the end of a warm summer day of sight-seeing elsewhere. The park stays open until 8 P.M. in summer.

On the other side of I-5 in the community of El Toro, **Heritage Hill Historical Park** offers a more educational experience. The hilltop park has four historic buildings you can tour. Kids are most interested in the El Toro Grammar School, a one-room schoolhouse built in 1890. Ring the bell in the tower and sit at tiny desks with ink wells to get a feel for old-fashioned school days. At the 1908 Bennet Ranch House you'll see a typical home of the period, where six children grew up. Next door at Serrano Creek Park, there are picnic tables, a children's playground, and hiking trails.

Laguna Beach, to the south, is a picturesque coastal town with several attractions for children. A series of cove beaches with tide pools line Laguna's shore. The beaches are small and secluded. You'll find the most gentle waves for kids at Shaw's Cove, Rock Pile Beach, and Crescent Bay. A good place to picnic is at **Heisler Park,** a winding strip of grass atop the bluffs along Cliff Drive. Paths descend from the park to beaches below. One mile north of the city is **Crystal Cove State Park,** a 3,000-acre park with three miles of beaches. The park extends inland through a hilly oak woodland with hiking trails.

Laguna's beauty attracts many artists to the area and has spawned the **Festival of the Arts,** held every year in July and August. Children who are interested in art enjoy browsing through the festival's maze of stalls. There are free, drop-in art workshops for children each afternoon at festival headquarters. The festival supplies art materials and encouragement, while kids supply the creativity. Youngsters also enjoy puppet shows that are presented several times daily in the Festival Forum Theatre. Across the street, the Sawdust Festival offers more arts and crafts items for sale in a casual street-scene atmosphere.

The **Pageant of the Masters,** held nightly in the Irvine Bowl on the festival grounds, is an easy introduction for kids to the works of famous artists. Local residents present tableaus of paintings, remaining motionless while lighting techniques and friezes create the illusion of two dimensionality. Children are quite fascinated watching a scene come together as sets, props, and actors are arranged to portray a famous painting. The pageant is extremely popular, so you'll need to make your reservations months in advance. After the two-hour show, take the kids backstage to see the sets and learn about the technical aspects of the production.

Dana Point, a hilly coastal community south of Laguna Beach, has other attractions for children. Stop at the **Marine Institute at Dana Point Harbor,** a sea-life museum at the west end of the harbor. The institute's aquariums, which are displayed low enough for young children to see, contain a variety of local sea life, such as octopuses and sea urchins. A large whale skeleton hangs from the ceiling of a spacious lab room. Below, kids can touch a variety of sea treasures—lobster shells, colorful corals, and giant turtle shells.

A paved walkway leads from the institute down to the beach where you'll find tide pools full of some of the creatures featured inside the building. The institute sponsors weekend classes for the entire family that offer such adventures as tide-pool exploration, snorkeling, and excursions aboard the institute's floating laboratory boat.

Adjacent to the institute is the brig *Pilgrim,* a full-size replica of the square-rigged vessel that brought writer Richard Henry Dana into the harbor in 1834. Dana called the area "the only romantic spot in California" in his book *Two Years Before the Mast.* You can take a living-history tour of the *Pilgrim* at certain times of the year. Schoolchildren live aboard the ship at sea for several days to learn nineteenth-century seafaring skills. During summer evenings, the *Pilgrim* serves as a stage for family-oriented musicals and concerts.

At this end of Dana Point Harbor, below steep cliffs, there's a calm swimming beach that is ideal for young children. You can rent paddleboats or sailboards on the beach. Picnic shelters with barbecues await on a grassy strip of park next to the sand. A bike path runs the entire length of the harbor. Sportfishing boats leave for daily half-day and twilight fishing trips. Between the end of December and the beginning of April, whale-watch cruises leave from the harbor full of passengers intent on seeing the huge mammals on their annual migration from Alaska to Mexico.

A good place from which to view the whales is **Lantern Bay Park,** a stretch of lawn atop the bluff in front of the gracious Dana Point Resort. Most days, it's also a good place to fly a kite. There are picnic tables, barbecues, and wide paved paths in the public park.

In town, the **Nautical Heritage Museum** occupies a replica of an old New England lighthouse. Permanent exhibits include dozens of historic ship models, shipbuilding tools, and scrimshaw. Children enjoy watching and talking to a model ship builder who creates miniatures at the museum most days. Another interesting exhibit for kids who have studied a bit of American History are the ships' papers, original documents used to identify the nationality of sailing vessels during the eighteenth and nineteenth centuries.

Documents on display bear signatures of such famous people as George Washington, Thomas Jefferson, and Abraham Lincoln.

The museum is administered by the Nautical Heritage Society, which built and maintains the *Californian,* the state's official tall ship. It's a replica of a coast guard cutter used during the gold rush. The ship is used primarily to give nautical training to high school and college students, but it also is available for four-hour public excursions. Children must weigh 45 pounds or more to go aboard for a cruise. During the trip, you learn about the history of this square rigger and you can help sail it if you wish. Tours leave from ports along the Southern California coast, but tour reservations are made through the museum.

South of Dana Point is **Doheny State Beach,** a wide stretch of sand and tree-shaded grassy parkland that is popular with families for day use or for camping. The visitors center near the park entrance features natural-looking touch-tank tide pools set at floor level. Kids can sit on surrounding rocks to watch and touch sea creatures. Surfing is good at the north end of the park, where swells are gentle for beginners.

Inland is the town of San Juan Capistrano and its famed mission. Built in 1776, **Mission San Juan Capistrano** is best known for its swallows, which are said to return to the mission from South America every year on March 19. In spring, you'll see some swallows at the mission building their mud nests, but the birds most in evidence throughout the year are pigeons. Buy some bird feed at the gift shop near the main fountain so the kids can feed these friendly creatures. The birds will land on outstretched arms or on shoulders to feed.

Take time to walk around the mission's flower-lined walkways. Visit the narrow Serra Chapel, which was built in 1777 and is one of the oldest buildings in California. Nearby, you'll see the ruins of a church that was built in 1797 and destroyed in an earthquake in 1812. Bells still hang from the archways of the church. Stroll through an excavated archaeological site that displays kitchens used by the Indians and a smelter for preparing metal tools. Be sure to see the well-laid-out **Mission San Juan Capistrano Museum,** which exhibits Indian artifacts and items brought to California by the Spaniards.

The museum offers children's programs on the first Saturday of each month. Saturday at the Mission gives kids ages 8 to 15 practical experience in living a mission-era life. In the varied programs, kids learn such skills as making adobe bricks, weaving Indian baskets, and excavating at a dig (alongside an archaeologist). Because of the popularity of these programs, you'll need to sign up several weeks in advance.

Across the street from the mission is the red-tile-roofed **San Juan Capistrano Depot.** This 1894 Santa Fe Railway station, along with several train cars permanently placed on adjacent tracks, now houses a popular restaurant and several small shops. The depot is a regular stop for Amtrak's San Diegan trains, and you can buy tickets in one box car in the complex. You also can take the train to San Juan Capistrano from elsewhere in Southern California for a special all-day excursion with kids. Once in town, you can tour the mission, then take a bus to the beach for a fun-filled day.

Attractions

CAPISTRANO DEPOT, 26701 Verdugo Street, San Juan Capistrano. (Across the street from the mission; see directions to mission below.) (714) 496-8181. Open daily at 10 A.M. Shops close at 5 P.M.; restaurant hours vary.

CRYSTAL COVE STATE PARK, on Pacific Coast Highway (1), one mile north of Laguna Beach. *Note:* Pacific Coast Highway becomes simply Coast Highway (both 1) south of Laguna Beach. (Exit San Diego Freeway [405] at Corona del Mar Freeway [73] south; continue on 73, which becomes MacArthur Boulevard, to Pacific Coast Highway [1]; left to park.) (714) 494-3539. Open daily, 6:30 A.M.–sunset. Day-use parking: $4 per car.

DOHENY STATE BEACH, south of Dana Point. (Exit San Diego Freeway [5] at Coast Highway [1]; west to Dana Point Harbor Drive; left to entrance.) (714) 496-6172. Open daily, 6 A.M.–10 P.M. Day-use parking: $4 per car.

FESTIVAL OF THE ARTS AND PAGEANT OF THE MASTERS, 650 Laguna Canyon Road, Laguna Beach. (Exit San Diego Freeway [5] at Laguna Freeway [133], which becomes Laguna Canyon Road; south to festival grounds.) (714) 494-1145. Grounds open daily during July and August, 10 A.M.–11 P.M. Adults, $2; seniors, $1; ages 12 and under, free with adult. Pageant held 8:30 nightly during festival. Admission varies with seating.

HEISLER PARK, along Cliff Drive, Laguna Beach. (Exit San Diego Freeway [5] at Laguna Freeway [133], which becomes Laguna Canyon Road; south to Coast Highway [1]; right to Cliff Drive; left to park.)

HERITAGE HILL HISTORIC PARK, 25151 Serrano Road, El Toro. (Exit San Diego Freeway [5] at Lake Forest Drive; north to Serrano Road; left to parking lot in shopping center below museum.) (714) 855-2028. Open daily, 8 A.M.–5 P.M. Guided tours: Tuesday–Friday, 2 P.M.; Saturday, Sunday, and holidays, 11 A.M.–2 P.M. Free.

LANTERN BAY PARK, in front of the Dana Point Resort. (Exit San Diego Freeway [5] at Coast Highway [1]; west to Dana Point Harbor Drive; left to Street of the Park Lantern; right to park.) Open daily.

MARINE INSTITUTE AT DANA POINT HARBOR and the *PILGRIM*, 24200 Dana Point Harbor Drive, Dana Point. (Exit San Diego Freeway [5] at Coast Highway [1]; west to Dana Point Harbor Drive; left to institute.) (714) 496-2274. Open daily, 10 A.M.–3:30 P.M. Free.

MISSION SAN JUAN CAPISTRANO, at Camino Capistrano and Ortega Highway (74). (Exit San Diego Freeway [5] at Ortega Highway [74]; west one block to mission.) (714) 493-1111. Open daily, 7:30 A.M.–5 P.M. Adults, $2; children under 11, $1.

• *Mission San Juan Capistrano Museum.* (See directions to mission.) Saturday at the Mission program, first Saturday of the month, 10 A.M.–1 P.M. Ages 10–15, $1.

NAUTICAL HERITAGE MUSEUM, 24532 Del Prado Boulevard, Dana Point. (Exit San Diego Freeway [5] at Coast Highway [1]; west to Street of the Amber Lantern; left to Del Prado Boulevard; left to museum.) (714) 661-1001. Open Tuesday–Saturday, 10 A.M.–4 P.M. Free. Call for reservations to sail on the tall ship *Californian.*

WILD RIVERS, 8800 Irvine Center Drive, Laguna Hills. (Exit San Diego Freeway [405] at Irvine Center Drive; south to park entrance.) (714) 768-WILD. Open mid-May–early June, weekends and holidays only, 11 A.M.–5 P.M.; mid-June–Labor Day, daily, 10 A.M.–8 P.M.; mid-September–early October, weekends only, 11 A.M.–5 P.M.

For More Information

Dana Point Chamber of Commerce, 34221 Street of the Golden Lantern, Box 12, Dana Point, CA 92629; (714) 496-1555.

Laguna Beach Chamber of Commerce, 357 Glenn Eyre, Box 396, Laguna Beach, CA 92652; (714) 494-1018.

San Juan Capistrano Chamber of Commerce, 31682 El Camino Real, San Juan Capistrano, CA 92675; (714) 493-4700.

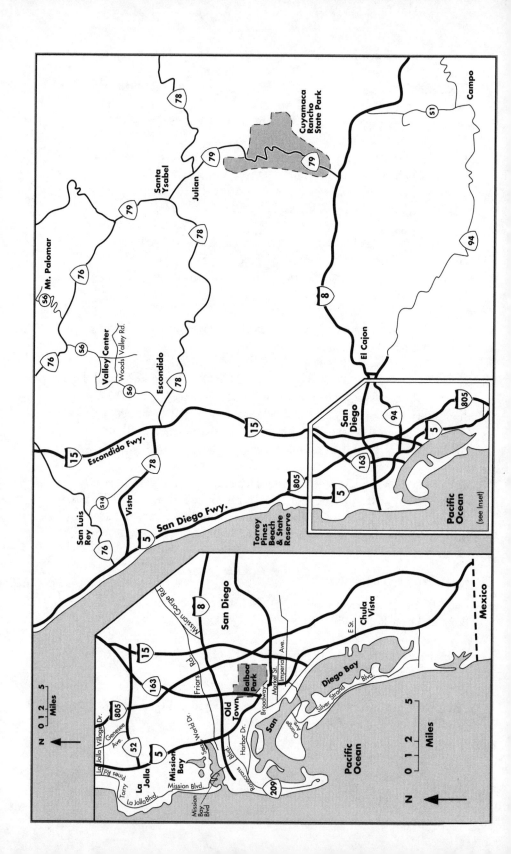

11

San Diego

California's second largest city is built on a huge natural bay, has a graceful, arching bridge, is a popular tourist destination . . . and is not named San Francisco.

Comparisons stop there. San Diego, unlike its northern counterpart, has a more homespun reputation, thanks to its many parks, world renowned zoo, and nearly ninety museums.

San Diego's appeal is due in part to its climate—a year-round average temperature of 70 degrees, with ample sunshine and ocean breezes—and in part to its physical setting; 70 miles of beaches, two large bays, and acres of greenery.

Given these advantages, it's little wonder that tourism is one of San Diego's principal industries. Transportation is convenient and directions to attractions are well marked. Especially helpful is the city's Molly Trolley (really a bus) that shuttles to and from all the main points of interest. The trolley runs daily from 9 A.M. to 7 P.M. An all-day pass, the only ticket you can buy, costs $5.

San Diego is 125 miles south of Los Angeles. That works out to a 20-minute plane flight, a 2½-hour drive down the freeway (I-5), or about the same amount of time by train. Amtrak's San Diegan schedules eight daily round-trips between Los Angeles and San Diego for $29 (kids 2–11 are half fare when riding with a paying adult).

The train ride can be part of a daylong round-trip excursion package from Los Angeles's downtown Union Station to San Diego's Sea World or Zoo. The $25 ticket ($17 for children) includes train fare, a one-hour San Diego Harbor cruise, transportation to and from the attraction, and its admission price. Along the way, the train stops near Anaheim Stadium and Mission San Juan Capistrano, travels through the huge U.S. Marine reservation of Camp Pendleton and along the sweeping coastline to San Diego.

SAN DIEGO ZOO AND SEA WORLD

Koala Bears and Killer Whales

San Diego's largest and most popular family attractions are the zoo and Sea World. Plan to spend a whole day to see each attraction.

The **San Diego Zoo** occupies 100 acres in the city's famed Balboa Park. One of the largest zoos in the world, the San Diego Zoo is home to 3,200 animals and an extensive (and expensive) display of plant life. For children, one of the zoo's nicest features is the absence of cages and bars. Many of the animals live in areas enclosed only by moats. You'll see birds at even closer range when you walk through their huge aviaries.

Arrive at the zoo when it opens at 9 A.M. to see it best. As the day wears on the crowds grow larger. A good way to orient kids to the zoo is with a 40-minute narrated tour aboard a double-decker bus. These open air trams cover about 80 percent of the zoo and give kids an appreciation for what there is to see. Lines for the tour grow rapidly, so you may want to make this one of your first activities.

After the bus tour, it's time to hit the highlights, which of course depend on your kids' interests. Almost everybody's favorite, the koala bear (not really a bear at all), lives in an enclosure just across the street from the tour bus unloading area. Don't expect too much, though, because these nocturnal creatures usually aren't very active during the day.

Among the newest attractions are the zoo's bioclimatic exhibits, which group animals, birds, and plants together in an environment that simulates their normal habitat. In Sun Bear Forest, you wander through a rain forest where there are romping sun bears, playful lion-tailed macaques, and colorful birds. The sun bears frolic in a large tree fitted with pumps that distribute a sweet syrup, and the bears remain active all day as they search the tree for syrup.

Tiger River, another bioclimatic exhibit, combines plants and animals from the Indian subcontinent. Youngsters will smell, feel, and see a tropical rain forest in this area. There are exotic flowers, web-footed fishing cats, strange-looking Malayan tapirs and, of course, the lordly Sumatran tiger.

The Children's Zoo, at the far left of the entrance, is built on a child's scale. Youngsters can walk through a tiny aviary, touch baby chicks, and watch (but not touch) fluffy guinea pigs. Notice the special little mouse house made from a loaf of bread. In the paddock, kids pet and feed barnyard animals, and there's a baby animal nursery that shows off some of the zoo's newest arrivals. One clever display lets kids measure their leaping ability against such well-known jumpers as the grasshopper, frog, springbok, and kangaroo.

For a change of pace and a different view of the zoo, climb aboard the Skyfari, just outside the Children's Zoo. This aerial tram takes you across the park to the Horn and Hoof Mesa, where you will find deer, gazelles and antelopes. Another spot to catch your breath is Wegeforth Bowl, near the Children's Zoo, where free animal shows are presented several times a day.

When the kids get hungry, stop at one of the zoo's numerous hot dog and hamburger stands, snack stands, or specialty restaurants. There is a picnic area next to the Children's Zoo, if you want to bring your own food.

Across town at **Sea World**, on the banks of man-made Mission Bay, the emphasis is on marine creatures and waterfowl. Dozens of exhibits and shows at this park introduce kids to the rich variety of life under, on, and even over the sea. The park's 135 acres accommodate large crowds without seeming crowded.

Sea World's most popular show stars its biggest performer, Shamu, the three-ton killer whale. He and his friends perform daily in the new Shamu Stadium that is part of the park's $25 million face-lift and expansion. Before you decide where to sit in the stadium, you should know that the glass walls of the huge tank provide fascinating views from the front rows of the whales as they swim and leap, but there is a trade-off. As with most shows in the park, you are likely to get wet if you're sitting within the first six rows (called the splash zone).

Other shows feature performing dolphins, whales, sea lions, walruses, otters, and even humans. The shows are repeated at staggered times throughout the day, so you can plan to see them all if you stay from opening to closing.

Sea World's Skytower Ride is visible for miles around and serves as a local landmark. A ride up and down this 265-foot tower can be a spectacular adventure on a clear day, with views of the park, Mission Bay, San Diego, and the Pacific Ocean.

A special feature kids like at Sea World is the chance for hands-on learning. At the Whale and Dolphin Petting Pool, they can feed and touch these smooth, slippery creatures. At the park's tide pool tanks, they touch starfish or sea urchins and look for other shallow water inhabitants.

Two of the most popular attractions don't involve shows at all. The Shark Exhibit allows youngsters to come face to face with the sea's most feared predators. Several different species of shark swim almost ceaselessly in the huge aquarium. Pictures above the windows help the kids identify them.

At the Penguin Encounter the mood is much more lighthearted. More than three hundred penguins and other Arctic and Antarctic birds inhabit a man-made, subfreezing ice shelf behind glass. While you move along an automated ramp, the penguins waddle, flap, toddle, and slide on the ice. They are much more graceful "flying" through their glassed-in ocean, chasing fish. As in the Shark Exhibit, children can refer to photos to help identify the different birds.

Not far from the Penguin Encounter is Captain Kid's World. This place is sure to revive kids who are starting to flag at the prospect of viewing another show or exhibit. With rope climbs, swings and a dozen more playground adventures, there is plenty to occupy them for an hour or more. The hard part comes when it's time to collect them and move on to the day's next event.

Behind Captain Kid's World is a huge geography lesson. A one-acre map of the United States allows children to walk "from sea to shining sea" in a matter of minutes, while learning the location of all the states and their capitals. Nearby there's a circle of state flags. See how many the kids can identify.

Near the big map is the Parent's Store. This large shop features books for all ages, educational toys, and science kits, plus a special area where children can play with selected educational materials.

It's a good idea to pace the family if you are planning to spend the entire day at Sea World. Alternate the shows with exhibits, or take a break from walking with an aerial tram ride along the shores of Mission Bay and back to the park again. During summer, Sea World is open until 11 P.M., so you may want to leave the park for dinner and come back for an evening show and spectacular fireworks. If you do leave, be sure to have your hand stamped for same-day return.

Attractions

AMTRAK, eight trains daily from Los Angeles to San Diego. Adults, $30 round-trip; children 2–11, $15.00 with full-fare paying adult. Call (800) 872-7245 for times and information.

SAN DIEGO ZOO, 2920 Zoo Drive, San Diego. (Exit I-5 at Pershing Drive; north to Florida Drive; left to Zoo Place; left to zoo parking.) (619) 234-3153. Open daily, 9 A.M. to 5 P.M. (July–Labor Day); 9 A.M. to 4 P.M. (post-Labor Day–June). Adults, $8.50; ages 3–15, $2.50; under 3, free. Children's Zoo: ages 3 and above, 50 cents; under 3, free. Skyfari (one way): adults, $1; ages 3–15, 75 cents; under 3, free.

SEA WORLD, 1720 South Shores Road, Mission Bay. (Exit I-5 at Teco-lote Road; west to Sea World Drive and continue to Sea World.) (619) 226-3901, 226-6363. Open daily, 9 A.M. to 6:00 P.M.; 9 A.M. to 11 P.M. (mid-June–Labor Day). Adults, $21.00; seniors and ages 3–11, $15.50; under 3, free.

For More Information

San Diego Convention and Visitors Bureau, 1200 Third Avenue, Suite 824, San Diego, CA 92101; (619) 232-3101.

San Diego Visitor Information Center, 2688 East Mission Bay Drive, San Diego, CA 92109; (619) 276-8200.

BALBOA PARK
Heart of the City

Balboa Park has been called the cultural heart of San Diego, and it is easy to see why. The park is home to 16 museums plus the city's famed zoo, live theaters, and pavilions for musical performances. You can easily spend an entire day in the park with kids. From space flight to dinosaurs, there is certain to be a museum or activity somewhere in Balboa Park to capture their interest.

The backdrop for all these attractions is 1,400 acres of lush gardens, rolling green lawns, and groves of shady trees north of San Diego's civic center. Located near the junction of Highways 5 and 163, the park is easy to reach. Parking lots are near most of the attractions and space is ample, although the lots are crowded most weekend afternoons. You'll also find picnic areas and food stands near most of the attractions.

The park's cultural center lies along El Prado, a wide thoroughfare that bisects Balboa Park on an east-west axis. On either side of El Prado, which changes from a street to a pedestrian mall midway through the park, you will find a complex of Spanish-baroque buildings that house most of the museums. If you park near El Prado, you will be able to walk to nearly all the park's attractions.

Pick up a Balboa Park Passport if you are planning to visit several of the museums. This $9 book of coupons will provide admission to as many as four of the seven participating museums. Passports are available at any of these museums or at the park's information center in the House of Hospitality building. The passport covers the Aerospace Historical Center, Museum of Art, Museum of Man, Museum of Photographic Arts, Natural History Museum, Reuben H. Fleet Space Theater and Science Center, and San Diego Hall of Champions.

Start your day in Balboa Park at one of its highlights for kids, the **Reuben H. Fleet Space Theater and Science Center**. The building is at the east end of El Prado's mall, just south of a large fountain. Allow plenty of time for the kids to explore the Science Center's more than sixty interactive exhibits. Each demonstrates a different law or phenomenon of physical science, and they all contribute to a general scene of chaotic activity spurred by young imaginations running full tilt. Principles of magnetism, acoustics, electricity, and much more come to life in the exhibits. While the kids are building arches, peering through a periscope, listening to heart sounds, or testing their sense of balance, you can reinforce the science lesson.

When not being intrigued by the exhibits, children will be awed by presentations in the Space Theater. In 1973 the theater pioneered the giant movie format known as Omnimax, which projects a movie on a dome screen that seems to surround viewers. Coupled with a sophisticated sound system, the theater's presentations envelop the senses to create an almost overwhelming experience. Movie programs last up to 50 minutes and alternate during the day. Admission to the theater is separate from that for the Science Center.

Directly across El Prado from the Reuben H. Fleet is the **Natural History Museum**. A far cry from the physical sciences, this museum nevertheless contains another subject that fascinates children—dinosaurs. A skeleton of the meat-eating Allosaurus is suitably impressive. Other exhibits cover insects, gems, birds, and whales. Kids can really come to grips with the problem of endangered species through the display On the Edge, where they touch the skins of such threatened animals as tigers, grizzly bears, and bison, while learning of efforts to save these creatures. Downstairs, the Chapman

Hall of Desert Ecology shows youngsters that the desert is not a wasteland. Exhibits cover North America's four largest deserts with dioramas of desert scenes, such live denizens as tarantulas and scorpions, and a video learning center.

From the Natural History Museum, turn right and head west up El Prado. On your left across the mall, the Casa de Balboa building houses four museums. The **Museum of San Diego History** is under development, but does have a 1,500-square-foot gallery of changing exhibits that depict the history of the city from 1850 to the present. In the **Museum of Photographic Arts** you'll see the work of photographers displayed in exhibits that are changed throughout the year. A 22-foot tall railroad semaphore stands at the entrance to the **San Diego Model Railroad Museum**. Inside, kids will see the largest collection of mini-gauge trains in the world, plus displays that portray the role of the train in San Diego's development. Sports heroes are honored in the **San Diego Hall of Champions**, where more than forty sports are represented. If your kids enjoy sports, they are likely to recognize names such as baseball greats Ted Williams and Don Larsen, boxer Archie Moore, and America's Cup skipper Dennis Connor.

Next door to Casa de Balboa is the House of Hospitality, where you will find the park's information center. At the Café del Rey Moro, also in the building, the family can enjoy sit-down dining on a landscaped terrace or at tables indoors. If you prefer, the café will prepare box lunches for your picnic.

To introduce the kids to the fine arts, head across El Prado to the **San Diego Museum of Art**. The museum collection has more than 10,000 works, with an emphasis on European and American painting and sculpture. East of the Museum of Art is the **Timken Art Gallery**, which also is devoted to European and American masterworks, from the Renaissance through the nineteenth century. A few steps east of this gallery is a building sure to catch the kids' attention. The Botanical Building at the end of the lily pond looks like an unfinished railroad station made out of redwood lath strips. One of the few structures remaining from the original 1915 Panama-California Exposition, it is now used to house tropical and sub-tropical plants.

West of the Museum of Art, beneath the distinctive Spanish baroque gingerbread of the California Tower, is another Balboa Park highlight for children—the **San Diego Museum of Man**. In the main gallery, Native Americans often are on hand to demonstrate such everyday skills as weaving and tortilla making. Upstairs the primate exhibit shows human evolution from the apes to modern man with the help of skeletons and models. Other exhibits depict the life of early humans, hunting societies, and ancient

Southwestern native cultures. Kids can look inside a full-scale Hopi Indian house to see exhibits of basket making, corn milling, and blanket weaving.

Across El Prado from the main museum building, an annex holds the Wonder of Life exhibit. This tasteful exploration of the reproductive system shows how the fetus develops from six weeks to 32 weeks, while models show the stages of birth in a normal delivery. The exhibit is so skillfully done that most children will be able to view it without any embarrassment.

Back outside, head east and follow the roadway as it turns south off El Prado. A short distance ahead, where the road bends, you will pass a large, semi-circular open-air pavilion in front of an ornate three-story structure. This is the Spreckle's Organ Pavilion, which houses one of the world's largest outdoor pipe organs. The huge instrument, with more than four thousand pipes, was a gift to the city by sugar barons John D. and Adolph Spreckles for the 1915 exposition. Every Sunday (except in February) at 2 P.M., you can hear this musical monarch in full-throated concert—and it's all free.

The distinctive round building at the end of the road is the Aerospace Historical Center, home of the **San Diego Aerospace Museum** and **International Aerospace Hall of Fame**. The Hall of Fame commemorates pioneers, industrialists, and heroes of aviation with portraits and biographies that chronicle their achievements.

The adjacent Aerospace Museum is even more likely to bring the romance of flight alive for the kids. Collected in a surprisingly small area are more than 55 aircraft and other exhibits in chronological tableaus that depict the many eras of flight. A special section honors the contributions of women to the history of aviation. In the center rotunda sits a replica of Charles Lindbergh's *Spirit of St. Louis.* Its place of honor is fitting in the city where the original plane was built. Kids will marvel at how Lindbergh flew this tiny plane all the way to Paris . . . without a front window. Just off the rotunda, a gift shop sells books, pictures, and models.

Depending on where you parked, you may want to drive to Balboa Park's last two attractions, which are sure to be a real hit with small children. At the eastern edge of the park take Park Boulevard north and turn right at Zoo Place. Turn right immediately into the small lot and stop to listen to the syncopated organ music that could only come from the park's famed merry-go-round. This beautifully maintained carousel was built in 1910 and moved to its present site from Coronado Island in 1922. It has been delighting youngsters ever since.

Another popular attraction with the young set is right next door, across from the entrance to the zoo. It's a miniature train—with a one-fifth scale diesel locomotive—that takes 48 passengers on a half-mile round-trip. Both the train and carousel operate on weekends and holidays, and during school vacations.

Balboa Park also happens to be one of the best places anywhere to introduce the kids to the plays of William Shakespeare. A replica of London's **Old Globe Theater** is the centerpiece of the Simon Edison Center for the Performing Arts, adjacent to the Museum of Man. The Old Globe is actually one of three theaters in the complex where the resident company stages 12 productions a year, including contemporary and traditional works. The Old Globe Theater usually offers three Shakespeare plays each summer. Each production is preceded by Renaissance dancing and entertainment. If you plan to attend, order your tickets weeks, if not months, in advance.

Attractions

(For directions to all attractions, see Aerospace Historical Center.)

MUSEUM OF PHOTOGRAPHIC ARTS, 1649 El Prado, San Diego. (619) 239-5262. Open daily, 10 A.M.–5 P.M. (Thursday night until 9 P.M.). Adults, $2.50; under 12, free.

MUSEUM OF SAN DIEGO HISTORY, 1649 El Prado, San Diego. (619) 232-6203. Open Wednesday–Sunday, 10 A.M.–4:30 P.M. Adults, $1; under 13, free.

NATURAL HISTORY MUSEUM, El Prado and Village Place, San Diego. (619) 232-3821. Open daily, 10 A.M.–4:30 P.M. (to 5 P.M., mid-June–mid-September). Adults, $5; ages 6–18, $1; under 5 and military in uniform, free.

OLD GLOBE THEATER, Box 2171, San Diego, CA 92112-2171. (619) 239-2255. Performances Tuesday–Sunday evenings and weekend matinees. Call theater for program and prices.

REUBEN H. FLEET SPACE THEATER AND SCIENCE CENTER, 1875 El Prado, San Diego. (619) 238-1233. Open daily, 9:30 A.M.–9:30 P.M.

- *Science Center:* adults, $2; ages 5–15, $1; under 5, free.
- *Space Theater:* adults, $5; seniors, $3.50; ages 5–15, $3; under 5, free (includes admission to Science Center).

SAN DIEGO AEROSPACE MUSEUM AND INTERNATIONAL AEROSPACE HALL OF FAME, 2001 Pan American Plaza, San Diego.

(Exit I-5 at Pershing Drive; east to Florida Drive; left to Zoo Place; left to Park Boulevard; left to President's Way or Village Place; right to parking.) (619) 234-8291. Open daily, 10 A.M.–4:30 P.M. Adults, $4.00; ages 6–17, $1; under 6, free.

SAN DIEGO HALL OF CHAMPIONS, 1649 El Prado, San Diego. (619) 234-2544. Open Monday–Saturday, 10 A.M.–4:30 P.M.; Sunday, noon–5 P.M. Adults, $2; seniors, military, and students, $1; ages 6–17, 50 cents; under 6, free.

SAN DIEGO MODEL RAILROAD MUSEUM, Casa de Balboa, San Diego. (619) 696-0199. Open Wednesday–Friday, 11 A.M.–4 P.M.; Saturday and Sunday, 11 A.M.–5 P.M. Adults, $1.

SAN DIEGO MUSEUM OF ART, 1450 El Prado, San Diego. (619) 232-7931. Open Tuesday–Sunday, 10 A.M.–4:30 P.M. Adults, $4; seniors and military, $3; students, $2; ages 6–12, $1; under 6, free.

SAN DIEGO MUSEUM OF MAN, 1350 El Prado, San Diego. (619) 239-2001. Open daily, 10 A.M.–4:30 P.M. Adults, $3; ages 12–18, $1; ages 6–11, 25 cents; under 6, free.

TIMKEN ART GALLERY, 1500 El Prado, San Diego. (619) 239-5548. Open Tuesday–Saturday, 10 A.M.–4:30 P.M.; Sunday, 1:30 P.M.–4:30 P.M. Free.

For More Information

San Diego Convention and Visitors Bureau, 1200 Third Avenue, Suite 824, San Diego, CA 92101; (619) 232-3101.

San Diego Visitor Information Center, 2688 East Mission Bay Drive, San Diego, CA 92109; (619) 276-8200.

SAN DIEGO BY THE SEA
Exploring a Maritime Tradition

When explorer Juan Rodriguez Cabrillo first dropped anchor in San Diego Bay in 1542, he described it as "a harbor, closed and very good." For four hundred years this very good harbor has been the key element in the city's growth. As a result, many of San Diego's sights and activities reflect a strong nautical influence. The best places to sample that influence are on or around San Diego Bay and man-made Mission Bay to the north.

For $1.50, you can board the San Diego ferry at the foot of Broadway for a ride to Coronado on the 297-passenger *Silvergate*. The mini-cruise takes about 15 minutes to deposit you at the Old Ferry Landing on Coronado, and along the way, you'll have a panoramic view of the dynamic downtown skyline.

The refurbished Old Ferry Landing now houses a complex of gift and specialty shops, restaurants, and snack-food eateries. Kids can fish from the pier at the landing, or rent bicycles. Coronado is ideal for bike riding because its streets are flat, mostly residential, and quiet. The town is only about 12 square blocks, but there is more exercise waiting if you head off down the wide bikeway that runs south along the Silver Strand, the narrow spit of land that connects Coronado with the mainland.

The setpiece of your Coronado tour will be the historic **Hotel del Coronado**. The century-old hotel is a National Historic Landmark, and its red gabled, conical roof is visible from almost anywhere in Coronado. To get there, head south on C Avenue from the Old Ferry Landing to Orange Avenue, then follow around to the left toward the hotel. If you're not biking, 50 cents will buy a ride on a motorized trolley that runs between the landing and the hotel. The Del Coronado was built to provide European elegance and cuisine in the boisterous American West of the 1880s. Over the years, it has entertained U.S. presidents, European royalty, and American movie stars. In the ornate Victorian lobby, you can point out the woodworking craftsmanship to the kids, then take them for a peek at the two-story, open beam ceiling of the Crown Room, the hotel's main dining room. If the youngsters are interested, visit the Hall of History displaying photographs and artifacts from the hotel's past. If the kids have their bathing suits, stop to play at Coronado Beach, next to the hotel. It is rarely as crowded as most of San Diego's other beaches.

To give the kids more time on the water after your return ferry ride, take a boat tour of San Diego Bay. This is one of the busiest ports in the nation, not to mention the home of the 11th U.S. Naval District. Several companies offer harbor cruises. Among the best known are the **San Diego Harbor Excursion** (the company also operates the Coronado ferry from the Broadway Pier), nearby **Invader Cruises**, and the **Red Witch** on Harbor Island. Most companies offer one-hour cruises that take you by U.S. Navy facilities, the fishing fleet, dry dock operations, and the Coronado Bridge. Two-hour tours add a trip around North Island and out to the bay's entrance.

Sit on the starboard side of the ship (the right side as you face the bow) for the best views and be sure to bring along a sweater or jacket because ocean breezes can be nippy. Kids will be impressed with the mammoth aircraft carriers *Constellation* and *Ranger*, berthed at North Island when they are in port. Jets frequently take off and land at the Naval Air Station on the island, a hub of the Navy's antisubmarine operations.

For kids who want to pilot a boat themselves, San Diego has plenty of charter companies that rent sailboats or speed boats by the hour or by the day. Many will include lessons as part of a beginner's package. Or try your hand with a rod and reel on a half-day, full-day, or overnight cruise. You can rent fishing gear from most charter services, and crew members are usually accommodating to beginners. They'll even bait your hook and clean your fish, if you catch one. Shelter Island in San Diego Bay and Mission Bay's Quivira Basin are two of the more popular sport fishing landings.

Nautical history is exhibited at San Diego's unique **Maritime Museum,** comprising three ships berthed at the Embarcadero. The *Star of India*, a square-rigged sailing ship, the *Berkeley*, a 90-year-old San Francisco ferry boat, and the *Medea*, a luxury steam yacht built in 1904, are at once museums and museum pieces.

The *Star of India* began her career in 1863 as a merchant ship, sailing around the Cape of Good Hope to India. Today, youngsters can walk her wooden decks and imagine what the age of sail might have been like. Several of the cabins have been restored. The captain's quarters reveal such "luxuries" as a chamber pot and a wash basin on gimbals. Another cabin shows evidence of a youthful passenger with an antique dollhouse and tiny high-button shoes as part of the baggage. A video presentation describes the days of iron men and wooden ships. Below decks, you'll see displays that cover navigation, knot tying, shipbuilding, and sail rigging.

On board the *Berkeley*, youngsters will find more historical displays, including models of several famous ships. Of particular note, however, is the *Berkeley*'s engine room, where one of the boilers holds a scary surprise. The upper deck retains the flavor of the *Berkeley*'s heyday as a passenger ferry, with stained-glass windows and carved wood paneling. The wheelhouse is open for youngsters to inspect and set forth on an imaginary voyage.

The *Medea* is the smallest of the three ships. As her elegant teakwood and oak appointments suggest, she was built for luxury cruising. Her main cabins have been restored to their original turn-of-the-century charm and are the only part of the ship open to the public.

On most weekends, the kids may have a chance to glimpse a more contemporary vessel. The Navy frequently holds an open house for one of its ships at Navy Pier, immediately south of Broadway Pier. The kind of ship on display depends on those the Navy has in port. The tour is free to the public on weekends from 1 P.M. to 4 P.M. On board these modern vessels you'll see obvious contrasts with the historic ships, but even today's sailors don't have a lot of room.

Depending on your stamina at this point, you and the kids can consider two alternatives. The first is to head less than a mile south on Harbor Drive to **Seaport Village**. More then seventy shops, boutiques, and restaurants make up this 14-acre development at the south end of the Embarcadero. For the kids, there is a carousel, magic shop, toy store, and kite shop. With steady ocean breezes, you will have a kite airborne in no time. For a change of pace, hop one of the steeds at the Broadway Flying Horses Carousel. Its colorful, hand-carved horses carried their first children eighty years ago on Coney Island, New York.

Your second choice is to take Harbor Drive north around the bay to Point Loma and the **Cabrillo National Monument**. Along the way, you will pass Harbor and Shelter islands, man-made additions to the bay that offer spots for strolling, bike riding, picnics, and sailing rentals.

Point Loma, at the end of Catalina Boulevard, is a large promontory that juts southward into the Pacific to form a part of the entrance into San Diego Bay. There is no better panoramic view of the city and bay than from the monument's visitors center. Inside the center are natural history displays, a huge lighthouse lens, and a small book and gift shop.

From the visitors center, take the trail south to the Old Point Loma Lighthouse. Built in 1855, the lighthouse served as both a coastal beacon and a harbor entrance light until it was taken out of service in 1891. Kids will be interested to learn that the last lighthouse keeper and his wife raised four children at this lonely outpost. The family quarters have now been restored and are open to the public during monument visiting hours. The tower to the light, however, remains closed for safety reasons.

For hikers, the national monument provides a two-mile Bayside Trail, formerly an asphalt road used by the military, that leads from the lighthouse down toward the bay side of the point. The trail is clearly marked with exhibits of the plants and animals in the area. Along the way, you will see the remnants of the coastal artillery batteries that defended San Diego Harbor during World Wars I and II.

On the west side of the point, take the road that leads down to the ocean where the kids can explore several tide pools. Starfish, tiny crabs, and feathery sea anemones live in this harsh environment. If you're patient, you might even spot an octopus. The best time to go is at low tide. Be sure everyone wears rubber-soled shoes that will provide traction on the wet rocks.

Point Loma also is an excellent vantage point for watching the annual migration of the Pacific gray whales. A glass-enclosed Whale Overlook includes information about the whales. Rangers offer daily talks on these giant mammals during their migration, which occurs between late December and the end of March.

Whale watching is a brisk industry in San Diego. Back in 1955, a San Diego fisherman was reportedly looking for some additional income after a poor fishing season and offered to ferry people out to see the whales at $1 a passenger. The price has gone up since then and so has the number of boats. Whale-watch cruises usually last a couple of hours and are offered by most of the excursion companies at San Diego Bay and several sportfishing charter services. Be sure to bring along a jacket or sweater, even on sunny days. Binoculars will help keep the kids amused until someone cries, "Thar she blows!"

San Diego's other major bay was carved out of marshy mud flats in the lowlands north of downtown and south of La Jolla. Mission Bay's principal industry is recreation. At 4,600 acres, it is the largest municipal aquatic park in the world. If the kids enjoy swimming, sailing, windsurfing, waterskiing, jet skiing, or fishing, then you can easily spend a day here. The shoreline includes 27 miles of beaches for sunbathing. Bayshore trails are popular with joggers and cyclists, and you can even find places to play golf and tennis. Mission Bay, of course, is also the home of Sea World, not to mention several resort hotels and a few shopping complexes.

About the only thing Mission Bay doesn't have is surf. For that you will have to follow West Mission Bay Drive to Mission Beach on the Pacific side of the peninsula. Lifeguards are on duty year round and you also will find places to rent roller skates, bicycles, and boogie boards along the beachfront. The beach has picnic tables and if you go several blocks farther south, you'll find barbecue facilities and fire rings at South Mission Beach.

Attractions

CABRILLO NATIONAL MONUMENT, San Diego. (Exit I-5 at Camino del Rios south to Rosecrans Boulevard [209]; right to Canon Street; right to Catalina Boulevard; left to the end of the road and the monument.) (619) 557-5450. Open daily, 9 A.M.–sunset. Admission: $3 per vehicle; $1 per hiker, bus, or bike rider; over 62 and under 13, free.

CRUISES

• *California Cruisin'*, B Street Cruise Ship Terminal, San Diego. (Exit I-5 at Front Street; south to Broadway; right to Harbor Drive; right to B Street terminal.) (619) 235-8600. Catalina departures: June–September, daily, 8 A.M.; October–May,

Wednesday, Friday–Sunday, 8 A.M. Round-trip: adults, $49; seniors, military, $43; ages 2–13, $33; under 2, free.
• *Ensenada Express*, B Street Cruise Ship Terminal, San Diego. (See directions to California Cruisin'.) (619) 232-2109. Ensenada, Mexico, departures: summer, Thursday–Tuesday, 9 A.M.; winter, Friday–Monday, 9 A.M. Round-trip: adults, $59; seniors and military, $56; ages 12–17, $49; ages 3–11, $29; under 3, free.
• *Invader Cruises*, 1066 North Harbor Drive, San Diego. (Exit I-5 at Front Street; south to Broadway; right to Harbor Drive; right to cruise office.) (619) 234-8687. Open daily. Call for departure times. One-hour cruises: adults $8. Two-hour cruises: adults, $11.50; seniors, children, and active military personnel, half price.
• *Red Witch*, 1380 Harbor Island Drive, San Diego. (Exit I-5 at Kettner Boulevard; south to Laurel Street; right to Harbor Drive; exit right to Harbor Island Drive and cruise office.) (619) 542-0646. Open Wednesday–Sunday. Call for departure times. Adults, $15; under 13, $7.50.
• *San Diego Harbor Excursion*, 1050 North Harbor Drive, San Diego. (See directions for Invader Cruises.) (619) 234-4111. Open daily. Call for departure times. One-hour cruises: adults, $8. Two-hour cruises: adults, $11.50; seniors and children under 12, half price.

HOTEL DEL CORONADO, 1500 Orange Avenue, Coronado. (Exit I-5 at Coronado Bridge [75] [$1 toll]; west to Orange Avenue; left to hotel. Or take the ferry from the Broadway Pier to Coronado). Open daily. Self-guided tour: $3 in the lobby.

SAN DIEGO MARITIME MUSEUM, 1306 North Harbor Drive, San Diego. (See directions for Invader Cruises.) (619) 234-9153. Open daily, 9 A.M.–8 P.M. Adults, $5; ages 13–17, seniors, and active military, $4; 6–12, $1.25; families, $10; under 5, free.

SAIL/SPEEDBOAT RENTALS

• *Glorietta Bay Marina*, 1715 Strand Way, Coronado. (See directions for Hotel del Coronado. Marina is across the street from the hotel on the bay side of the peninsula.) (619) 435-5203. Open daily, 9 A.M.–5 P.M. Call for rental rates and boat sizes.
• *Mission Bay Sportscenter*, 1010 Santa Clara Place, San Diego. (Exit I-5 at Mission Bay Drive; south to Garnet Avenue; right to Mission Boulevard; left to Santa Clara; left to sportscenter.) (619) 488-1004. Open daily. Call for rental rates and craft descriptions.
• *San Diego Baysailors*, 2040 Harbor Island Drive, Suite 102, San Diego. (See directions to Red Witch under Cruises above.) (619) 291-4759. Open daily, 9:30 A.M.–5 P.M. Call for rental rates and boat sizes.

• *Seaforth Boat Rentals,* 1641 Quivira Road, Mission Bay. (Exit I-5 at Tecolote Road; west to Sea World Drive; continue to Midway Drive; exit at West Mission Bay Drive; west to Quivira Road; left to rental shop.) (619) 223-1681. Open daily. Call for rental rates and boat sizes.

SEAPORT VILLAGE, Harbor Drive at Kettner Boulevard, San Diego. (Exit I-5 at Kettner Boulevard; south to Seaport Village.) (619) 235-4014. Open daily, 10 A.M.–9 P.M.

WHALE WATCHING

(The following companies offer whale-watch trips of varying length and prices during the migration from late December through March. Most three-hour cruises cost about $12 for adults and $9 for children. Call for exact departure times and prices.)

• *Fisherman's Landing,* 2836 Garrison Street, San Diego. (Exit I-5 at Camino del Rio; south to Rosecrans Boulevard; right to Garrison Street; left to landing at foot of street.) (619) 222-0391.
• *H & M Landing,* 2803 Emerson Street, San Diego. (Exit I-5 at Camino del Rio; south to Rosecrans Boulevard; right to Emerson Street; left to landing). (619) 222-1144.
• *Invader Cruises* (See listing, page 267.)
• *San Diego Harbor Excursion* (See listing, page 267.)

For More Information

San Diego Convention and Visitors Bureau, 1200 Third Avenue, Suite 824, San Diego, CA 92101; (619) 232-3101.

San Diego Visitor Information Center, 2688 East Mission Bay Drive, San Diego, CA 92109; (619) 276-8200.

OLD TOWN, DOWNTOWN
Windows on the Past

San Diego is California's oldest city. Introducing the youngsters to its colorful past will take most of a day in downtown San Diego. If too much history makes them yearn to get back to the present, you might combine portions of this one-day itinerary with other city attractions.

Start your day where Father Junipero Serra began many of his, at the

Mission Basilica San Diego de Alcala. Father Serra was the Franciscan missionary who founded the famous string of 21 California missions that reach all the way to Sonoma, north of San Francisco. Mission San Diego was the first to be built, which is why it claims to be the Mother of Missions. Actually, it was built at the city's Presidio in 1769, and relocated to its present spot in 1774.

The mission is six miles east of the Presidio ruins, near the junction of I-8 and I-15, in a largely residential neighborhood. The gift shop has audio taped tours you can rent, or you may want to just stroll around the grounds and through the exhibits, which include the sparsely furnished quarters of Father Serra himself. The church, sanctuary, gardens, and rectory are all open during visitors hours. A small museum contains artifacts of early mission life. Point out to the kids the photos of the mission before it was restored. Like many of the California missions, San Diego de Alcala still is the site of daily religious services.

The city's first European settlement was founded in 1769 and the remnants of the original structure, a fortress, are at **Presidio Park**. Beautifully landscaped and dotted with memorial statues, this outdoor museum covers almost fifty acres of a hilltop that commands a panoramic view of the city. The park's grass-covered knolls and hollows are all that remain of the original settlement. You can see where archaeologists are painstakingly excavating these ruins to put together the record of this first European community on the West Coast.

The huge white building at the top of the hill, **Junipero Serra Museum**, is often mistaken for the San Diego mission, thanks to its mission-revival architecture. The museum commemorates the era of missions and ranchos and the Native American culture that preceded them. Among the exhibits you will see several artifacts from the park's excavations.

By the 1820s local residents felt safe enough to move out of the Presidio's confines to establish the "old town" of San Diego. The bustling community that grew up at the foot of the hilltop Presidio is now clearly evident in **Old Town State Park**. The six-block area is cordoned off from traffic and contains at least 12 vintage buildings along with several newer structures designed to blend in. With four shopping areas and several restaurants, it is a combination history lesson and shopping mall rolled into one attraction.

In the 1800s, Old Town was for nearly half a century the commercial, political, and social center of San Diego. Several of the original buildings have been restored to evoke life during this era. Park Service rangers conduct a free one-hour walking tour of Old Town every day at 2 P.M. The tour leaves from in front of the Machado-Silvas House on San Diego Street.

If you can't time your visit to coincide with a tour, you can see some of the highlights by starting from the same place and heading east on San Diego to Mason Street. Just around the corner to the right on Mason is the **Mason Street School**, a popular attraction with kids. Built in 1865, it was San Diego's first schoolhouse. Walk into the one-room structure to see the potbelly stove and old-fashioned books and desks. The message is clear to most youngsters—school days were pretty austere a hundred years ago.

Back on San Diego Avenue, continue east one block to **Casa de Altamirano**. This 1851 residence was the first frame building in Old Town, but its real claim to fame was as the home of the San Diego Union newspaper, which began printing there in 1868. The Union has restored the offices and now maintains the structure as a museum.

Another block east, at San Diego Avenue and Harney Street, is **Whaley House Museum**. It was Old Town's first two-story mansion, built by San Francisco merchant Thomas Whaley in 1856. Over the years, the building has served as a home, store, theater, courthouse, and even a church. Most intriguing for kids, however, is the ghost that is supposed to haunt the premises.

Double back on San Diego Avenue and turn right on Twiggs Street to Juan Street. Turn left on Juan and in the middle of the block you'll find the **Seeley Stables**. Inside this former stagecoach stop, you will see an impressive collection of horse-drawn vehicles, including a Wells Fargo mail coach. The eclectic exhibits include musical instruments, nineteenth-century toys, and Native American artifacts. Another reason to stop at the stables is a slide show on early California, presented three times a day.

One block west on Juan Street is **Bazaar del Mundo**, a large white-washed structure of several buildings that once served as the Casa de Pico Hotel. Take a break from history by browsing in a few of the 17 shops. You also can stop for a bite to eat at one of four restaurants in the complex, and on most weekends, the Bazaar offers entertainment.

To experience history firsthand, sign the kids up for one of the park's living-history programs held on Saturday morning. Park docents lead participants on a variety of craft endeavors, from making adobe bricks to constructing cornhusk dolls. Attendance is limited and you will need to call (619) 238-3193 to make a reservation.

From Old Town, resume your historic tour by rejoining I-5 and heading south toward the civic center. Not far from the corner of Cedar and Columbia streets is the **Firehouse Museum**. The history of firefighting in San Diego is on display in exhibits and equipment that crowd the museum's quarters, the former home of Engine Company No. 6. There is so much to see in such a small space that some youngsters might be overwhelmed. Take the time to make sure they see the fine collection of model fire engines and appreciate some of the early equipment. The 1841 hand pumper was used before there were water mains in San Diego and the city had to rely on bucket brigades for its water. You'll see a 1903 steam pumper that was drawn by three horses. All polished enamel and shining silver, these machines have been lovingly restored. Other collections that might interest kids include historical fire helmets, badges, and patches.

The largest collection of historic buildings downtown is in the **Gaslamp Quarter**, southeast of the civic center, where about a hundred buildings from the Victorian era have been restored and now house various businesses. The effect is pleasingly nostalgic, but the more gritty waterfront establishments that once occupied the area are still in evidence around the perimeter.

The quarter's most popular attraction for families is **The Old Spaghetti Factory**, at 5th and K streets, which occupies an 1898 Romanesque structure that originally housed a printing company. One of the city's better-known family restaurants, it's so popular you are almost certain to have a half-hour wait to get in, no matter when you arrive. While the food may not be spectacular, the turn-of-the-century memorabilia crowding the rooms make the wait worthwhile. Much of the restaurant's decor came from old California hotels. Be sure to notice the barber chair, parlor stove, and stained glass windows. There's even a 1917 streetcar in the middle of one room that serves both as atmosphere and an eating venue. As an added touch, youngsters can fold their children's menu into a paper streetcar by following instructions on the menu. The food is reasonably priced and portions are generous, but be warned that the restaurant does not take credit cards.

One of San Diego's most elaborate survivors of the Victorian era is east of the Gaslamp Quarter on K Street at 20th Street. **Villa Montezuma** was built in 1887 during a boom-town period as part of a housing-development promotion. The home is now a museum, with changing art exhibits occupying an upstairs gallery. The best way to see the house is on a docent-led tour. The docents are adept at making the house's history come alive for youngsters, having them try to guess the uses of certain household objects. In the process of learning about butter churns and rug beaters, the kids gain insight into the quality of life enjoyed by the children of a well-to-do family before the turn of the century.

If all this history is proving overwhelming for the youngsters, you can switch to more up-to-date diversions nearby. One of the most unusual is **Horton Plaza** on the edge of the Gaslamp Quarter at 4th Street and Broadway. Sprawling over 11 acres, this outdoor shopping center reflects an amalgam of more than a dozen architectural styles. Buildings, courtyards, walkways, ramps, and stairs come together at odd angles and in splashes of colors and bold patterns that are as whimsical as they are distinctive. The plaza has numerous specialty shops, bookstores, gift shops, large department stores, restaurants, snack stands, and movie theaters.

Attractions

FIREHOUSE MUSEUM, 1572 Columbia Street, San Diego. (Exit I-5 at Front Street; south to Cedar Street; right to Columbia Street and the museum.) (619) 232-FIRE. Open Thursday–Sunday, 10 A.M.–4 P.M. Free.

GASLAMP QUARTER, Downtown San Diego; bordered by Broadway (north), Harbor Drive (south), 6th Street (east), and 3rd Street (west). (Exit I-5 at Front Street; south to Broadway; left to 4th Street.)

• The Old Spaghetti Factory, 5th and K streets, San Diego. (See directions to Gaslamp Quarter; follow 4th Street south; left on K Street to restaurant.) (619) 233-4323. Open Monday–Thursday, 5 P.M.–10 P.M.; Friday and Saturday, 5 P.M.–11 P.M.; Sunday, 4 P.M.–10 P.M.

HORTON PLAZA, 4th Street and Broadway, San Diego. (Exit I-5 at Front Street; south to Broadway; left to 4th Street; right to plaza parking structure.) (619) 239-8180.

JUNIPERO SERRA MUSEUM, 2727 Presidio Drive, San Diego. (Exit I-8 at Taylor Street; west to Chestnut Street; left to Presidio Drive; left to museum.) (619) 297-3258. Open Tuesday–Saturday, 10 A.M.–4:30 P.M.; Sunday, noon–4:30 P.M. Adults, $2; under 13, free.

MISSION BASILICA SAN DIEGO DE ALCALA, 10818 San Diego Mission Road, San Diego. (Exit I-8 at Mission Gorge Road; north to Twain Avenue; left to mission [becomes San Diego Mission Road after one block].) (619) 281-8449. Open daily, 9 A.M.–5 P.M. Adults, $1; under 13, free.

OLD TOWN SAN DIEGO STATE HISTORIC PARK. Six-block area bordered by Juan Street (north), Congress Street (south), Twiggs Street (east), and Wallace Street (west). (Exit I-8 at Taylor Street; west to Juan Street and parking.) (619) 237-6770. Open daily. Guided walking tours daily at 2 P.M.

• *Bazaar del Mundo*, 2754 Calhoun Street. (619) 296-3161. Open daily. Call for individual shop and restaurant hours.

• *Casa de Altamirano*, 2626 San Diego Avenue. Open Tuesday–Sunday, 10 A.M.–5 P.M. Free.

• *Mason Street School*, Mason Street and San Diego Avenue. Open daily, 10 A.M.–4 P.M. Free.

• *Seeley Stables*, 2648 Calhoun Street. Open Memorial Day–Labor Day, daily, 10 A.M.–6 P.M.; Labor Day–Memorial Day, daily, 10 A.M.–5 P.M. Adults, $1; ages 6–17, 50 cents; under 6, free.

• *Whaley House Museum*, 2482 San Diego Avenue. (619) 298-2482. Open Wednesday–Sunday, 10 A.M.–4:30 P.M. Adults, $3; seniors, $2.50; ages 12–16, $1; ages 5–11, 50 cents; under 5, free.

PRESIDIO PARK (see Junipero Serra Museum).

VILLA MONTEZUMA, 1925 K Street, San Diego. (Exit I-5 at Imperial Avenue; east to 20th Street; left to K Street and the house.) (619) 239-2211. Open Wednesday–Sunday, 1 P.M.–4:30 P.M. Adults, $3; under 13, free.

For More Information

San Diego Visitor Information Center, 2688 East Mission Bay Drive, San Diego, CA 92109; (619) 276-8200.

La Jolla
A Gem by the Sea

North of San Diego, perched on a bluff overlooking the sea, the city of La Jolla is blessed with cove beaches and shoreline parks. Pronounced "La Hoya," the word means "jewel" in Spanish. In any language the city is a gem and its many facets provide youngsters with attractions that teach, challenge, and entertain in the arts and sciences.

If you have young children, drive first to the **Children's Museum of San Diego**. It is located in the La Jolla Village Square shopping center off La Jolla Village Drive near I-5. Designed for children ages 4 to 14, this cheery museum has a dozen hands-on exhibits that invite kids to participate. In Shapespace, kids build structures out of hundreds of Lego pieces and plastic tubes. At the Health Center, they can play with an operating table and a dentist's chair, or inspect a human skeleton and a plastic model of a human body which has removable inner parts. Kids borrow crutches and wheel-chairs from the center to use all over the museum. In a TV studio, children create the KKID evening news before a video camera, while others watch the show on a color monitor. Next door, budding thespians present plays on a curtained stage using the props and costumes provided. At the Art Studio, teachers help youngsters create projects from paint, paper, and household objects. A small shop at the museum exit sells children's books and educational toys.

La Jolla has another museum designed with kids in mind, **Scripps Aquarium-Museum**, part of Scripps Institute of Oceanography at the University of California at San Diego. On walls lining the darkened perimeter of the museum, 18 well-lit tanks display marine life from the La Jolla area, Mexico, and Micronesia. Each tank has something to catch the kids' attention—stingrays, leopard sharks, giant sheep crabs, and treelike anemones. Schedule your visit for Wednesday or Sunday at 1:30 P.M. to see the fish being fed.

In the central exhibit area, children learn about wave action when they push buttons to generate water movement in a wave machine. A three-dimensional map of the ocean floor along the Southern California coast shows the deep trenches and underwater mountains we can't see from the surface. Outside the museum entrance a man-made tide pool simulates intertidal conditions. Kids peer into the clear water to see starfish, anemones, and other sea creatures. Parking is limited around the aquarium so you may need to park at metered slots in a well-marked lot up the hill.

After learning about what lives in the ocean, you may want to spend the rest of the day relaxing with the kids along the shore. La Jolla's seven-mile coast beckons with small cove beaches, cliff-top parks, and tide pools. A good place to swim with youngsters is at **Children's Pool Beach**, south of La Jolla Cove Park along Coast Boulevard. A concrete breakwater keeps the shallow lagoon calm. There are lifeguards on duty and restrooms with changing facilities. North of this beach at **La Jolla Cove**, kids who are good swimmers can snorkel in the clear water. The younger set will enjoy the tide pools, and there's a small sandy beach with lifeguards on duty. The grassy park on the blufftop above the cove is a good spot for a picnic with a priceless view.

A number of caves have been carved by waves into the sandstone cliffs along La Jolla Cove, but only one is accessible from land. To reach **Sunny Jim Cave**, enter through the **La Jolla Cave and Shell Shop** on Coast Boulevard east of La Jolla Cove Park. You'll pay a small entrance fee at the cash register. Kids who are old enough not to be frightened by a dark tunnel and a cave, are intrigued with the adventure of climbing down 141 steps to the cave below. From a sturdy platform in the cave, you'll watch the water surge out of the entrance and crash in again with each wave. Try to time your visit with high tide for the most exciting view.

Parking spaces are a precious commodity in La Jolla, so if you have a spot, stay there and walk to nearby attractions. From the shell shop, walk across Coast Boulevard and up some steps to Prospect Street, the main commercial thoroughfare of La Jolla. Head south on this elegant, curving street past small stylish shops, ice-cream parlors, and restaurants to the **La Jolla Museum of Contemporary Art**. This columned building with beautiful ocean views offers changing exhibits of post-1950 American art. Children are often fascinated with the colorful pop-art pieces and fanciful sculptures on display. Docents lead tours through the collection in the afternoons, and if they have youngsters along in the group, they will try to help the children appreciate the art.

On Girard Street, La Jolla's other main street, **The White Rabbit Children's Books** is worth a stop. This cheerful store carries more than six thousand titles for children from infants through high school, plus a small selection of educational toys and games. There's a cozy reading area in the back, and toys to play with beside curving carpeted seats. Every Wednesday morning at 10:30 is story hour for young children, and there are special programs on holidays and some weekends.

La Jolla has one more museum that kids will enjoy, the **Mingei International Museum of World Folk Art**. Located in the University Towne Centre on La Jolla Village Drive at Genessee Avenue, this large museum gives kids a fascinating look at cultures from around the world. Changing exhibits feature such items as costumes, folk toys, jewelry, and masks. Every exhibit is accompanied by music and films that usually appeal to kids. The Collectors Gallery shop features educational toys and some inexpensive folk craft items. The museum offers school tours. You'll find the museum on the second level of the shopping center, south of Nordstrom and west of Robinsons department stores.

North of La Jolla on North Torrey Pines Road (S-21) is **Torrey Pines State Beach and Reserve**, a 1,750-acre park established to protect the world's rarest pine tree. The gnarled Torrey pine is native only to San Diego and Santa Rosa Island off the coast of Santa Barbara. Well-marked trails along a bluff above the beach lead through stands of thousands of the trees. If you are lucky, you may see some of the wildlife that lives in the reserve, such as deer, coyotes, and foxes. New displays and a video presentation at the Visitor Center showcase the reserve's environment. Rangers conduct guided nature walks on weekends at 11:30 A.M. and 1:30 P.M. The beach below has lifeguards on duty during summer.

Attractions

CHILDREN'S MUSEUM OF SAN DIEGO, 8657 Villa La Jolla Drive, La Jolla. (Exit I-5 at La Jolla Village Drive; west to Villa La Jolla Drive; left to Noble; left to parking lot of La Jolla Village Square. Enter shopping center between May Company and Bullocks Wilshire and walk to the museum on the first level.) (619) 450-0768. Open Wednesday–Friday, Sunday, noon–5 P.M.; Saturday, 10 A.M.–5 P.M. Admission: ages 2–65, $2.75; over 65, $1.25; under 2, free.

LA JOLLA CAVE AND SHELL SHOP (SUNNY JIM CAVE), 1325 Coast Boulevard, La Jolla. (Exit I-5 at La Jolla Village Drive; west to Torrey Pines Road; left to Prospect Place; right to Coast Boulevard; right to shop.) (619) 454-6080. Open daily, 10 A.M.–5 P.M. Adults, $1; ages 3–11, 50 cents.

LA JOLLA MUSEUM OF CONTEMPORARY ART, 700 Prospect Street, La Jolla. (Exit I-5 at La Jolla Village Drive; west to Torrey Pines Road; left to Prospect Place; right and continue after street becomes Prospect Street to Silverado Street. Museum is on Prospect Street at Silverado Street.) (619) 454-3541. Open Tuesday–Sunday, 10 A.M.–5 P.M.; Wednesday, 10 A.M.–9 P.M. Adults, $3; seniors and students, $1; under 12, 50 cents. Wednesday nights, 5–9 P.M., free.

MINGEI INTERNATIONAL MUSEUM OF WORLD FOLK ART, 4405 La Jolla Village Drive, La Jolla. (Exit I-5 at La Jolla Village Drive; east to Genessee Avenue and park in lot at University Towne Centre on southeast corner of intersection. Walk to museum on upper level adjacent to footbridge, near Forum Hall, opposite Nordstrom.) (619) 453-5300. Open Tuesday–Thursday, Saturday, 11 A.M.–5 P.M.; Friday, 11 A.M.–9 P.M.; Sunday, 2 P.M.–5 P.M. Adults, $2; under 12, free.

SCRIPPS AQUARIUM-MUSEUM, 8602 La Jolla Shores Drive, La Jolla. (Exit I-5 at La Jolla Village Drive; west to North Torrey Pines Road; right to La Jolla Shores Drive; left to museum.) (619) 534-6933 or (619) 534-FISH. Open daily, 9 A.M.–5 P.M. Free (donation encouraged).

THE WHITE RABBIT CHILDREN'S BOOKS, 7755 Girard Avenue,

La Jolla. (Exit I-5 at La Jolla Village Drive; west to Torrey Pines Road; left to Girard Avenue; right to store.) (619) 454-3518. Open Monday–Saturday, 9 A.M.–5:30 P.M.

TORREY PINES STATE BEACH AND RESERVE, eight miles north of La Jolla. (Exit I-5 at La Jolla Village Drive; west to North Torrey Pines Road; right to beach at bottom of hill; left through gate and up hill to Visitor Center.) (619) 755-2063. Reserve open daily, 9 A.M.–dusk. Visitor Center open daily, 11 A.M.–4 P.M. Guided nature walks on weekends, 1:30 P.M. Parking: $4 per vehicle.

For More Information

La Jolla Town Council, Inc., 1055 Wall Street, Suite 110, Box 1101, La Jolla, CA 92038; (619) 454-1444.

INLAND SAN DIEGO
On Safari in San Diego County

The mountains and valleys that surround San Diego are filled with activities for families with all kinds of interests. From the picturesque streets of a century-old gold mining town to the awesome grandeur of a starry galaxy seen through a giant telescope, San Diego County's rural attractions span both time and distance. To do it all, you will need two or three days.

The most popular attraction for kids in north San Diego County is **Wild Animal Park**. A few miles east of Escondido on State Highway 78, the 1,800-acre park is operated by the San Diego Zoo. Wild Animal Park differs from a conventional zoo in that most of its 2,200 animals are allowed to roam freely over habitats that duplicate the terrain in Africa and Asia. You won't get as close as you can to animals in conventional zoos, but you will see them interacting—butting heads or galloping across an open savannah—as you never do in zoo confines. Don't worry, though, the lions and tigers are kept separate from their normal prey.

The only way to see most of the animals is from the Wgasa Bush Line monorail train that takes you on a five-mile, 50-minute narrated tour of the habitats. The best seats are on the right side and binoculars can help the kids get that close-up feeling. The waiting line for the monorail can grow long by midday, so it's best to ride the train early. The animals usually are most active in the morning or late afternoon and take it easy in the midday sun.

The round-trip begins and ends at Nairobi Village, the park's commercial center. The village covers about 17 acres and has animal shows, gift shops, and eating facilities. Animal enclosures in the village allow kids to watch gorillas, monkeys, cheetahs, wolves, and birds at close range, and they offer information about the animals as well. Visit the petting "kraal" with young children to feed and pet small deer and more conventional barnyard critters. If it's a cool day, take the 1¼-mile hiking trail that starts near the village's picnic area to see the animals at your pace. Near the start of the trail is Pumzika Point, a shaded and elevated observation tower that overlooks animals in a simulated East African savannah. You can view the animals up close with a telescope.

There is plenty to keep you busy for most of the day at the park, so it's probably wise not to schedule too much else. But you have only scratched the surface of what there is to see in the rest of the north county area.

Mission San Luis Rey, a few miles east of Oceanside on State Highway 76, is often called the King of the Missions. Within several years of its founding in 1789, the mission grew to be the largest, wealthiest, and arguably the most beautiful of all 21 California missions. Restored by the Catholic Church at the end of the nineteenth century, the mission is open to visitors daily. A self-guided tour directs you to the church, cemetery, chapel, and a museum. The kids will be interested in the museum's reproduction of a friar's bedroom, kitchen, weaving room, and workroom.

On Route S14 between the mission and the town of Vista, the youngsters will encounter artifacts of a different sort at the **Antique Gas & Steam Engine Museum**. The collection includes steam and gas engines, horse-drawn equipment, and machinery used in logging, mining, and oil drilling—more than a thousand objects in all. There is even a one-third scale steam locomotive for children to ride. But the principal appeal of this living-history museum is its re-creation of turn-of-the-century American farm life. The museum building occupies only a small part of its 40-acre site in Guajome Regional Park. Twenty acres are given over to growing crops like wheat and barley with the aid of the collection's antique equipment, which is all in working order. From the brightly painted tractors outside to the crafty animal-powered treadmill inside, most of the equipment is so elemental that many youngsters can see exactly how the pistons, pulleys, and belts of these machines worked.

The best time to see the machinery in action is during the Threshing Bee & Antique Engine Shows on the third and fourth weekends of June and October. Kids gain a real appreciation of old time farm life by watching museum volunteers demonstrate planting, harvesting, and threshing. They also will glimpse volunteers going about household chores, and working at early American crafts.

If you head up into the mountains toward Mount Palomar, take Route S6 out of Escondido and stop in Valley Center at **Bates Bros. Nut Farm**, an odd combination of enterprise and recreation. Once solely devoted to cultivating walnut groves, the family enterprise is now limited strictly to packing and shipping nuts, dried fruits, candy, and preserves all over the world. At the Valley Center Store on the farm, you can buy nuts and inquire about a tour of the packing operation led by Clifford Bates, one of the original brothers. After the tour, small children will enjoy the farm zoo, with goats, geese, chickens, and other animals they can feed and pet (food packets are available in the store for 20 cents each). If you visit in October, the kids can pick out a perfect pumpkin from the thousands scattered around the grounds. The rest of the year, the Nut Farm's grounds are given over to picnicking.

From Valley Center, continue on Route S6 into the Cleveland National Forest and **Mount Palomar Observatory** at the end of the road. The major attraction at Mount Palomar is the 200-inch Hale telescope housed in a distinctive white-domed building. You can peer into the dome and see its telescope from a glassed-in observation room. The kids may have trouble identifying the telescope because it isn't the long tube they usually associate with the word. This is a reflecting telescope, the largest in the United States. A diagram on the wall explains how it works.

Be sure to stop at the Greenway Museum on the path between the parking area and the observatory. A videotape presentation describes the telescope's construction and some of its astronomical work. The walls are lined with spectacular photographs of galaxies and star explosions that were taken through the telescope. A cement replica of the giant mirror will give the kids a real appreciation for just how big 200 inches can be. The museum also houses a small gift shop.

From Mount Palomar, return on Route S6 to State Highway 76, head south to join State Highway 79, and continue on to Santa Ysabel. **Dudley's Bakery** sits near the only intersection in town. Visitors come from miles around to buy the bakery's fresh bread. From New England hearth to Danish apple nut, Dudley's bakes more than a dozen distinctive varieties of bread each day, but you have to get there early to have the widest selection. The shelves usually are stocked with other temptations, ranging from cookies to Danish pastries, so you're sure to find a treat for every member of the family.

From Santa Ysabel, continue south on State Highway 79 to **Julian**. Picturesque Main Street, with its board sidewalks and historic buildings, recalls the town's heyday in the 1880s as a gold-mining center. Today Julian is the apple-growing center of Southern California, thanks to its 4,200-foot elevation. Consider staying overnight at the town's historic hotel or at one of several bed and breakfast establishments in order to appreciate Julian at an unhurried pace.

On Main Street, peek in at the Julian Hotel, built in 1897 (the lobby is open to guests only). The hotel has 15 rooms, all of which retain their Victorian atmosphere right down to the four-poster beds and the bathroom at the end of the hall.

At Main and Washington streets take the kids into the Julian Drug Store for a milk shake or an ice-cream sundae at the old soda fountain counter. A block down Washington Street is the **Julian Pioneer Museum**, with artifacts chronicling everyday life from the gold-rush days. Overlooking the museum from a hill on 4th Street is the **Witch Creek School**. This one-room schoolhouse was built in 1880 and later moved from Witch Creek to its present site where it serves as the town's library.

Julian's mining boom, which lasted less than a decade, took $5 million out of the local mountains. The **Eagle & High Peak Mines** preserve the spirit of those long-dead days with a tour through 1,000 feet of underground hard rock tunnels. The only way to see the mines is with a tour guide, who will likely spin yarns about powder monkeys and miners that will give youngsters a whole new perspective on the glamour of gold mining. Be sure to bring a sweater. The mines are cool and drafty, even on the hottest days.

From the last week in September to mid-October, when Julian harvests its apples, the population swells to several thousand tourists. The apple cider runs deep and the aroma of hot apple pie fills the air during harvest time. You can arrange to pick your own apples, but you will need to "rent" a tree from a local grower many months in advance.

South out of Julian, State Highway 79 climbs into the mountains, through dense forests of oaks, alders, and sycamores into stands of pines and white firs. The lush foliage testifies to the unusually frequent rainfalls that soak these hillsides in **Cuyamaca Rancho State Park**. The 25,000-acre park has campgrounds and hiking trails if you want to spend more time exploring these backwoods. A museum at Park Headquarters introduces the kids to the park's original Native American inhabitants, who lived there for centuries. At the small interpretive center near Paso Picacho Campground, exhibits describe the area's natural history. Stonewall Mine, at the north end of the park, tells the story of Southern California's richest gold mine. Today, the only gold to be spotted in the area is in the leaves of the park's many deciduous trees at the onset of fall. This is one of the few places in

Southern California where children can appreciate the full spectacle of the term *fall colors.*

From Cuyamaca, continue south on State Highway 79 to I-8 and make a choice. You can go west back to San Diego, or head east to Route S1 and go south to Campo, where volunteers have built a living memorial to the golden age of railroading at the **San Diego Railroad Museum**. The facility, which is only open on weekends and holidays, houses restored railroad cars and equipment, but its real charm is in the enthusiasm of the volunteers who guide you through the railroad yard and the old trains. Twice a day on weekends, volunteers hitch a restored steam or diesel locomotive to a string of passenger cars to take visitors on a 16-mile train ride through Campo's rugged high desert. It's an excellent way for a youngster infatuated with trains to get in touch with the golden age of railroading.

Head west out of Campo on State Highway 94 to get back to San Diego, and detour south on I-5 to the bayside community of Chula Vista for a visit to one of the few remaining salt marshes in California. What looks to be a shallow, marshy wasteland comes alive for kids at the **Chula Vista Nature Interpretive Center**. From an observation tower, you can watch the many different kinds of migratory birds as they rest during their travels. Inside the center, exhibits bring you closer to the creatures that live in the water and along the shoreline. A petting pool allows youngsters to touch and hand-feed small sharks, bat rays, and stingrays, which have been debarbed to allow for safe handling. A bookstore offers educational materials, and the kids also will enjoy a video presentation on the salt marsh.

Attractions

ANTIQUE GAS & STEAM ENGINE MUSEUM, 2040 North Santa Fe Avenue, Vista. (Exit I-5 at State Highway 76; east to Santa Fe Avenue [Route S14]; right to museum.) (619) 941-1791. Open daily, 10 A.M.–4 P.M. Donations accepted.

BATES BROS. NUT FARM, 15954 Woods Valley Road, Valley Center. (Exit I-15 at Valley Parkway [Route S6]; east to Valley Center Road; left to Woods Valley Road; right to farm.) (619) 749-3333. Open daily, 8 A.M.–5 P.M. Free.

CHULA VISTA NATURE INTERPRETIVE CENTER, 1000 Gunpowder Point Drive, Chula Vista. (Exit I-5 at E Street; west to Bay Boulevard and center parking lot. Shuttle runs between parking lot and center.)

(619) 422-BIRD. Open Tuesday–Sunday, 10 A.M.–5 P.M. Free. (Shuttle, adults, 50 cents; under 17, free).

CUYAMACA RANCHO STATE PARK, 12551 State Highway 79, Descanso. (Exit I-5 at State Highway 78; east to State Highway 79; east to park. Exit I-8 at State Highway 79; north to park.) (619) 765-0755. Open daily, sunrise–sunset. Day-use fee: $3 per car.

DUDLEY'S BAKERY, Santa Ysabel. (Exit I-5 at State Highway 78; east to State Highway 79. Bakery is at junction of the two highways.) (619) 765-0488. Open Wednesday–Saturday, 8 A.M.–5:30 P.M.; Sunday, 8 A.M.–4 P.M.

JULIAN. (Exit I-5 at State Highway 78; east to State Highway 79; east to town.)

• *Eagle & High Peak Mines.* (East on C Street to Old Miners Trail; left to end; right to mine.) (619) 765-0036 or 765-9921. Open daily, 9 A.M.–4 P.M. Adults, $6; under 13, $3.
• *Julian Pioneer Museum,* 2811 Washington Street. (619) 765-0227. Open Memorial Day–Labor Day, daily, 10 A.M.–4 P.M.; Labor Day–Memorial Day, Saturday and Sunday, 10 A.M.–4 P.M. Free.

MISSION SAN LUIS REY, 4050 Mission Avenue, San Luis Rey. (Exit I-5 at State Highway 76; east to mission.) (619) 757-3651. Open daily, Monday–Saturday, 10 A.M.–4 P.M.; Sunday, noon–4 P.M. Adults, $2; under 12, $1.

MOUNT PALOMAR OBSERVATORY, Palomar Mountain. (Exit I-15 at State Highway 78; east to Route S6; left to end of road and observatory.) (619) 742-3476. Open daily, 9 A.M.–4 P.M. Museum open daily, 9 A.M.–4:45 P.M. Free.

SAN DIEGO RAILROAD MUSEUM, Campo. (Exit I-8 at Route S1; south to Campo.) (619) 697-7762. Open Saturday and Sunday, 9 A.M.–5 P.M. Train ride: adults, $7; ages 6–12, $3.50; under 5, free.

WILD ANIMAL PARK, 15500 San Pasqual Valley Road, Escondido. (Exit I-5 at State Highway 78; east to park.) (619) 480-0100, (619) 747-8702. Open daily, late June–Labor Day, 9 A.M.–6 P.M.; Labor Day–late

June, 9 A.M.–4 P.M. Admission including entrance, monorail, animal shows, and exhibits: adults, $12.95; under 16, $6.20; under 2, free.

For More Information

Chula Vista Chamber of Commerce, 233 4th Street, Chula Vista, CA 92010; (619) 420-6602.

Escondido Convention and Visitors Bureau, 720 North Broadway, Escondido, CA 92025; (619) 745-4741.

Julian Chamber of Commerce, Box 413, Julian, CA 92036; (619) 765-1857.

1 2

Annual Events for Kids and Adults

January

TOURNAMENT OF ROSES PARADE, Pasadena. Headquarters, 391 South Orange Grove Boulevard, Pasadena. (818) 449-4100. World-famous parade of floral decorated floats, bands, and equestrian units takes place on New Year's Day.

SANTA MONICA PIER KITE FESTIVAL, Santa Monica Pier, Santa Monica. (213) 822-2561. (Held the last Sunday in January, March, June, and October.) Kite-flying demonstrations, fanciful designs, and kite-flying lessons are part of these one-day events.

MOOSEHEAD SLED DOG CLASSIC, Palm Springs Aerial Tramway, Palm Springs. (619) 325-1449. Sled dogs race at the top of Mount San Jacinto, weather permitting.

February

CHINESE NEW YEAR, Chinatown, downtown Los Angeles. (213) 617-0396. (Held in conjunction with the Lunar New Year.) Several days of celebration include beauty pageant, community carnival, and Golden Dragon Parade through city streets with bands, floats, and dragon dancers.

NATIONAL DATE FESTIVAL, Festival Fairgrounds, Indio. (619) 342-8347. Two-week festival includes Arabian Nights pageant, national horse show, camel and ostrich races, and exhibits.

LAGUNA BEACH WINTER FESTIVAL, Laguna Beach. (714) 494-1018. Four days of festivities feature international foods, music, dancing, and arts, along with a parade and sand-castle–building contest.

FESTIVAL OF THE WHALES, Dana Point. (714) 496-2274. Famous scientists, lecturers, and sailors gather to celebrate the annual migration of the Pacific gray whale from Alaska to Mexico with seminars, talks, and a film festival on weekends over a three-week period.

OCEANSIDE WHALE FESTIVAL, Oceanside. (619) 943-1910. Two-day beach celebration of the Pacific gray-whale migration features sand sculpture, entertainment, arts and crafts, and food.

March

BLESSING OF THE ANIMALS, El Pueblo de Los Angeles State Historic Park, downtown Los Angeles. (213) 625-5045. (Held Holy Saturday before Easter.) Children bring their decorated pets to the Plaza Church to be blessed by priests.

AMERICAN INDIAN FESTIVAL, Los Angeles County Museum of Natural History, Exposition Park. (213) 744-3466. Three-day festival salutes Native American culture with displays and demonstrations of painting, pottery, weaving, and dancing.

SANTA MONICA PIER KITE FESTIVAL, Santa Monica Pier, Santa Monica. (See January listing.)

FIESTA DE LAS GOLINDRINAS, Mission San Juan Capistrano. (714) 493-5911 or (714) 493-4700. Community fair and parade mark this three-week celebration of the swallows' return to the mission from their annual migration to Argentina.

ST. PATRICK'S DAY PARADE, San Diego. (619) 299-7812. Parade begins at noon at 6th and Juniper and heads south, concluding at 6th and Laurel with an Irish Festival that features bands and Irish dancing.

OCEAN BEACH KITE FESTIVAL, Ocean Beach, San Diego. (619) 223-1175. One-day event is open to all comers with kites judged for design, decoration, and flying ability.

April

RAMONA PAGEANT, Hemet. (714) 658-3111. Outdoor presentation of a famed Indian love story involves cast of more than 350.

PALM SPRINGS BALLOON CLASSIC, Palm Springs. (619) 325-1577. Colorful hot-air balloon races during morning give way to helium-filled crafts competing in the Gordon Bennett International Balloon Race.

APPLE BLOSSOM FESTIVAL, Oak Glen. (714) 797-6833. Week-long event features competition for and crowning of the Apple Blossom Queen, a barbecue, and the Blossom Parade.

BUD LIGHT LA JOLLA GRAND PRIX, La Jolla. (619) 296-5165. City streets are transformed into a Monte Carlo–style bicycle race, one of the five largest held in the United States, that draws top riders from the United States and abroad.

May

CHILDREN'S DAY, Little Tokyo, downtown Los Angeles. (213) 626-3067. A combination of traditional Japanese holidays for boys and girls; event features magicians, special shows, clowns, and dancing.

CINCO DE MAYO (MAY 5), El Pueblo de Los Angeles State Historic Park, downtown Los Angeles. (213) 625-5045. Festival of several days' length commemorates a popular Mexican holiday with dancing, music, parades, and puppet shows.

CALIFORNIA STATE SCIENCE FAIR, California Museum of Science and Industry, Exposition Park, Los Angeles. (213) 744-7432. Week-long show displays best of state's high school students' science projects in competition for prizes and scholarships.

UCLA MARDI GRAS, UCLA Athletic Field, Westwood. (213) 825-4321. Charity carnival features rides, games, music, fireworks, and a lot more.

CALIFORNIA STRAWBERRY FESTIVAL, Vintage Marina of Channel Islands Harbor, Oxnard. (805) 485-8833. Two-day festival celebrates one of the main crops of the Oxnard plain with music, food, games, contests, and a children's fun center.

CHILDREN'S CELEBRATION OF THE ARTS, Ventura. (805) 654-7837. Arts projects for children involve puppet making, face painting, and other crafts workshops.

ANNUAL OLD TOWN DAYS CELEBRATION, Saugus Depot, Newhall. (805) 254-1275. (Held first Saturday in May.) Daylong festivities celebrate historic times with demonstrations of sheepshearing, horseshoeing, wool spinning, quilting, and hayrides.

CALICO SPRING FESTIVAL, Calico Ghost Town, Yermo. (619) 254-2122 or (714) 780-8810. A three-day bluegrass hootenanny includes fiddle, banjo, guitar, and band contests, clogging, square dancing, and ragtime entertainment.

STRAWBERRY FESTIVAL, Garden Grove. (714) 638-0981. Four days of festivities on the village green mark Garden Grove's role as the nation's leading strawberry-producing area with pie-eating contests, carnival rides, crafts booths, and a parade.

CINCO DE MAYO DAYS FESTIVAL, Old Town State Historic Park, San Diego. (619) 237-6770. Two-day festival features authentic Mexican entertainment and a buffalo barbecue.

June

SANTA MONICA PIER KITE FESTIVAL, Santa Monica Pier, Santa Monica. (213) 822-2561. (See January listing.)

SUMMER SOLSTICE CELEBRATION, State Street, Santa Barbara. (805) 965-3396. Commemorates longest day of the year with carnivallike parade followed by music, mimes, dance, and theater performances in Alameda Park.

SANTA MONICA MOUNTAINS FOLKLIFE FESTIVAL, Paramount Ranch, Santa Monica Mountains National Recreation Area. (818) 888-3770. One-day event features music concerts, folk dances, craft workshops, ethnic food, and art displays.

HUCK FINN'S JUBILEE, Mojave Narrows Regional Park, Victorville. (619) 245-2226. The life and times of Huck Finn and Tom Sawyer come alive on Father's Day weekend with a raft-building contest, fence painting, buried-treasure hunt, country crafts fair, and country, western, and bluegrass music.

THRESHING BEE and *ANTIQUE ENGINE SHOW*, Antique Gas & Steam Engine Museum, Vista. (619) 941-1791. (Held third and fourth weekends of June and October.) Volunteers demonstrate traditional farm-life activities, including planting, harvesting, threshing, household chores, and crafts, with plenty of food and entertainment.

DEL MAR FAIR, Fairgrounds, Del Mar. (619) 259-1355 or (619) 755-1161. San Diego's daylong county fair features flower shows, arts and crafts displays, livestock shows, entertainment, and a carnival.

INDIAN FAIR, Museum of Man, Balboa Park, San Diego. (619) 239-2001. Native Americans representing several southwestern tribes demonstrate dances and arts and crafts during a two-day gathering.

July

INTERNATIONAL SURF FESTIVAL, Hermosa, Manhattan, and Redondo beaches. (213) 545-4502. Activities include body-surfing competition, volleyball, sand sculpture, and lifeguard competitions on the beaches.

FESTIVAL OF THE ARTS AND PAGEANT OF THE MASTERS, Laguna Beach. (714) 494-1145. More than a hundred artists and craftspeople display their work at the festival site and at the nearby Sawdust Festival. Children's art workshops, music, dance, and the famed pageant's live recreation of well-known artworks are part of the festival.

ORANGE COUNTY FAIR, Costa Mesa. (714) 751-3247. Ten-day event features amusements, entertainment, arts, crafts, exhibits, and a rodeo.

ANNUAL SAND CASTLE DAYS, Imperial Beach, San Diego. (619) 424-3151. The U.S. Open Sand Castle Competition, one of the largest in the nation, helps mark the city's birthday. A parade and fireworks also are part of the weekend celebration at the south end of San Diego Bay.

August

NISEI WEEK JAPANESE FESTIVAL, Little Tokyo, downtown Los Angeles. (213) 626-3067. Weeklong festival celebrates Japanese cultural heritage with parades, dancing, carnival, and karate and judo tournaments.

LONG BEACH SEA FESTIVAL, Long Beach. (213) 421-9431. Week-long summer festival includes sailboat regattas, sand-sculpture contest, life-guard and volleyball competitions.

OLD SPANISH DAYS, Santa Barbara. (805) 962-8101. Weeklong celebration of Spanish heritage with events throughout city, including parades, a carnival, rodeo, Latino music, singing, and dancing.

ANTELOPE VALLEY DISTRICT FAIR AND ALFALFA FESTIVAL, Lancaster. (805) 948-4518. Rodeo, 4-H Roundup, rides, entertainment, and exhibitions are featured during the month-long fair.

THUNDERTUB REGATTA, Mission Bay, San Diego. (619) 232-1289. Bathtubs of every shape and design take to the waters of Enchanted Cove off Fiesta Island to compete for prizes in this daylong regatta.

September

MEXICAN INDEPENDENCE DAY, El Pueblo de Los Angeles State Historic Park, downtown Los Angeles. (213) 687-4344. Fiesta lasts several days to commemorate Mexico's independence with dancing, music, and parades.

LOS ANGELES COUNTY FAIR, Los Angeles County Fairplex, Pomona. (714) 623-3111. Two-week county fair includes exhibits, entertainment, and a carnival midway. One of California's largest, most colorful fairs, it draws more than a million people.

CELEBRATION OF HARVEST TIME, Oak Glen. (714) 797-6883. (Held the third week of September.) Weeklong festival features apple harvest, wagon rides, square dances, country music, and barbecues at ranches along Oak Glen Road. Apple harvest and some festivities continue throughout autumn months.

CABRILLO FESTIVAL, San Diego Harbor Area. (619) 557-5450. A two-day festival of music, dancing, exhibits, and ethnic foods mark the anniversary of Juan Cabrillo's 1542 landing in what became San Diego Harbor.

FIDDLE & BANJO CONTEST, Julian. (619) 765-1857. Bluegrass and country music are on the bill at this daylong family-oriented event at Frank Lane Memorial Park.

October

INTERNATIONAL FESTIVAL OF MASKS, Hancock Park, Mid-Wilshire District, Los Angeles. (213) 934-8527. (Held in even-numbered years only.) Weekend celebration before Halloween marks city's cultural diversity with music, dance, mask-making workshops, and a parade.

SANTA MONICA PIER KITE FESTIVAL, Santa Monica Pier, Santa Monica. (213) 822-2561. (See January listing.)

SAND CASTLE AND SCULPTING CONTEST, East Beach, Santa Barbara. (805) 966-6110. Nonprofit teams compete for cash prizes in building structures in different categories.

GOLETA VALLEY DAYS, Goleta. (805) 967-4618. Weekend celebration promotes Goleta with a parade, hoedown, fiddlers' convention, and arts and crafts shows.

VENTURA COUNTY FAIR, Ventura Fairgrounds, Ventura. (805) 648-2075. Parade, rodeo, and carnival highlight this colorful county fair.

LITTLE PEOPLE'S FESTIVAL, Ventura. (805) 654-7800. One-day festival introduces preschoolers to a variety of arts and crafts.

MARITIME DAYS, Oxnard. (805) 485-8833. Event commemorates Oxnard's maritime heritage with boat races, clambake, entertainment, and crafts and games at a Children's Fest area.

THEATER ARTS FESTIVAL FOR YOUTH (TAFFY), Peter Straus Ranch, Santa Monica Mountains National Recreation Area. (818) 888-3770. Artisans demonstrate their crafts as part of everyday life demonstrations. Day includes music concerts, folk dances, craft workshops, ethnic food, and art displays.

VALYERMO FALL FESTIVAL, St. Andrew's Priory, Valyermo. (805) 944-2178. (Held last weekend in October.) Folk music, drama, petting zoo, and art projects are featured on the grounds of the Benedictine monastery.

CALICO DAYS, Calico Ghost Town, Yermo. (619) 254-2122 or (714) 780-8810. Calico comes to life for a three-day celebration of its gold-rush heyday with a Wild West parade, burro run, 1880s games and contests, and the National Gunfight Stunt Championships.

OKTOBERFEST, Big Bear Lake. (714) 866-4607. Carnival booths, music, dancing, sing-alongs, log sawing, and yodeling take place for nine weekends, plus German food and selection of an Oktoberfest queen.

SAND CASTLE AND SAND SCULPTING CONTEST, Corona del Mar State Beach. (714) 644-8211. Amateurs and professionals, young and old, all take part in this one-day event, competing in many different categories.

THRESHING BEE and *ANTIQUE ENGINE SHOW*, Antique Gas & Steam Engine Museum, Vista. (619) 941-1791. (See June listing.)

FALL APPLE HARVEST FESTIVAL, Julian. (619) 765-1857. On each weekend of the month, local residents welcome visitors with a variety of entertainment and a chance to take part in harvesting the area's famed apple crop.

DEL MAR GREEK FESTIVAL, Del Mar. (619) 744-7396 or (619) 942-0920. Children's games, pony rides, and entertainment mark this one-day celebration of Greek culture.

YE OLDE ENGLISH FAIRE, Rancho Santa Fe. (619) 744-1270. Revellers, musicians, and craftspeople re-create a fifteenth-century English country marketplace and pleasure faire with two days of music, magic, food, and crafts.

November

HOLLYWOOD CHRISTMAS PARADE, Hollywood. (213) 469-2337. (Held the Sunday after Thanksgiving.) Hollywood celebrities participate in parade of bands, mounted units, floats, and Santa Claus through the city's streets.

BEVERLY HILLS HOLIDAY PAGEANT, Beverly Hills. (213) 271-8126 or (800) 345-2210. Santa Claus and real reindeer join entertainers and choirs to light city's multimillion-dollar street decorations.

HOLIDAY HOUSE OF MAGIC, San Diego. (619) 297-4216. Beginning in early November and continuing through Christmas Eve, evenings at the Presidio Garden Center become an animated Christmas fantasy with decorations collected from all over the world.

NORTH PARK TOYLAND PARADE, San Diego. (619) 543-0730. The colorful parade travels along University Avenue to the North Park Recreation Center, where food, games, and free llama rides await children.

MOTHER GOOSE PARADE, El Cajon. (619) 444-8712. (Held the Sunday before Thanksgiving.) The parade of floats, bands, and clowns celebrates childhood with a Mother Goose theme.

December

LAS POSADAS, El Pueblo de Los Angeles State Historic Park, downtown Los Angeles. (213) 687-4344. (Held the week before Christmas.) Nightly candle-light processions depict the journey of Mary and Joseph into Bethlehem and includes traditional piñata.

MARINA DEL REY CHRISTMAS BOAT PARADE, Marina del Rey. (213) 821-7614. More than a hundred boats decorated with Christmas motifs circle the marina's main channel.

LONG BEACH CHRISTMAS WATER PARADE, Naples Canals, Long Beach. (213) 436-3645. Boat owners cover their boats with Christmas lights and parade past decorated homes along Naples canals.

PORT OF LOS ANGELES CHRISTMAS BOAT PARADE, Ports o' Call Village, San Pedro. (213) 519-3508. (Held the weekend before Christmas.) Boat owners parade and compete for prizes for the best decorated boats.

PARADE OF LIGHTS, Oxnard. (805) 485-8833. (Held the second weekend in December.) Boats decorated in holiday motifs parade through the harbor.

CHRISTMAS BOAT PARADE OF LIGHTS, Newport Beach. (714) 644-8211. Some two hundred decorated and lighted boats parade through Newport Beach harbor for six nights before Christmas.

TOYS ON PARADE, Santa Ana. (714) 647-6561. Giant helium-filled balloons join floats, bands, equestrian units, celebrities, and Santa Claus in this parade through city streets.

CHRISTMAS ON THE PRADO, Balboa Park, San Diego. (619) 232-3101. During a two-day celebration, Balboa Park's museums offer a special holiday program, carolers, storytellers, candlelight procession, and traditional crafts.

SAN DIEGO HARBOR PARADE OF LIGHTS, San Diego. (619) 222-4081 or (619) 224-8211. Colorfully decorated and lighted boats parade past Shelter and Harbor islands during this one-evening event.

Acknowledgments

This book is the work of many people whom we would like to thank for their valuable contributions. Michelle and Tom Grimm provided the inspiration and encouragement that got us started. Barbara Lowenstein, our agent, guided our involvement at the early stages and got us working in the right direction. Shirley Wohl, our editor, asked questions and offered suggestions that helped us fashion a manuscript of greater clarity. Finally, we wish to thank our children and their friends, who helped us evaluate most of the attractions in this book from their youthful perspectives.

Index